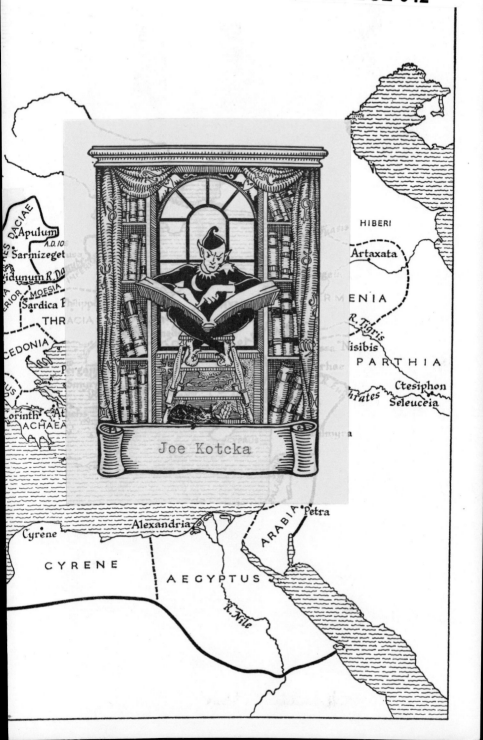

Joe Kotcka

ever been. As a zealous Stoic he attempted
to remain faithful to that creed through-

MARCUS AURELIUS

MARCUS AURELIUS

ANTHONY BIRLEY

with photographs and maps

LITTLE, BROWN AND COMPANY · BOSTON · TORONTO

PRINTED IN THE UNITED STATES OF AMERICA

CONTENTS

MAPS AND PLATES

MAPS

PLATES

Acknowledgements and thanks are due to the following for permission to
reproduce photographs:

The Mansell Collection: plates 1, 3b, 4, 8a, 8b.

Musei Capitolini, Rome: plates 2a, 5, 7a, 7b; and all the photographs (plates
   9–16) from the Aurelian column.

Amt der Niederösterreichischen Landesregierung: plate 2b.

The Trustees of the British Museum: all the coins shown in plates 3a and 6a.

Divine Mercy College, Fawley Court, Henley-on-Thames: plate 6b.

PREFACE

'L'histoire des Cours n'est plus à la mode', as an eminent French historian of Rome recently commented.[1] This is a question of fashion, dictated by political changes of the past fifty years. But, by the same token, it was pointed out emphatically thirty years ago that 'it is precisely during the period of the Antonines that the significance of the individual ruler declines steadily',[2] and thus that it may be positively harmful to study imperial history by reigns. The present work is the biography of an individual, not a 'Life and Times'—if it were, it would have to be a history, social and economic as well as political and military, of the age of the Antonines. Nonetheless, Marcus spent most of his life in close contact with power, and for nineteen years was master of the Roman Empire. In some respects it may not have mattered much who was emperor. But whoever was emperor was faced with a constant and enormous stream of official duties and decisions: governmental activity became the major part of his life. Court history may be unfashionable, but Marcus Aurelius and the court to which he belonged for forty-two years had simple tastes, and Marcus himself deserves to be considered as a man, not merely as a prince or a monarch.

It has always been as the author of the *Meditations* that he has attracted attention, and to a lesser degree as the correspondent of Fronto—the perfect pupil of a slightly pedantic if warmhearted tutor who was also an outstanding forensic lawyer. Not surprisingly, his life and character and the dilemma or paradox of the Stoic in the imperial purple have been frequently portrayed, generally in 'Hamletian or Faustian colours'.[3] Though I have laid greater

[1] H.-G. Pflaum, 'Les gendres de Marc-Aurele', *Journal des Savants*, 1961, p. 28.
[2] R. Syme, reviewing a work by W. Weber, *Class Rev.*, 53, 1939, 79.
[3] L. A. Stella, *Marco Aurelio*, Roma, 1943, p. 8.

emphasis than my predecessors on the detailed history of his wars, that dramatic emphasis is surely right. One may wonder regretfully what Shakespeare or any Renaissance dramatist might have made of the essentially tragic life of this deeply human man, brought up in easy and pleasant circumstances, imbued with noble and enlightened beliefs, then thrust after long preparation into autocratic power over millions as ruler of 'the fairest part of the earth'. But the materials were lacking: Cassius Dio's Greek too inaccessible and fragmentary; the biography in the Augustan History known to Petrarch and others but not edited till 1603; Fronto's letters lying unrecognized in the Vatican library; the sublime *Meditations* long supplanted by a forgery and not translated into English till 1634. At least, any Renaissance dramatist could have produced something truer to the spirit of Marcus Aurelius than a twentieth-century film company: Sir Alec Guinness' graceful performance as Marcus in *The Fall of the Roman Empire* could not redeem a plot which travestied and falsified history without any gain in dramatic effect.

It remains for me to acknowledge the assistance of those who have made a pleasant task pleasanter. Professor Sir Ronald Syme guided my early investigations into the age of the Antonines and did me the kindness of reading chapters II–IV in typescript. My father, Professor Eric Birley, read the whole typescript and made many helpful suggestions. My friends, Dr Barri Jones, Dr John Wilkes and Mr David Francis Jones, read a large part of it and enabled me to remove various errors. I owe much, in a more general way, to discussion with Dr John Morris and M. H.-G. Pflaum. To all these I express my thanks, the more necessarily as I have not always followed their advice, and must be held responsible for any errors of fact which may remain and for the views expressed. Over ten years ago I first had the privilege of meeting and working with Erich Swoboda, the excavator of Carnuntum, where Marcus spent three of his most difficult years. While this book was in process of completion the news came of his death. I would like to take this opportunity of expressing my admiration for a great scholar and my sorrow at the loss of an inspiring friend. I began collecting material in 1960, but most of the book was written in autumn 1964, while I was a Research

Fellow at the University of Birmingham: to that university and in particular to my head of department, Professor D. R. Dudley, I am most grateful for their support. Mr John Bright-Holmes of Eyre and Spottiswoode has provided energetic and thoughtful help which has greatly improved my text. I dedicate the book to my wife as a token of gratitude for her unsparing encouragement.

A.R.B.

November 1965

MARCUS AURELIUS

TO SUZANNA

I

INTRODUCTION:
THE AGE OF THE ANTONINES

'IF A MAN were called to fix the period in the history of the world during which the condition of the human race was most happy and prosperous, he would, without hesitation, name that which elapsed from the death of Domitian to the accession of Commodus.'[1]

So wrote Edward Gibbon of the 'happy period of more than four-score years,' from A.D. 96–180, during which the Roman Empire was ruled by the 'Five Good Emperors' – Nerva, Trajan, Hadrian, Antoninus Pius and Marcus Aurelius. Marcus' own life (A.D. 121–80) spanned therefore almost three-quarters of this epoch while his reign (A.D. 161–80) occupied its last nineteen years. In fact it was in describing Marcus' death, and the accession of his son Commodus, that the historian Cassius Dio, who was born soon after Marcus' accession, wrote: 'My history now descends from a kingdom of gold to a kingdom of iron and rust, as affairs did for the Romans at that time.'[2]

The 'five good emperors' were individuals of widely differing character and training. One factor linked them: none was the son of his predecessor. Hence it seemed to some contemporary observers and to many subsequent commentators, including Gibbon, that a new principle was then governing the imperial succession: 'the adoption of the best man'. In fact there was no principle or conscious policy at work, merely chance. All but Marcus had no son to succeed him, and in any case kinship linked Trajan and Hadrian, Pius and Marcus. Still, the sensitive upper classes felt happier that they were

[1] E. Gibbon, *Decline and Fall of the Roman Empire*, chapter 3.
[2] Dio, 71, 36, 3.

no longer 'inherited with the rest of the family property' as had been the case under the previous imperial dynasties.[1]

In his first work, the biography of his father-in-law Agricola, written at the outset of the new era, Tacitus voices the relief of the senate that their time of servitude was over: 'Now at last our spirits revive.' Nerva had succeeded Domitian, assassinated in A.D. 96, and had achieved the impossible: the principate and liberty could co-exist. Tacitus' contemporary, Pliny, expatiated at far greater length, a few years later, on the change which had begun that year. It was no longer necessary to flatter the ruler as though he were a god; he contrasted the humanity, frugality, clemency, generosity, kindness, self-restraint, industriousness and bravery of Trajan who followed Nerva in A.D. 98, with the pride, luxury, cruelty, spitefulness, lust, inactivity and cowardice of Domitian. Tacitus and Pliny were speaking for the senate. To the provincial bourgeoisie and peasantry, on the other hand, the personality of the emperor did not perhaps matter very much. The wayward general Petillius Cerialis is made by Tacitus to remind an assembly of Gallic rebels in A.D. 70: *saevi proximis ingruunt*, i.e. savage emperors vent their spleen on those closest to them – the senators at Rome – and the average inhabitant of the provinces does not suffer. Besides, bad emperors often had good advisers (as Trajan is once supposed to have remarked).[2]

The favourable verdict of history on 'the Golden Century of the Antonines' depends largely on the fact that senators felt more secure when an emperor had been chosen from their own number, rather than when he succeeded to the throne solely by dynastic inheritance. This was a kind of safeguard. At any rate, since most Roman historians and biographers were members of the senate or linked with that order in their sympathies, the dominant theme of Roman imperial historical writing was the relationship between the emperor and the senate.

[1] 'Family property': Tacitus, *Histories*, 1, 16.

[2] Tacitus, *Agricola*, 3: 'nunc demum redit animus; et quamquam primo statim beatissimi saeculi ortu Nerva Caesar res olim dissociabilis miscuerit, principatum et libertatem, augeatque cotidie felicitatem temporum Nerva Traianus, etc. . . .' Trajan's remark: *V. Sev. Alex.*, 65, 5. Pliny, *Panegyricus*, 2, 3; 3, 4. Cerealis: Tacitus, *Histories*, 4, 74.

To understand more clearly why this was so, it is worth looking back at the origins of the imperial system.[1] Rome had been dominated by one man before, at various stages in the history of the republic, but autocracy began with the victory of Octavian at Actium in 31 B.C. Octavian cunningly and wisely concealed his powers, however, or at least did not flaunt them, and so disarmed opposition and allowed his opponents to preserve a semblance of self-respect. After years of civil war men were anxious for stability and the historical accident of his remarkable talent for survival (forty-five years sole rule) allowed the innovations which he had introduced gradually, at every stage appealing to ancient precedent and feeling his way, to harden.

By Augustus' death, Rome was in effect an empire, however hard his successor Tiberius tried to disguise it. Exactly when the republic had ceased and the empire had begun was not so obvious. Writing during Tiberius' reign, Velleius Paterculus, one of the new men favoured by the new system, felt able to say complacently that Augustus had merely 'recalled to existence the pristine and ancient constitution of the republic'.[2] Augustus wanted to appear as no more than *primus inter pares*. But the man who began life as plain C. Octavius was much more than that.

He had first changed his name to C. Julius Caesar Octavianus when posthumously adopted by the assassinated dictator Julius Caesar. Through the efforts of Antony and others, Caesar was proclaimed a god, or something very like one, and this enabled Caesar's heir to draw attention to his unique ancestry – Imperator Caesar divi filius (son of the deified). *Imperator*,[3] once a title for all Roman com-

---

[1] See Table I, page 5, for Roman emperors from Augustus to Severus.

[2] Velleius Paterculus, 2, 89, 3: 'prisca illa et antiqua rei publicae forma revocata'. On the career of Augustus it may be permissible in this context to refer to Syme, *The Roman Revolution*, Oxford, 1939 (repr. 1952), 1, without in any way imputing to him responsibility for the treatment here given. 'Outlasting the friends, the enemies, and even the memory of his earlier days, Augustus the *Princeps*, who was born in the year of Cicero's consulate, lived to see the grandson of his granddaughter and to utter a prophecy of empire concerning Galba, to whom the power passed when the dynasty of the Julii and Claudii had ruled for a century.' (R. Syme, op. cit., p. 1).

[3] Anomalously, the old use of Imperator continued as well as the new. Even ordinary senators continued to be hailed by their troops as Imperator. But after the year A.D. 22 this privilege was reserved to emperors alone.

manders, had become a special title of honour, used after their names by generals whose soldiers had thus hailed them at a victory. Octavian abusively turned the title into a kind of name, giving up Caius – and Julius too, for Caesar now became his family name. In 27 B.C. the senate granted him yet a further name by which he became generally known: Imperator Caesar divi filius Augustus.[1] In 23 B.C. Augustus received the new 'tribunician power', a creation of his own which gave him wide powers of interference in a multitude of spheres. Other powers and honours followed at various stages in his long life.

Augustus recognized that he could not survive unless he allowed the senate, once the supreme arbiter of Roman destinies, to participate in his rule – indeed, he could not do without senators. The old magistracies of the republic also continued. He himself held the consulship thirteen times, and one or two of his close associates whom he wished to mark out with special honour also became consul more than once. In order to satisfy the aspirations of ordinary senators whose ambition remained the tenure of the *fasces* of the ancient supreme magistracy, he regularized the institution of the suffect consulship, established originally to replace consuls who had died or been removed from office. The *consules ordinarii*, who gave their names to the year, now resigned before completing their year of office to make way for *suffecti*. This practice greatly increased in subsequent years.

Entry into the senate (a body nominally 600 strong) was hereditary, but suitable persons with the requisite property qualification of one million sesterces could apply for the *latus clavus*, the broad-stripe of the senator's toga, which allowed them to enter the senate through election as quaestor at the age of 24 or 25, after preliminary service in minor magistracies (and with the army). Thereafter they could climb the ladder of the senatorial hierarchy, becoming aedile or tribune of the people, praetor, and, finally, consul. Patricians, the hereditary aristocracy (enlarged by Augustus and some of his successors), could move direct from quaestor to praetor and could become

[1] Cf. R. Syme, *Historia*, 7, 1958, 172 ff., on the details of his changes of nomenclature.

4

31 B.C.	*September* 2: Octavian, great-nephew of Julius Caesar, gains sole power after defeat of Antony at Actium.
27 B.C.	Octavian given name AUGUSTUS.
23 B.C.	Augustus given *tribunicia potestas*.
A.D. 4	Augustus adopts stepson Tiberius Claudius Nero, who becomes Tiberius Julius Caesar.
A.D. 14	TIBERIUS succeeds to Augustus' position on latter's death.
A.D. 37	GAIUS ('CALIGULA'), great-nephew of Tiberius, great-grandson of Augustus, succeeds Tiberius on latter's death.
A.D. 41	Murder of Caligula. His uncle CLAUDIUS proclaimed emperor.
A.D. 54	NERO, stepson of Claudius, nephew of Caligula, great-great-grandson of Augustus, succeeds Claudius on latter's death.
A.D. 68	*June* 6: Suicide of Nero after revolts in western provinces. GALBA recognized as emperor.
A.D. 69	*January* 2–3: VITELLIUS proclaimed emperor by Rhine armies.
	January 15: OTHO instigates murder of Galba and is proclaimed emperor at Rome.
	April 15: Vitellius' army defeats that of Otho in N. Italy.
	July 1–3: VESPASIAN proclaimed emperor by eastern armies.
	October 27–28: Defeat of Vitellius' forces in N. Italy.
	December 20: Vitellius killed at Rome.
A.D. 79	Death of Vespasian, succeeded by elder son TITUS.
A.D. 81	Death of Titus, succeeded by younger brother DOMITIAN.
A.D. 96	*September* 18: Murder of Domitian at Rome. NERVA made emperor.
A.D. 97	*October*: Nerva adopts Trajan as his son.
A.D. 98	*January* 28: TRAJAN succeeds on death of Nerva.
A.D. 117	HADRIAN, after ostensible death-bed adoption, succeeds his cousin Trajan.
A.D. 136	*Spring or early summer*: Hadrian adopts L. Ceionius Commodus, who becomes L. Aelius Caesar.
A.D. 138	*January* 1: Death of L. Aelius Caesar.
	February 25: Hadrian adopts T. Aurelius Antoninus, who becomes T. Aelius Hadrianus Antoninus and adopts Marcus and L. Commodus junior.
	July 10: ANTONINUS succeeds on Hadrian's death.
A.D. 161	*March* 7: MARCUS succeeds on death of Antoninus (Pius), jointly with L. Commodus junior who becomes L. VERUS.
A.D. 169	*January*: Death of L. Verus.
A.D. 177	Marcus' only surviving son COMMODUS made joint emperor.
A.D. 180	*March* 17: Death of Marcus, COMMODUS sole emperor.
A.D. 192	*December* 31: Commodus murdered.
A.D. 193	*January* 1: PERTINAX proclaimed emperor.
	March 25: Pertinax murdered, DIDIUS JULIANUS proclaimed emperor (Rome).
	April 9: SEPTIMUS SEVERUS proclaimed emperor (Danube).
	June 1: Julianus killed at Rome.
A.D. 197	*February* 19: Defeat of Severus' last rival, at Lyons.
A.D. 211	*February* 4: Death of Severus at York.

TABLE I Roman Emperors from Augustus to Severus

consul at 32, ten years earlier than the rest. The patricians had more chance of becoming consul *ordinarius*. But very few were consul more than once.

Alongside the old magistracies a new career developed. If they chose, senators could ignore the emperor's existence, serve only as magistrates at Rome and as proconsuls of provinces administered by the senate in the old republican way. But Augustus and his successors governed a vast *provincia*, virtually all the provinces which had armies and many others besides, and could also interfere in the senatorial provinces. The imperial provinces and armies were administered and commanded by the emperor's deputies, *legati*, and a career in the emperor's service formed the real basis of the senatorial hierarchy, with the ancient republican magistracies merely stepping-stones, formal stages of qualification for further advancement. Some provinces were not given to senators to administer, for various reasons, but to knights, members of the next highest order in the state, who had the title of procurator or prefect. Other new offices grew up in Rome – prefectures of the treasuries, and of the city of Rome, for senators: of the corn-supply, the city-police and the praetorian guard for knights.[1]

At Rome, Augustus had to keep up appearances. In the provinces, he was worshipped as king and god, and his family were sacred. 'It is not necessary to praise political success or to idealize the men who win wealth and honours through civil war.'[2] At his death in A.D. 14 almost everyone did – a few through fear, but most inhabitants of the empire from a sense of awe, admiration and gratitude for the stability which he had created, or allowed to form. Augustus was deified by decree of the senate. So had Julius Caesar been. But although Augustus had at first used the 'deified Julius' to further his own plans, the memory of the murdered dictator had not been unduly emphasised at a later stage. 'Divus Augustus', with his college of priests, his temple and the festivals to commemorate significant days in his earthly life, played a profound role in the subsequent

---

[1] On senatorial careers, cf. E. Birley, *Proc. Brit. Acad.*, 39, 1953, 197 ff.; J. Morris, *Listy Filologické*, 87, 1964, 317 ff.

[2] Syme, *Roman Revolution*, p. viii.

history of the Roman Empire: his successors were assessed in large measure in comparison with him. All his successors (except Tiberius and Vitellius) used his three names, Imperator Caesar Augustus, as part of their official style, and with some modifications their powers were those which he had gradually built up during his long decades of ascendancy.[1]

Tiberius, thanks to his stepfather Augustus' grudging and unwilling use of him, was by far the most distinguished Roman of his day at his accession: he had been consul more often, had commanded more armies and provinces than his peers, and was son by adoption of Augustus, sharing enough of his special powers to make the succession inevitable. He lacked Augustus' pliable qualities (the qualities of a chameleon, the emperor Julian was to call them[2]), and was never popular with the senate, indeed by the time of his death in A.D. 37 he was generally feared and hated, and he was not deified. His successor was his great-nephew, Augustus' great-grandson, Gaius 'Caligula'. Caligula had no other claim to be '*Princeps*' except his Julian blood: he was only 24 and had no higher rank than that of quaestor. This made the autocracy obvious and Caligula went on to exaggerate even further the concept of 'divine kingship'.

When Caligula was murdered in A.D. 41, there was an abortive attempt to restore the republic, but the imperial bodyguard discovered another member of the 'divine family', Claudius, uncle of Caligula, who was a laughing-stock to the aristocracy through his personal failings and dominated by his wives and freed slaves. Under him the autocracy and the bureaucracy increased their powers. Claudius was succeeded in A.D. 54 by his 16-year-old stepson Nero, who began his rule with professions of deference to the senate, sedulously instilled into him by his tutor and minister Seneca. But soon his behaviour became intolerable to the senate – *saevi proximis ingruunt*. Eventually Nero took fright at a rebellion in Gaul, and, deserted by the praetorian guards, committed suicide in the summer of A.D. 68.

---

[1] On emperor-worship, cf. L. R. Taylor, *The Divinity of the Roman Emperor*, Middletown, Conn., 1931.

[2] Julian; *Caesares*, p. 309.

There was no attempt to restore the republic now some ninety-nine years after the battle of Actium. The aim of all parties in the civil war of A.D. 68–69 seems to have been (in principle at least) to return to the harmonious state of affairs that had prevailed under Augustus. In A.D. 69, the year of the four emperors, the premium on birth fell sharply with successive occupants of the throne – and the secret had already been revealed 'that emperors could be made elsewhere than at Rome'. Vespasian, the eventual victor, was a parvenu. Paradoxically, his having two sons was regarded as a point in his favour by some of his supporters: he could found a dynasty which would, it was thought, stabilize the succession. Opposition from senators influenced by the ideals of Stoic philosophy was stifled. Vespasian refused to allow his powers to be limited and was determined that his sons should succeed him. He was duly succeeded by Titus at his death in A.D. 79, and Titus two years later by his younger brother Domitian. Vespasian and Titus had been efficient and popular emperors, and they had cultivated the support of the senate. Domitian, who had been a youth in his late teens at his father's accession, had a suspicious and sensitive personality and, as he had never been a normal member of the senate, had little sympathy with senatorial feeling. He was competent, even talented, as a ruler or administrator, but opposition was provoked by his behaviour (for instance, his insistence on being addressed as 'Lord and God', and his holding the consulship ten times as emperor out of a maximum possible of fifteen). His rule ended with a reign of terror, and he was murdered in September A.D. 96.

His successor, Nerva, had not had a very creditable past – he had been an agent of Nero, and then had been honoured by Vespasian and Domitian, for no very obvious reason, except that he was well-connected and, surely, a useful counsellor of the Flavian emperors. In A.D. 97 opposition to Nerva became open and his position in grave danger. The situation was saved when he adopted as his son and heir the governor of the Upper Germany, M. Ulpius Traianus[1]

[1] The fact that Trajan had been in command of three legions on the far side of the Great St Bernard route into Italy at the moment when Nerva selected him may well have been more significant than the 'divine inspiration' to which Pliny piously attributed the choice.

who became emperor in his own right on Nerva's death early in A.D. 98.

Trajan, a provincial, had been made a patrician as a young man by Vespasian in recognition of his father's services to the new dynasty. He had served Domitian loyally, as had others of his class like Agricola, also a neo-patrician of provincial extraction, whose biography Tacitus had written to demonstrate that good men could exist and perform worthy deeds even under bad emperors. At the death of Domitian a good deal of cant had been talked about opposition to the tyranny: there had in fact been the Stoic group of senators who had suffered 'martyrdom' under Nero and the Flavians. But most of the senate had knuckled under. Trajan became a hero to virtually everyone – a conqueror abroad, he respected senators at home (for example, he was consul only four times in his reign of twenty years, which was but one of the many studied contrasts to Domitian). The senate gave him the title *Optimus* – best of emperors. His name became a proverb for centuries, for he seemed to fulfil everyone's ideals.[1]

Hadrian, a cousin of Trajan and married to his great-niece, was the obvious choice to succeed, but the succession was not made obvious. Trajan died in the east in August A.D. 117 and Hadrian, commanding the Syrian army, had no difficulty whatever in gaining the adherence of the troops. But he did not have time to wait for the senate's approval, and within a short time of his accession a number of leading senators, including some of Trajan's closest collaborators, were put to death. On his arrival in Rome Hadrian clearly had met some suspicion and hostility, and although he tried hard to regain the senate's favour, the manner in which his reign opened was never forgotten or forgiven.

Hadrian was a tremendous organizer and systematizer. Trajan's final conquests (in the east) were abandoned, and he reverted to the ultimate policy of Augustus of avoiding further expansion. He was outside Italy for most of his reign, visiting the provinces and armies

[1] On Nerva and Trajan, cf. especially R. Syme, *Tacitus*, Oxford, 1958, especially I, ix–xii; 1–58; II, 627–33. On the hereditary principle, cf. J. Béranger, *Rev. Ét. Lat.*, 17, 1939, 171 ff.

and reorganizing the frontier defences of the new empire, one of the most celebrated results of which is the wall that bears his name in Britain.

Hadrian's reign gave the empire a breathing-space. Efficiency was increased. By now the imperial household which had administered so many important departments of state had given way to a regular equestrian civil service in which knights could have as varied and important a career as senators continued to have in their own sphere. For a knight, the summit was still – as it had been for a hundred years – the prefecture of the praetorian guard. Below this were the other great prefectures – of Egypt, of the city-police (the *vigiles*), and of the corn-supply (*annona*), the financial department (*a rationibus*), the Secretariat (*ab epistulis*) and similar offices in Rome itself, and appointments as financial procurator throughout the empire and as presidial procurator (i.e. governor) in a number of provinces. Entry into the service was controlled solely by the emperor, but there seem to have been various standard means of starting on the ladder. Some men obtained commissions as regimental commanders of auxiliary units, others began as praetorian guardsmen, obtained a centurion's commission, and then after further military service became procurators; a few, such as the writer Suetonius (who was *ab epistulis* early in Hadrian's reign), seem to have entered the higher grade directly without prior military service.

The major strength of the army lay in the legions, and these were all commanded by senators, with the exception of the two in Egypt. At any one moment some twenty-eight senators would be legionary legates. Most would be men in their thirties, and some of these would be governing a province simultaneously. In provinces where there was more than one legion, the governor was an ex-consul, hence generally in his forties or older. A few key provinces had as many as three legions – Britain, Syria, Upper Pannonia and Lower Moesia. The British and Syrian commands, in more isolated positions than were the Danubian armies, required a correspondingly greater degree of responsibility. Hence the governors of Britain and Syria were usually the two outstanding generals of their day.

But the military senators – the *viri militares* – were not the only figures of influence. Indeed, as they were away from the centre of affairs for long periods their voice was often not of much weight in imperial councils. For although the emperor of Rome was still – even increasingly – an autocrat, importance was attached to the opinions of the senate and, by the reign of Hadrian, even more to the emperor's Privy Council – the *consilium principis*. This had grown up gradually (like most Roman institutions) from the time of Augustus, and its members – the emperor's friends, *amici Caesaris* – must have played an important role in influencing policy decisions. Unfortunately, as more than one ancient writer complained, from the end of the republic policy was decided in secret and few significant details are preserved of the discussions where the real business of policy-making was carried on.[1]

The emperor's power rested ultimately on his control of the armies. He also controlled the finances of the state, whatever legal fictions there might have been to assert the senate's share in this. He was the source of rewards both titular and financial. Legates and · procurators, legionaries and auxiliaries, were all paid by him. A legionary in the reign of Augustus received 225 denarii a year (it had risen to 300 by Hadrian's day). The senator's property-qualification was more than one thousand times as great as this (one million sesterces or 250,000 denarii). In fact, a procurator eager and able to obtain entry to the senate could soon accumulate the required wealth many times over. The lowest grade of procurators were paid 60,000 denarii a year, and higher grades were paid at 100,000, 200,000 and 300,000. Senatorial salaries in imperial service were higher (and there were many ways of increasing one's earnings). To translate this into modern terms would be meaningless. But the legionaries, on their retirement from the service, were reckoned among the better-off members of society.[2]

[1] Dio, 53, 19.
[2] See the *vita Hadriani, passim*, and on particular questions, E. Birley, 'Hadrianic Frontier Policy', in *Carnuntina*, ed. E. Swoboda, Graz-Köln, 1956, 26 ff.; B. d'Orgeval, *L'Empereur Hadrien: oeuvre législative et administrative*, Paris, 1950; H.-G. Pflaum, *Les procurateurs équestres*, Paris, 1950, 58 ff.; M. G. Jarrett, *Historia*, 12, 1963, 209 ff.; J. Crook, *Consilium Principis*, Cam-

The empire ruled by Hadrian was a cosmopolitan world-state, with a varied polyglot population. But there were only two official languages, Latin in the west and Greek in the east. The highest orders in the state were bi-lingual, and educated Romans of Latin-speaking descent looked increasingly to Greek language and culture. Theorists liked to see the empire as a confederation of city-states, fulfilling the aspirations of the great age of Greek history. This was a myth, and the civilization of the empire was basically urban. The communities of the empire were granted considerable autonomy in local government, although by the second century A.D. this was coming to be regarded as a burden by the town bourgeoisie and provincial landed gentry who had to reach into their own pockets to support their home towns. In the west city-life was something new, but under Hadrian townbuilding was flourishing even in Britain, and Gaul had for some while been very Romanized. Spain was one of Rome's oldest provinces and, as the home of Trajan and Hadrian, was, not surprisingly, well up to the level of Italy in its social and economic development. The North African provinces had a brilliant city-life along the coast. Morocco was less civilized and the mountains in the south of Mauretania were the home of brigands who constantly disturbed the peace of both Mauretania and Spain. Nevertheless, both the Iberian peninsula and North Africa were deemed sufficiently protected by the presence of one legion each, stationed in Tarraconensis and Numidia respectively. This garrison was, of course, supplemented by the presence of non-citizen auxiliary regiments in substantial numbers. The Gallic provinces also were undefended by legions. But there were three legions in Britain and four in the two Rhineland provinces of Upper and Lower Germany. In Numidia, Upper Germany and Britain

---

bridge, 1955. It may be useful to state briefly the nature of Roman currency, which was bi-metallic, based on the gold *aureus* (42 to a pound of gold) and the silver *denarius* (84 to a pound of silver). One *aureus* was worth 25 *denarii*. But the unit in which money was generally reckoned for official purposes was the brass *sestertius* weighing 1 oz., of which there were four to 1 *denarius*. The smaller units (e.g. *quinarii*, *asses*, *dupondii*) need not be mentioned here except in passing.

abundant traces of Hadrian's activity as a renovator of imperial frontier-defences have been discovered.

The hinge which bound the western and eastern parts of the empire together was the area north of the Alps, notably the provinces of Upper and Lower Pannonia, with three legions and one legion respectively. The two Moesian provinces formed a military zone right along the Danube to the Black Sea; and from the time of Trajan's conquests the Dacian provinces formed a great bastion to the north of the river. Dalmatia was a province of contrasts: the Adriatic coast, opposite Italy, had a brilliant city-life; inland the country was mountainous and wild. The rest of the empire was Greek in language and culture, but as with Latin in the Celtic, Iberian and Berber lands, this was in many areas merely a superficial veneer. Nevertheless, Achaea and Macedonia and the province of Asia were thoroughly Hellenic, with cities that had flourished when Rome was a village. Thrace and Bithynia, Pontus, Lycia-Pamphylia, Cilicia, Galatia, Cappadocia, Syria, Palestine, Arabia, all had benefited in some degree from the presence, before Rome absorbed them, of Greek and Hellenistic settlers. Egypt was in a special category. Only Alexandria was a true city – the next after Rome itself in size – but it was denied local autonomy, and it and the province of Egypt were ruled as the emperor's personal fief through his Viceroy, the Prefect, and a civil service which followed closely the bureaucratic pattern laid down by the Ptolemies.

The empire had enemies of various kinds. Britain, Spain and Morocco were disturbed by brigands, but the damage they inflicted was essentially local. The long river-frontier in the north was more vulnerable: the 'cordon-system' of frontier control is unsatisfactory in many ways, as Napoleon and others have pointed out. The Teutonic tribes of northern and central Europe were often restless, as were their eastern neighbours of whom the Sarmatians are the best-known, particularly the Jazyges of the Hungarian Plain. Trajan's creation of a province of Dacia had helped to solve the problem of frontier control in the Lower Danube region, but it had created tensions as well. Rome aimed to stifle possible threats by exercising a protectorate over the peoples which bordered her frontiers. The system of 'client-states' in treaty-relationship with the emperor provided Rome with 'invisible frontiers' which stretched far beyond the tangible barriers of the empire.

In the east, the problem was different. In the Parthian Empire Rome had a potential adversary of apparently much higher calibre than the disunited tribes to her north. The Parthians too were loosely-knit, but the conquests of Alexander had extended Hellenic civilization far beyond the Tigris, and in any case the Parthian kings were the inheritors of a Mesopotamian civilization stretching back for several millennia. The main bone of contention between Rome and Parthia was the kingdom of Armenia which each wished to dominate. But Mesopotamia too was sometimes coveted by Rome. The client-state system was used extensively on the eastern frontiers: Rome found it profitable to have allies as far away as the Caucasus; and the Black Sea was virtually a Roman preserve, for the Greek cities of its coasts were under careful supervision.

Augustus had expanded the empire to its natural limits. A number of additions had been made by his successors, but Hadrian gave up Trajan's eastern conquests – Armenia, Mesopotamia, Assyria – and concentrated on making the empire a viable, secure and flourishing concern. In this he evidently succeeded, for he was reaping the harvest sown in the first century. The Hellenized provinces of the east, after long decades of civil peace, were richer than ever before. The rougher west, even distant Britain, now began to enjoy the fruits of the Roman peace. The whole world could lay down its arms as if at festival time, the fulsome young East Greek orator Aelius Aristides could proclaim five years after Hadrian's death. The cities of the empire had no other concern, he said, but to adorn themselves with public buildings – gymnasia, fountains, arches, temples, workshops, schools. They gleamed with radiance and grace. The earth was now indeed the common mother of all men. An encamped army ringed the world like a rampart, from the inhabited part of Ethiopia in the south to the Phasis in the north, from the Euphrates in the east 'to the great outermost island towards the west'. He might equally have said, with more precision, that from the Upper

Nile to the Don, from the Euphrates to the Clyde, from the Sahara to the Rhine, the Danube and Transylvania, the Roman law and the Roman peace prevailed. War was a thing of the past. Rome alone of great empires had ruled such a vast area, and she alone ruled with equity and restraint.[1]

Not everyone profited. Aristides spoke for the upper classes. And the economic system was based on slavery. Many, even the better-off, sought escape from a somewhat soulless materialism in exotic new cults. The cultivated Pliny, on his arrival in Pontus-Bithynia, found that the temples of the ancestral gods were becoming deserted and neglected. The reason soon appeared. There was a sect called Christians – sober, decent people, he found, in spite of the monstrous allegations against them – who preferred their own private cult. Trajan told the governor that these people had to be punished, if, after proceedings had been initiated, they were found to be Christians – punished with death. This was not a new ruling. After the great fire at Rome, under Nero, it had probably become imperial policy that to be a confessed Christian was a capital offence. But Trajan told Pliny that these people should not be searched out. They should be left alone. If they were accused, confessed and refused to recant, the law had to take its course. This is remarkable judicial practice. But it seemed to work.[2]

There were other exotic cults also, Egyptian and Oriental for the most part.[3] Hadrian himself had been initiated into the ancient (and respectably classical) cult of the Mysteries of Eleusis. Others sought consolation in philosophy. What had once been a dangerous and expensive eccentricity or fad – even a deeply believed inner defence against despotism – could now be practised with decorum, publicly. Also, there arose crowds of bogus philosophers.

In the fields of architecture and the plastic arts there was genuine achievement. The gleam of the cities has left its traces. The Hadrianic and Antonine architects and sculptors produced works of con-

[1] Cf. J. H. Oliver, *The Ruling Power* (Trans. American Philosophical Society, 43), Philadelphia, 1953, 971 ff.

[2] Pliny, *Epp.*, 10, 96–7; and see Appendix IV.

[3] Cf. J. Beaujeu, *La religion romaine a l'apogée de l'empire*, I, Paris, 1955.

15

siderable grace and beauty, and left a permanent mark on the face of the empire, not least of Rome itself.[1]

There is somehow an air of the eighteenth century about the Antonine Empire. The aristocracy which had been ennobled in the struggles of the previous century wanted now to relax and enjoy their dignity and wealth. The provincial Romans and the Italian municipal families had come to the top. Their worth was solid, and their possessions satisfyingly secure. The old aristocracy had almost disappeared. 'Freedom' had long been a catchword under the early principate. It never really meant what the younger Cato had meant by it. 'Freedom' meant order, stability, regularity. An emperor was a necessity. If he preserved social distinctions and allowed the senate an honoured place in the state, all would be well. The new Roman aristocracy had no disturbing memories of ancient glories under the free republic. But they did prefer an enlightened autocracy to the grim, uneasy and suspicious days of Domitian. The Annii Veri, the Ceionii, the Vettuleni, and their peers, with their riches and their assured place in public life, gained by faithful service even under bad emperors, had come into their own. The virtues which Tacitus had praised in the *Agricola* had gained their reward. Also, it was now safe and laudable to admire the valiant few who had dared to speak out against tyranny in the past, Thrasea Paetus, Helvidius Priscus – the Stoics. Tacitus had in fact preferred the example of the unrebellious but still untarnished Agricola. But both types could now be admired simultaneously.[2]

The society revealed by the letters of Pliny is contented and industrious, conscious of its own virtues. These men and women, and their imitators in the provinces, provided the gleam of the age of the Antonines. They were, many of them, of provincial origin, as were Trajan and Hadrian. But they did not see themselves as

[1] Cf. P. G. Hamberg, *Studies in Roman Imperial Art*, etc., Copenhagen-Uppsala, 1945. U. E. Paoli, *Rome, Its People, Life and Customs*, Eng. tr., London, 1963, 1 ff. and 292 ff., gives an eloquent picture of the changing face of Rome.

[2] Tacitus, *Agricola*, 42, 5. See R. Syme, *Tacitus*, Oxford, 1958, *passim*, esp. 1, 59 ff.; II, 585 ff.; ibid., *Colonial Elites*, London, 1958, 1 ff.; also C. Wirszubski, *Libertas as a Political Idea at Rome*, Cambridge, 1950.

Spaniards or Gauls or Africans, except as an occasional affectation. They were Romans, and the leading Romans of their day. Greek culture was once more on the upsurge. But things Hellenic were permissible, in fact essential (in moderation) to an educated Roman. (Hadrian, the restless cosmopolitan, went a little to extremes, in this as in other respects.) Wealthy men from Greek-speaking provinces were themselves entering the senate in increasing numbers, in any case, adapting themselves with varying success or enthusiasm to the manners of Rome.

Some of the friends and correspondents of Pliny undertook arduous work in the service of the emperor, governing his provinces and commanding his armies. Others lived in sedate but cultivated retirement. Others still could confine their public as well as their private life almost entirely to Rome and Italy. Those, in particular, who had the rank of patrician, did not need to do more, for patricians were assured of access at an early age to the ancient magistracies of Rome, which remained the leading aspiration of the upper class. Pliny obviously did not know personally (to his regret, perhaps) *all* the leading figures of his time. But his correspondence gives a remarkable picture of Roman high society in the last decade of the first and the first decade of the second centuries A.D. Its self-satisfied and urbane atmosphere mirrors more accurately than the sombre pages of Cornelius Tacitus, the world into which Marcus Aurelius was born.

The effect of the new stability on the literary world was not entirely happy. The early second century saw the genius of two of the greatest figures of Latin literature, Tacitus and Juvenal. They were also two of the last great Latin writers, and both were dead before Hadrian. There was also Suetonius, the young friend of Pliny. Pliny and Suetonius wrote unexceptionable prose, and are still widely read. But tastes were changing. There was a move back to the past, back to the days before Caesar Augustus had established his New Order. The emperor Hadrian's own tastes accorded well with this. In Greek literature he preferred Antimachus (of whom scarcely anyone had heard) to Homer. There were writers of some distinction in both

Greek and Latin in the age of the Antonines – notably Apuleius and Lucian. Of the rest, what has survived is perhaps judged by unfair standards, but much is incredibly tedious. Few now would read all the works of Aelius Aristides.[1]

A by-product of the literary sterility of the age is that little historical writing has survived on which the modern historian can draw to fashion his picture of the period. Certainly there is nothing comparable with Tacitus' account of the Julio-Claudians and of the upheaval which followed them, or with Suetonius' reliable portrayal of the first *Twelve Caesars*. The 'kingdom of rust and iron' which followed the age of the Antonines, was equally barren, in fact more so. Conditions were too disturbed to favour great writing or to ensure the survival of much of what was written. The prime source is the historian Cassius Dio, born in A.D. 163 or 164, a native of the Greek city of Nicomedia in the province of Bithynia, who followed his father into the senate early in the reign of Commodus. Dio wrote in Greek a complete history of Rome in eighty books, from the earliest origins to his own day – his account ends with some sombre reflections in the middle years of Severus Alexander, the late A.D. 220s. Dio's work is preserved in various forms. Some of the original work survives, but for the life and reign of Marcus Aurelius there are only epitomes and excerpts; and the entire account of the twenty-three years' reign of Antoninus Pius (A.D. 138–61) is lost. Cassius Dio, like most of his class, idealized Marcus Aurelius and hated Commodus. His outlook is biased therefore, but it does not appear to distort the facts unduly and provides an invaluable chronological framework.

Marcus Aurelius' own writings naturally offer a unique insight into the man. There are the letters to his tutor Fronto which cover his life between the ages of about seventeen and forty-five, with varying completeness. The letters are difficult to date exactly in many cases, but enough clues are provided to give an approximate indication. The *Meditations* were written late in life, and only the first book dwells in any detail on named persons. This provides an

[1] Cf. Tacitus, *Dialogus, passim*. In general, cf. A. S. L. Farquharson, *Marcus Aurelius*, 2nd ed., Oxford, 1952, esp. 89 ff.

18

invaluable series of character-sketches of his friends and family. Here and there in the later books casual references are historically illuminating. But the *Meditations* as a whole are informative about the inner life of Marcus, rather than his actions.

Marcus' correspondence with Fronto was re-discovered in the early nineteenth century. Marcus Cornelius Fronto had been known of as his tutor of course; but he had also been spoken of by writers of late antiquity as the second glory of Roman oratory after Cicero, and this judgement was accepted without question until his letters to Marcus and others were recovered. Then there was amazement and scorn. The letters were full of small-talk and gossip, vignettes of the unpretentious family life of the Antonines, and therefore they disappointed historians who had hoped for light on matters of greater moment. Students of literature were unimpressed with the artificial style. Fronto, a native of Cirta (Constantine) in Numidia and a member of the senate, had been credited with the revitalizing of Latin by his *elocutio novella*. This 'new speech' was revealed by the letters as a self-conscious effort to get away from the purist dictatorship exercised by writers such as Cicero and Seneca, and to enrich or revive the literary language by drawing on authors earlier than Rome's Golden Age of literature and on the language of daily life. The intention was good though the result seems a little half-baked. But his speeches, which have not survived, were supposedly renowned for the splendour and seriousness of their style, and it is obviously unfair to judge Fronto by his 'off-the-cuff' productions.

In view of the failings as historical sources of Dio, Marcus himself and Fronto, much reliance has inevitably to be placed on another work, the mysterious 'Augustan History'. This is a collection of biographies of the emperors from Hadrian to Carinus (A.D. 117–284) with a gap in the third century. It was ostensibly composed in the late third and early fourth centuries, by six authors. A peculiarity of the work is that biographies are included not only of emperors but of usurpers and Caesars (in effect, heirs to the throne). It has long been recognized that these latter 'minor lives' are worthless and, in particular, the 'documents' which they contain – supposedly original letters, speeches, and the like – are bogus, the work of the authorship rather than of those to whom they are assigned. There is more to the mystery than that, however. It has seemed to many that the 'authors' – Aelius Spartianus, Julius Capitolinus, Aelius Lampridius, Vulcacius Gallicanus, Trebellius Pollio and Flavius Vopiscus – never existed, and that whoever was responsible for the Augustan History was writing later than he (or they) pretends. Quite when, why and by whom remains a mystery. Many attempts have been made to identify the hand behind it, but none has convinced for long. In the present context no attempt need be made. But it is relevant to ask how the work was composed, in other words, from what materials. The work gives every appearance of having been put together in haste – by a hoaxer perhaps, in the fourth or early fifth century A.D., as a literary 'spoof'. But although the 'minor lives' of second-century characters are virtually worthless, and the lives of the third-century figures contain about 50 per cent fiction, the 'major lives' of second-century figures – the emperors from Hadrian to Severus, at least – are full of factual material, put together haphazardly in many cases, but providing irreplaceable information. This must be derived from a sound source. Personally I accept the view that this source was Marius Maximus, cited occasionally by the Augustan History. Maximus evidently wrote a second *Twelve Caesars* on the model of Suetonius, probably in direct continuation of him, and he is undoubtedly identical with L. Maximus Perpetuus Aurelianus, a contemporary of Cassius Dio, a leading general in the civil wars of Septimius Severus and a very prominent figure in the reigns of Caracalla, Macrinus, and of Severus Alexander, when the opportunity for composing a second *Twelve Caesars* first arose. The lives of all the emperors from Hadrian to Severus, particularly of Marcus himself, contain much valuable material which has to be used with caution, admittedly. The material in the second-century 'minor lives', on the other hand, has been incautiously used in many earlier biographies of Marcus and other second-century figures, and I have rejected almost all of it.

After that, there is little left. Herodian, a mediocre eastern Greek litterateur who was a younger contemporary of Dio and Maximus, wrote a history of the period from A.D. 180–238. He opened with the death of Marcus, and his account has nothing of value to add (and on some points is demonstrably false). In this context he is of interest solely as representative of the viewpoint of the third century on the passing of the golden age of the second. Much more useful are contemporary non-historical writers who provide background information and occasional historical facts. Aulus Gellius, an earnest hanger-on of the literary circles of the reign of Pius, provides a number of entertaining accounts of the philological discussions at the salons presided over by Fronto. In a slightly different category, Philostratus, a Greek intellectual who was a contemporary of Cassius Dio and a protégé of the empress Julia Domna, has left in his *Lives of the Sophists* useful information on the literary and intellectual life of the age of the Antonines, particularly in his life of Herodes Atticus, one of Marcus' tutors. Other writers such as Lucian, a Greek from Samosata, and Apuleius, a Latin-speaking native of Roman North Africa, are sometimes helpful, and Galen, the great physician who served Marcus Aurelius, mentions in one or two places episodes in the life of Marcus or his family.

Later historians are flimsy. Ammianus Marcellinus began his History with the accession of Nerva, but his account of the late first, second and third centuries is totally lost, and only in occasional flashbacks does he provide information of any value to the study of Marcus Aurelius. The other historians of the fourth century and after are no better than terse chroniclers, often confused and ignorant. Some Christian writers from the second century onwards throw light on the course of events, but their prime interest was naturally the history of the Christian Church and the vicissitudes of individual Christians. The legal sources are in a separate category. Roman jurisprudence was reaching its apogee during Marcus' lifetime, and the compilations of law of the late empire preserve a large number of decisions made by him which illuminate his personality and are informative on social conditions of the age.

Finally there is the evidence of coins, inscriptions and papyri, and of archaeology (including the historical reliefs). Coins can provide a chronological framework, and they can also reveal imperial policy:

they certainly expressed in their legends and design imperial atti-tudes. Inscriptions too are vital for dating purposes. They also reveal the entire careers of individuals otherwise entirely or almost entirely unknown but who played an important historical role. This was a by-product of the Roman love of self-advertisement. Archaeology rarely reveals facts which alter the historical picture at one stroke, but the collation of the results of excavations scattered throughout the empire can and does produce significant changes of outlook. The historical reliefs, notably the Column of Marcus Aurelius, are tan-talizing, as it seems to be impossible to understand the details which they show and to construct a valid narrative history from them. But they do help in our understanding of Marcus and his age by their graphic portrayal of the emperor and his army on campaign.[1]

Thus the sources for the life and reign of Marcus Aurelius are varied and incomplete. But whatever the loopholes in the history of the period, the personality of Marcus himself comes to life more vividly perhaps than that of any other single emperor.

[1] The sources are treated in more detail, with references, in Appendix I.

II

FAMILY AND EARLY YEARS

THE FAMILY into which Marcus was born, the Annii Veri, did not bear a name celebrated in the annals of Rome. The only Annius to have achieved fame (or notoriety) was the brutal and vicious political gang-leader of the late republic, T. Annius Milo. Nevertheless, the year of Marcus' birth, A.D. 121, was known in Roman records as the year when his paternal grandfather, Marcus Annius Verus, and Cn. Arrius Augur were the consuls. Annius Verus was holding the office for the second time, and was also prefect of the city of Rome. These two facts reveal that Marcus' grandfather was at the peak of social distinction and that he enjoyed the closest confidence of the emperor Hadrian. He had by then become the controlling figure in a complex network of family alliances. The ancient writers scarcely comment on the key political importance of this man. But something of his history and his connections can be pieced together, shedding valuable light on Marcus' origins and early life, and on the reasons for his ultimate rise to supreme power.[1]

The family came from Spain, from Uccubi (near Cordova) in the province of Baetica. The great-grandfather, also called Annius Verus, was 'made a praetorian senator', i.e. he was given the rank of ex-praetor.[2] It was clearly a reward for services rendered – no doubt

---

[1] For details of the family of Marcus see, in addition to the passages cited in the notes, Appendix II with family tree. Most members of the family are treated by R. Syme, *Tacitus* (Oxford, 1958), esp. II, 792–5, to which I am much indebted. For Marcus himself see *PIR 2*, A 697. The basis is in *v. Marci*, 1. On Milo, cf. *PW*, 1, 1894, 2271 ff. There is no obvious reason to suppose any connection between the Annii Veri and the Annii Milones (the *gens Annia* was very widespread). On the grandfather, see *PIR 2*, A 694.

[2] This need not imply that he had not been a senator before. It might mean that he was promoted within the senatorial order.

in the civil war in A.D. 69. Many who supported the winning Flavian side received high favour from Vespasian. His son, the grandfather of Marcus, was made patrician as a boy, by Vespasian in A.D. 73 or 74. The son of a key supporter of Vespasian, M. Ulpius Traianus, was also made patrician at the same time. This was the future emperor Trajan – colonial origin by this time was no drawback for he was from Baetica too, from the town of Italica, as was his cousin and successor Hadrian.[1] The first-known Annius Verus evidently died without achieving further honours. The son had to make his own way.

The young patrician married well, into a family of some pretensions. His bride was Rupilia Faustina, daughter of one Rupilius Libo or Libo Rupilius Frugi. The Rupilii were never distinguished, but the names Libo and Frugi indicate connection with descendants of Pompey and Crassus. Rupilius' wife no doubt had useful family connections – and the mother as well as the father of an ambitious young senator's bride would be an important person in furthering his career. But Rupilia's mother is unknown.[2]

How Annius Verus occupied himself under Domitian is not recorded. He reappears in the troubled year A.D. 97, when an unusually large number of carefully selected persons held office as consul. One of the suffect consuls was Annius Verus, now in his thirties. His colleague was the jurist L. Neratius Priscus, a south Italian and a new patrician of the same vintage as himself. Their tenure of office was remembered for one thing only, a decree of the senate forbidding the castration of slaves. Also consul in A.D. 97

---

[1] *v. Marci*, 1, 4: 'proavus paternus Annius Verus praetorius ex [S] Uccubitano municipio ex <H>ispania factus senator'. Cf. *v. Pert.*, 2, 6, for a parallel use of 'praetorium facere'. On the elder Trajan, cf. R. Syme, op. cit., I, 30 ff.

[2] On Rupilius, see Appendix II (note iii to stemma C). The wife of Rupilius might have been a Galeria (even a daughter of Vitellius with that name, cf. *PIR* 2, G 33), for this would explain how the name came into the Annian family. Some have suggested that he married Matidia, mother of Hadrian's wife Vibia Sabina, as her second husband, cf. J. Carcopino, *Rev. Ét. Anc.*, 51, 1949, 314 ff. – but this is highly conjectural. Later Annii bore the names Flavius and Sabinus: *PIR* 2, A 648 (M. Annius Flavius Libo) and 688 (M. Annius Sabinus Libo), which might suggest some link with the imperial Flavian house.

was one Arrius Antoninus, holding office for the second time with, as his colleague, L. Vibius Sabinus, the husband of Trajan's niece Matidia. Antoninus had been consul for the first time in another troubled year, A.D. 69, the year of the four emperors. He would not congratulate his friend Nerva, when the latter was made emperor in September A.D. 96: he congratulated the senate, the people, the provinces, but not the man unlucky enough to be chosen emperor. The younger Pliny was a friend and admirer of this cultivated person, whose grandson was the future emperor Antoninus Pius.[1]

Annius Verus and Rupilia Faustina had three children, two sons, Verus and Libo, and a daughter, Annia Galeria Faustina. The elder son married Domitia Lucilla, daughter of another patrician, P. Calvisius Tullus Ruso and of the elder Domitia Lucilla. Lucilla the elder inherited an enormous fortune, the wealth mainly of her maternal grandfather, Curtilius Mancia, and of her paternal grandfather by adoption, the orator Cn. Domitius Afer. The inheritance from Mancia is described at length in one of Pliny's letters.[2]

The circumstances were that Curtilius Mancia (consul in A.D. 55, at the beginning of the reign of Nero) had taken a violent dislike to his son-in-law, Domitius Lucanus. In his will he left Lucilla his fortune, but only on condition that she was released from paternal control – he did not want Lucanus to touch a penny of it. Lucanus complied. But the girl was at once adopted by Lucanus' brother, Tullus. The brothers held their possessions in common, 'and thus the purpose of the will was defeated', Pliny explained. He adds interesting details about the two Domitii brothers, prominent members of the new aristocracy. They had been adopted themselves by Domitius Afer – who had taken steps to ruin their real father, Curvius. The occasion for Pliny's letter was the death of Tullus; 'crippled and deformed in every limb he could only enjoy his wealth

---

[1] On the events of A.D. 97, cf. R. Syme, op. cit., esp. I, 1–18; on the consuls of that year, ibid., II, 640 ff. Arrius Antoninus: *PIR* 2, 1086 and R. Syme, op. cit., II, 640. The anecdote is in Victor, *de Caes.*, 12, 3.

[2] The father: *PIR* 2, A 696. Libo: A 667. Faustina: A 715. Elder Lucilla: D 182. Younger Lucilla: D 183. Tullus Ruso: C 357. Mancia: C 1605. Domitius Afer: D 126. The brick-factories: cf. *CIL*, XV, 979 ff. (tile-stamps of Afer), ibid., 127–32, etc. See further references in *PIR* 2, D 183.

by looking at it, and he could not even turn round in his bed without being helped. He also – a squalid and miserable detail – had to have his teeth cleaned and brushed for him.' The death of Tullus meant that all the family's wealth now came to Lucilla. Pliny's letter retails in full the complicated and embarrassing family history. It was a welcome source of gossip. 'You now have all the city gossip – for all the gossip is about Tullus,' he concludes, adding a final titbit about the forthcoming auction of the effects, and a sententious comment: 'if you have any news worth writing about in return, do not grudge it me – for men's ears are cheered by news, and through examples we are educated in the art of living.'[1]

Lucilla had other children besides the daughter with her own name, perhaps by another husband. But the younger Lucilla acquired much of her fortune, including vast brick factories on the outskirts of Rome.[2]

The younger Lucilla and her husband Verus had two children, Marcus, born in A.D. 121 and his younger sister, Annia Cornificia Faustina, born probably within the next two years.[3] Marcus' father died young, during his praetorship.[4] As a patrician he should have become consul at thirty-two, the minimum age, two years after his praetorship. His younger brother Annius Libo was consul in A.D. 128 and can hardly have been praetor later than A.D. 126. Verus must have been praetor earlier than this and A.D. 124 is the likeliest year of his death. Thus Marcus can scarcely have known his father, but he was later to say of him: 'From my father's reputation and from my memory of him [I learned] modesty and manliness.' Similar qualities were in fact ascribed to Marcus by the biographer.[5] Lucilla was faithful to her husband's memory and did not remarry. The younger Verus, had he lived, would have been assured of achieving a distinguished place in Roman public life.

In the year A.D. 126 Marcus' grandfather Verus was consul again, for the third time, a great mark of honour, for Hadrian himself did not

---

[1] Pliny, *Epp.*, 8, 18.   [2] *PIR 2*, D 183.   [3] *PIR 2*, A 708.
[4] *PIR 2*, A 696. Generally thought to have died *c.* A.D. 130, which I regard as too late.
[5] *Med.*, 1, 2. Cf. *v. Marci*, 6, 7–8; 12, 7; 17, 2.

hold the office more than three times.¹ Catilius Severus, Marcus' 'step-grandfather', had been consul for the second time a year before Verus, in A.D. 120, and there were others with more seniority. There were no rules or precedents governing such exceptional honours, of course; they were in the emperor's gift – and this goes to underline the enormous importance and prestige of the family. Verus' junior colleague was a man named Eggius Ambibulus (among many other names), perhaps a relative of Verus' daughter-in-law Lucilla – yet another illustration of the closely interwoven nature of Roman public and private life.²

Perhaps old Annius Verus had shown some kindness to Hadrian when he was a young man from Spain trying to make his way in Rome, embarrassed by his provincial accent.³ There may even have been a direct relationship: Cassius Dio certainly states that Hadrian favoured Marcus because of 'his kinship'.⁴ If this kinship existed it might have been through another Spanish Roman family, the Dasumii. The family of Marcus was alleged to have been descended from 'the Sallentine king, Malemmius, son of Dasummus, who founded Lupiae'. This is the kind of fictitious descent from a semi-mythical figure which Romans loved to concoct on the basis of some family name. One of the Annii in the past might have married a Dasumia.⁵ It certainly appears that one of the Dasumii had married an Aelia, a lady of Hadrian's family, for a Dasumius of the early second century bore the name Hadrianus.⁶ Dio might have been referring to this. Alternatively, he might have meant simply that Hadrian favoured Marcus' family. In a later passage he states that Marcus 'while still a boy so pleased all his many powerful and

---

¹ The statement in *v. Had.*, 8, 4, that H. made many men consul for the third time and even more for the second time is false. See A. Degrassi, *I Fasti Consolari, etc.*, Roma, 1952, 34–40.

² *PIR* 2, E 6. Cf. R. Syme, op. cit., II, 793, No. 6.

³ *v. Had.*, 3, 1: 'agrestius pronuntians' (as quaestor in A.D. 101).

⁴ Dio, 69, 21, 2: διά τε τὴν συγγένειαν αὐτοῦ. For the theory of Carcopino, see n. 2, p. 24 above and Appendix II.

⁵ *v. Marci*, 1, 5. Cf. Suetonius, *Galba*, 2 (descent from Jupiter and Pasiphae); ibid., *Vitellius*, 1 (descent from Faunus, King of the Aborigines).

⁶ *PIR* 2, H 5 (not quite certain, cf. R. Syme, op. cit., II, 794, No. 11).

wealthy relations that they all loved him' – and that Hadrian adopted him chiefly for this reason.[1]

Marcus was brought up as a boy in his parents' house on the Caelian, one of the seven hills of Rome, which he was later to call, with affection, 'my Caelian'. Under the empire the Caelian was the fashionable district of Rome for the leading families. It had few public buildings, but many splendid aristocratic mansions, of which the most splendid was the Lateran Palace, once the possession, by confiscation, of Nero, and thenceforward imperial property, standing where the Basilica of San Giovanni Laterano now stands. In Roman times it was next to the barracks of the Imperial Horse Guards, the *equites singulares*. Also next to the Lateran was the palace of Marcus' grandfather, where Marcus spent much of his childhood. The Caelian was on the southern edge of Rome. From it, to the north, one could look across to the Circus Maximus, to the Palatine with its imperial palaces, the Forum, the Colosseum and the Baths of Trajan. In the foreground was the massive temple of the Divine Claudius, and, straddling the area between the Lateran and the heart of Rome, the great aqueduct which brought the *Aqua Claudia* and part of the *Aqua Marcia* into the city.[2]

If Marcus' parents followed the traditional practice, his father would have had to acknowledge the child as his by lifting him up from the hearth at his feet. On the ninth day after this came the ceremony of purification, at which the child was named. It was then that the *praenomen* Marcus was given him, the only one of his names which he bore for the rest of his life. The child would be given presents at this ceremony, a rattle formed of a string with tinkling objects attached to it (*crepundia*) and an amulet of gold (*bulla*), a charm against the evil eye which he would wear round his neck until he assumed the *toga virilis*, the dress of manhood – in Marcus' case this was to be at the age of 14.[3]

After the birth, Lucilla probably had little to do with her son for

[1] Dio, 71, 35, 2–3.
[2] *v. Marci*, 1, 5–7; Fronto, *ad M.C.*, II, 6, 2 (Haines, I, 142). On the Caelian, cf. A. M. Colini, *Mem. Pont. Acc. Arch.*, 1944, 138 ff.
[3] Cf. Marquardt, *Handbuch*, VII, 1, Leipzig, 1879 (Privatleben), 10, 81 ff.

some time. The historian Tacitus, who may have been still living when Marcus was born, had written with some bitterness in his *Dialogue on Orators* of the changed habits of the nobility in the up-bringing of children: 'In the old days, each Roman child born in wedlock was not brought up in the back-bedroom of some slave-girl nurse, but in its mother's bosom and lap. The mother's especial glory was to keep her house and serve her children. . . .Thus we read how Cornelia the mother of the Gracchi and Aurelia the mother of Julius Caesar were in charge of the upbringing of their sons and brought them up to be leaders. . . . Now the new-born infant is handed over to some little Greek serving-maid, who has the help of some other slave chosen from the rest of the household, usually the most worthless and totally unfitted for an important task. The child's green and untaught mind is filled with their stories and mistakes. No one in the whole household thinks it of any importance what is said and done in the presence of the young master.'[1]

It is recorded that Marcus was in the care of 'nurses'.[2] This would certainly have included, at first, a wet-nurse, who would have the duty of feeding the new-born child. This impression is confirmed by a mention of his nurse in the *Meditations*: 'I follow the way of nature until I lie down and rest, breathing my last breath in the air from which I now breathe, lying down on the earth from which my father drew his vital seed, my mother her blood and my nurse her milk.'[3] The fact that the nurses were usually Greek was no accident. It was essential for an educated Roman to master Greek, and if the child's nurse spoke Greek, this would be a great help – although there was a slight danger that the child would then speak Latin with a foreign accent.[4]

Not everyone approved of the practice of using wet-nurses, but it was deep-rooted. Aulus Gellius records how he accompanied the philosopher Favorinus to visit one of the latter's pupils, a senator of noble family. The wife had just had a son, and Favorinus wished to bring his congratulations: 'When he had been told how long the

[1] Tacitus, *Dial.*, 28–9.
[2] *v. Marci*, 2, 1: 'annos qui nutricum foventur auxilio'.
[3] *Med.*, 5, 4.   [4] Quintilian, *Inst.*, 1, 1, 12 ff.

birth had taken, and how difficult the labour had been, and that the girl, worn out with her efforts and lack of sleep was now sleeping, he began to talk at some length. "No doubt," he said, "she will feed her son with her own milk?" But the girl's mother said that she had to be spared this, and that wet-nurses had to be provided, so that the tiring and difficult task of breast-feeding need not be added to the pains which she had suffered in labour.' This produced an outburst from Favorinus – '"Do you think that nature provided women with nipples as a kind of beauty-spot",' and so on, for some time. The arguments he used were a little fallacious, for he claimed that'"if she whom you provide to give milk is a slave or of servile background, and, as usually happens, of foreign and barbarous origin, if she is dishonest, ugly, immodest, a drunkard,"' some of her unfortunate qualities would be transferred to the child she fed, through her milk. Modern authorities might agree in principle, although the effect that they would postulate would be psychological rather than physiological. Favorinus, a Hellenized Gaul from Arles, said credibly to have been a hermaphrodite, was a philosopher prominent in the reign of Hadrian and the early part of the reign of Antoninus Pius. He was an intimate of the same circles as the family and friends of Marcus, and the young mother whose conduct occasioned his outburst could well have been Domitia Lucilla. Aulus Gellius gives no names.[1]

At his father's death Marcus was adopted by his grandfather, Verus.[2] But in his early years another man played an important role in supervising his life – L. Catilius Severus. Marcus bore the names Catilius Severus for some years in addition to Marcus Annius Verus. Catilius Severus is described as his *proavus maternus*, which must mean 'step-grandfather' rather than, as more normally, 'great-grandfather'. (He cannot have been the grandfather of the younger Lucilla.) Catilius Severus may have married the elder Lucilla after the death of Calvisius Tullus Ruso: this alliance would be valuable to Severus' ambitions – he was a man of talent but with no known family ties with the aristocracy, old or new. He had been one of the

[1] A. Gellius, *Noct. Att.*, 12, 1. Favorinus: *PIR 2*, F 123.
[2] *v. Marci*, 1, 7 and 10. Cf. *Med.*, I, 17, 2.

most prominent allies of Hadrian at the stormy period of his accession, when Hadrian transferred him from Armenia to take over the Syrian army at a time when loyalty in the largest army of the east was particularly vital.[1]

Virtually nothing is known of Marcus' uncle Annius Libo, except that he was consul in A.D. 128, as junior colleague to one of the old aristocracy; and that he had a son, also named Libo, and a daughter named Annia Fundania Faustina. His daughter's second name suggests that Libo had married a Fundania. If so, a good match.[2] Marcus' aunt Annia Galeria Faustina is naturally much better known,[3] for she was married to the future emperor Antoninus Pius – T. Aurelius Fulvus Boionius Arrius Antoninus, who had been junior colleague to Catilius Severus in the consulship of A.D. 120.

Aurelius Antoninus was also from a provincial family, which had its origin at Nemausus (Nîmes) in Gallia Narbonensis.[4] The founder of his family's fortunes had been his grandfather, T. Aurelius Fulvus, whose career had first shown brilliance when he was a legionary legate under the great Corbulo in Nero's reign. He had gone from strength to strength under the Flavian emperors, being made prefect of the city and consul for the second time. His son, Antoninus' father, probably yet another of the new patricians of A.D. 73–74, had died when Antoninus was a boy, and his mother Arria Fadilla, daughter of the celebrated Arrius Antoninus, remarried.[5] Her second husband was P. Julius Lupus, a distant connection of the Flavian imperial house.[6] Antoninus had been born in A.D. 86, and

---

[1] Catilius Severus: *PIR* 2, C 558. Marcus' use of his names: *v. Marci*, 1, 9 (cf. 1, 4, in both cases giving the relationship as 'proavus maternus'); Dio, 69, 21, 1. Cf. also *Med.*, 1, 4. See E. Groag, *Jahreshefte*, 29, 1935, Beibl. 181 ff.; also in *PIR* 2, D 182, and R. Syme, op. cit., II, 793, n. 3 (whose suggestion is followed here).

[2] Libo: *PIR* 2, A 667. The name of the cos. ord. 116 is now known to be L. Fundanius Lamia Aelianus (*AE*, 1947, 4). This man was of aristocratic origin, cf. *PIR* 2, A 204. Libo's son: *PIR* 2, A 668. His daughter: *PIR* 2, A 713.

[3] *PIR* 2, A 715.

[4] The Aurelii Fulvi: *PIR* 2, A 1509, 1510, 1513 (Antoninus).

[5] Fadilla: *PIR* 2, A 1509. Arrius Antoninus: *PIR* 2, A 1086.

[6] *PW*, 10, 1919, 664; *v. Pii*, 1, 5–6. For the possible Flavian connection, cf. G. Townend, *JRS*, 51, 1961, 57 ff.

had thus probably married Faustina in about A.D. 110, some years before Marcus was born. They had four children, two sons and two daughters. Three died young, the two boys and the elder daughter, Aurelia Fadilla (she survived long enough to be married to Lamia Silvanus, a young man from one of the noblest families, but died in, probably, A.D. 134). The younger daughter, named after her mother, was to marry her cousin Marcus. Her date of birth is not known, but as she married Marcus in A.D. 145 and was still young enough to bear children in the A.D. 160s, it is probable that she was born about A.D. 130.[1]

Marcus was 'a solemn child from his earliest infancy',[2] in spite of being brought up by his grandfather, a genial and sporting old man, one of whose favourite pastimes was a new ball game, played with a glass ball, the details of which are not known. It was evidently for two players. Old Annius Verus was the patron of the champion at this game, a man named Ursus. He could give the champion a good game – and on many occasions beat him, as Ursus was proud to inform the world in his metrical epitaph: he, Ursus, 'excelled all his predecessors', in the ball game, 'in touch, grace and subtlest art'; but, he concluded, 'I was beaten myself, I confess –

> By the thrice consul Verus, my patron,
> Not once, but often, and I will gladly
> Sing his praises.'[3]

The great doctor Galen wrote a short treatise on the benefits to health that devotion to ball games provided, and Marcus himself became a tolerably good player.[4] He does not dwell on this aspect of his grandfather's character in his *Meditations*, but he placed his name at the head of the list with which the *Meditations* open, of those

[1] Aurelia Fadilla: *PIR 2*, A 1653. Lamia Silvanus: *PIR 2*, A 206. He may have been a Fundanius, cf. n. 2, p. 31. The younger Faustina: *PIR 2*, A 716. The sons were M. Aurelius Fulvus Antoninus (*PIR 2*, A 1511) and M. Galerius Aurelius Antoninus (*PIR 2*, G 26).

[2] v. *Marci*, 2, 1: 'fuit a prima infantia gravis'.

[3] Cf. n. 1, p. 33. For the ball-game, Dessau, *ILS*, 5173=*CIL*, VI, 9797 (Rome).

[4] Galen, περὶ τοῦ διὰ τῆς μικεᾶς σφαίρας γυμνασίου, V, 899–910 K. Cf. also Galen, VI, 406 K; v. *Marci*, 4, 9: 'et pila lusit adprime'.

from whom he had benefited: 'From my grandfather Verus; good character and avoidance of bad temper.'[1] On the other hand, some time after the death of his wife Rupilia Faustina, the old man took a mistress, with whom he lived openly. Marcus was grateful in later years that the course of events prevented him from being brought up in the same household as this lady any longer than he was: evidently something about her or her entourage might have placed temptation in his path.[2]

Marcus' mother played a large role in his life, even if she did not feed him in infancy herself. The qualities in her which he remembered as influencing him were 'religious piety, generosity, not only refraining from wrongdoing but even from thoughts of it, simplicity in diet, and to be far removed from the ways of the rich'.[3] The last perhaps a particularly surprising tribute, considering the exceptional wealth inherited by Lucilla. Marcus in middle age was grateful that 'although my mother was fated to die young, yet she spent her last years with me'.[4] His correspondence with Fronto is full of natural and affectionate references to her. She was a lady of some talent and education, well-versed in Greek. The great Athenian orator Herodes Atticus, who was to be the instructor of her son, had been brought up in her father's house for a time – presumably to learn Latin – and this no doubt played a part in giving her a fondness for Hellenic culture.[5]

When Marcus reached the age of seven in A.D. 128, the time had come when a Roman boy began his elementary education, although he had probably, following Quintilian's principles, already been taught to read.[6] It may have been then that the question arose whether he should be sent to school or should be taught at home by tutors. Formerly the most conscientious fathers instructed their sons in the most elementary subjects in person, as was the case with the great Cato, nearly 300 years before the birth of Marcus, who

---

[1] *Med.*, 1, 1.   [2] Ibid., 1, 17, 2.   [3] Ibid., 1, 3.   [4] Ibid., 1, 17, 7.

[5] For the references in Fronto (and the connection with Herodes), cf. in *PIR 2*, D 183.

[6] Quintilian, *Inst.*, 1, 1, 16. For the background to what follows, cf. H.-I. Marrou, *A History of Education in Antiquity* (Eng. tr. of *Histoire de l'Education dans l'Antiquité*, 3rd ed., Paris), London, 1956, esp. 229 ff.

'as soon as his son showed signs of sufficient intelligence, took personal charge of him and taught him to read, even though he had an accomplished slave who was a schoolmaster. . . . He thought that it was wrong that his son should be scolded and have his ears pinched by a slave for being slow at his lessons – still less that he should owe to a slave such a priceless benefit as education. He took on himself the task of being his son's reading-master, law-tutor and physical training instructor . . . he even wrote out in his own hand, in large letters, a *History of Rome* for the boy.' Still, Cato was exceptional, even in his own time. His wife not only fed her babies herself, but sometimes provided milk for her slaves' babies, which was going to the opposite extreme.[1] In any case, Marcus had no father by the time he was old enough to begin reading. And even Pliny, who was in favour of boys attending a school when it was run by a man like his friend Julius Genitor, applied this only to secondary education: 'Up to the present your son has been too young to leave your side,' he wrote to Corellia Hispulla, recommending Genitor's school for her son, 'and has had teachers at home where there is little or no opportunity for going astray.'[2]

There was obviously some discussion among the family as to what should be done, although the discussion may not have arisen until Marcus was ready for his secondary education. The deciding voice was that of Catilius Severus, whom Marcus later remembered gratefully for this: 'From my step-grandfather: not to have attended public places of teaching but to have enjoyed good teachers at home; and to have learned that it is a duty to spend liberally on such things.'[3]

The basis of Roman education, after the elementary lessons in reading, writing and arithmetic, was to teach a boy Greek language and literature, which the Romans regarded as essential for a civilized person. His first teachers were called Euphorion and Geminus.[4] Euphorion was, to judge from his name, Greek, and was presumably

---

[1] Plutarch, *Cato Maior*, 20, 2 ff.   [2] Pliny, *Epp.*, 3, 3, 3.   [3] *Med.*, 1, 4.
[4] *v. Marci*, 2, 2. (The mention of Andron here is misplaced, cf. J. Schwendemann, *Der historische Wert der vita Marci bei den Scriptores Historiae Augustae*, Heidelberg, 1923, 6–7.)

responsible for elementary instruction in that language. Geminus, whose name is Latin, is described as an actor, and his task may therefore have been to supervise the boy's Latin pronunciation and elocution in general. Both Euphorion and Geminus, who are otherwise unknown, would undoubtedly have been family slaves or freedmen of the Annii Veri. A third teacher was in general charge of Marcus, as his *educator* (τροφεύς in Greek), to watch over his moral welfare and general development. His name is unknown, but Marcus speaks of him with gratitude in the *Meditations*: 'From my tutor: not to be a supporter of the Greens or the Blues at the races, nor of the Thracian or Samnite gladiators; to bear pain and be content with little; to work with my own hands, to mind my own business, to be slow to listen to slander.'[1]

In A.D. 127, at the age of six, probably a year before he began his education, he was enrolled in the order of the *equites* by the nomination of Hadrian himself. This gave him the right to wear a gold ring and a tunic with a narrow border. The honour was not completely exceptional – other cases are known where boys of very tender years were appointed – but Marcus was unusually young.[2] The following year, when he was seven, he was enrolled by Hadrian into the priestly college of the Salii. The qualification for membership was to be of patrician birth and to have both parents living. In Marcus' case the second qualification was lacking, since his father was dead, but perhaps the adoption by his grandfather met the legal requirements; although the fact that he was enrolled by Hadrian, rather than co-opted in the normal way, suggests that there was an irregularity and special favour from the emperor.

The name Salii came from the word *salire*, to leap or dance, which indicates the nature of the ceremonies which they performed: ritual dances. These priests were found in various towns of Italy from earliest times. At Rome itself they were associated with the worship of Mars, the god of war. There were two companies, each with twelve members, called the Collini and Palatini. Their priestly costume was

---

[1] *Med.*, 1, 5. Note *v. Pii*, 10, 5.
[2] *v. Marci*, 4, 2. Cf. A. Stein, *Der römische Ritterstand*, München, 1927.

the old Italian war-uniform, the *tunica picta*, with a breast-plate covered by a short military cloak, and a felt hat of conical shape. They wore a sword and on their left arm they carried *ancilia*, shields of figure of eight shape, which were supposed to be copies of an original which fell from heaven, as a gift from the god Jupiter to Rome's second king Numa Pompilius. They carried a spear or staff in their right hand. Twice a year they played a prominent part in religious ceremonies which marked the opening and close of the campaigning season, at the Quinquatrus on March 19, and the Armilustrium on October 19. On some other days in these two months they went in procession through the city carrying their shields. At intervals they halted to perform their complicated ritual dances, beating their shields with their staffs and singing their hymn, the Carmen Saliare, an obscure religious chant in archaic Latin, the words of which were by this time almost unintelligible. In the evening they feasted.

Marcus took his duties as a member of this order very seriously. He fulfilled various of the offices in the priesthood in turn, being the leader of the dance, the *vates* (prophet), and the master of the order. In his last function it was his task to initiate new members and formally to dismiss those who left the order. He learned the archaic formulas by heart, so that it was never necessary in his case for them to be read out for him to repeat. While Marcus was a Salian priest an omen occurred, which was remembered (long after, no doubt) as signifying his future rule. When the members of the college were casting their crowns on the banqueting couch of the god, as was the custom, Marcus' crown fell on the brow of the god Mars, as if he had placed it there, whereas the others fell in random places. At the time, quite possibly, it was thought no more of than that Marcus was an especially good shot (or especially bad, if he was aiming somewhere else).[1]

---

[1] For this argument on the enrolment (which is also an argument in favour of a date earlier than c. A.D. 130 for the death of his father), cf. R. Dailly-H. van Effenterre, *Rev. Ét. Anc.*, 56, 1954, 357 ff. Marcus' enrolment and performance as a Salius, v. *Marci*, 4, 2–4. On the Salii in general, see *PW*, IA, 1920, 1874 ff., and more recently R. Bloch, *The Origins of Rome* (Eng. tr., revised), London, 1960, 134 ff.

No further details of his earliest years of education are recorded. When he approached his twelfth year, he would be ready for secondary education, under *grammatici*. In his case, two other teachers are also recorded. The first, Andron, was 'a geometrician and musician'. His instruction in mathematics probably did not begin until Marcus was eleven. The music teaching may have been mainly in singing.[1] At about the same time he was given another teacher, the painting-master Diognetus.[2] Diognetus was more than a painting-master to Marcus, however. It seems to have been he who first showed Marcus the attractions of philosophy – as a way of life, at least. Marcus remembered in his *Meditations* the lessons he had learned from this man: 'From Diognetus: to avoid passing enthusiasms; to distrust the stories of miracle-workers and impostors about incantations and exorcism of spirits and such things; not to go cock-fighting or to get excited about such sports; to put up with outspokenness; and to become familiar with philosophy; to hear first the lectures of Baccheius, then of Tandasis and Marcianus; to write philosophical dialogues in my boyhood; to aspire to the camp-bed and the skin coverlet and the other things which belong to the Greek training.'[3] It was when he entered his twelfth year (in April A.D. 132) that Marcus was first fired with eagerness to follow the austere way of life of the philosopher, the biographer records. 'He adopted the dress, and a little later the habits of endurance, of the philosopher. He followed his studies clad in a rough Greek cloak. He slept on the ground, and it was only at his mother's insistence that he consented, with reluctance, to sleep on a little bed strewn with skins.'[4]

Magicians and miracle-workers of all kinds were flourishing as never before at this time, and were to flourish even more. Marcus as emperor was to come across a charlatan of this kind on the grand scale – Alexander of Abonuteichos. The philosophic way of life that the 11-year-old Marcus adopted sounds from its description like an attempt to imitate the Cynics, who were the most obvious practising philosophers of the time, to the average person, for they made a

---

[1] *v. Marci*, 2, 2; cf. n. 55.
[2] Ibid., 4, 9 (in the wrong context, cf. Schwendemann, op. cit., 20).
[3] *Med.*, 1, 6.   [4] *v. Marci*, 2, 6.

cult of the simple life to the point of aggressiveness. The sardonic essayist Lucian portrayed one of the leading practitioners of the Cynic philosophy, Peregrinus, in terms almost as scathing as he used to tear in shreds the bogus claims of Alexander, the false prophet and miracle-worker.[1]

The boy's solemn and serious devotion to his studies made an impression on Hadrian, who took a close interest in his upbringing from an early stage. The emperor, playing on his name Verus ('true', 'truthful', or 'genuine'), nicknamed him Verissimus, 'truest'. The name stuck, and has even been found on coins and on an inscription.[2] It is clear however, that Hadrian cannot have seen much of Marcus during these boyhood years. In A.D. 121, when Marcus was born, he was in Gaul and on the Rhine. In A.D. 122 he was in Britain, he passed through Spain in A.D. 123 on his way to the east, and conferred with the Parthian king on the frontier. The years A.D. 124 and 125 were spent in the Greek-speaking lands – in fact Hadrian may not have returned to Rome until A.D. 127. In A.D. 128 he was away again, on a visit to Africa, and after a brief return to Rome left for Athens, the eastern provinces and Egypt. He was back in Rome in A.D. 131, but the Jewish war which broke out in A.D. 132 and lasted for four years demanded his attention.[3] On his visit to Egypt Hadrian had lost his favourite, the beautiful Bithynian youth, Antinous.[4] He was inconsolable for a time, and the dead youth was deified – a subject for considerable gossip among the aristocracy. Hadrian was no longer as fit as he had been, although in

---

[1] Cf. S. Dill, *Roman Society from Nero to Marcus Aurelius*, London, 1904, repr. New York, 1956, 354 ff. and 443 ff.; also B. Baldwin, *CQ*, N.S. 11, 1961, 199 ff. For Alexander and Peregrinus, see the works of Lucian bearing their names. On the Cynics, cf. D. R. Dudley, *A History of Cynicism, etc.*, London, 1937, esp. 143 ff.

[2] *v. Marci*, 1, 10; 2, 1: 'educatus est in Hadriani gremio, qui illum, ut supra diximus, Verissimum nominabat'. Dio, 69, 21, 2 (the reason given here is, in addition to that quoted earlier, p. 27 above, 'his exceptional strength of character'). For the coins, cf. the references in *PIR 2*, A 697 (p. 120). The inscription: *AE*, 1940, 62 (Ostia).

[3] See the extensive bibliography of works dealing with Hadrian's travels in A. Garzetti, *Storia di Roma*, VI, Bologna, 1960, 678–80.

[4] *PIR 2*, A 737.

A.D. 132 he was only 56 years old.[1] The question of the succession began to loom up. In A.D. 134 Hadrian made his brother-in-law, the aged Servianus, now nearly 90, consul for the third time. Servianus should have realized that the honour was only an honour, yet it excited his hopes[2] – only Annius Verus, Marcus' grandfather, had received a like honour. But Servianus had a grandson, Pedanius Fuscus Salinator, a young man in his late teens who was also Hadrian's great nephew.[3]

Hadrian's last years were spent at his country palace at Tivoli on the edge of the Sabine hills, twenty miles east of Rome. This vast complex of halls, baths, theatres, lakes, porticoes, temples and ornamental gardens was Hadrian's pride and joy. It covered over a hundred acres, with a circumference of several miles. Hadrian had built it himself – and had no doubt taken a personal hand in the architectural design. He filled it with originals or copies of works of art from all the places he had visited in his travels, or copies of buildings – from Thessaly, Athens, Alexandria.[4]

Hadrian began in A.D. 135 to build himself a mausoleum as well, for the imperial vaults built by Augustus on the Campus Martius were now full. Hadrian's tomb was to be erected opposite the new bridge he had given Rome, the Pons Aelius. Bridge and tomb have since become more famous as the Ponte and Castel Sant' Angelo.[5] It may have been in these years at Tivoli that Hadrian came to know and acquire a liking for Lucius Ceionius Commodus, now married to the daughter of Avidius Nigrinus, one of the men Hadrian had disposed of at the beginning of his reign.[6] Ceionius Commodus was a young man of taste who may have appealed to Hadrian. His family

---

[1] *v. Had.*, 23, 1, places the onset of illness shortly after his return and before the death of Servianus, i.e. between A.D. 134 and 136. For his age, *v. Had.*, 1, 3; complete details in *PIR 2*, A 184.

[2] *v. Had.*, 15, 8; 23, 2-3, 8; 25, 9, and 8, 11 (the third consulship, in a different context). Dio, 69, 17, 1. See also *PW*, 20, 1919, 882 ff., and R. Syme, op. cit., II, 636.

[3] *PW*, 19, 1937, 19 ff.; R. Syme, op. cit., esp. I, 247; II, 600.

[4] See H. Kähler, *Hadrian und seine Villa bei Tivoli*, Berlin, 1950, and S. Aurigemma, *Villa Adriana*, Roma, 1961.

[5] See G. Lugli, *I Monumenti Antichi*, III, Roma, 1938, 693 ff.

[6] *PIR 2*, C 605 (Commodus); A 1408 (Nigrinus).

was one of those that had risen to the peak of social eminence on the foundation of meritorious service under the Flavian dynasty. His grandfather had been consul in the fourth last year of Vespasian, one of only four men who had the honour of the ordinary consulship in the reign of Vespasian, who were not from the imperial family – (the other sixteen places were filled regularly by Vespasian and his sons). He had then been governor of Syria.[1] This distinction was sufficient to allow succeeding generations to settle down to a life of confident and opulent ease, enjoying as a hereditary right the traditional honours of the Roman state, without the need to work as soldier and administrator in the service of the emperors. The second Ceionius Commodus was consul in A.D. 106, thirty years after the first,[2] and this Commodus, the third, was to be consul in A.D. 136, after another thirty years. His colleague was his step-brother, Sextus Vettulenus Civica Pompeianus – their fathers had been colleagues in A.D. 106. The grandfather of Civica Pompeianus, like the grandfather of Commodus, had commanded legions – and had met a violent end through the jealousy of Domitian. These days were done with now.[3] Commodus' mother must have been a remarkable woman. Only her name, Plautia, is known, no details of her personality, but she had three husbands, of whom Commodus' father was only the first. Following his death she married Avidius Nigrinus, so that Commodus' wife, Avidia, had been for a time his step-sister. Finally, after the unfortunate end of Nigrinus, she married Civica Cerialis, the father of Pompeianus, by whom she had another son, Civica Barbarus, born probably about A.D. 124. Ceionius Commodus had a son, born in December A.D. 130, and two daughters, Ceionia Fabia and Ceionia Plautia. It was to one of these daughters, Fabia, that Hadrian was to arrange the betrothal of Marcus in A.D. 136.[4]

---

[1] *PIR 2*, C 603.   [2] *PIR 2*, C 604.

[3] *PW*, 8A, 1958, inexplicably omits this family. Cf. R. Syme, *Historia*, 8, 1959, 207 ff.

[4] Civica Barbarus: *PIR 2*, C 602, where he is thought to be a Ceionius. But see *AE*, 1958, 15, and the important article by R. Syme, *Athenaeum*, 35, 1957, 306 ff., where details of this family nexus are revealed. The son (named after his father): *PIR 2*, C 606. Ceionia Fabia: *PIR 2*, C 612. Ceionia Plautia: *PIR 2*, C 614.

But the introduction of Lucius Commodus and his family at this stage is anticipating, very slightly, the known details in the life of Marcus. As already mentioned, it was normal for a boy at about eleven or twelve to pass from the care of the *litterator* to that of the *grammaticus*. This was perhaps the time when the question seriously arose whether Marcus should be taught at home or should go to school. In the event, more tutors were chosen, one Greek, Alexander of Cotiaeum, and three Latin, Trosius Aper, Pollio and Eutychius Proculus of Sicca Veneria in North Africa.[1] They must have taken over Marcus' education in about A.D. 132 or 133. The task of the *grammaticus* was to instil in his pupil a knowledge of literature. The students had to read aloud and learn by heart passages from classical writers, and the teacher commented on matters of style and inculcated the moral or philosophical lessons to be found in the works.[2] Little is known of the three Latin teachers. Pollio was perhaps a lover of Horace, if what Marcus was to write some years later refers to him: 'Horace died for me with Pollio.'[3] Trosius Aper is only a name, but Eutychius Proculus was later rewarded by Marcus with public office, in this case a proconsulship.[4] Alexander of Cotiaeum, the Greek master, was a well-known literary figure of the early second century, the leading authority on Homer. He was also the teacher of the orator Aelius Aristides, who wrote an elaborate obituary of him in the form of a speech addressed to the people of Cotiaeum, a Phrygian city in the province of Asia. Marcus had favourable memories of Alexander when he wrote his *Meditations*: 'From Alexander the *grammaticus*: to avoid finding fault and not to criticise in a carping spirit those who use outlandish expressions, solecisms or an awkward style; but to use the right phrase oneself, neatly and precisely, by way of answer or confirmation or handling of the actual subject in question, not its description in words, or by some equally happy reminder.'[5] Something of this training by

---

[1] *v. Marci*, 2, 3.
[2] H.-I. Marrou, op. cit., 274 ff.
[3] Fronto, *ad M.C.*, 2, 10, 3 (Haines, I, 138–40). For the identification, cf. A. S. L. Farquharson, *Marcus Aurelius, His Life and World*, Oxford, 1952, 18.
[4] *v. Marci*, 2, 5.
[5] *PIR* 2, A 502; *Med.*, 1, 10; Aristides, *or. 32 K.*

Alexander – the emphasis on matter rather than elaborate style, the careful choice of language, the occasional use of Homeric expressions – has been detected in the Greek of Marcus' own *Meditations*.[1]

When Marcus was fourteen he assumed the *toga virilis*, the garment of manhood. He would discard the gold amulet and striped toga of his childhood, and assume the plain white toga of a man. He was now a full citizen, ready for a part in public life. But his education had to go on – it was in fact to continue for many years more, by necessity of the station in which he was to find himself, and by his own inclination. Shortly after this, Hadrian expressed the wish that the betrothal should take place of Marcus and the daughter of Ceionius Commodus.[2] Marcus' fourteenth birthday was in April A.D. 135, but it is not known whether he became engaged to Ceionia Fabia in A.D. 135 or 136. It was probably A.D. 136, for the ceremony of the assumption of the *toga virilis* customarily took place at the festival of the Liberalia, on March 17 – hence A.D. 135 would be impossible.[3] An additional reason is that soon after the betrothal he was given a new honour, that of being prefect of the city during the *feriae Latinae*. This 'Latin festival' was held every year at Albano in April, at a date appointed by the consuls, who had to be present in person at the ceremonies. Since this meant that they had to be absent from the city they appointed a prefect of the city to carry on the administration in their place. After the institution of a full-time prefect by Augustus this archaic office had lost any real significance, but it was retained and was customarily held by young members of the aristocracy or imperial family. As it was the consuls who made the appointment, it seems probable that it was Ceionius Commodus who appointed his intended son-in-law. According to the biographer Marcus 'conducted himself very brilliantly when acting on behalf of the magistrates and at the banquets of the emperor Hadrian'.[4]

[1] Cf. Farquharson, *Meditations*, II, 453.
[2] *v. Marci*, 4, 5.
[3] See *PW*, 12A, 1937, 1450 ff. (art. *Tirocinium fori*).
[4] *v. Marci*, 4, 6.

The entry into the family circle of the Ceionii Commodi had another important effect on the life of Marcus. He met a Stoic philosopher, Apollonius of Chalcedon, who had taught Commodus. Stoicism was by now the fashionable school of philosophy and Apollonius one of its leading expounders. There is no question but that Marcus was enormously influenced by this man whom he names, with two others only, as one of those whom he thanks the gods for having met. He was later to study regularly with Apollonius.[1]

Another family event must have taken place at about this time – the marriage of Marcus' younger sister, Annia Cornificia, to a certain Ummidius Quadratus, a member of a now noble family, the fortunes of which had been founded in the reign of Augustus.[2] It was presumably at the time of this wedding that Domitia Lucilla asked Marcus if he would give his sister part of the inheritance left him by his father. Marcus replied that he would give it all to his sister. He was content with his grandfather's fortune (although his grandfather was, it would seem, still alive), and he added that his mother could leave all her own fortune to his sister, so that she might not be poorer than her husband.[3] Her father-in-law had been, as a young man, a friend of Pliny, who was delighted with his promise as a barrister (especially, no doubt, as Pliny had had a hand in his training in public speaking), and approved, in a somewhat sententious letter, the way the young man managed 'to spend his youth and early manhood untouched by scandal', in spite of living with his grandmother, a riotous old lady noted for the troupe of dancers that she kept at her house. This Quadratus married before he was twenty-four but had not had children in A.D. 107 when Pliny wrote this

[1] *v. Marci*, 2, 7: 'usus est etiam Commodi magistro, cuius ei adfinitas erat destinata, Apollonio Chalcedonio, Stoico philosopho'. (I prefer here the text given by Magie in the Loeb edition – following a conjecture of Obrecht – to that of E. Hohl.) Schwendemann, op. cit., 12, thinks that this reference is misplaced, but the detail about the prospective relationship dates it closely to A.D. 136–7. Cf. *Med.*, 1, 8, and 1, 17, 5; *PIR* 2, A 929; and see below, p. 46.

[2] *v. Marci*, 4, 7; 7, 4. Cf. *PW*, 9A, 1961, 597 ff.

[3] *v. Marci*, 4, 7. The son of this marriage was consul in A.D. 167, and can hardly have been born much after A.D. 134. This would make Cornificia only 12 at her marriage, but this is quite feasible.

letter, so his son, Cornificia's husband (it must be presumed, for no other Ummidii are known), would certainly have been under thirty at the time of the marriage.[1] At some time in the reign of Hadrian the elder Quadratus was persecuted by the emperor, but the details of this are unknown. It may even have been part of the events of the last two years of the reign.[2]

In late A.D. 136 an event occurred which shook the leading circles at Rome. Hadrian had been ill – he had almost died from a haemorrhage. The uncertainty about the future which the state of his health occasioned gave rise to speculation about his successor. While Hadrian was bedridden in the early stages of his illness he thought first of Servianus, his 90-year-old brother-in-law, whom he had appointed consul for the third time in A.D. 134.[3] Men remembered how Hadrian had once asked his friends at a banquet to name him ten men who were competent to become emperor, and had then added – 'No, I need to know only nine, for one I have already, Servianus.'[4] But then he had the haemorrhage at Tivoli, and in his illness certain actions of Servianus were construed by him as suspicious – 'he had given a feast to the imperial slaves, had sat in a royal chair close to his bed, and although nearly ninety used to get up and go forward to meet the praetorian guardsmen when on duty'. Meanwhile Hadrian also heard reports that Servianus' grandson, Pedanius Fuscus Salinator, had been spurred on by certain prophecies and omens to hope for the imperial power. But Hadrian had another man in view, and Servianus could not conceal his displeasure. The unfortunate pair were forced to commit suicide.[5] Many others, according to the biographer of Hadrian, were put to death at this time, either openly or by treachery: and when the empress Sabina died, probably in A.D. 136, it was rumoured that Hadrian had poisoned her.[6]

At last Hadrian publicly announced his choice of heir. He adopted

---

[1] Pliny, *Epp.*, 7, 24.
[2] *v. Had.*, 15, 7; and see below, p. 54.
[3] *v. Had.*, 23, 1–3, 7; Dio, 69, 17, 1.
[4] Dio, 69, 17, 3.
[5] Dio, 69, 17, 1–2; *v. Had.*, 23, 3 and 7–8; also 15, 8; 25, 8.
[6] *v. Had.*, 23, 9; probably in A.D. 136.

Ceionius Commodus as his son.[1] According to the biographer his sole recommendation was his beauty.[2] Hadrian's tastes in this matter, after the affair of Antinous, were only too well known, and the reason suggested is only too obvious – and unlikely.[3]

The adoption might have been an act of conscience on Hadrian's part, to make amends for what had been done to Avidius Nigrinus, the father-in-law of Ceionius Commodus. Nigrinus had even – it was said – been intended as Hadrian's successor in the opening months of the reign, until he was executed in A.D. 118 for 'plotting against the emperor's life'.[4] On the other hand, it might have been sheer perversity – Hadrian's desire to infuriate other aspirants. The adoption certainly did have this effect. It was done *invitis omnibus* – 'against the wishes of everyone'.[5] Combined with this might have been the desire not unknown in great men to be succeeded by someone of lesser stature, so that their own reputation might be enhanced by the comparison in the eyes of history. Some believed that Hadrian had sworn some oath to adopt Ceionius Commodus, but when, and for what reason, is not recorded.[6] But none of these motives seem

---

[1] *v. Had.*, 23, 10 ff.; Dio, 69, 17, 1. For full references, cf. *PIR 2*, C 605. The exact moments at which the disgruntled Servianus and Fuscus met their end, and at which the adoption was carried out, are uncertain. In the text it is assumed that the adoption was known about, but not yet final, when Servianus and Fuscus died.

[2] *v. Had.*, 23, 10: 'sibi forma commendatum'.

[3] The biographer, in a misguided attempt to give his work some novelty value, decided to present not only biographies of reigning emperors, but of all who had borne the name of Caesar (a decision not carried out in meticulous detail), in spite of the fact that the only historical evidence that he possessed was for the lives of the emperors themselves. Thus although a biography of L. Aelius Caesar (the name Ceionius Commodus took, although the biographer, for some curious reason, always calls him Helius Verus Caesar) has survived, the information in it has little independent value: the stories about him being a noted gourmet, his invention of a mattress filled with rose petals, on which he lay with his mistresses after anointing himself with Persian perfumes, his habit of fastening wings to his slave-boys so that they would be like Cupids – these charming stories might be true, but the likelihood is that they were invented by the biographer to pad out the life of a man about whom virtually nothing was remembered in the fourth century. Cf. *v. Hel.*, 5. For the worth of this biography and the rest of the mysterious Augustan history, see Appendix I.

[4] *v. Had.*, 7, 1–2; 23, 10; Dio, 69, 2, 5.

[5] *v. Had.*, 23, 11.

[6] *v. Hel.*, 3, 8–9.

plausible. The only one which seems credible is that Ceionius Commodus was adopted because of his whole family connection – in particular, because of his prospective relationship with Marcus, which Hadrian had himself brought about. But this again in a sense begs the question. If Hadrian wanted to choose a man who would act as a placeholder until Marcus was old enough, why did he choose Commodus? The answer must be that he felt Commodus was a man of the right type to take on such a position. A factor may have been that Hadrian knew that Commodus was unlikely to be long-lived, which would assure the succession of Marcus after a reasonable interval. The biographer records that Hadrian was acquainted with the man's horoscope, which predicted a short life for him.[1] However this may be, he was a man of poor physique as well. More than that cannot be discovered. Possibly Ceionius Commodus was in fact the illegitimate son of Hadrian but there is no proof of this.[2] It is just as possible – and implausible – that Marcus was Hadrian's bastard.[3]

The adoption was the culmination of Hadrian's growing unpopularity with the senate. The death of Servianus had made a deep impression. As he prepared for his end he asked for fire to be brought to him, offered incense and then said: 'You know, you gods, that I am guilty of no wrong; as for Hadrian, this is my only prayer, that he may long for death, and may be unable to die.'[4] The tragic end of Servianus and his grandson is the more distressing when one reflects that cultured circles in the capital were probably familiar with the reference to Servianus and his family in the letters of Pliny: 'I am pleased to hear that your daughter has been betrothed to Fuscus Salinator and I congratulate you. The family is patrician,

---

[1] v. Hel., 3, 8: 'scisse genituram' – interpreted otherwise by J. Carcopino, Rev. Ét. Anc., 51, 1949, 301. J. Schwendemann, op. cit., 18 ff., believes that the connection with Marcus was decisive – but this was brought about by Hadrian, and the question why this was so remains to be answered. See now also H.-G. Pflaum, Historia-Augusta-Colloquium, Bonn, 1964, 95 ff.

[2] J. Carcopino, op. cit., esp. 301 ff. See the bibliography of the question in A. Garzetti, op. cit., 688–9.

[3] As Professor Sir Ronald Syme has pointed out to me (Hadrian was in Rome in A.D. 120).

[4] Dio, 69, 17, 2.

his father a most honourable man, his mother equally praiseworthy; he himself is scholarly, well-read, something of an orator. He combines a childlike simplicity and youthful charm with the seriousness of a man of mature years ... I can assure you that he will be a son-in-law who will prove better than your fondest hopes. It remains for him to give you grandchildren like himself as soon as possible. ...'[1]

The adoption was celebrated publicly with games in the Circus Maximus and with a distribution of bounty to the people of Rome and the soldiers. Commodus took the name Lucius Aelius Caesar, and was designated consul for a second time, for the year A.D. 137; at the end of A.D. 136 he was also given the tribunician power – the *summi fastigii vocabulum*, 'the name for the highest dignity', as Tacitus, a few years before, had described this creation of Augustus. Hadrian decided that the new Caesar must go to the armies. He had not made a good impression at the beginning of his new duties – he had been unable, through illness, to appear in the senate to make his speech of thanks to Hadrian for his adoption. Hadrian no doubt felt that a tour of military duty might have a beneficial effect. Aelius was sent to the Danube, to Carnuntum, with proconsular power over the two Pannonian provinces.[2] There was some unrest among the German tribes in Slovakia. The presence of a member of the imperial family would be calculated to restore the tribes beyond the Danube to their allegiance, in particular the Quadi, a powerful Suebian tribe that the Roman emperors did their best to keep under a protectorate. The Quadi were settled in the valley of the River March or Morava, which flows into the Danube about a mile downstream from the fortress of the legion XIV Gemina at Carnuntum. The governor of Upper Pannonia had his residence in the town outside the fortress, and it was here that Aelius Caesar had his headquarters. The valley of the March was part of an important north-south trade route between the Baltic and the Adriatic, the Amber Road. Carnuntum and its province of Upper Pannonia, astride this

---

[1] Pliny, *Epp.*, 6, 26. He received another letter (3, 17) and is several times mentioned in affectionate and laudatory terms (7, 6, 8; 8, 23, 5; 10, 2, 1).

[2] For details, *PIR 2*, C 605; Tacitus, *Annals*, 3, 56.

trade-route, was the hinge which bound the western and eastern parts of the empire together.[1]

In the winter of A.D. 137 Aelius Caesar returned to Rome. He was to deliver an important speech in the senate on the first day of the year A.D. 138, the Kalends of January. But in the night he fell ill. The medicine which he was given made his condition worse, and he died the same day. It sounds, from the references to his coughing blood even before his adoption, and from his death being caused by a haemorrhage, as if he was tubercular. Hadrian forbade public mourning, which would have prevented the important ceremonial taking of New Year vows on behalf of the state.[2]

The curse of Servianus was now apparently having its effect. Hadrian was weary of life and was suffering from dropsy; he wished to die but could not.[3] Already in the month of January A.D. 138 the observant and superstitious noticed premonitions of his death (or claimed afterwards that they had done so). On the day before his birthday, January 23, someone came into the senate wailing. The emperor was visibly disturbed. He appeared to be talking of his own death, but his words were unintelligible. Then he made a slip of the tongue. He meant to say 'after my son's death' (Aelius Caesar), but said 'after my death'. He had disquieting dreams as well, evidently. He dreamed that he had asked his father for a sleeping draught; and that he had been overcome by a lion.[4] The next day, his sixty-second birthday, January 24, he ended the speculation about his successor. He called a meeting at his house of the most prominent and respected senators, possibly in the form of a meeting of his *consilium*. Lying on his couch he made a short speech to them, the gist of which is recorded by Cassius Dio: 'Nature has not permitted me to have a son, my friends, but you have made it possible through law. There is this difference between the two sorts of son: a son that one has begotten turns out to be whatever sort of man heaven pleases; an adopted son is one that a man takes to himself as the

[1] On Carnuntum, cf. esp. E. Swoboda, *Carnuntum, Seine Geschichte und seine Denkmäler*, 4th ed., Graz-Köln, 1964. On the Quadi and their neighbours, J. Klose, *Roms Klientelrandstaaten am Rhein und an der Donau*, Breslau, 1934.
[2] *v. Had.*, 23, 15–16; Dio, 69, 20, 1 (cf. 69, 17, 1: καίτοι αἷμα ἐμοῦντα).
[3] Dio, 69, 20, 1; *v. Had.*, 24, 1.   [4] *v. Had.*, 26, 8–10.

result of deliberate choice. A son that is born may be mentally defective or a cripple. One that is chosen will certainly be of sound body and mind. For this reason I formerly selected Lucius [Ceionius Commodus] from all others – a person such as I could never have expected any son of mine to have become. But since heaven has taken him from me, I have found as emperor for you in his place the man I now give to you, one who is noble, mild, tractable and prudent, who is not young enough to do anything rash or old enough to be neglectful, one who has been brought up according to the laws and who has exercised authority in accordance with our ancestral customs, so that he is not ignorant of any matters which concern the exercise of imperial power but can deal with them all well. I am speaking of Aurelius Antoninus here. I know that he is not the least inclined to be involved in affairs and is far from desiring such power, but still I do not think that he will deliberately disregard either me or you, but will accept the rule even against his will.' Thus were Hadrian's intentions announced, and he formally commended Antoninus to the gods.[1]

Afterwards several of those who had been present must have retailed various anecdotes about the occasion. One story in particular records the effect which the entry of Antoninus to a meeting of the senate had produced, some time in that January. He had entered supporting the steps of his venerable father-in-law, Marcus Annius Verus. This Hadrian found such a moving scene that he decided to adopt Antoninus. But the same scene is also given as a reason why Antoninus later received the name of Pius.[2] Others recorded that when Hadrian was commending Antoninus to the gods his bordered toga slipped for no apparent reason, baring his head which he had covered to pray after the Roman custom. And his signet-ring, on which a portrait of himself was carved, suddenly slid off his finger. Both omens of his approaching end, men said.[3]

[1] Dio, 69, 20 (the speech, apparently at his house); v. Had., 26, 6 (the date: 'natali suo ultimo, cum Antoninum commendaret').
[2] v. Pii, 4, 1–2; Aur. Victor, de Caes., 14, 11. The same story occurs in v. Had., 24, 3, and v. Pii, 2, 3 – but there a different result is ascribed to it, see below, p. 64.
[3] v. Had., 26, 6–7.

A.D. 121	*April* 26: Birth of Marcus (Rome); his grandfather Verus consul fo second time and prefect of the city.
A.D. *c.* 122	Birth of Marcus' sister Cornificia.
A.D. *c.* 124	Death of Marcus' father while praetor.
A.D. 126	Marcus' grandfather consul for third time.
A.D. 127	Marcus enrolled in order of *equites*, aged 6.
A.D. 128	Marcus made *salius Palatinus*, aged 7. His elementary education begins
A.D. 132	Marcus first attracted by 'philosophy', aged 11.
A.D. *c.* 133	His secondary education begins.
A.D. 135	Hadrian begins to live at Tivoli.
A.D. 136	Marcus assumes *toga virilis*, aged 14 (perhaps on March 17). He is mad honorary prefect of the city during the Latin festival. After his fifteenth birthday, he is betrothed to Ceionia Fabia, daughte of L. Commodus, consul that year. He meets Apollonius the Stoic L. Commodus adopted by Hadrian, becomes L. Aelius Caesar. Marcus sister Cornificia marries Ummidius Quadratus. Suicide of Hadrian's brother-in-law Servianus and Servianus' grandsor Fuscus Salinator.
A.D. 137	L. Aelius Caesar in Pannonia.
A.D. 138	*January* 1: Death of L. Aelius Caesar. *February* 25: Marcus' maternal uncle T. Aurelius Antoninus adopted b Hadrian. Marcus, aged 16, and L. Commodus junior (Lucius), adopte by Antoninus. Faustina, daughter of Antoninus, betrothed to L. Com modus junior. Marcus moves to Hadrian's house in Rome. Marcu designated quaestor for A.D. 139. Antoninus designated consul fo A.D. 139. *July* 10: Death of Hadrian (Baiae), accession of Antoninus. Marcus betrothal to Ceionia Fabia and Lucius' betrothal to Faustina cancelled Marcus betrothed to Faustina. Hadrian deified. Antoninus given nam Pius.
A.D. 139	Pius consul, Marcus quaestor (aged 17). Marcus designated consu for A.D. 140. Marcus acts as a *sevir turmarum equitum Romanorum* becomes *princeps inventutis*; is given the name Caesar; and is co-opte into the major colleges of priests. He moves into the palace. Hi higher education has by now begun, his best-known teacher bein M. Cornelius Fronto.
A.D. 140	Marcus, aged 18, consul for first time, with Pius. Marcus studies witl Fronto and attends imperial councils.
A.D. 143	Marcus' tutors Herodes Atticus and Fronto hold consulship (Januar and July).
A.D. 145	Marcus consul for second time, with Pius. *Late spring*: Marcus, aged 24, marries Faustina.
A.D. 146–7	Marcus turns wholeheartedly to philosophy.
A.D. 147	*November* 30: Faustina bears Marcus a daughter (Faustina). *December* 1: Marcus receives *tribunicia potestas*, Faustina called Augusta
A.D. 148	900th anniversary of founding of Rome.

TABLE II Events

A.D. 149	*March* 7: Faustina bears a second daughter (Lucilla).
A.D. 152	Death of Marcus' sister Cornificia. Lucius designated quaestor.
A.D. 153	Lucius quaestor.
A.D. 154	Lucius consul.
A.D. 155	Marcus' friend Victorinus, son-in-law of Fronto, consul.
.D. 150–61	More children born to Marcus and Faustina.
.D. 155–61	Marcus' mother Domitia Lucilla dies.
A.D. 161	Marcus consul for third time, with Lucius.
	March 7: Death of Antoninus Pius. Marcus, aged 39, becomes emperor as Imperator Caesar M. Aurelius Antoninus Augustus, with Lucius, who becomes Imperator Caesar Lucius Aurelius Verus Augustus.
	August 31: Birth of twin sons (Antoninus and Commodus) to Faustina. Military crisis in the east. Flooding and famine at Rome.
A.D. 162	Lucius sent to the east.
	Birth of son to Faustina (Annius Verus).
A.D. 163	Roman victories in Armenia.
A.D. 164	Lucius marries Lucilla (at Ephesus).
A.D. 165–6	Death of Marcus' son Antoninus.
	Roman victories against Parthia.
A.D. 166	Return of Lucius to Italy.
	October: Triumph for eastern victories celebrated.
A.D. *c.* 166	Death of Fronto.
A.D. 167	Plague rampant at Rome.
	Military threat on northern frontiers.
A.D. 168	Marcus and Lucius set off for the north. They winter at Aquileia.
A.D. 169	*January*: Death of Lucius, aged 39.
	Marcus (now aged 47) returns to Rome. Lucilla marries Pompeianus. Death of Marcus' son Annius Verus, aged 7.
	Autumn: Marcus returns to northern armies.
A.D. *c.* 170	Birth of Marcus' youngest child (Sabina).
A.D. 170–1	Defeat of Roman offensive. Greece and Italy invaded.
A.D. 172	Marcus defeats invaders. Roman offensive begins. Marcus based at Carnuntum.
A.D. 173	Marcus based at Carnuntum.
A.D. 174	Marcus at Sirmium, is joined by Faustina and Sabina.
A.D. 175	Rebellion of Cassius in the east. Marcus makes armistice with Sarmatians. Commodus summoned from Rome. Marcus and court go to east.
A.D. 176	*Spring*: Death of Faustina, aged about 46.
	Late autumn: Marcus and Commodus return to Rome.
	December 23: Marcus and Commodus hold triumph.
A.D. 177	*January* 1: Commodus made co-emperor, aged 15, and is consul with his brother-in-law Quintillus.
A.D. 178	Commodus, aged 16, marries Crispina.
	August 3: Marcus and Commodus go to northern front.
A.D. 179	Roman victory over northern tribes.
A.D. 180	*March* 17: Death of Marcus (at Vienna), aged 58.

ime of Marcus Aurelius

The motive for the choice of Antoninus as heir was not a sudden impulse. The biographer gives a sufficiently detailed description of his personality for other ostensible reasons to emerge. He was very rich. He was of a calm and benevolent nature. He was cultured and a good speaker. He was thrifty and a conscientious landlord. All these qualities he possessed in their proper proportion and without ostentation.[1] His public service had not, however, given him very wide experience. Apart from the quaestorship, praetorship, and consulship in Rome, he had had only two appointments: as one of the four consulars appointed by Hadrian (a newly instituted post) to administer Italy: and as proconsul of Asia, for one year, probably the summer of A.D. 134 to the summer of A.D. 135.[2] The consular administrators of Italy were an innovation of Hadrian's which the senate had resented – it was an infringement of the senatorial prerogative (to administer Italy through the urban magistrates), and it hinted that Italy was on the way to being regarded as just a province. Antoninus was assigned to the area 'in which most of his own possessions lay', hence, probably, Etruria and Umbria.[3] It was later retailed that an omen of his future rule occurred during his administration. When he ascended the tribunal to give judgment, someone cried out: 'the gods preserve you, Augustus' – i.e. the imperial name, instead of his own name. His proconsulship of Asia was likewise marked by an omen. The priestess at Tralles greeted him with the expression 'Hail, emperor', instead of 'Hail, proconsul', her normal greeting at what were apparently regular visits by proconsuls. At Cyzicus, another city in the province of Asia, a crown was inadvertently transferred to a statue of Antoninus from the statue of a god. Still earlier omens could be adduced to please the credulous. After his service as consul, in A.D. 120, a marble bull was found in his garden, hanging by its horns from a tree. His house was struck by lightning from a clear sky – but was not damaged. Certain large jars that had been buried in the ground, in Etruria, reappeared above the surface. Swarms of bees settled on his statues throughout Etruria.

[1] v. Pii, 1, 9–2, 2.   [2] Ibid., 2, 9–11; 3, 6–8. Cf. PIR 2, A 1513.
[3] v. Pii, 2, 11 ('in qua plurimum possidebat'); on the four consulars, v. Had., 22, 13. Cf. W. Hüttl, Antoninus Pius, I, Prag, 1936, 34 ff.

Finally, he was frequently warned in dreams that he should include a statue of Hadrian among his household gods.[1] The significance of most of these wonders is obscure, to say the least.

The omens aside, Antoninus was an amiable and wealthy man, who had played an honourable but not remarkable part in public life. It would seem in fact that he had only spent the year of his proconsulship outside Italy. For the rest, he had not seen the provinces, let alone the armies – for no military service is recorded for him, and, indeed, none was likely.[2] A man of his standing, whose grandfathers had both been consul twice, did not need to prove himself in this way if he had not the inclination. Antoninus did not have the inclination. He was a man of peace. This was probably a not unimportant factor in Hadrian's choice, for the whole policy of the reign had been one of peace with security. Hadrian would not have been eager to see as his successor a man with lurking military ambitions.

Thus far the personality and qualifications of Antoninus himself. But there was another factor. A condition of his adoption was that he in turn should adopt the young surviving son of Lucius Aelius Caesar, now aged seven – and his own nephew, Marcus.[3] The adoption of Antoninus caused ill-feeling, as had the adoption of Ceionius Commodus. 'All were opposed' to the adoption of Commodus. The adoption of Antoninus 'caused pain to many' – not least to the prefect of the city of Rome, L. Catilius Severus, Antoninus' colleague in the consulship in A.D. 120 (but his senior colleague, for Severus was then consul for the second time). Catilius Severus was evidently making plans to secure the throne for himself. His plans, or at any rate his reaction to the choice of Hadrian, were discovered, and he was removed from office, to be succeeded by an undistinguished aristocrat who bore the noble names of Servius Cornelius Scipio Orfitus.[4]

The behaviour of Catilius Severus is another indication that

---

[1] v. Pii, 3, 1–5.

[2] W. Hüttl, op. cit., I, 32–3, has no warrant for the assertion that Pius must have been a tribunus militum laticlavius and a legatus legionis (or proconsulis).

[3] v. Had., 24, 1; v. Pii, 4, 5; v. Marci, 5, 1; v. Veri, 2, 1–2; Dio, 69, 21, 1–2.

[4] v. Had., 24, 6–7. Severus: PIR 2, C 558; Orfitus: C 1446.

Hadrian's intention all along had been to secure the succession for Marcus, his favourite 'Verissimus' – and that these intentions were known about, or suspected, in the ruling circles in Rome. Catilius Severus was the young man's 'step-grandfather', and Marcus as a boy had included the names Catilius Severus in his nomenclature. It is in the highest degree plausible that Catilius Severus regarded himself as a more suitable candidate than the boy's uncle, Antoninus, to become the boy's place-holder. From the point of view of seniority and administrative experience he was justified. Consul twice and city prefect, Severus had also been proconsul of Africa, and before that had had a remarkable civil and military career. He had commanded one of the German legions, had served in no less than three junior prefectures at Rome, had governed Cappadocia and then Armenia in the Parthian war (he was the only man ever to govern Armenia, a new province given up by Hadrian in A.D. 117) and had been decorated by Trajan. And Hadrian, of course, at the critical time of his accession, had transferred him to the Syrian army, a position of the highest importance.[1]

Catilius Severus may have had allies in his bid for power. The disfavour into which Ummidius Quadratus, father-in-law of Marcus' sister, fell is linked with the disgrace of Catilius, together with a third name, that of the former praetorian prefect Q. Marcius Turbo.[2] A young member of Turbo's family had been selected to serve as quaestor to L. Aelius Caesar in his consulship in A.D. 137, but the role played by the former prefect in these critical months is not known. (He may have been dead some while, and the conjunction of his names with those of Severus and Quadratus mere hazard.)[3]

At any rate, Antoninus was chosen. He asked for time to consider his answer. This confirmed the opinion of Hadrian that he was not ambitious.[4] His grandfather Arrius Antoninus had found no cause

[1] His *cursus honorum* is given by *CIL*, X, 8291=Dessau, *ILS*, 1041 (cf. vol 3, p. clxxiii), and Cagnat-Merlin, *ILAfr.*, 43.

[2] *v. Had.*, 15, 7.

[3] The relative is T. Flavius Longinus Q. Marcius Turbo (*PIR 2*, F 305); on the family see also R. Syme, *JRS*, 52, 1962, 95 ff., and H.-G. Pflaum, *Les carrières procuratoriennes, etc.*, Paris, 1960, No. 94.

[4] *v. Pii*, 4, 4; cf. Dio, 69, 205 (πόρρω τοιαύτης ἐπιθυμίας).

for envy or congratulation when his friend Nerva had become emperor in A.D. 96.[1] On the other hand, had his answer been negative, his position in any future reign, let alone for the remainder of that of Hadrian, would have been almost intolerable. One who had been pointed to by Hadrian as emperor-to-be, and had spurned the offer, would have been the object of envy and suspicion in the reign of another.[2]

How soon Antoninus accepted the offer is not recorded. But the ceremony of adoption did not come for another four weeks, on February 25.[3] In accordance with Hadrian's wishes, Antoninus, who now became Imperator T. Aelius Aurelius Caesar Antoninus,[4] adopted in his turn his nephew Marcus and the young Lucius Commodus. These boys now became M. Aelius Aurelius Verus and L. Aelius Aurelius Commodus. Further, at Hadrian's request, the surviving daughter of Antoninus, Faustina, was betrothed to Lucius.[5]

Antoninus received powers and titles consonant with his new dignity. He became Imperator, and could place this title before his name, but not yet Augustus. He received the tribunician power and the proconsular *imperium*.[6]

The night of his adoption Marcus had a dream, that he had shoulders of ivory, and when asked if they were able to bear a burden, he discovered that they were much stronger than before. He had been 'appalled, when he learned that Hadrian had adopted him'. It was with reluctance that he moved from his mother's house on the Caelian to Hadrian's private house (not yet, evidently, to the 'Tiberian House', as the imperial residence on the Palatine was known). 'When members of his household asked him why he was sorry to be adopted into the imperial family, he listed to them the evils that the

---

[1] *epit. de Caes.*, 12, 3; *v. Pii*, 1, 4.

[2] The position of L. Verginius Rufus, who had refused the throne on more than one occasion in the civil wars of A.D. 68–9, was not really comparable. Rufus had been urged to the throne by soldiers – he could live on, as an example to other generals, through several reigns (cf. *PW*, 8A, 1958, 1536 ff.).

[3] *v. Pii*, 4, 6.

[4] For his titulature, cf. W. Hüttl, op. cit., I, 50 ff.

[5] *v. Veri*, 2, 3; *v. Hel.*, 6, 9; *v. Marci*, 5 and 6, 2. If *v. Marci* 5, 6 may be pressed, Marcus was not adopted before his seventeenth birthday (April 26).

[6] Cf. W. Hüttl, op. cit., I, 45.

imperial power contained in itself', the biographer records.[1] The biographer gives a sufficiently pleasing portrait of his character and habits at the time of his adoption: 'he was so complaisant that he allowed himself to be taken, at times, to hunt or the theatre or the spectacles. He loved boxing, wrestling, running and bowling. He played the ball-game well and hunted well too. But the zeal for philosophy led him away from all these pursuits and made him serious and reserved. Still, this did not spoil the friendliness in him which he showed to his household and his friends, and even to those less well known to him. He was austere but not unreasonable, modest but not inactive, reserved but not gloomy.'[2] In another passage he makes a revealing comment on the young Marcus' habits after his adoption: 'he had such a high regard for his reputation, moreover, that even as a boy he always used to warn his procurators – those in charge of his estates and financial affairs – not to do anything in a high-handed fashion. He also often refused legacies that were left him, returning them to the next of kin.'[3] He did not want to take any unfair advantage from his position. There is a portrait bust of Marcus as a young man in the Capitoline Museum. It shows a beardless youth with head turned slightly to his right side and leaning forward a little. The chin is firm, the lips full, slightly parted and serious, even solemn, the eyes are wide apart and deepset. The head is crowned by luxuriant curly hair worn long over the forehead and ears as was then the custom. This is certainly a grave young man.

In the spring the time came for the designation in advance of the magistrates for the following year, A.D. 139. Antoninus was to be consul, for the second time. It may be that Hadrian intended to be his colleague. Hadrian requested in the senate that Marcus should be exempt from the law which barred him from taking office as quaestor before his twenty-fourth birthday, and he was designated to be the quaestor of Antoninus, now by law his father.[4] In April Marcus was seventeen, and in the normal course of events would not have begun public life until the following year, when he could have

---

[1] v. Marci, 5, 2–4; cf. Dio, 71, 36, 1.
[2] v. Marci, 4, 8–10.
[3] Ibid., 7, 1.   [4] Ibid., 5, 6.

been appointed to one of the junior posts reserved for future senators, a group of offices known as the vigintivirate. Marcus' family background would undoubtedly have secured for him the office of *triumvir monetalis*, the most highly regarded of the available posts, involving token administration of the state Mint. Thereafter it would have been open to him to serve for a year or more as tribune with a legion, its nominal second-in-command. It is unlikely that Marcus would have chosen to undertake this military service. The intervening years would have been spent in travel and further education. This was not to be. His career from henceforth was to be set apart from that of his contemporaries.[1] Nevertheless, his character was unaffected by the change. 'He still showed the same respect to his relations as he had when he was an ordinary citizen, and he was as thrifty and careful of his possessions as he had been when he lived in a private household; and he was willing to act, speak and think according to the principles of his father'[2] – that is, of Antoninus. Antoninus' own attitude is exemplified by his reply to his wife, the elder Faustina, who had reproved him for not being generous enough to his household in some minor matter, shortly after his adoption: 'Foolish woman, now that we have gained an empire we have lost even what we had before.'[3] He realized that for a man in his position, as a private citizen undoubtedly one of the wealthiest men in the empire, the additional possession of imperial funds was far outweighed by the financial outgoings his new status demanded – for a start, largesse to the people of Rome to celebrate the occasion, and public entertainment.

Hadrian was now filled with disgust for life, the biographer records, and ordered a slave to stab him with a sword. When Antoninus heard this, he came to Hadrian with the prefects and begged him to bear bravely the hard necessity of illness: he himself would be no better than a parricide if he, as Hadrian's adopted son, allowed him to be killed. The betrayal of the secret angered Hadrian, who ordered the slave to be put to death, but Antoninus protected

[1] Cf. E. Birley, *Proc. Brit. Acad.*, 39, 1953, 197 ff., for the varying types of career, and J. Morris, *Listy Filologické*, 87, 1964, 317 ff.
[2] *v. Marci*, 5, 7–8.   [3] *v. Pii*, 4, 8.

him.[1] Cassius Dio tells the same story in slightly more detail. The slave was a barbarian captive named Mastor, a Jazygian. Hadrian had used him as a huntsman because of his strength and daring. The emperor had planned his own death with some care, drawing a coloured line round a place beneath the nipple as his doctor, Hermogenes, had shown him, so that Mastor could hardly fail to achieve his task.[2] When this attempt failed, he drew up his will, nevertheless continuing to take part in administering the empire. He then tried to stab himself, but the dagger was taken from him. He became violent and demanded poison from his doctor, but the doctor preferred to commit suicide himself.[3]

Two curious episodes then occurred. A woman appeared, who claimed that she had been told in a dream to persuade Hadrian not to kill himself, for he was destined to recover. For her failure to do this before, she had gone blind; the order had been repeated; and she was told to kiss the emperor's knees, after which she would recover her sight. She carried out the instructions and recovered her sight after bathing her eyes in water from the temple from which she had come. (It sounds as if she had been taking a 'dream-cure'.) Then a blind old man from Pannonia came to Hadrian when the emperor was feverish; when the old man touched him he regained his sight and Hadrian's fever left him. The cynical Marius Maximus, the biographer's source for these anecdotes, declared that both episodes were hoaxes.[4]

Hadrian finally left for the seaside resort of Baiae on the Campanian coast, leaving Antoninus to carry on the work of government at Rome. But he did not improve and sent for Antoninus.[5] On his death-bed the literary-minded emperor wrote the brief, tantalizingly untranslatable poem which might serve as a kind of epitaph to his restless spirit:

> Animula vagula blandula,
> Hospes comesque corporis,

---

[1] v. Had., 24, 8–10. [2] Dio, 69, 22, 1–3.
[3] v. Had., 29, 11–13. [4] Ibid., 25, 1–4.
[5] Ibid., 25, 5–6. For a supposed letter of Hadrian to Antoninus from this time, çf. P. J. Alexander, H.S.C.P., 49, 1938, 170 ff.

Quae nunc abibis in loca
Pallidula, rigida, nudula,
Nec ut soles dabis iocos?

Little soul, little wanderer, charmer,
Body's companion and guest,
What places will you leave for now,
Little pale thing, stiff, little naked thing,
(And you won't make your usual jokes)?[1]

He had abandoned the diet prescribed by his doctors and was indulging in unsuitable food and drink, according to Dio. At the end, as he lay dying, 'he shouted aloud the well-known saying: "Many doctors have killed a king".' He died in the presence of his adopted son on July 10 A.D. 138.[2]

Hadrian was never popular with the senate. The circumstances of his accession, and the executions of senators which had come shortly after, made the establishment of good relations nearly impossible. The ugly affair of Servianus at the end of the reign, when Hadrian's illness made him act in a suspicious and overbearing way, even to his old friends – 'although he ruled with the greatest mildness', as Dio admits[3] – merely confirmed the opinions of leading circles in Rome. But this must not obscure the fact that Hadrian's achievement as ruler was colossal. His travels from one end of the empire to the other gave the provinces a new sense of belonging to Rome, and his reorganization of the Roman frontier system gave a solid basis to the defences of the empire. Cassius Dio, writing nearly a century later, was no admirer of Hadrian – his description of the suspicious circumstances of the accession in A.D. 117 shows he was not biased in Hadrian's favour[4] – but his verdict on Hadrian's military policy is a remarkable tribute: 'To sum up,' he concludes, 'by his example and by his instructions he trained the armed forces throughout the whole empire, and disciplined them, to such an extent that even today the measures he introduced are the armies' law of campaigning. This is why his reign was one of peace with

---

[1] *v. Had.*, 25, 9.   [2] Dio, 69, 22, 3–4; *v. Had.*, 25, 6.
[3] Dio, 69, 2, 5.   [4] Ibid., 69, 1.

foreign peoples, since they, for the most part, seeing his state of preparedness and that they were not subject to aggression (but even received financial aid), did not cause trouble. In fact his troops had been so well trained that the Batavian cavalry, as they are called, swam the Danube fully armed. The barbarians observed this state of affairs, and had a healthy respect for the Romans. They turned to their own internal affairs and even employed Hadrian as a mediator in their disputes.'[1]

'Other faults which people found in him,' Dio says in another passage, after describing Hadrian's rows with an architect, 'were his great strictness, his curiosity and his interference in other people's affairs. Yet he balanced and made up for these faults by his careful administration, his prudence, generosity and ability – besides which, he did not stir up any war' – in contrast, it is implied, with the militaristic Trajan – 'and he deprived no one of money unjustly, while he presented many, communities and individuals, including senators and knights, with large sums of money, without waiting to be asked.'[2] Trajan too had been a supporter of Hellenic culture, but under Hadrian – derisively nicknamed 'the little Greek'[3] – the Greek-speaking half of the empire began a great step forward. It was no accident that his grandson by adoption, Marcus, was to write his *Meditations* in Greek.

[1] Dio, 69, 9, 4–6.   [2] Ibid., 69, 5, 1–2.
[3] *v. Had.*, 1, 5. Many more judgments on Hadrian might be cited, but they would be out of place here. The reader is referred to the bibliography in A. Garzetti, op. cit., 676–89, which covers the material published 1936–60.

AURELIUS CAESAR

AT HADRIAN'S DEATH it was the duty of Antoninus to make the immediate arrangements for the remains. As a temporary measure Hadrian was buried quietly at Puteoli above the Bay of Naples, at the villa once owned by Cicero, for the massive mausoleum on the right bank of the Tiber was not yet completed.[1] The ceremony at Puteoli was in private: Hadrian was buried 'unseen by all'.[2]

'Marcus was left in Rome and discharged his (adoptive) grandfather's funeral rites', the biographer records, which may have included the announcement through heralds of the date and arrangements of the public funeral. 'He also gave a gladiatorial spectacle, in his private capacity, although he was quaestor,' the biographer adds – Marcus was presumably still only quaestor-designate, and he would not become quaestor until the start of A.D. 139.[3]

Immediately after Hadrian's death, Antoninus approached Marcus through his wife Faustina, Marcus' aunt, and asked if he would be willing to alter his marriage arrangements. They wanted him to dissolve his betrothal to Ceionia Fabia and to become betrothed to their daughter, the younger Faustina, his first cousin.[4] This involved also the dissolution of the betrothal between Faustina and Ceionia's brother Lucius Commodus, now the younger adopted son of Antoninus. Faustina was still far too young to be married – her marriage was in fact not until A.D. 145, so in A.D. 138 she was probably only 8 or 9 years old. This meant that Marcus had to wait seven years

[1] v. Had., 25, 7.
[2] Ibid.; cf. E. Hohl, Klio, 31, 1938, 172, for the meaning of invisus, which is taken by many to mean 'hated'; but the context here makes it clear that it must mean 'unseen'. [3] v. Marci, 6, 1. This cannot refer to old Annius Verus.
[4] Ibid., 6, 2; cf. v. Veri, 2, 4; v. Hel., 6, 9.

before he could marry. Ceionia Fabia was probably older than Faustina – she was certainly married several years before A.D. 145 – so, if Marcus had been allowed to keep to his original betrothal, he would not have had to wait so long.[1] In spite of the temptations to which, he hints in the *Meditations*, he had been exposed while living in the same house as his grandfather's mistress, Marcus had probably not had sexual experience – and perhaps did not have, until his marriage, for he says: 'I preserved the flower of my manhood and did not make proof of my virility before the right time, but even deferred the time.'[2] In any case, the match with Ceionia Fabia had been arranged by Hadrian; and Lucius and Faustina were fairly clearly ill-matched in ages, certainly by Roman standards – Faustina was probably just a little older than Lucius, at any rate very little younger, whereas Roman custom normally required the bridegroom to be several years older than the bride. Marcus consented without demur to the new arrangements. Betrothal did not, in any case, carry very binding legal obligations and could be dissolved without difficulty.[3]

A record of Marcus participating in public life in A.D. 138, under his new names, happens to be preserved. The city of Cyzicus in the province of Asia (on an island in the Propontis) had set up an organization for the young men, a *corpus iuvenum*, in which training for public life was provided. They sent to the senate for their action to be confirmed (a very necessary precaution, as the Roman state regarded clubs and societies of all kinds with suspicion, as breeding-grounds for political opposition). Antoninus presided and a motion was passed in his name after a speech by one of the consuls designate, Appius Annius Gallus. Seven witnesses were required to legalize a motion of this kind (as for all legal documents). At the head of the list came 'Marcus Aelius, son of the emperor Titus Aelius Hadrianus Antoninus, of the Papirian voting district,

---

[1] She married Plautius Quintillus, consul in A.D. 159, and their son (a son-in-law of Marcus) was consul in A.D. 177, hence born at latest in A.D. 144. On him see H.-G. Pflaum, *J. des Savants*, 1961, 34 ff.

[2] *Med.*, 1, 17, 2; 1, 17, 7, where he says that he did *not* 'touch Benedicta and Theodotus', in spite of which R. Dailly and H. van Effenterre, *Rev. Ét. Anc.*, 56, 1954, 363–4, regard these two as Marcus' first partners in sexual experience.

[3] Cf. P. E. Corbett, *The Roman Law of Marriage*, Oxford, 1930, 1–23.

Aurelius Verus.' The name which followed his has not been completely preserved, but it looks as if the name of Marcus' grandfather, M. Annius Verus, may be restored. Fourth on the list stood the name of his paternal uncle, Libo. The family was evidently turning out in strength – but Marcus was now senior in rank to them all, except Antoninus. Marcus was probably entitled to be present in his capacity as quaestor or quaestor-designate. Ironically, the answer to the request of the city of Cyzicus is not known, as the stone is broken after the beginning of the decree of the senate. But as the stone which records it was set up in Cyzicus, presumably the answer was in the affirmative.[1]

The events of the rest of the year A.D. 138 did not greatly concern Marcus personally. But Antoninus was involved from the outset in a struggle with the senate. The unpopularity of Hadrian, and Antoninus' own democratic demeanour and easy-going personality, emboldened some members to make a stand against him. Antoninus felt in duty bound to have the memory of Hadrian officially consecrated; he was to be Divus Hadrianus, the Deified Hadrian. The senate was unwilling to consent. Not only that, it was proposed that Hadrian's acts should be annulled. Antoninus resisted: if Hadrian's acts were annulled, his own adoption would automatically become void also. This he could not, of course, allow.[2] He also felt that he owed it to Hadrian to have him deified. Otherwise he would fall into the same category as Tiberius, Caligula, Nero and Domitian: all the other emperors (excluding the ephemeral rulers of A.D. 68 and 69, Galba, Otho and Vitellius) had become Divus – Julius Caesar as well. Hadrian might not compare with Augustus – who could? But he deserved consecration as much as, for example, Titus and Nerva – except, of course, that from the senators' point of view these two rulers were especially distinguished for their benign attitude to the senate itself. That was the crux. But Antoninus forced the measure through, 'against universal opposition'.[3]

---

[1] *CIL*, III, 7060=Dessau, *ILS*, 7190. Cf. H.-G. Pflaum, *Historia-Augusta-Colloquium*, Bonn, 1964, 110 ff.   [2] *v. Pii*, 5, 1; 6, 4–5; *v. Had.*, 27, 1–2.
[3] *v. Pii*, 5, 1: 'repugnantibus cunctis'. Note the interesting analysis by H. Mattingly, *BMC*, IV, pp. xl–xli, xlviii ff.

Thus Hadrian was to be worshipped as a god. Quinquennial games were to be held in his honour. A temple was to be built for him in Rome – and elsewhere, for example at Puteoli, where his body was first buried. A priesthood bearing his name was formed from senators, the *sodales Hadrianales*, with a *flamen* to minister to the cult.[1] When the Mausoleum was ready, the body was transferred to the Garden of Domitia in which it stood, for the official funeral ceremony and *consecratio*, which no doubt followed the by now traditional lines. After the ceremony the ashes were placed in the massive tomb, accompanied by the remains of L. Aelius Caesar and of Antoninus' three older children who had died before his adoption.[2] In spite of Antoninus' rigidity over the official honouring of Hadrian's memory, he demonstrated the change of atmosphere of his own administration by releasing political prisoners and recalling exiles, and by commuting sentences of death imposed by Hadrian in his final months of tortured existence. He had in any case taken steps before Hadrian's death to prevent sentences being carried out.[3]

Antoninus' dignified stand, coupled with his favourable attitude to the senate, won a warm response. He was asked to accept a new name, Pius, and from henceforward was generally known as Antoninus Pius, or, briefly, as Pius. Various versions have survived which purport to explain the origin of this name, which had in fact been borne by a senator named Aurelius mentioned in Tacitus' *Annals*, who could well have been an ancestor of (Aurelius) Antoninus. In other words, Pius may have been a family name, which Antoninus felt entitled to produce for himself. (But none of the sources refer to this.) The most popular version refers to the occasion shortly before the adoption of Antoninus, when he entered a meeting of senators, supporting his aged father-in-law, Annius Verus: this evoked to men's minds, fairly obviously, the legendary founder of the Roman race, Aeneas the Trojan, 'pius Aeneas' as Virgil describes him constantly, who earned the epithet – meaning 'dutiful' – not least by

---

[1] *v. Pii*, 5, 1–2; *v. Had.*, 27, 3.
[2] Dessau, *ILS*, 350–2, records the funerary inscriptions.
[3] *v. Had.*, 25, 8; *v. Pii*, 6, 3.

his action in rescuing his aged father Anchises from the flames of Troy and carrying him out of the burning city on his back. There was an antiquarian revival in Rome at this time, and the comparison of Antoninus to Aeneas would have come readily to men's minds. Certainly representations of Aeneas carrying Anchises occur on coins and medallions of Antoninus. However, even if such an episode as this prompted someone, for example, to exclaim 'Pius Antoninus' (and the episode was clearly misunderstood, for it is even asserted that Hadrian's choice of Antoninus as heir in the first place was prompted by his pleasure at this incident, which is clearly an exaggeration), this was not sufficient reason in itself for a Roman emperor to take a new official name. Other considerations were relevant: Antoninus' own deep religious convictions; his dutiful respect to the memory of his adopted father Hadrian; his efforts to prevent Hadrian from killing himself; his success in protecting senators against Hadrian; and his general 'clemency' or mildness (*clementia*).[1]

On January 1 A.D. 139, Pius was consul for the second time. His colleague was C. Bruttius Praesens, also consul for the second time. Praesens was a man who had been a friend of Hadrian for many years and owed his career to him. His family was eventually to become connected with the Antonine dynasty, for his granddaughter Crispina married Marcus' son Commodus – but this was nearly forty years later. However, Praesens and his son were influential figures throughout the reigns of Pius and Marcus.[2]

Pius made few initial changes in the administration. He did not

---

[1] Pausanias, 8, 43, 5; cf. Dessau, *ILS*, 341; Dio, 70, 2, 1; *v. Had.*, 24, 3–5; 27, 2–4; *v. Hel.*, 7, 9–10; *v. Pii*, 2, 3–7; *v. Av. Cass.*, 11, 6; Eutrop., 8, 8, 3. Aurelius Pius: Tacitus, *Annals*, 1, 75. For the medallions, Gnecchi, IV, 90, 158. For the coins, cf. *BMC*, IV, Antoninus Pius, Nos. 237, 1264, etc. See also W. Hüttl, op. cit., I, esp. 54, n. 20.

[2] Praesens may have been named consul for A.D. 139 by Hadrian before his death. Alternatively it is perhaps likelier that Hadrian himself might have been intending to be consul for A.D. 139 with Antoninus, and that Praesens was a replacement. Praesens: *PIR 2*, B 164, but this is out of date, cf. *AE*, 1950, 66, and *IRT*, 545; also R. Syme, *Historia*, 9, 1960, 374 ff. The son: *PIR 2*, B 165. The granddaughter: *PIR 2*, B 170. The family was still prominent in the third century, cf. *PIR 2*, B 163 and 167.

replace any of Hadrian's nominees, according to the biographer.[1] This accession of Pius, indeed, in spite of the initial embarrassments over the treatment of Hadrian's memory, was peaceful and stable. Even so, there were a few changes. Scipio Orfitus, the prefect of the city, 'asked permission' to resign, says the biographer, giving no dates or details. He did not receive the honour of a second consulship, which prefects usually acquired at some stage, and it is possible that the request was a cloak for a swift dismissal. He may have been replaced by Bruttius Praesens.[2] Another change was in the powerful province of Britain, with Syria one of the two senior appointments of this kind for a senator where a new governor was appointed by Pius in A.D. 139. His name was Quintus Lollius Urbicus, African in origin, the third son of a knight and the first of his family to enter the senate. He had been prominent in the Jewish war of A.D. 132–135, after which Hadrian had made him consul and then governor of Lower Germany. It was common for governors of Lower Germany to be promoted to Britain, and the appointment of Urbicus by Pius is not therefore unusual; and his predecessor may have been due for replacement in any case. But as Urbicus was soon to take action which reversed an important and very expensive policy decision of Hadrian, his arrival in Britain seems a significant move.[3]

---

[1] v. Pii, 5, 3: 'factus imperator nulli eorum quos Hadrianus provexerat successorem dedit, fuitque ea constantia ut septenis vel novenis annis in provinciis bonos praesides detineret'. The second part of the statement – about long tenures – is worthless, although accepted and elaborated by Hüttl, op. cit., I, 329, n. 12, and others; cf. A. Birley, in forthcoming memorial volume for E. Swoboda. In the early third century, when the biographer's source for this statement, Marius Maximus, was writing, such behaviour may have seemed unusual and surprising. The events of A.D. 217 and 218, not to speak of the civil wars of A.D. 193–7, must have been fresh in the mind of Marius Maximus, and they demonstrated the precarious position of governors of provinces when there was a change of ruler. Indeed, the accession of Hadrian had also seen some significant replacements. Cf. R. Syme, Tacitus, Oxford, 1958, I, 243.

[2] v. Pii, 8, 6: 'successorem viventi bono iudici nulli dedit nisi Orfito praefecto urbi, sed petenti'; cf. R. Syme, Historia, 9, 1960, 375 ff., for the interpretation here followed.

[3] For Urbicus, cf. PW, 13, 1927, 1392 ff.; Hüttl, op. cit., II, 65. The career is given mainly by Dessau, ILS, 1065. For his presence in Britain: AE, 1936, 75 (A.D. 139); EE, IX, 1146 add. (A.D. 140). v. Pii, 5, 4: 'nam et Britannos per Lollium Urbicum vicit legatum', etc.

He may have been recommended by the leading general of Hadrian's reign, Sextus Julius Severus, his commander-in-chief in the Jewish war. Julius Severus had previously been governor of Britain himself and may well have found the policy initiated there by Hadrian and Platorius Nepos very difficult to put into operation.[1] Another move of Pius which reversed a decision of Hadrian was the abolition of the posts of the four consulars who administered Italy (a post which Pius himself had held, it will be remembered). The ending of direct imperial control over Italy must have been welcomed, especially by the senate.[2]

In A.D. 139, Pius took further steps to enhance the dignity of his nephew and elder adopted son. Marcus was designated consul for A.D. 140, and Pius himself was to be his colleague. (It may have been announced at the same time that they would hold office together again in A.D. 145.) Marcus was also given other honours. He was made one of the six *seviri turmarum equitum Romanorum*, a purely formal office, the duties of which consisted in leading one of the six squadrons of knights at the annual mounted parade on July 15. It was normally given to a young senator or future senator of good family, the only other requirement being, clearly, that he should be a good horseman. As heir apparent, Marcus was also *princeps iuventutis*, head of the equestrian order. He now received the name Caesar, and from this time until the death of Pius his name was officially Marcus Aelius Aurelius Verus Caesar.[3] He had only the name, not yet any of the imperial powers. But it was no ordinary name, as Marcus himself realized: 'see that you do not turn into a Caesar,'[4] he reminded himself in his *Meditations* in later years, 'do

---

[1] Sex. Iulius Severus: *PW*, 15, 1932, 1813 ff. A. Platorius Nepos (the constructor of Hadrian's Wall): *PW*, 20, 1950, 2545 ff.
[2] Cf. Hüttl, op. cit., I, 34.   [3] *v. Marci*, 6, 3–4; Dio, 71, 35, 5. See *PIR 2*, A 697.
[4] *Med.*, 6, 30. P. Maas, *JRS*, 35, 1945, 145 (reviewing Farquharson, *Meditations*), prefers the alternative reading ἀποκαισαριανωθῇς, which he takes to mean 'do not become one of the *Caesariani* – which he translates as 'courtiers'. But *Caesarianus* and καισαριανός both normally meant 'Caesarian', i.e. supporter of Julius Caesar in the civil war, as opposed to *Pompeianus*, cf. Appian, *BC*, 3, 91, for its use in this sense in Greek by a contemporary of Marcus. The normal word for members of the imperial household is καισάρειος, cf. Dio, 78, 18. Both readings give otherwise unattested words. The one translated here, ἀποκαισαρωθῇς, gives a better sense.

not be dipped into the purple dye – for that can happen'. The implication is clear. But at one of his first official appearances, Cassius Dio records, when as *princeps iuventutis* 'he had become leader of the knights', it created a favourable impression that 'he entered the Forum with the rest, although he was a Caesar'.[1]

At the senate's command Marcus was made a member of the priestly colleges, the four principal ones being the *pontifices*, the *augures*, the *quindecimviri sacris faciundis* and the *septemviri epulonum*. An ordinary senator could not expect to belong to more than one of these, and the majority had to be content with membership of one of the less distinguished bodies – the Arval Brethren, the *fetiales*, and the *sodales* of the imperial cult, to all of which Marcus, as a matter of course, was probably co-opted, although direct evidence is available only in the case of the Arval Brethren.[2]

Pius himself acquired a new distinction in A.D. 139: he received the title of *pater patriae*, 'father of the fatherland', one which all emperors particularly coveted, but of which it was customary to defer acceptance for a while. Hadrian had waited eleven years. Pius' acceptance of the title after only one year is therefore a little surprising, but it was probably at the pressing request of the senate. 'He refused it at first when the senate offered it, then accepted with an elaborate speech of thanks.'[3]

Pius now required Marcus to take up his residence in the House of Tiberius, the imperial palace on the Palatine hill, and provided him with the outward and visible signs of his new station, the *aulicum fastigium*, the 'pomp of court', in spite of Marcus' objections.[4] The difficulty of living a normal life – or a good life – in a palace is a theme which recurs on several occasions in the *Meditations*: 'where life is possible, then it is possible to live the right life; life is possible in a palace, so it is possible to live the right life in a palace'. In a later

[1] Dio, 71, 35, 5. H. Mattingly, *BMC*, IV, p. lviii, denies that this refers to Marcus being *princeps iuventutis*.

[2] *v. Marci*, 6, 3: 'et in collegia sacerdotum iubente senatu receptit'. For the Arvals: *CIL*, VI, 32, 379 (cf. 1012=Dessau, *ILS*, 360).

[3] *v. Pii*, 6, 6; cf. Hüttl, op. cit., I, 63 ff. (probably early in January 139).

[4] *v. Marci*, 6, 3: 'et in Tiberianam domum transgredi iussit et aulico fastigio renitentem ornavit'.

passage in the *Meditations* Marcus tells himself: 'let no one, not even yourself, ever hear you abusing court life again'.[1] He must have realised that it was too easy for him to make his position an excuse for not being able to live up to his own high standards. But he must have known the lines of the Stoic poet Lucan:

> Let him leave the palace,
> Who wishes to be pious.[2]

Antoninus Pius helped Marcus 'to strip off all my pride and brought me to realise that one can live in a palace and yet not need bodyguards, embroidered uniforms, candelabra or statues carrying lamps, and things like that, all that goes with pomp and ceremony; but that one may live very nearly as a private citizen, without thereby losing any dignity or being less active in the duties necessary for a prince on behalf of the state'.[3] As quaestor in A.D. 139 Marcus' role in the senate was a subordinate one. His main duties, as the emperor's own quaestor, would be to read letters of the emperor to the senate when Pius was not present himself, and in general to act as a kind of parliamentary private secretary. In A.D. 140, as consul, he would have more important duties: as one of the two senior representatives of the senate during his period of office he would be required to preside over meetings and perform official and religious ceremonies, and take a leading part in the senate's administrative functions.[4]

He was now in fact to take an important part in his adoptive father's administration, initially by attending meetings of the imperial council to observe how the business of the empire was carried out: 'he had to be prepared to rule the state', as the biographer puts it.[5]

The influence of Pius on the young Marcus was enormous; and of all the tributes in the first book of the *Meditations* to those whose effect on him he remembered with gratitude, the tribute to Antoninus

---

[1] *Med.*, 5, 16; cf. 8, 9.   [2] Lucan, 8, 493.   [3] *Med.*, 1, 17, 3.
[4] See M. Hammond, *The Antonine Monarchy*, Rome, 1959, 288 ff.
[5] *v. Marci*, 6, 5: 'cum formandus ad regendum statum rei publicae patris actibus interesset'.

Pius is by far the longest. The picture of the emperor and the man that it presents is so vivid that it deserves to be quoted in full:

'From my father – gentleness and to be unshakeably resolute in judgments made after full investigation; no vain-glory about outward honours; love of work and perseverance; readiness to listen to any who had something to contribute to the good of the state; his practice of rewarding every man impartially according to his deserts; knowing from experience where to tighten the reins, where to relax them.

'He prohibited homosexual practices. He was tactful in his social relations. He excused his friends from attending all his banquets and from accompanying him every time he made a progress outside Rome – but those who could not attend on him because of some necessary engagements of their own always found him the same towards them when they did see him. At meetings of his council he made a careful scrutiny and was persistent – he was not content with first impressions, avoiding further investigations. His practice was to keep the same friends' – the term 'friend' here has an official significance, not only a private one: the members of the imperial council had the title of 'friends of the emperor'[1] – 'and not to tire of them: he was not subject to sudden mad changes of feeling. He was always satisfied and cheerful. He had the foresight to plan well in advance and could deal with the most trivial matters without any theatrical fuss. He restrained applause by the people and all forms of flattery. He always kept a watch on the needs of the empire and was a good steward of its resources. To criticism in everything of this kind he was long-suffering. His attitude to the gods was not superstitious and he did not court the favour of men – he did not try to cultivate people by gifts or flattery, but was temperate in every respect, without any mean behaviour or love of novelty for its own sake.

'As for the material comforts of life, in which fortune had been lavish to him, he used them without ostentation and at the same time without apology – when they were there he enjoyed them, when they were not, he did without. No one could have said of him that he was

---

[1] See J. Crook, *Consilium Principis*, Cambridge, 1955.

a sophist, an impostor or a pedant. He was acknowledged to be a mature and complete personality, who was above flattery and competent to deal with his own affairs and those of others. As well as this he had a respect for genuine followers of philosophy, but did not find fault with the other sort – yet was not taken in by them. He was affable and good-humoured, but not excessively so. He took care of his health, in moderation, not in the way that a man does who is attached to life or thinks of his personal appearance. He did not neglect himself, but he rarely needed a doctor, or to take medicine, or to have some external application.

'A particular characteristic was his readiness to give way without ill-feeling to the experts in special fields, whether it was in the use of words, the knowledge of civil law or traditions, or anything else – he even shared in the enthusiasm of the expert so that they could get the credit that their special qualifications deserved. In everything he followed traditional ways, without making a fetish of it. He was not inclined to alter his position or change his mind. He liked to stay settled in the same places and to do the same things. After his sudden attacks of headache he returned to his usual tasks fresh and vigorous. He did not have many secrets, only very few, quite exceptionally, and these only for reasons of state. He was prudent and economical in his provision of shows, in carrying out public building, in largesse to the people and so forth. It was the behaviour of a man who is interested in what has to be done, and not in the reputation that he gets' – this perhaps a recollection by Marcus of his own boyish concern for his good name, a tendency to mind what other people thought of him which he had to fight against for the rest of his life.[1]

'He was not the kind of person who took his bath at odd hours. He did not have a mania for building, did not mind what he ate, did not worry about the colour or material of his clothes, or about the personal beauty of his slaves. His clothes were brought from Lorium, his country house down on the coast. [I remember] his way of life at Lanuvium, and how he treated the tax-collector who apologized at Tusculum, and all his behaviour in that sort of matter. He was in no way harsh, merciless or violent – never carried any-

---

[1] *v. Marci*, 7, 1; 22, 6; cf. *Med.*, 5, 3.

thing "to fever pitch", as you might say. Everything was examined and divided up carefully, as if he had plenty of leisure. No rush, but complete orderliness, with vigour and consistency. What is recorded of Socrates would fit him exactly – that he could equally well abstain from or enjoy what many are too weak to abstain from and too self-indulgent in enjoying. He was strong enough to bear the one and could be sober in the other – the mark of a man of perfect and invincible spirit, like Maximus in his illness'[1] (a reference to Marcus' friend Claudius Maximus).[2]

High on the list of subjects for discussion at the imperial council meetings in A.D. 140 must have been Britain. Because of his military inexperience, Pius relied a good deal on experts, prominent among whom were the two praetorian prefects, M. Petronius Mamertinus and M. Gavius Maximus. The previous careers of these two men are little known. One of Mamertinus' grandsons was to marry a daughter of Marcus.[3] Gavius Maximus was of Italian origin, from Firmum in Picenum, near the Adriatic coast. He had been procurator of Mauretania Tingitana some ten years previously and then procurator of the province of Asia. It is not improbable that he had met Pius there when the future emperor was proconsul, and that he had made a favourable enough impression to be selected for the vital task of praetorian prefect without going through the normal stages of promotion beforehand. Maximus was to remain prefect for nearly twenty years – an unparalleled length of tenure. He was not universally liked – 'a man of great severity' – but he must have been competent and was in a position to influence profoundly the military policy of the reign.[4]

Other advisers were available to give their views on Britain. Sextus Julius Severus has already been mentioned. Platorius Nepos, the builder of Hadrian's Wall, may still have been living, but his

[1] *PIR 2*, C 933–4; cf. *Med.*, 1, 15, quoted below.
[2] *Med.*, 1, 16.
[3] *PW*, 19, 1937, 1217 ff. Cf. H.-G. Pflaum, *J. des Savants*, 1961, 36 ff.
[4] The long tenure: *v. Pii*, 8, 7. Cf. *PIR 2*, G 104, and H.-G. Pflaum, *Les carrières procuratoriennes*, Paris, 1960, No. 105 *bis*. For his row with Censorius Niger, see below, p. 148.

views were perhaps not much valued. P. Mummius Sisenna had been in Britain as governor only five years before and his son Sisenna Rutilianus was at that moment legate of the Sixth Legion under Urbicus.[1] A young man named Pontius Laelianus, whose military abilities were highly thought of in this reign, had gone to Britain from Lower Germany with Platorius Nepos and the Sixth Legion, as tribune.[2] And there were others who had served there.[3]

In the autumn of A.D. 140 Pius and Marcus called on another former governor of Britain. Marcus recalled the occasion in A.D. 143: 'Three years ago, I remember, as I was returning from the vintage with my father, we turned aside to the estates of Pompeius Falco. I saw there a tree with many branches which he called *catachanna*. It seemed to me a wonderful new sort of tree, having on one trunk the shoots of practically every kind of tree. . . .' Here the manuscript of the letter breaks off. Even if the complete text had survived there would probably not have been any reference to Britain. But there is little doubt that Pius would have discussed developments there with Falco, as well as admiring his experiments in grafting. Falco had been governor immediately before Platorius Nepos, and probably had quite different ideas as to how the truculent north Britons should be treated.[4]

In effect Lollius Urbicus abandoned the expensive permanent stone frontier barrier erected by Nepos for Hadrian, and invaded southern Scotland. There had been, no doubt, provocation, but the reprisal need not have involved the giving up of the frontier wall unless the Roman High Command had begun to find it unsatisfactory. Urbicus won victories, and began the construction of a new

---

[1] The Mummii Sisennae: *PW*, 15, 1933, 528 ff.

[2] M. Pontius Laelianus Larcius Sabinus: *PW*, 22, 1953, 39 ff. His career is given by Dessau, *ILS*, 1094+1100 (without doubt parts of the same inscription). For the date of transfer of VI Victrix, cf. *JRS*, 27, 1937, 247. See further below, esp. p. 166.

[3] For example, L. Minicius Natalis Quadronius Verus, son of a leading marshal of Trajan (Dessau, *ILS*, 1029), and legate of VI Victrix under Hadrian. After a promising start his career had languished, but he was made consul by Pius in A.D. 139, then governor of Lower Moesia (Dessau, *ILS*, 1061, and *AE*, 1960, 19, which makes earlier discussions obsolete).

[4] Fronto, *ad M.C.*, 2, 11 (Haines, I, 140). For Falco, cf. *PW*, 21, 1952, 2270 ff.

frontier, between the Forth and Clyde, only half the length of Hadrian's wall and built of turf not stone, hence much cheaper (but easier to outflank, especially down the west coast).[1]

The success in Britain prompted Pius to accept the acclamation by the victorious troops of the British legions, in A.D. 142. The following year the title IMP. II appeared on the coinage.[2] It was the only such military title that Pius was to accept throughout his entire reign, a sign of the special importance attached to the British war – and also a sign of the peaceable nature of the reign as a whole. Pius himself was credited by his flatterers with personal direction of operations from Rome: 'Although he committed the conduct of the campaign to others,' said the orator Fronto, 'while remaining in the Palace at Rome, yet like the helmsman at the tiller of a warship, the glory of the whole navigation and voyage belongs to him.'[3]

Although the war in Britain was the only major one, there was trouble in Dacia also. Under Hadrian Dacia had been divided into three provinces, two of which were governed by procurators with no legionary troops under their command. Disturbances of an unknown nature which affected Lower Dacia made it necessary to send in legionary troops, which could normally only be commanded by a senator, with the title *legatus*, to reinforce the procurator's garrison. It was evidently felt impolitic to send a senator to campaign in Lower Dacia, so, although Pius did not like to tamper with the prerogatives of the senate, the procurator was given special powers as *pro legato*. The man in question was a close relative of Hadrian's great praetorian prefect Q. Marcius Turbo, who had himself taken military action in Dacia with special powers in A.D. 118.[4] Meanwhile

---

[1] Cf. Collingwood in R. G. Collingwood and J. N. L. Myres, *Roman Britain and the English Settlements*, 2nd ed., Oxford, 1937.

[2] Dessau, *ILS*, 340 (A.D. 142); for the coins, cf. *BMC*, IV, Antoninus Pius, No. 1640 ff.: the dating to A.D. 143 seems acceptable.

[3] Eumenius, *Paneg. Constantii*, 14 (Fronto Haines, II, 250).

[4] *v. Pii*, 5, 4. For the division of Dacia under Hadrian (formerly assigned to Pius), cf. C. Daicoviciu and D. Protase, *JRS*, 51, 1961, 63 ff. For Turbo and his relative (T. Flavius Priscus Gallonius Fronto Q. Marcius Turbo): R. Syme, *JRS*, 52, 1962, 87 ff. (whose dating is preferable to that suggested by H.-G. Pflaum, *Les carrières procuratoriennes*, Paris, 1960, No. 157 *bis*).

on the middle Danube there was a diplomatic success. The trouble-some Quadi accepted a Roman nominee to the throne, an event announced on the imperial coinage with the legend REX QUADIS DATVS.[1]

There was also diplomatic activity in the east. The Armenians too accepted a Roman nominee to the throne, and the king of the distant Hiberi from the Caucasus (useful allies of Rome in any difficulties with Parthia), came on a state visit to Rome in about A.D. 140. He treated Antoninus with great respect – more than he had shown to Hadrian, it was said.[2]

In addition to these matters of state, Marcus was – 'with great eagerness' – pursuing his studies. The taking of the *toga virilis* was normally the moment for the beginning of the third stage of educa-tion, in oratory or rhetoric. Although Marcus was only fourteen in A.D. 135 when he took the *toga virilis*, he may well have been ad-vanced enough to begin oratorical training. This meant far more in ancient times than we understand by the term today. The simplest definition of the term *orator* was that given by Cato the Elder several centuries before: 'a good man skilled in speaking'. This emphasises the importance attached to training in morals and character-building, for the aim was not simply to produce a man who could make a good, or even a brilliant speech, although this was then a far more important qualification than it is now. In ancient times to make a speech was the *only* way of communicating with a mass audience, in the absence of printing and broadcasting. To be trained as an orator was to be trained for the whole of public life. On the other hand, this must not be exaggerated – even its leading expo-nents sometimes admitted, in any case, that the practical aspect of the oratorical training was not always very great. It was nevertheless

---

[1] *BMC*, IV, Antoninus Pius, No. 1274 (A.D. 140–4). Note the award of *ornamenta triumphalia* to the governor of Upper Pannonia, T. Haterius Nepos (Dessau, *ILS*, 1058). No doubt L. Aelius Caesar had played a part in A.D. 137, see above p. 47.

[2] Coins with REX ARMENIIS DATVS: *BMC*, IV, Antoninus Pius, No. 1272, etc. The Hiberi: *v. Pii*, 9, 6 (cf. *v. Had.*, 13, 9); Dio, 69, 15, 3=70, 2, 1, Boissevain. See now H. Nesselhauf, *Athenaeum*, 36, 1958, 219 ff.

a humane university education that was offered, covering philology, literature, history and philosophy.[1]

Marcus had three tutors in Greek, Aninius Macer, Caninius Celer and Herodes Atticus, and one in Latin oratory, Cornelius Fronto; although Fronto and Herodes probably did not become his tutors until his adoption by Antoninus.[2] As always, it was felt important that Greek should receive particular attention.

Marcus also had a tutor in law, Lucius Volusius Maecianus. Maecianus was a knight, whom Pius had taken on to his staff at his adoption, and he was now holding office as director of the public posting-service (*praefectus vehiculorum*), a job given him so that he could remain in Rome, where he would be available to give advice on legal problems in the council – one of those experts to whom, Marcus relates, Pius was so ready to listen.[3]

The great educationalist of the preceding age, Quintilian, appointed to a state chair of rhetoric by the emperor Vespasian, had held that philosophy could not decently be omitted from the syllabus for a future orator, although there was a traditional rivalry between the orators and the philosophers, as educationalists, stemming back to the days of Isocrates and Plato.[4] But the Roman prejudice against philosophy, which had made the mother of Agricola restrain her son when 'he was drinking in philosophy too deeply for a Roman and a senator' at the university of Marseilles,[5] no longer obtained. Marcus had previously been attending classes given by the Stoic Apollonius. The philosopher was now back in his native Chalcedon, and Pius sent for him. He came, his detractors

---

[1] *v. Marci*, 6, 5: 'per eadem tempora, cum tantis honoribus occuparetur, et cum formandus ad regendum statum rei publicae patris actibus interesset, studia cupidissime frequentavit'. Cf. H.-I. Marrou, op. cit., 284 ff. Cato's definition: Quintilian, *Inst.*, 12, 1, 1 (cf. 1, pr., 4).

[2] *v. Marci*, 2, 4–5. J. Schwendemann, op. cit., argues that Fronto began teaching Marcus in A.D. 136. This is very uncertain – the correspondence, at least, did not begin until A.D. 138 at the earliest.

[3] *v. Marci*, 3, 6. Cf. H.-G. Pflaum, *Les carrières procuratoriennes*, Paris, 1960, No. 141. The career is known from *CIL*, XIV, 5347–8 (Ostia) and – fuller – *AE*, 1955, 179 (Ostia).

[4] Quintilian, *Inst.*, 1, pr., 13; cf. H.-I. Marrou, op. cit., 210 ff. and 285.

[5] Tacitus, *Agricola*, 4, 4.

said, like a Jason after the Golden Fleece, in reverse. On his arrival in Rome he was summoned to the palace to teach Marcus. But his answer was: 'The master ought not to come to the pupil, but the pupil to the master.' Pius made fun of him – 'It was easier for Apollonius to come from Colchis to Rome than from his house in Rome to the Palatine.' But Marcus went to the house of Apollonius, all the same.[1] Pius is reported to have found Apollonius greedy over the matter of his salary. Marcus' own memories of Apollonius in the *Meditations* were quite different, and he is mentioned as one of the three people that he was especially grateful to the gods for having come to know. From Apollonius he learned 'the meaning of moral freedom, not to expose myself to the uncertain cast of fortune; to look to nothing else, even briefly, except reason. To be always the same, in sharp attacks of pain, in the loss of a child, in long illnesses. To see clearly from his living example that a man could be at the same time completely serious and yet relaxed. Not to find fault when explaining something. To see a man who obviously regarded his technical accomplishment and his facility in expounding philosophical principles as the least important of his gifts. The lesson how one ought to accept the pretended favours of friends, without either lowering one's self-respect on their account or tactlessly returning them.' This last point is interesting in the light of Pius' opinion: Marcus seems to be thinking of how Apollonius had reacted to presents from him in return for his teaching, presents which as mere material objects could not be compared in value with his lessons.[2]

How much attention Marcus paid to his training in philosophy with Apollonius at this stage is not known; probably the practical Pius insisted that the major emphasis be placed on oratory. Not much is known about two of Marcus' tutors. A chance mention in Philostratus reveals that Caninius Celer was the author of a work entitled *Araspes the Lover of Panthea* – which presumably told the

---

[1] *v. Pii*, 10, 4 (reading 'Colchide' for MSS. 'Calchida') – a joke by Pius, playing on the similarity of names between Apollonius' native Chalcedon and Colchis, home of the Golden Fleece. Cf. also *v. Marci*, 3, 1.
[2] *Med.*, 1, 8; 1, 17, 5. Cf. Farquharson, *Meditations*, II, 449.

tale of the wife of the Persian king Abradatus, who fell in love with her Median captor Araspes. Celer also wrote on rhetoric, and 'although he was a good imperial secretary [apparently to Hadrian], he lacked proficiency in declamation'.[1] If Aninius Macer, however, is the same person as the Marcus mentioned by Philostratus (the name is certainly incorrectly rendered in the manuscript of the biography), a few anecdotes are preserved about him. He was from Byzantium, of ancient lineage, an orator of natural but polished style, a man of grave countenance and steady gaze, unkempt in his personal appearance. He was admired by the emperor Hadrian.[2] Celer is mentioned once, in passing, by Marcus in the *Meditations*.[3] Macer, or Marcus, not at all.

Marcus' other two teachers, Herodes Atticus and Cornelius Fronto, were the two most celebrated practitioners of oratory of the age, in Greek and Latin respectively, and many details of their lives are known. Herodes – Tiberius Claudius Atticus Herodes – was a controversial figure.[4] His connection with Marcus' family went back to the period when he had lived for a time as a young man in the house at Rome of Marcus' maternal grandfather, Calvisius Tullus Ruso. Herodes was an Athenian, from an ancient family, and enormously wealthy. 'No man used his wealth better', says his biographer Philostratus.[5] But he could be tactless and hot-headed as well. His father had been consul under Trajan, so entry into the senate, and ascent to the highest honours in the state, were assured to him. He had been in contact with Antoninus when the latter was proconsul of Asia and he himself was administering some of the communities there as a special commissioner. The versions of their meeting differed: some said the self-assured Greek jostled the proconsul in the street – and no more. Philostratus is forced to admit the authenticity of the story – 'they did shove one another aside, after a fashion, as happens in a rough place and a narrow road; still, they did not break the law by coming to blows'.[6] The episode is

---

[1] Philos., *v. soph.*, 1, 22, 3; Aristid., *or. 50 K; PIR 2,* C 388.
[2] Philos., *v. soph.*, 1, 24, 1–3.   [3] *Med.*, 8, 25.
[4] See *PIR 2,* C 802, and P. Graindor, *Hérode Atticus, etc.,* Le Caire, 1930.
[5] Philos., *v. soph.*, 2, 1, 1.   [6] Ibid., 2, 1, 8.

curious. Possibly both exalted senators were in carriages and the quarrel was over who had the right of way. The affair did not, however, jeopardize his future when Antoninus became emperor.[1]

Herodes was not merely rich. He was probably the richest man in the eastern half of the empire. But the proud Athenians resented his patronizing manner and from time to time complaints were made, beginning with his father's death, when it was alleged that he had tried to defraud them of a legacy in his deceased parent's will.[2] But he could be generous. One public building which he had built at his own expense at Athens still testifies to this – the well-known Odeum. Cities in other parts of the empire likewise benefited.[3] Herodes was married to Appia Annia Regilla, a daughter of an Italian noble house. The marriage was not welcomed by all the members of Regilla's family, and it was to end in tragedy, with unpleasant recriminations.[4]

Herodes' oratorical abilities were lightly acquired – 'no man ever found it easier to learn than he', Philostratus declares. 'He did not neglect hard work, but he used to study while drinking wine, and at night, in periods of sleeplessness. Hence he was called "The Stuffed Orator" – by the lazy and small-minded.' He was a restrained speaker, whose speciality was subtlety rather than vigorous attack, according to Philostratus. 'His language was pleasing and full of metaphors – graceful.'[5]

The second century was the heyday of the sophist – the professional lecturer and teacher, the travelling professor (but some had university chairs endowed by the state).[6] Public men like Herodes and Fronto were the doyens of the profession in a sense, although

---

[1] Philos., *v. soph.*, I, 25, 3. Antoninus was good-humoured with the ebullient Greeks, as his treatment of the arrogant sophist Polemo, who had also dealt high-handedly with him as proconsul, illustrates. Pius as proconsul of Asia had been given lodgings in Polemo's house in Smyrna (the best in the city) in its owner's absence, and was unceremoniously ejected at midnight on his return. As emperor he was able to joke about it – and Polemo apparently received honours from him (ibid.).

[2] Ibid., 2, I, 4.

[3] Ibid., 2, I, 5.   [4] Ibid., 2, I, 8 ff.   [5] Ibid., 2, I, 14.

[6] H.-I. Marrou, op. cit., 303; A. S. L. Farquharson, *Marcus Aurelius*, 2nd ed., Oxford, 1952, 89 ff.

they would not regard themselves as being in the same category as Favorinus, for example, or even as Caninius Celer. Fronto especially, as a forensic orator, would have justification in looking down on the theorists. The earnest Aulus Gellius was an admirer of both Herodes and Fronto and related in his *Attic Nights* the occasions on which he had had the privilege of hearing the great men hold forth. Two of the stories about Herodes are of occasions when he put so-called philosophers firmly in their place. 'When we were students at Athens,' one story begins, 'Herodes Atticus the consular, of true Greek eloquence, often invited me to his country house near the city, with the senator Servilianus and several other Romans who had come to Greece from Rome in search of culture. At that time, when we were there at his villa called Cephisia, we used to be protected against the unpleasant heat in the summer or the burning autumn sun by the shade of his spacious groves, the long avenues and the cool position of the house. It had elegant baths with abundance of sparkling waters and as a whole was a charming place, with a melodious sound of running water and birdsong.

'There was with us on one occasion a young student of philosophy, "of the Stoic persuasion", as he himself used to put it – intolerably talkative and presumptuous. During the normal after-dinner conversation he used to lecture away at immoderate length about philosophical principles, in a quite inappropriate and ridiculous way, claiming that in comparison with himself all the Greek authorities and all the toga-wearers – all the Latin name in general – were ignorant boors . . .' and so on. But, Gellius concludes,'Herodes waited for him to finish' and then silenced him by having the first volume of *The Discourses of Epictetus*, edited by Arrian, brought in and having a passage read out, in which the great Stoic had given a simple definition of the distinction between good and evil. The self-confident young man was reduced to embarrassed silence.[1]

On another occasion Herodes dealt with a man who asked him in the street for money to buy bread. 'The man was dressed in a cloak with hair and beard down to his waist' – the normal appearance of a

[1] A. Gellius, *Noct. Atticae*, 1, 2. Gellius was also able to convalesce at Cephisia from an attack of dysentery (ibid., 18, 10).

certain type of philosopher. 'Herodes asked him who he was, which annoyed the man. "I am a philosopher," he replied. "Why do you ask what should be obvious?" Herodes said that he could see a beard and a cloak but not a philosopher. "By what evidence do you think I can recognize you as a philosopher?" he asked. Some of those with Herodes told him that the man was a well-known tramp of low character.' Herodes then in munificent manner gave the tramp enough money to buy bread for thirty days, afterwards deploring the practice of men posing as philosophers.[1]

On a third occasion Gellius heard Herodes attacking Stoicism. 'I once heard the consular Herodes Atticus speaking at length, in Greek, in which language he was outstanding among all the men of our time in the seriousness, fluency and elegance of his diction. He was speaking at the time against the "lack of feeling" of the Stoics' – their belief that emotions should be kept in check. The emotional Herodes could not accept this attitude and compared the Stoics with an ignorant barbarian, who having learned that pruning is good, proceeds to chop down all his vines and olives. ' "Thus", said Herodes, "these disciples of the cult of the unemotional, who want to be considered calm, brave and steadfast because they show neither desire nor grief, neither anger nor pleasure, cut out the more active emotions of the spirit and grow old in a torpor, a sluggish, enervated life".'[2]

Marcus was to become a Stoic. As a young man when he was mourning the death of one of his teachers, some of the palace staff restrained him. Pius intervened: 'Let him be human for once – for neither philosophy nor the empire take away natural feelings.'[3] Perhaps the teachings of Apollonius had been having some effect on Marcus. Little is known about Herodes as Marcus' teacher. They were to come into contact a good deal for the rest of their lives. But Marcus does not refer to Herodes at all in the *Meditations*.

The urbane Marcus Cornelius Fronto rivalled Herodes in popular

[1] A. Gellius, *Noct. Atticae*, 9, 2.

[2] Ibid., 19, 12.

[3] *v. Pii*, 10, 5. The man who died is called his *educator* – hence perhaps his unnamed τροφεύς of *Med.*, 1, 5 (above, p. 35).

esteem.[1] Fronto, from Cirta (Constantine) in the Latin-speaking province of Numidia, did not care greatly for his flamboyant rival, although Marcus later managed to bring them on to terms of polite acquaintanceship. As an orator Fronto was highly regarded in ancient times – he was thought to be second only to Cicero, or even to be an alternative choice as 'the glory of Roman eloquence' – a choice which is puzzling now when only fragments of his speeches and some letters and anecdotes survive.[2] One anecdote, not startlingly amusing, but pleasant enough, is found in Cassius Dio. 'Cornelius Fronto, who held first place at the bar among the Romans of those times, one night was returning home from a banquet very late. A man he was to plead for told him that Turbo was already sitting in court. He went to the court as he was, in his banqueting dress, and greeted the prefect with "ὑγίαινε" (good night), instead of "χαῖρε" (good morning)'.[3]

But the stories in Aulus Gellius give a better picture of Fronto, the man of letters, and help to show him in the context of the literary society of the time. 'When I was at Rome as a young man, before I left for Athens, when my sessions with my teachers and my attendance at lectures allowed me the spare time, I used to go to Cornelius Fronto, for the pleasure of seeing him and to enjoy his conversation, which was full of useful instruction expressed in the most classical way. Invariably we went away more cultured and better educated than before, after seeing him and listening to him talking – as for instance with that discussion of his on one particular day, on a minor matter certainly, but not irrelevant to the study of the Latin language. For when a certain acquaintance of his, a well-educated man and a well-known poet of the day, said that he had been cured of the dropsy by the application of heated "sands" (*arenae*), Fronto said, in a bantering way:

'"You are cured of your disease, to be sure, but not of corrupt usage of words. For Gaius Caesar the life dictator [Julius Caesar],

[1] *PIR* 2, C 1364. See also Appendix I, on his letters.

[2] Eumenius, *Paneg. Constantii*, 14: 'Romanae eloquentiae non secundum sed alterum decus'. See Haines, I, ix–x, for further verdicts from late antiquity.

[3] Dio, 69, 18, 3. The story is really told to illustrate the zeal for hard work of the prefect Marcius Turbo.

1. Hadrian: marble bust

2*a*. Marcus Aurelius as a boy

2*b*. Antoninus Pius: gem portrait

the father-in-law of Gnaeus Pompeius, from whom the family and name of Caesars are derived, a man of the foremost intellect and distinguished beyond all his contemporaries for the purity of his diction, holds in his work *On Analogy*, dedicated to Marcus Cicero, that 'sands' is an incorrect usage and that sand is never used in the plural any more than sky or wheat. . . ." Fronto went on to give more examples, and his acquaintance argued the other side, quoting from Plautus and Ennius. Fronto produced his copy of Caesar's work, and then was asked by his poet friend to justify the dictator's arguments.' Aulus Gellius took the opportunity of memorizing the opening words of the book by Caesar (of which, presumably, he did not possess a copy). Fronto's exposition ended with a recommendation to look out for 'sands' plural, or other words normally plural only used in the singular – 'not, I presume,' says Gellius 'because he thought that they were in fact to be found in any of the classical authors, but so that he could give us practice in reading by our search for rare words'.[1]

Gellius later visited Fronto with his friend Favorinus when the great man had gout, but was nevertheless in full swing at a literary *salon*. The learned men present were discussing the words used to describe colours. Favorinus put forward the view that Greek had more words to describe, for example, shades of red. Fronto was not to be outdone and produced seven alternative Latin words for different shades of red, in addition to the three which were the only ones Favorinus had been able to think of – and had maintained to be exact synonyms in any case. Favorinus had only been able to think of four Greek words, and gracefully conceded to Fronto's brilliance in argument.[2]

At another discussion Fronto dealt with a critic who maintained that 'many mortals' was an absurd expression for the historian Claudius Quadrigarius to use, when he could have said simply 'many men' or 'many people'. Fronto firmly explained the subtle distinction of atmosphere that Quadrigarius had intended to convey.[3] Details of this kind were meat and drink to Fronto. 'I remember

[1] A. Gellius, *Noct. Atticae*, 19, 8.
[2] Ibid., 2, 26. [3] Ibid., 13, 28.

once that Julius Celsinus Numida and I went to see Cornelius Fronto, who was then suffering from gout. When we were shown in we found him lying on a Greek-style couch, surrounded by many men of eminent learning, noble birth, or wealth. Several architects were present who had been called in to construct a new bath-house, and were showing sketches of various types of baths, drawn on little parchment scrolls. When he had chosen one type and sketch, he asked what the estimate of the cost for completing the work was. The architect said it would be about 300,000 sesterces. "Plus another 50,000, or thereabouts (*praeter propter*)", said one of his friends.' Fronto suddenly put off further discussion of the new baths and began an investigation into the use of the expression *praeter propter*.[1]

A final illustration will give another glimpse into the atmosphere of these literary circles. Fronto was standing in the entrance-hall of the palace, talking with Postumius Festus, another senator from Numidia, and Gellius' own teacher, the great scholar Sulpicius Apollinaris (also the teacher of Pertinax, the future emperor, at that time a young man of low origin and no prospects). 'I was standing near at the same time with the others, eagerly listening in to their conversation on literary topics' – the debate was going on about the alternative Latin words for dwarf.[2] But all was grist to Gellius' mill. In some ways he would have made a perfect Boswell, but perhaps he lacked a single Johnson whose every word he could have recorded. The spirit of Gellius' curious work and of the things which he found interesting is perhaps best conveyed by giving a few of the headings of the short essays in his *Attic Nights*: 'The vigorous assertion by Julius Hyginus that he had read a manuscript of Virgil from the poet's own household, which had the version "et ora tristia temptantum sensus torquebit amaror", instead of the usual version "sensu torquebit amaro"'; 'Concerning a shameful error of Caesellius Vindex, which we find in his work *Early Words*'; 'A story taken from the works of Tubero about a snake of unprecedented length'; 'In what manner and how severely the philosopher Peregrinus, in my

[1] A. Gellius,., *Noct. Atticae*, 19, 10.
[2] Ibid., 19, 13. Cf. *v. Pert.*, 1, 3 (Pertinax was born in A.D. 126, *v. Pert.*, 15, 6).

hearing, rebuked a young Roman of equestrian family, who was standing in front of him inattentively yawning all the time'; 'About the strange suicide of the virgins of Miletus'.[1]

This then was the literary world in which Marcus was to immerse himself under the guidance of Fronto. It was above all a world which was trying to look back to the early days of Latin literature for its inspiration. The greatest figures of the golden age, Cicero and Virgil, could not be ignored, of course. But later writers, such as Seneca, Lucan, Martial, Juvenal, Pliny, Suetonius and Tacitus were ignored. Fronto and his friends went back to Ennius and Cato, Plautus, Terence, Gaius Gracchus and, although he was comparatively modern, to Sallust.[2] The movement back to the early days of Latin literature is reminiscent of the nineteenth-century English literary world, when Keats and Charles Lamb looked for their inspiration to the Elizabethan period rather than to the writers of the eighteenth century. But for orators and historians there was a dilemma. The death-throes of the Roman republic had been the great age of Roman literature, precisely because of the political upheavals. It was difficult to find inspiration under a stable and benevolent autocratic régime, as Tacitus complained.[3] The students of rhetoric or oratory had to go back to the past to find subjects for debate. As Juvenal mockingly pointed out, Hannibal's remarkable career – for example – might have been especially designed to provide debating themes or essay subjects for the schools.[4]

Nevertheless, Fronto had a prince to educate, which meant that his pupil was required to speak in the senate on subjects of high importance during his actual period of instruction, which was, for the times, an enviable state. Quintilian had died before his two imperial pupils, who were in any case much younger than Marcus was in A.D. 138, could put his instruction into effect.[5]

[1] 1, 21, L; 6, 2, L; 7, 3, L; 8, 3, L; 15, 10, L.
[2] See esp. R. Marache, *La critique littéraire de langue latine et le développement du goût archaïsant au IIe siècle*, Rennes, 1952.
[3] Tacitus, *Dial.*, esp. 38, 2 and 41, 5.   [4] Juvenal, 10, 147–67.
[5] See *PIR* 2, F 59 (Quintilian), and 257, 397 (the pupils).

IV

THE EDUCATION OF A CAESAR

BY A FORTUNATE chance the correspondence between Fronto and Marcus has been preserved, and although few of the letters are precisely dated, they give a unique insight into the education of a future emperor. In one of the later letters in the collection, written when Marcus was already emperor, Fronto recalls the early days of their association. 'Do you remember that speech of yours which you delivered in the senate when you were scarcely more than a boy? You used in it the simile of "a leather bottle" to illustrate a point, and were very anxious in case you had made use of a linguistic image little suited to the dignity of the place and of a senator. I wrote that first fairly long letter to you, and in it I said that I inferred from this – quite rightly, in fact – that it was a sign of great ability to meet the dangers involved in expressing thoughts of that kind with boldness, but that you would rise to what was needed, by your own study and with help from me, namely, to the command of language sufficiently luminous to match such great thoughts.'[1]

The letter to which he referred has also survived. 'Fronto to my Lord. In all the arts, I think, complete inexperience and ignorance are better than half-experience and half-knowledge. For a man who realizes that he knows nothing of some art will attempt less, and consequently is less likely to come to grief – in fact, diffidence prevents rashness. But when someone ostentatiously pretends to have mastered something of which he has merely a superficial knowledge, he makes mistakes of all kinds because of his false confidence. They say that it is better never to have touched the teaching of

---

[1] *Ad Anton. Imp.*, 1, 2, 3=Haines, II, 38.

philosophy, as well, than to have tasted it superficially, with the edge of the lips, as the saying is – and that those who enter the corridors of some art and turn aside before they have penetrated within, turn out the most perfidious.' This reference to philosophy was undoubtedly a direct piece of advice to Marcus to watch where he was going. Fronto never had much sympathy for philosophy and philosophers and cannot have viewed Marcus' sessions with Apollonius and others with great enthusiasm.

In other arts one might be able to get away with it for a time, he went on, 'but in the choice and arrangement of words the ignorant are shown up at once. . . . Comparatively few of our classical writers gave themselves up to the laborious and hazardous pursuit of seeking out words with real industry. M. Porcius [Cato] was alone among all the orators, and his constant imitator C. Sallustius; of the poets especially Plautus, and above all, Q. Ennius and his great rival L. Coelius, not to omit Naevius, Lucretius, Accius too and Caecilius, Laberius also. In addition to these you might notice certain writers who are elegant in specialized fields, Novius and Pomponius and that sort in country dialect and facetious or amusing language, Atta in women's talk, Sisenna for erotic language, Lucilius for the technical language of each art and business.

'At this point you will perhaps have been wanting to know for some time in what category I place M. Tullius [Cicero], who is famed as the head and fount of Roman eloquence. He used the most beautiful language on all occasions, I think, and was magnificent – above all other orators – in embellishing what he wished to set forth. However, he seems to me to have been far from disposed to search out words with extra effort, perhaps from his high-mindedness, or to avoid the effort, or because he felt confident that he would always have ready to hand what others find with difficulty after careful search. . . . In all his speeches you will find only very few words that are surprising and unexpected, the kind that can only be hunted out by careful study and watchfulness and by memorizing a lot of classical poetry. By a surprising and unexpected word I mean one which is produced when the listener or reader is not expecting it or thinking of it, yet could not think of any substitute himself or one to express the particular meaning if you took the word out and asked him to find another. So I commend greatly your hard work and industrious application to the task of digging deep for your word and fitting it in to what you mean. . . .' He went on to emphasize the dangers of doing this half-heartedly, and added, 'I may say that I noticed, when you were reading out to me what you had written, and I altered a syllable in one word, that you did not pay attention to it and thought that it did not matter much. So I do not want you to be ignorant of the great difference which one syllable can make' – and he went on to illustrate his point with different words for 'washing' – *colluere* and *pelluere*, *lavare* and *lavere*, *eluere* and *abluere* – and so forth, depending on what was being washed.

'Possibly someone might ask: "Who is to prevent me from saying *vestimenta lavere* rather than *lavare*, *sudorem lavare* rather than *abluere*?" And you, certainly – no one will have the right to interfere with you in this or set up standards for you, you who are a free man, born of free parents, who have more than the knight's property qualification, who are asked for your opinion in the senate. But we who have dedicated ourselves in dutiful service to the ears of the men of learning, we must of necessity study these slender minutiae with the greatest care. . . . It will be better for you, if you are to search out words more expertly, to remember when you have been corrected, and not to reject criticism or slacken your efforts when caught out. For if you give up searching you will not find; if you go on, you will. Finally, you seemed to me even to have made light of it when I changed your word order, to make you say "three-headed" before "Geryon" ' – and he explained why the change was necessary – 'then again, when you were pointing out why the Parthians wore rather loose long sleeves, you wrote, I think, to the effect that heat was *suspended* by the gaps in the garment.' Fronto commended Marcus for looking for the right word to express what he intended here, but felt that 'suspended' was an impossible choice in this instance. 'After that I advised you what you should study to prepare yourself for the writing of history, since you requested it. That subject would need rather a long discussion, so I will end here, to avoid extending this letter beyond due limits. If you want me to write to you on that subject as well, you must remind me again and again.'[1]

Not long afterwards Fronto wrote another letter, as a letter from Marcus with some work he had been doing had 'crossed in the post' with his own previous letter. 'To my Lord. Gratia [his wife] returned here last night. But my delight at having her back was no greater than my pleasure at seeing that you have translated your [Greek] sentences so splendidly; the one I received today was almost perfect and could be inserted into a book of Sallust without being out of place or inferior in any way. I am happy, merry, healthy, even young again when you make such progress. What I shall require of you is difficult, but I must ask you to do what I remember was so useful in my own case. . . . If the gods are favourable, when you return to Rome I will exact your daily verses from you again. Greet my Lady your mother.'[2]

Marcus was evidently in the country, probably at one of Pius' two main family estates, at Lorium north of Rome on the *via Aurelia*, or at Lanuvium, near Albano in the hill-country south of the city. Marcus received both these letters by messenger. 'To my master. I have received two letters from you at the same time. In one of them you reprove me and show that I had written a sentence carelessly; but in the other you strove to encourage my work with praise. But I swear to you by my health, by my mother's too and by yours, that the first letter gave me the greater pleasure and that as I read it I exclaimed several times "How lucky I am!" "Are you then so lucky?", someone will say, "to have a teacher who will show you how to write a translation of your Greek maxims more expertly, more clearly, more briefly, more elegantly?" No, that is not my reason for calling myself fortunate. Why then? It is because I learn to speak the truth (*verum dicere*) from you' – there may perhaps have been a play of words here: he was still Marcus Aurelius *Verus*. He was delighted to have a master who was not afraid to criticize him and treated him as a normal person. 'Farewell my good master, best of masters – I am

---

[1] *ad M.C.*, 4, 3=Haines, I, 2 ff.
[2] *ad M.C.*, 3, 11=Haines, I, 12 ff. The relative dating of the last two letters quoted is, of course, conjectural. See further Appendix I on the chronology of the correspondence.

delighted that you have come to be my friend in this way. My Lady [his mother] greets you.'[1]

This exchange of letters may well date from the end of the year A.D. 138. In A.D. 139, when he received the name or title Caesar, Marcus had a good deal more public speaking and, in particular, had to make a speech of thanks in the senate for the grant of the name. In a letter from somewhere in the country he told Fronto of his anxieties. 'Hail, my best of masters. If any sleep returns to you after the sleepless nights of which you have been complaining, do write to me, and I beg you this first of all, to take some care of your health. Then, as for that axe of Tenes that you are threatening us with [a proverbial expression meaning 'strict justice'] – hide it away somewhere and bury it and do not give up your intention of pleading in court – or let all other mouths be dumb as well. You say you have composed something or other in Greek which pleases you as little else you have written has. Wasn't it you that was giving me a severe reprimand lately for writing in Greek? As a matter of fact I feel the need now more than ever to write in Greek. "Why?" you ask. I want to make an experiment to see if what I haven't learned comes to me easier, seeing that what I *have* learned is failing me. But if you loved me you would have sent me that new piece that you say you like. Still I read you here even if you are unwilling and by this alone do I live and am sustained.

'The theme you have sent me is a bloodthirsty one. I haven't read the extract from Coelius that you sent me yet – and I shan't read it until I can collect my wits together. But my Caesar speech is gripping me with hooked claws. Now I finally realize what a task it is to shape three or five lines and to take time over writing something. Farewell, my soul – should I not burn with love for you, you who have written to me as you have. What shall I do? I cannot resist telling you –last year at this very time and place I was consumed with passionate longing for my mother. This year it is you that inflame my longing. My Lady greets you.'[2]

The piece written in Greek which Marcus mentioned is included in the correspondence. It is a 'Discourse on Love', very much a

[1] *ad M.C.*, 3, 12=Haines, I, 14 ff.   [2] *Epist. Graecae*, 6=Haines, I, 18 ff.

mannered piece of writing, in which Fronto takes on the role of Socrates to Marcus' Phaedrus. It is the kind of thing which is almost embarrassing to read now.[1] Still, Marcus appreciated it and thanked Fronto in an effusive way; 'This I can swear without rashness: if that Phaedrus of yours ever really existed, if he was ever away from Socrates, Socrates never felt for Phaedrus a greater longing than I have felt for the sight of you all these days – do I say days? I mean months. . . .'[2]

In another letter from this period Marcus mentions that he is working on another literary exercise set him by Fronto. 'To my master. When you rest and do what is good for your health you do me good as well. Have a pleasant time and be lazy. My opinion is that you have done right in taking care to cure your arm. I too have done something today. I have been on my couch from the seventh hour and have finished about ten similes. In the ninth one I must call you in as my ally and adjutant, because my efforts to pin it down haven't been too successful. It is the one about the island of Aenaria [Ischia] which has a lake in it; in the lake is an island and it too is inhabited, "from which we draw a certain simile". Farewell, sweetest soul. My Lady greets you.'[3] Fronto wrote back to explain the simile. What he had had in mind was that 'your father carries on his shoulders all the troubles and difficulties of the Roman Empire and keeps you safe in his own calm breast, the partner in his rank, glory and all his possessions' – just as the island protected the little island in its lake from the raging of the sea. Marcus was to make use of this simile in his speech of thanks, either for the Caesar-speech in A.D. 139 or for his speech on the consulship in A.D. 140, presumably.[4]

The firm bond between pupil and master is further illustrated by a letter written by Marcus for Fronto's birthday. 'Hail, my best master. I know that on everyone's birthday his friends undertake vows. But I, because I love you as I love myself, want to make today,

[1] *Epist. Graecae*, 8=Haines, I, 20 ff.   [2] Ibid., 7=Haines, I, 32.
[3] *ad M.C.* 3, 7=Haines, I, 32 ff.
[4] Ibid., 3, 8, 1=Haines, I, 34 ff. Note 'Igitur hac imagine multimodis uti potes ubi patri tuo gratias ages' (Haines, I, 36).

your birthday, a good prayer for myself. I call on all the gods, therefore, who anywhere among the nations of the world offer their present and ready power to men, who give aid and show their power in dreams or mysteries or cures or oracles, wherever it may be, I call on each and every one of these gods with my vows, and I place myself, according to the nature of each vow, in the place where each god who is endowed with that power may hear me the more readily. Therefore I now climb first the citadel of Pergamum and call on Aesculapius to regulate well and protect the health of my master. Then I go to Athens and clasping Minerva around the knees beseech and beg her that if ever I know anything of literature this knowledge may enter my heart above all from the lips of Fronto. Now I return to Rome and implore the gods of the roads and the seas that in every journey of mine you may accompany me and that I may not be worn out by so fierce a longing for you. Lastly I ask all the gods who watch over all peoples, and the very grove whose rustling is heard on the Capitol hill, to grant this to me, that I may keep with you this day on which you were born for me, with you in strength and happiness. Farewell my sweetest and dearest master – I ask of you that you take care of your health so that when I come I shall see you. My Lady greets you.'[1]

Fronto's reply was brief but grateful. 'To my Lord. All is well with me since you wish it so for me, for there is no one who deserves more than you to have his prayers granted by the gods – or rather, when I pray for you, there is no one who better deserves the fulfilment of prayers on his behalf than you do. Farewell, my sweetest Lord. Greet my Lady.'[2] Marcus' prayers for Fronto's health were more than conventional for Fronto was often ill – at times the letters give the impression that he was a constant invalid, suffering from a variety of ailments. 'Hail my best master,' wrote Marcus on another occasion, 'am I to study when you are in pain, especially when it is my fault? Shall I inflict myself of my own accord with every kind of discomfort? I deserve it, by Hercules. For who else was responsible for that pain in your knee which you write was worse last night, who else but Centumcellae, not to mention myself?' Fronto had evidently

[1] *ad M.C.*, 3, 9=Haines, I, 50.   [2] Ibid., 3, 10=Haines, I, 52.

been visiting Marcus at Centumcellae (Civita Vecchia) on the Etrurian coast, about fifty miles from Rome, where there was an imperial palace built by Trajan. 'What then shall I do, when I cannot see you and am tortured with such anxiety? Add to that the fact that even if I want to study the courts prevent me – they will take up whole days according to those who know. Still I am sending you yesterday's Greek sentence and the day before yesterday's commonplace. We spent the whole day yesterday on the road. Today it is difficult to find time for anything except the evening's Greek sentence. "Do you sleep all night through?" you will say – "Yes, I can do that, for I am a great sleeper, but it is so cold in my bedroom that I can hardly put my hand outside the bedclothes." But as a matter of fact what really puts me off studying is the thought that my excessive love for reading caused you discomfort at the Harbour, as it turned out. So farewell Catos and Ciceros and Sallusts, until *you* are well and I see you in good health even with no books. Farewell my chief delight, sweetest master. My Lady greets you. Send me three Greek sentences and commonplaces.' The Harbour refers to Centumcellae and it sounds as if Fronto had come there with some books for Marcus, or to advise him about his reading, and Marcus blames himself for being the indirect cause of Fronto's knee-trouble, which must have come on there.[1]

Some of the letters give a little more insight into Marcus' other activities, when he describes what else he has been doing. One letter begins tantalizingly with a gap in the manuscript and then the words 'and my wrestling-trainer had me by the throat'. It goes on to describe a day in the country. 'But what was the story, you ask? When my father got home from the vine-yards, I as usual mounted my horse and set off along the road and went on a little way. Then I met a lot of sheep crowded together in the middle of the road as usually happens in narrow places, with four dogs and two shepherds – nothing else. Then one shepherd said to the other when he saw our little group of horsemen: "Watch out for those fellows on horseback – they're the ones who usually steal the most." When I heard

---

[1] *ad M.C.*, 5, 59=Haines, I, 52 ff. Cf. Pliny, *Epp.*, 6, 31, 15–17, for a brief description of Centumcellae forty years before.

that I spurred my horse and galloped straight at the sheep. They were terrified, and scattered in all directions, bleating and wandering all over the place. The shepherd hurled his crook at us. It fell on the knight who was following me, and we got away. So the man thought he was going to lose his sheep and lost his crook instead. You think I'm making the story up? It's true and there is more that I could write to you about it, but a messenger is calling me to the bath. Farewell my sweetest master, most honourable and most rare of men, my dearest joy and delight.'[1]

Another occasion in the country which Marcus described to Fronto was a visit to Anagnia. 'After getting into the carriage, when I had said goodbye to you, we did not have too bad a journey although we got a slight soaking from the rain. But before we got to the villa we turned aside to Anagnia, about a mile off the road. Then we looked round the ancient town, which is very tiny, certainly, but has many antiquities and buildings, and a vast number of religious ceremonies. There isn't a corner in the place that doesn't have a sanctuary or shrine or temple. There are many books written on linen too, which has a religious significance. Then as we were going out we saw an inscription on the gate, written twice: *flamen sume samentum*. I asked one of the locals what the last word meant. He said it was Hernician for the sacrificial victim's skin which the priest puts on his peaked cap when he enters the city. We learned quite a lot of other things that we wanted to know – but the only thing that we do not want is your absence. That is our chief concern.

'When you left us did you go to the Aurelia or to Campania? Be sure to write and tell me, and whether you have begun the vintage, and whether you have brought a multitude of books to your villa, and this too – if you are missing me, which is a foolish question, for you will do that of your own accord. Well, if you do miss me and if you love me, send me letters often to console and cheer me. For I would ten times rather sip your letters than wine from all the Massic or Gauran vineyards. For the vines of Signia have too rank clusters and bitter grapes – I'd rather drink wine made from them than the must, though. Besides, it is pleasanter to chew parched

[1] *ad M.C.*, 2, 12=Haines, I, 150 ff.

grapes than pulpy ones. I would rather tramp pulpy ones with my feet than champ them with my teeth. . . .'[1]

Marcus managed to keep at his books when he was in the country for the vintage. 'Today by a careful arrangement of meal-times I worked from the ninth hour of the night until the second hour of the day. From the second hour until the third I walked about in my slippers outside my bedroom in a happy state of mind. Then I put on my boots and my cloak – for we had been told to come in that dress - and went to greet my Lord. We set off for the hunt and did valiant deeds. We heard that boars had been taken but were not lucky enough to see it. Still, we climbed quite a steep hill, and in the afternoon came home – I to my books. I took off my boots and my clothes and lay on my bed for nearly two hours reading Cato's speech *On the Property of Pulchra*, and another one in which he impeached a tribune. "Ho!" you will cry out to your boy, "go as fast as you can and bring me those speeches from the Libraries of Apollo." It is no use you sending for them, for those volumes as well have followed me here. So you must get round the Palace Librarian – a small bribe will be necessary (which he and I can share when I come back to the city!) Well, when I had read these speeches I wrote out a little miserable stuff which I ought to dedicate to the gods of water and fire. Really I have been unlucky in my writing today – certainly that was one of the hunters' or a vintager's little bit of work, one of those whose songs are resounding through my bedroom – a noise quite as hateful and tiresome as the pleaders in the law-courts. What did I say? No, it's all right, my master is an orator (not just a pleader). I think I must have got a chill, either from walking about in my slippers this morning or from writing badly. I don't know which. Certainly I am usually quite full of rheum anyway and today I am drivelling more than ever. So I will rub some oil on my head and go off to sleep – I'm not going to pour a drop of oil into my lamp to-night. I'm so worn out from my riding and sneezing. Farewell my dearest and sweetest master whom I would rather see than Rome itself, I dare to say!'[2]

---

[1] *ad M.C.*, 4, 4=Haines, I, 174 ff. Anagnia (Anagni) is south-east of Rome, east of Lanuvium.   [2] Ibid., 4, 5=Haines, I, 178 ff.

In another letter the description continues, 'We are well. I slept rather late because of my slight cold, which seems to have subsided. From the eleventh hour of the night till the third hour of the day I spent part of the time reading Cato's *Agriculture* and part in writing – not quite such miserable stuff as yesterday. Then, after greeting my father, I soothed my throat, rather than gargled (though the word *gargarisso* is found in Naevius and elsewhere I think), by swallowing honeywater as far as the back of my throat and spitting it out again. After seeing to my throat I went off to my father and accompanied him when he made a sacrifice. Then we went to have lunch. What do you think I had to eat? I only had a little bit of bread, while I watched the others tucking into beans, onions and herrings with plenty of roe. Then we worked hard at gathering the grapes, sweating away and merry and, as the poet has it "left some high-hanging survivors of the vintage". After the sixth hour we came home. I studied for a little bit and what I did hadn't much sense in it. Then I had a long gossip with my little mother as she sat on the bed. My conversation was as follows: "What do you think my Fronto is doing now?" Then she said, "And what do you think my Gratia is doing?" Then I said, "And what do you think the little sparrow is doing, our tiny little Gratia?" While we were chattering away and arguing which of us loved one or the other of you two the more, the gong sounded, the signal that my father had gone to the bath-house. So we had supper after we had bathed in the oil-press room – I don't mean we bathed in the oil-press room, but we had supper there after the bath and enjoyed hearing the country people making jokes at each other. Then back here and before I turn on my side and start snoring I am doing my duty and giving an account of the day to my sweetest master – and if I could miss him more I would not mind tormenting myself a little more. Farewell my Fronto, wherever you are, my most sweet love and delight. How is it between you and me? I love you and you are not here.'[1]

The description of the vintage and their other country activities confirms the brief statement in the biography that Pius 'took great delight in fishing and hunting and in walks and conversation with

[1] *ad M.C.*, 4, 6=Haines, I, 180 ff.

his friends. He used to spend the vintage-time like a private citizen with his friends.' It also records that 'he never performed any sacrifice by proxy except when he was ill', although the sacrifice that Marcus mentions would only be a normal family sacrifice. In the *Meditations* Marcus mentions that his tutor had taught him 'to work with my hands', so he must have been used to helping at the vintage from an early age.[1]

The two Gratias mentioned in the last letter quoted were, of course, Fronto's wife and daughter. The daughter was still a tiny girl. She was the only one of Fronto's six children to survive infancy. Eventually she was to marry another of Fronto's pupils, Gaius Aufidius Victorinus, who is mentioned in the biography as being one of Marcus' special friends from among his fellow-pupils, along with another young man of senatorial family, Seius Fuscianus, and two of equestrian family, Baebius Longus and Calenus. Both Victorinus and Fuscianus remained lifelong friends and Victorinus in particular was an important adviser and leading general in the reign of Marcus. He is mentioned on several occasions in the letters.[2] Between December 140 and July 141 (the exact date is not known) the empress Faustina died, but there is no certain reference to her, or to her death, in the letters. Faustina's character is little known, but apparently there were a lot of stories about her, because of her 'excessive frankness and levity' – an ambiguous expression (*ob nimiam libertatem et vivendi facilitatem*), which might refer to almost anything. At her death she was deified and a temple built for her above the Forum. Both before and after her death the coin issues were at pains to emphasize her good relations with her husband. The issues continued for many years after her death, in fact, and there is no doubt that Pius wanted it to be known that he remembered her with respect and affection.[3] Pius took a mistress after the death of Faustina, a freedwoman of his wife, Galeria Lysistrate. The fourth-century emperor Julian describes Antoninus in his satirical *Caesars* as

[1] *v. Pii*, 11, 2 and 5; *Med.*, 1, 5 (τὸ αὐτουργικόν).
[2] *de nepote amisso*, 2=Haines, II, 222 (on the five who died); Marcus' friends: *v. Marci*, 3, 8. On Victorinus, cf. *PIR* 2, A 1393+*add.*, and H.-G. Pflaum, *CRAI*, 1956, 189 ff.
[3] *v. Pii*, 3, 7; 6, 7–8. Cf. H. Mattingly, *Harv. Theol. Review*, 41, 1948, 147 ff.

'a wise statesman – not a wise lover'. But otherwise little is known about this part of his private life – except that at the end of the reign Lysistrate influenced Pius in making important appointments, which caused some scandal.[1] However, at least Pius did not have homosexual leanings, as did Hadrian. He was the epitome of normality in everything he did. It must be remembered that it would have been out of place for him to remarry at the age of fifty-five. It would have had political repercussions especially if he had had more children, which might have been difficult to avoid.

At some date between A.D. 140 and 143 an embarrassing episode occurred, which needed all Marcus' tact to sort out. Herodes Atticus had to face legal charges brought against him by some fellow-Athenians. The charges sound serious enough: Herodes was accused of unfilial behaviour, cruelty, avarice and even of murder. But the point at issue was that the plaintiffs had engaged Fronto as their leading counsel – undoubtedly a shrewd move if the hearing was to be at Rome, for Fronto was at the head of his profession. But Marcus naturally found the prospect of one of his teachers appearing in court to prosecute another an appalling one. 'Aurelius Caesar to his own Fronto, greeting. I know that you have often said to me "What can I do that will please you most?" Now is the time. If my love for you *can* be increased, you can increase it now. The trial is approaching at which men will not only listen favourably to your speech but will also observe with displeasure any expression of indignation. And I don't see anyone who might dare to advise you in this affair. Those who are not your friends would rather see you acting unlike yourself, and those who are more friendly to you are afraid of seeming too friendly to your opponent if they prevent you from conducting the prosecution in the way that you are entitled to. Then again, if you have composed some particularly neat passage for your speech in this action, they cannot bear to deprive you of the chance of delivering it, by enforcing silence on you. So, even if you think that I am being inconsiderate in giving you advice, or an im-

[1] *v. Pii*, 8, 9 (unnamed 'concubinam principis'); *CIL*, VI, 8972=Dessau, *ILS*, 1839. He may, of course, have had more than one. See also Julian, *Caes.*, p. 312A, and *Med.*, 1, 16, 2.

pertinent little boy, or too favourable to your opponent, I still won't hesitate to give you the advice that I think is right. But why have I said "advice"? It is a favour that I am asking from you and, if you grant it, I promise to lay myself under obligation to you in return. But you will say "What! If I am attacked am I not to repay it in like terms?" But you will win yourself greater praise if you do not reply when you are attacked. Still, if he is the first to attack, it will be pardonable for you to answer as best as you can. But I have asked him not to begin it and I think that I have gained my request. For I love both of you, each for his own merits – and I remember that he was brought up in the house of my grandfather Publius Calvisius, and that I have been educated with you. So for this reason I am most anxious that this most hateful business should be handled as honourably as possible. I hope that you will approve my advice, for you must commend my goodwill. I would certainly rather make a fool of myself by writing than fail in friendship by not saying anything. Farewell, my Fronto, my dearest and most loving friend.' Because Marcus does not describe Herodes here as his teacher some think that he cannot have begun instructing him yet. The truth possibly is that Herodes was never Marcus' tutor on such a regular basis as Fronto, but that he supplemented by occasional sessions the regular teaching in Greek oratory of Caninius Celer and Aninius Macer.[1]

Fronto's reply was generous, although it was a very awkward situation for him. 'Fronto to my Lord Caesar. I have been right to devote myself to you, I have been right to invest all the gains of my life in you and your father. What could be more like a friend, more pleasant or more true' – *verius*, here again alluding to Marcus' name Verus – 'Away with this "impertinent little boy" and this "inconsiderate in giving advice", I beg you.' Marcus had more good sense than many much older men, Fronto told him, and he agreed that there was no point in making a spectacle out of the business. He said that he had not realized that Marcus counted Herodes as a friend, which seems strange, in view of the apparent intimacy between Fronto and Marcus. One might have thought that he would be

[1] *ad M.C.*, 3, 2=Haines, I, 58 ff., cf. 60, n. 2.

fully acquainted with all the details of Marcus' life, but obviously this cannot have been the case. Fronto was not a full-time tutor, with nothing else to do except devote his whole time to his teaching of Marcus. He had his practice at the bar as well, as this itself shows, and he had other pupils besides Marcus, in any case. But when he had said this, that he would never have ventured to say a word against any friend of Marcus, he had to affirm that the facts of the case were going to make his position difficult. 'I have no doubt that I ought not to say anything which might harm Herodes which does not bear on the case itself. But the facts of the case – they are undoubtedly frightful – how am I to deal with them? That is what I *am* in doubt about and I need your advice. An account has to be given of men cruelly beaten and robbed, of one of them even killed. An account must be given of an unfilial son unmindful of the prayers of his father. Cruelty and avarice must be denounced. A man has to be proved to be a murderer in this trial. But if you think I ought to attack and press my opponent in those charges with all my might, inform me, best and sweetest Lord, if that is your advice. But if you think I ought to let him off to some extent in these, I shall consider what you advise to be the best thing to do. At any rate you may take it as certain and definite that I won't say anything about his character and the rest of his life outside the case itself. But if you think that I must serve my own side, I warn you that I won't even use in a disproportionate way the opportunity that I have in my case, for the charges are frightful and must be spoken of as frightful. Those in particular which refer to the beating and robbing I will describe in such a way that they savour of gall and bile. If I happen to call him an uneducated little Greek it will not mean war to the death. Farewell, my Caesar, and see that you love me to the utmost. I even love your handwriting – so when you write to me I would like you to write in your own hand.'[1]

Another letter followed straight after. 'Hail, my Lord. I had closed and sealed the previous letter when it occurred to me that those who plead in this case – and it looks as if many will be pleading – may say something quite unkind against Herodes. So be care-

[1] *ad M.C.*, 3, 3=Haines, I, 62 ff.

ful not to think that I am the only one involved in the affair. Farewell my Lord and live, that I may be happy. Capreolus, who is away at present, and my friend Marcianus seem likely to plead; also Vilianus.' These three men are otherwise unknown, although Vilianus was probably from a Greek-speaking family and Marcianus, whom Fronto describes as his friend, may be the same as P. Julius Geminius Marcianus, a young senator from Fronto's home town of Cirta.[1]

Marcus was relieved at Fronto's reaction. 'Hail, my dearest Fronto. I must render you my thanks at once, dearest Fronto, for not only not rejecting my advice but actually approving of it. As for the points on which you consult me in your most friendly letter, my opinion is this. Everything relevant to the case which you are representing should obviously be put forward. What concerns your own private feelings, although justifiable and provoked, should, all the same, be left unsaid.' In this way, he ended, Fronto would not lose his self-respect – and the others could say what they liked.[2] In a reply Fronto said that he was satisfied with this – but even so, 'my gaze will be quite piercing and my voice earnest and my words stern, and I must show anger by pointing a finger here and there – and your man ought to be able to put up with that'.[3]

After this urgent exchange of letters the matter was dropped for a while, although the case was still in the air. Another letter from Fronto, in the portion now preserved, mentions it indirectly. The letter as we now have it starts with a discussion of the legend of Orpheus, then makes a significant comment: 'If ever anyone had power by his character to unite all his friends in mutual love for one another, you will surely accomplish this much more easily, since you were born to practise all the virtues before you had any training in them. For before you were old enough to begin education you were already perfect and complete in all noble accomplishments, before adolescence "a good man", before manhood "skilled in speaking". But of all your virtues this is the most admirable, that you unite all your friends in harmony. I cannot conceal my opinion

[1] *ad M.C.*, 3, 4=Haines, I, 66 ff. Marcianus: *PW*, 10, 1917, 610 ff. Vilianus might have some connection with the Vilii of Patara in Lycia (*IGR*, III, 500, 664; also Dessau, *ILS*, 8835).

[2] *ad M.C.*, 3, 5=Haines, I, 66 ff.   [3] *ad M.C.*, 3, 6=Haines, I, 68 ff.

that this is much more difficult than to tame wild beasts and lions with the lyre.' Thus Fronto elegantly says that his pupil is greater than Orpheus. The letter ends with a reference to a certain Julianus. 'I love Julianus – for this conversation started from him – I love all those who love you. I love the gods who watch over you. I love life for your sake. I love literature with you. With your friends I take in deep draughts of love for you.' The reference to Julianus is slightly puzzling, because the tone of Fronto's elaborate metaphor of Orpheus the reconciler seems to mean that Marcus was persuading him and Herodes to be friends. Julianus may be the same as the great lawyer Salvius Julianus, in which case it is possible that Herodes had retained him as counsel in the forthcoming trial. If so, the matter would be understandable.[1] Marcus, in his reply, reveals that the first part of Fronto's letter (of which the manuscript is missing) had described his visit to Julianus when the latter was ill. Marcus had possibly asked him to do that. At any rate Marcus was most grateful that Fronto, when 'he was so busy with important affairs at home and abroad nevertheless made a point of going to see Julianus, chiefly on my account – I would be ungrateful if I did not realize that'. After expressing his thanks for this at length, Marcus reverts to the trial. 'As for Herodes, go on with what you were saying, I beg you; as our Quintus [Ennius] has it, "prevail with pertinacious persistence!" Herodes loves you, and I am doing my best in that direction – in fact, anyone who does not love you neither understands with his heart nor sees with his eyes. I won't say anything about the ears, for the ears of all listeners have passed under the yoke and are the slaves of your dear voice. To me this day seems and will seem longer than a spring day and the coming night more long drawn-out than a winter's night, because I so much want to greet my Fronto, to embrace the writer of this last letter.

'I have written this in a hurry, because Maecianus was pressing and it was only fair that your brother should return to you in good time. So if you find any solecism or confused expression or shaky writing here, please put it down to my haste. For although I am so

---

[1] *ad M.C.*, 4, 1=Haines, I, 70 ff. For Julianus, cf. W. Kunkel, *Herkunft und Soziale Stellung der römischen Juristen*, Weimar, 1952, 157 ff.

very fond of you as a friend I still ought to remember that I must show as much respect to you as my master as I show you love as my friend. Farewell, Fronto, dearest and above all things sweetest to me. The *Sota* of Ennius which you have sent back seems to be on cleaner paper, in a better looking volume and in pleasanter writing than before. There is no risk of Gracchus fermenting out, so he can remain with the barrel of new wine till we come. Fare ever well, my sweetest soul.'[1]

This letter reveals that Fronto may have actually been engaged in the trial – 'go on with what you are saying' – and that Herodes was grateful for the line that Fronto was taking. It also reveals, in passing, that Marcus was getting some tuition in the law from Volusius Maecianus. The brother who was going to take the letter to Fronto was his younger brother, Quintus Cornelius Quadratus.[2]

It is irritating that the result of the case is not known. No further contemporary letters refer to it, although a much later letter of Fronto's alludes to it. But it seems that Herodes must have been acquitted of the most serious charges or have come to a settlement. It sounds, from what Fronto said about 'unfilial son unmindful of the prayers of his father', as if this may have been an action brought to force Herodes to pay out the legacy to the people of Athens in his father's will, which apparently, as mentioned earlier, he had attempted to hold back. A judgment against him in a case of that kind could leave him financially worse off but otherwise not greatly damaged. But the accusations of murder must have failed.

The best evidence, in fact, that the charge against Herodes failed, is that shortly afterwards, in January 143, he became consul.[3] Fronto

[1] *ad M.C.*, 4, 2=Haines, I, 74 ff. For Maecianus, see above, p. 76.

[2] For Quadratus, cf. *PIR* 2, C 1426; also A. Degrassi, *I Fasti Consolari, etc.*, Rome, 1952, 42, for date of his consulship, now known to be A.D. 147, and E. Birley, *JRS*, 52, 1962, 225, for his probable command in Numidia.

[3] For the date, cf. *ad M.C.*, 1, 7=Haines, I, 162 ff., which refers to Fronto's consulship (1, 7, 2=Haines, I, 164). This letter is the reply to *ad M.C.*, 1, 6= Haines, I, 154 ff., which includes (1, 6, 7=Haines, I, 162) Marcus' request that Fronto should write to Herodes, clearly subsequent to the trial. The letter belongs to A.D. 143, cf. *PIR* 2, C. 802 (p. 178), citing R. Hanslik, *Opusc. phil. d. kath. phil.* (Vindob.), 6, 1934, 29 ff. (not accessible to me). On the case see also Philos., *v. soph.*, 2, 1, 4.

was also consul in A.D. 143, but only as consul suffect, for July and August. There are a great many letters between him and Marcus from this period, which refer in one way or another to this honour. In none of them is the impression given that Fronto felt offended that Herodes had been given a greater honour – the year A.D. 143, in fact, would be known as 'the year when Torquatus and Herodes were consuls', in the Roman records. It was left to the fourth-century orator Ausonius, whose pupil the emperor Gratian made him ordinary consul for the year A.D. 379, to complain on Fronto's behalf; when he alluded to the consuls in whose consulship Fronto was consul. In fact, Herodes as the son of a consular had a clear claim to priority. At that time it was most exceptional, and would have caused ill-feeling, for a new senator, i.e. a man from a non-senatorial family, to have become *consul ordinarius*. The fact that Fronto became consul in the same year as Herodes, and not later, shows that an effort was made to give him parity.[1]

Fronto would probably have been the first to admit that his only qualifications for supreme office were his skill as an orator and the fact that he had been teaching Marcus. In a letter to Marcus written at about this time he asks Marcus, in a joking way, what he had done to deserve such affection – such affection that 'my Lady your mother often says jokingly that she envies me for being loved so much by you'. 'What benefit has your Fronto conferred on you that you have such affection for him? Has he given his life for you or for your parents? Has he undergone dangers in your place? Has he successfully administered some province? Has he commanded an army? None of these things.'[2] The last two of these questions might have been asked by anyone who wondered why Fronto was being made consul.

While Fronto remained in Rome in the summer of A.D. 143, Marcus and the imperial family were on the coast at Baiae. Fronto had evidently written Marcus a little essay *In Praise of Sleep*, probably partly to persuade Marcus to sleep longer and not wear

[1] For the consulships of Herodes and Fronto, cf. A. Degrassi, op. cit., 40. See Ausonius, *grat. act.*, 7, 32–3.
[2] *ad M.C.*, 1, 3, 2 and 3=Haines, I, 84–6.

himself out by studying late. Marcus took up the challenge. 'Marcus Caesar to Fronto his master, greeting. Accept now a few little points in favour of sleeplessness against sleep – although, I think, I am in collusion with the other side, considering that I'm always in the presence of sleep day and night and don't desert him and he does not desert me, we are such intimates. But I hope that he may be offended by this accusation and leave me for a while and allow me the chance of burning the midnight oil at last. Now for some crafty arguments: of which the first I shall use is this, that if you say I have taken on an easier subject in accusing sleep than you in praising it – for who, you say, cannot easily accuse sleep? – I reply: what is easy to accuse is hard to praise, and what is hard to praise can serve no useful purpose. But I let that pass. Well, as we are staying at Baiae in this long labyrinth of Ulysses, I will take from Ulysses a few little points relevant to this matter. For he surely would not have only finally come "back to his fatherland in the twentieth year", nor would he have wandered about in that lake for so long, nor suffered all the other things which make up the *Odyssey*, "if sweet sleep had not come over him in his weariness". ' He went on to quote more from Homer, then from Ennius and Hesiod. 'Enough of this, which I have indulged in more from love of you than from any confidence I have in it.' He ends, 'Now, after a fine accusation of sleep I am off to sleep – for I have spun this out for you in the evening. I hope sleep will not pay me back.'[1]

The chief moment of Fronto's two months tenure of office in July and August 143 was to be his speech thanking Antoninus Pius for the honour – it was an opportunity for a public man to have his say about the course of events. Pliny's *Panegyricus* is the best-known example of this type of speech. It was difficult for the orator to avoid being banal, repetitious and obsequious. Fronto wrote to Marcus of his plans for his speech. 'You asked me in your last letter why I have not delivered my speech in the senate yet. Well, I have to return thanks to my Lord your father by proclamation too, and I am going to issue that at my Circus Games. The beginning of the proclamation will be as follows: "On the day on which by the favour of our

[1] *ad M.C.*, 1, 4=Haines, I, 90 ff.

greatest Prince I am exhibiting a spectacle most pleasing to the people and exceedingly popular, I thought it opportune that I should render thanks to him, so that the same day" – followed by some Ciceronian ending. My speech itself I will deliver in the senate on the Ides of August (August 13). Why so late? you may ask. It is because I am never in a hurry to discharge a solemn duty at the first possible opportunity, and in any fashion. But seeing that I ought to deal with you with no disguises, and unambiguously, I will tell you what I have in mind. I often praised your grandfather, the deified Hadrian, in the senate, with considerable effort – and with a ready effort too (and those speeches are still constantly in people's hands). Yet if your family loyalty will pardon me, I wanted to propitiate and please Hadrian in the same way as Mars Gradivus or Father Dis, rather than loved him. Why? Because to love requires some confidence and intimacy. I lacked confidence, hence I dared not love one whom I revered so greatly. Antoninus, however, I love and am devoted to, like the sun and the day and life and breath, and I feel that I am loved by him. I will be ungrateful to you too if I do not praise him in such a way that my praise is not hidden away in the *Acts of the Senate*, but rather so that it comes into the hands and before the eyes of men. As they say that the courier who ran away said: "I have run sixty miles for my master, I'll run a hundred for myself, to escape." So I too, when I praised Hadrian, was running for my master, but today I am running for myself – for myself, I say, and I am writing this speech to please myself. So I will do it at my ease, slowly, in a leisurely, gentle fashion. If you are impatient for it, amuse yourself some other way in the meanwhile. Kiss your father, embrace him, and finally, praise him yourself. But you may certainly expect to hear something on the Ides of August that you will want to hear, expressed in the way you wish. Farewell, Caesar, and be worthy of your father, and if you want to write anything, write slowly.'[1]

With Fronto's assumption of office Marcus could address him in a new way: 'My Fronto, most glorious consul.' In another letter he speaks again in the extravagant half-joking way of their friendship,

[1] *ad M.C.*, 2, 1=Haines, I, 108 ff.

but added 'Now Gratia will be a rival, and I fear that I cannot defeat her. For, as Plautus says, in her case, "The rain of love has not only soaked her dress with great drops but has rained in to her very marrow." [This was in reply to a letter in which Fronto had reaffirmed his affection.] That other letter of yours, in which you pointed out why you were going to put off making your speech in the senate in praise of my father, pleased me so much that I could not resist – and you must see whether I acted rashly – reading it out to my father himself. I don't need to go into detail about the great pleasure it gave him, because you know his very great good-will towards you and the splendid elegance of your style. But out of this a long conversation arose between us about you, much longer than yours and your quaestor's about me. So I don't doubt that your ears must have been tingling in the Forum at about that time. My Lord approves then, and is sympathetic to the reasons for your putting off the delivery of your speech till later. . . .'[1]

Finally Fronto gave his speech and wrote to describe the occasion to Marcus, but told him that he could hear from 'our friend Aufidius' [Victorinus] about the shouts of applause with which it was greeted. With his letter he sent back to Marcus some verses which he had written by Victorinus as courier. 'I have sewn the paper up carefully and have sealed the thread in such a way that that little mouse will not be able to poke in through a crack anywhere. For he has never shared any information about your hexameters with me, he's such an evil and malicious fellow – he says you always recite them so fast that he cannot memorize any of them. So he is paid back by me, quite fairly – he won't hear a single line. I remember, as well, that you reminded me not to show your verses to anyone.'[2]

Antoninus Pius was pleased with Fronto's speech and wrote to him. 'You have done well to find something new in such a hackneyed and worn-out subject. . . . I will not be guilty of defrauding you of your very well-deserved praise for fear of insolently praising your praise of myself! You have done well then and in a most appropriate fashion, for which – quite apart from the subject matter – you deserve all honour. But as for showing me your mind – it has not

[1] ad M.C., 2, 2=Haines, I, 112 ff.   [2] ad M.C., 1, 8=Haines, I, 118 ff.

done much. For I know well that you interpret *all* my actions and words in the most favourable way. Farewell, my dearest Fronto. That part of your speech which you most kindly gave up to honouring my Faustina seemed to me no less true than eloquent. For the fact is this: I would rather live on Gyara with her than in this palace without her.' The Faustina here is his daughter, his only surviving child and Marcus' betrothed. Gyara was an island to which banished persons were sometimes sent.[1]

Marcus wrote his letter of congratulations as well, of course, in the most glowing terms. 'In future be careful not to tell so many lies about me,' he ended, 'especially in the senate. This speech of yours is horribly . . . well written.'[2] With his last letter Fronto had enclosed one for Domitia Lucilla, written in Greek as a compliment to her high standard of education. The letter is an elaborate literary exercise, in which he apologizes for not having written before with the excuse of having had to make his speech, and says little else, but says it gracefully, ending with an apology for his barbarous Greek, 'for I am a Libyan of the Libyan nomads'.[3]

Marcus was still hard at work. 'You very kindly ask for my hexameters,' he says in another letter, 'and I would have sent them at once if I had them with me. But my secretary – whom you know, I mean Anicetus – did not send any of my writing with me when I set off. He knows my weakness and was afraid that if I got hold of them I should do as usual and put them in the oven. In fact those particular hexameters were in practically no danger. For, to tell my master the truth, I am fond of them. I do my studying at night here because the daytime is spent at the theatre. So I don't do all that much in the evening and I get up sleepy in the morning!' Marcus was missing Fronto and found time passing slowly. The two months of Fronto's consulship seemed like two years.[4]

Another letter of Marcus to Fronto in one of these two months of July and August 143 describes his life at Naples. 'Marcus Aurelius Caesar to his own consul and master, greeting. Since I last wrote to you there has been nothing worth writing about or that you would

---

[1] *ad Ant. Pium*, 2=Haines, I, 126 ff.   [2] *ad M.C.*, 2, 3, 3=Haines, I, 130.
[3] *Epist. Graec.*, 1=Haines, I, 130 ff.   [4] *ad M.C.*, 2, 10, 2=Haines, I, 138 ff.

be particularly pleased to know about. For we have spent more or less whole days in the same activities – the same theatre, the same dislike for it, the same longing for you. What? – do I say the *same*? I mean a longing that is renewed and increased every day, and, as Laberius says about love, in his own fashion and his own special style:

Your love grows as fast as an onion, as firm as a palm.

What he says about love I apply to my longing. I want to write a longer letter to you, but there is nothing to write about.

'But wait, I have thought of something. We have been listening to the official speeches in our honour here. The speakers are Greeks, of course, but amazing creatures, as far removed from Greek literature as my own Caelian hill is from the land of Greece – so much so that I could even rival Theopompus (for I hear that he is the most eloquent of the Greeks), in comparison to them. So these people, whose "ignorance", as Caecilius says, "is assured", have almost driven me, clownish mortal that I am, to write in Greek.

'The weather at Naples is certainly pleasant but violently changeable. Every few minutes it turns colder, or warmer, or wilder. To start with, at midnight it is warm, like Laurentum. At cockcrow it's chilly, like Lanuvium. The first part of the night, the small hours and dawn, till sunrise, is cold, just like Algidus. Then the morning is sunny, as at Tusculum. At midday it is boiling, like at Puteoli. But when the sun has gone off and dipped in the Ocean the temperature at last becomes more reasonable, the sort we have at Tibur. It stays like this for the evening and when you first get off to sleep, until, as Marcus Porcius [Cato] says, "the dead of night flings itself on you". But why am I collecting these bits of Masurius-type nonsense, when I said that I would only write a few words? So farewell most kindly master, most glorious consul, and long for me as you love me.'[1]

Fronto had to stay in Rome for the whole two months of his period as consul, although once he had given his speech he began to want to be away (or said that he did). 'The consul to his own Caesar. Lucky brother of mine to have seen you for those two days. I stick

---

[1] *ad M.C.*, 2, 6=Haines, I, 140 ff.

at Rome, bound fast with golden fetters. I am waiting for the Kalends of September as the superstitious do for the star at whose appearance they break their fast. Farewell Caesar, glory of your country and the Roman name. Farewell my Lord.' Fronto was referring to the Jews with his mention of the star and fast.[1]

Not only his brother Quadratus went to Naples to stay with the imperial family. His wife Gratia went too, to join the festivities for Domitia Lucilla's birthday. Fronto had to content himself with writing a birthday letter to Lucilla, again in Greek, and again, like his previous letter to her, full of elaborate compliments. 'Women from all over should have come to greet you on your birthday,' he said, 'those that love their husbands and children and are virtuous, the genuine and truthful, the kind-hearted, friendly, accessible and humble, and many others – since you possess all these virtues.' Marcus was not without occupation in the meantime – listening to lawyers. Presumably he had to sit in judgment as an assessor to his father.[2]

On an occasion not long after Fronto's consulship, if not during it, Fronto had been appearing in court and the speech he made won much approval. He sent it to Marcus, who declaimed passages of it to Pius. He wrote back to Fronto telling him that the emperor greatly admired it. Fronto was delighted – it pleased him more than his consulship, he said, that something he had written should be performed by Marcus, so to speak, with Pius as the audience. Marcus quotes a lengthy extract from the speech in his letter, although it does not now seem very impressive – and Fronto's interpretation of the law has even been criticized (it was a case involving an inheritance in one of the provinces, in which one of the parties had appealed to the emperor). But it is perhaps fairer not to judge when only a portion of the speech, and no other details of the case, are known.[3]

Marcus mentioned at the end of his letter that Herodes Atticus

---

[1] *ad M.C.*, 2, 7=Haines, I, 144.

[2] *ad M.C.*, 2, 8–9, 13–14=Haines, I, 144 ff., 152 ff.; *Epist. Graec.*, 2=Haines, I, 146 ff.

[3] *ad M.C.*, 1, 6–7=Haines, I, 154 ff. For the date, cf. R. Hanslik, op. cit. (p. 103, n. 3 above).

had just suffered a misfortune. His new-born son had died. Marcus asked Fronto to write him a note of condolence and the letter Fronto wrote has survived in part. There is no trace of their former antagonism in it. Herodes was not too old to have other children, Fronto tells him (he would not be much more than forty). He added that his own means of consolation had always been to reflect that others whom he loved had been preserved. 'If you too love a certain noble youth, distinguished for virtue and education and fortune and prudence, you will not go wrong if you attach yourself to him and set all your assurance of good things on him, for as long as he remains to us – and I confess that I am a rival for his love, I make no secret of it – everything else can easily be remedied and is a long way second in importance.'[1]

No events of particular importance for the private or public life of Marcus, or indeed in the external history of the empire, are known from the period from the end of A.D. 143 until Marcus' marriage in April 145. But it was in the spring or summer of A.D. 144 that the young Greek orator Aelius Aristides delivered at Rome his famous speech of praise for the Roman empire, which is the main basis for the favourable verdict of history on the age of the Antonines.

Aristides' speech is imbued with Platonic concepts, and is thoroughly literary in its style and construction. He was also being deliberately flattering, making no attempt to see the darker side of the picture. But the tribute remains remarkable, when all allowances have been made. He speaks of the vastness and universality of Rome's empire, and compares it favourably with those of the past, such as the Persian and the Macedonian. The pre-eminence of Rome lay as much in its perfection as in its great size. The government was carried on in a just and orderly fashion. The emperor was not a despot but a 'great governor', and he ruled free men not slaves. The whole world was now like one city-state. But the emperor protected the weak, which did not happen in a city-state 'democracy'. The Roman constitution embodied the best elements of democracy, aristocracy, oligarchy and monarchy. The greatest single 'work of

---

[1] *Epist. Graec.*, 3=Haines, I, 168 ff.

perfection' in the empire was the army – in its method of recruit-ment, its conditions of service, its deployment, its training, its discipline. If there happened to be a few peoples who were not in the empire, they could only be pitied. War was a thing of the past, even if there might be a few madmen like the Getae (Dacians), wretches like the Libyans (Moors) or ill-doers like the dwellers on the Red Sea. (Thus he alludes to military operations in Dacia and Mauretania, and, probably, to a minor revolt in Egypt.) Aristides would not prophesy the future of Rome, but he felt convinced that its 'Golden Race' would be there until the end of the world. He concluded with a prayer that the city and the empire should last for ever, and that the 'great governor and his sons' should be pre-served and provide good things for men.[1]

[1] The Roman Oration (XXVI K) has been edited with translation, full notes and introduction, by J. H. Oliver, *The Ruling Power*, *etc.*, Trans. American Philosophical Society, N.S. 43, 4, Philadelphia, 1953. I adopt the traditional date of A.D. 144, rather than A.D. 143, proposed with force by Oliver, pp. 886 ff.

V

THE STOIC PRINCE

THE YEARS A.D. 145 to 147 were of great importance in the life of Marcus. On January 1, 145, he became consul for the second time, an honour that a private citizen could rarely expect and only at a fairly advanced age, whereas Marcus was twenty-two. His father was his colleague, holding the office for the fourth time. Marcus' tenure of office required another important speech from him, and it may have been at this time that he was unwell and Fronto wrote him a brief note, urging him to have plenty of sleep 'so that you may come into the Senate with a good colour and read your speech with a strong voice'.[1] Marcus' illness may be the one he referred to himself in another letter. 'My present condition, as you can easily judge, is revealed by the shakiness of my handwriting. As far as my strength is concerned, I am beginning to get it back; and there is no trace of the pain in my chest. But that ulcer . . . [here the manuscript is uncertain] . . . I am having treatment and taking care not to do anything that interferes with it. For I feel that a long illness can only be made more tolerable by conscientious care and following doctors' orders. Anyway, it would be a bad business if a physical illness should last longer than one's mental determination to regain one's health. Farewell, my most delightful master. My mother greets you.'[2]

Marcus was never very strong physically. Cassius Dio speaks with admiration of his devotion to duty in spite of the handicap of physical weakness. He himself, in a passage already quoted, tells

---

[1] A. Degrassi, *I Fasti Consolari, etc.*, Roma, 1952, 41. Fronto, *ad M.C.*, 5, 1 =Haines, I, 188.

[2] *ad M.C.*, 4, 8=Haines, I, 184 ff.

how his teacher in philosophy, Apollonius, had taught him to preserve his equanimity, even in long illnesses. Twenty or more years later, as emperor, he suffered constantly from chest and stomach complaints, and had to take drugs to alleviate them. Speculation about the nature of these is perhaps unprofitable, in view of the small amount of data available. In any case, there is no evidence that the 'pain in the chest' he had as a young man, which had left him when he wrote the letter to Fronto just quoted, was from the same cause as 'the poor condition of his stomach and chest' twenty-five years later.[1]

In the year A.D. 145 there were military problems to deal with once more, and as Pius must have been very busy Marcus would have had to play his part. Serious revolts in Mauretania developed into a full-scale war. Neither of the two Mauretanian provinces had legionary garrisons, and reinforcements had to be brought in on a large scale, not only of legionaries, but of auxiliary units as well. Some reinforcements came from Britain, now relatively tranquil, brought by an officer named Sextus Flavius Quietus. At first, the same man who had dealt with the trouble in Dacia, Flavius Priscus, was made *pro legato*. But the situation soon demanded a senator to take command of the large new army-group concentrated for the war. A certain Uttedius Honoratus was appointed. The praetorian prefect Gavius Maximus would undoubtedly have been able profitably to capitalize on his experience as procurator of Mauretania Tingitana fifteen years previously, when the selection of officers and other matters concerning the war had to be discussed at the imperial council.[2]

It may have been at this period that Marcus wrote to Fronto complaining about the amount of correspondence he had to deal with. 'Hail my sweetest master. At last the courier is setting off, and I can

[1] Dio, 71, 36, 3; 71, 1, 2; 71, 6, 3-4 (taking drugs); 71, 24, 4; *Med.*, 1, 8; cf. 1, 17 *ad fin.* (bloodspitting and fits of dizziness). R. Dailly-H. van Effenterre, *Rev. Ét. Anc.*, 56, 1954, 352 ff., offer a diagnosis. Cf. Galen, 14K, 3 ff., 201 ff.

[2] Cf. R. Syme, *JRS*, 52, 1962, 92 ff., whose dating is more plausible than that of H.-G. Pflaum, *Les carrières procuratoriennes*, Paris, 1960, No. 157 *bis*. Uttedius Honoratus: *AE*, 1931, 36 and 38. Flavius Quietus: Pflaum, op. cit., No. 156 *bis*. Gavius Maximus in Tingitana: *CIL*, XVI, 173 (cf. Pflaum, op. cit., No. 105 *bis*). On the Mauretanian war cf. J. Baradez, *Libyca*, 2, 1954, 89 ff.

3a. Roman coins showing Marcus Aurelius in his late teens (*above left*), and aged about 23 (*above right*), 28 (*centre*), 34 (*below left*); Faustina in A.D. 138 or 139 (*below right*)

3b. Faustina, wife of Antoninus Pius

4. Apotheosis of Antoninus Pius and Faustina, presumably from their Temple above the Forum (now the Church of San Lorenzo in Miranda)

send you at last an account of my doings in the last three days. But I cannot *say* anything – I am so out of breath from dictating nearly thirty letters. For as to the opinion that you recently expressed about the letters, I haven't mentioned it to my father yet. . . .'[1] The word used for letters here (*epistulae*) is that also used for official correspondence, and from the number involved Marcus had obviously been performing official duties. It may be that Fronto had expressed some indignation about this, but that is only guesswork.

It was probably in A.D. 145, on March 17, at the Liberalia, that Marcus' adopted brother Lucius Aurelius Commodus assumed the *toga virilis*, as he would then be fourteen. Pius made the occasion even more festive by dedicating the temple to the deified Hadrian and largesse was given to the people of Rome.[2] Little is heard of Lucius in these early years. In fact he does not emerge into the fullest light until after Pius' death, when some of his correspondence with Fronto is preserved. But having now officially entered the status of manhood he was ready to be taught by Fronto. Hitherto he had received instruction from *grammatici* named Scaurinus in Latin and Telephus, Hephaestio and Harpocration in Greek. He was now handed over to Caninius Celer and to another Greek rhetorician named Apollonius, and to Herodes Atticus and Fronto. He also had philosophy teaching from Apollonius of Chalcedon and Sextus of Chaeronea (who also taught Marcus). A general eye was kept on his upbringing by a faithful freedman of his (real) father named Nicomedes, whom Antoninus had honoured for his devotion by bestowing on him the rank of knight (normally forbidden to freedmen). Less is related about Lucius' character in these early years than about Marcus, not surprisingly. He is said to have been deeply fond of all his teachers, and to have been loved by them; and to have tried his hand at composing verses as a boy.[3]

[1] *ad M.C.*, 4, 7=Haines, I, 184.

[2] *v. Veri*, 3, 1. But the dedication of the temple may be later, cf. *BMC*, IV, p. lxix. The date suggested for Lucius' entry into manhood is by analogy with Marcus (aged 14, *v. Marci*, 4, 5). The largesse (*liberalitas IV*) has problems attached to it, cf. *BMC*, IV, pp. lxiv ff.

[3] *v. Veri*, 2, 5-7; 2, 9. For Nicomedes, cf. H.-G. Pflaum, op. cit., No. 163, interpreting Dessau, *ILS*, 1740.

Marcus and Faustina were married at last in April 145. As Marcus was by adoption son of Pius, Faustina was his adoptive sister. One or other of them must have been formally released from Pius' paternal authority (*patria potestas*), to allow the ceremony to take place. Pius made it a noteworthy occasion. Coins were struck with the heads of the young couple. The soldiers were given a special bounty to commemorate it. As the couple were both patrician, the ceremony would undoubtedly have been that of *confarreatio*, few details of which are known. Pius, as Pontifex Maximus, would have been required to officiate. At some stage in the ceremony a cake of spelt (*far*) would be used. But there is no need to attempt to describe the occasion. All that is known is that it was 'noteworthy'.[1]

None of the letters refers to the marriage itself, unless Marcus is doing so in an oblique way when he talks about something that was to happen 'in two days time', in a letter that is incompletely preserved. 'I am beginning to be fastidious, as often happens with those who at last have in their grasp what they long for. . . .' But that is guesswork. The only mention of Faustina in the earlier letters had been by Pius when he had said that he would rather live in exile with her than without her in the palace.[2] The first reference to her in the letters after her marriage speaks of her as being ill. Fronto mentions that Victorinus had told him that 'your Lady is more feverish than yesterday. Gratia had reported that everything was getting better'. Fronto too was ill – 'The reason why I have not seen you is because I am weak from a cold.'[3] In his reply Marcus reported that Faustina was still feverish but was a good patient. In another letter from this period he describes a small chapter of accidents in the family. 'This is how I have spent the last few days. My sister was suddenly attacked with such a violent pain in her private parts that her face was dreadful to look at. Then my mother, in her worry, accidentally

---

[1] *v. Marci*, 6, 6; *v. Pii*, 10, 2; for the date, see now *Inscr. It.*, XIII, 1, 205. For marriage regulations and ceremonies, see P. E. Corbett, *Roman Law of Marriage*, Oxford, 1930. Allusions on the coinage: *BMC*, IV, pp. lxv, lxxxvii; Antoninus Pius, Nos. 611–12, 1236 ff., 1774 ff., 1801.

[2] *ad M.C.*, 5, 5=Haines, I, 192. The mention by Pius: *ad Ant. Pium*, 2 =Haines, I, 128.

[3] *ad M.C.*, 5, 10=Haines, I, 144.

hit her side on the angle of a wall, which caused a great deal of pain to us as well as to her. As for me, when I went to lie down I found a scorpion in my bed – but I managed to kill it before lying on it. If you are in better health that is a consolation. My mother is now a bit better, thank the gods. Farewell, my best and sweetest master. My Lady greets you.' There are more letters which describe mutual illnesses and convalescences, and some of the later correspondence, as Fronto grew older, seems to have been almost exclusively concerned with the subject of ill-health.[1]

In September 145 a puzzling episode took place. A certain Cornelius Priscianus was condemned by the senate 'for hostile action disturbing the peace of the province of Spain', as the official records describe it. The historians add that Priscianus was attempting to seize the throne and that he committed suicide, but give no more details. He must have been the governor of the province of Hispania Tarraconensis at the time – if he was genuinely seeking to make a *coup d'état*. On the face of it this seems an unlikely place from which to start a rebellion. The governors of Britain, Syria, and above all the strategically placed Upper Pannonia, were better equipped since each was armed with three legions, and within ready reach of possible allies. The Iberian peninsula was isolated, and had only one legion. On the other hand it had been a governor of Tarraconensis – Galba – who overthrew Nero in A.D. 68. But Galba took power when others had done the work for him and Nero was losing support fast. Two other facts may have weighed with Priscianus, however. First, he was himself of Spanish origin, and may have been confident of local support. Second, in A.D. 145 strong reinforcements for Mauretania were being sent south from Britain and the Rhine-Danube frontier. A high proportion of these troops might have passed through Spain, giving Priscianus a fatal temptation. But his motivation remains baffling, and it still seems more likely that he was involved in some more purely local trouble than overt rebellion. For example he might have disagreed violently with commanders of troop-detachments moving through his province,

---

[1] *ad M.C.*, 5, 11=Haines, I, 194; ibid., 5, 8=Haines, I, 196; cf. ibid., 5, 12, 17 =Haines, I, 196–200, for some letters on illnesses.

and have allowed his own men too much licence, thus causing an affray.

One other rebel or conspirator is heard of during Pius' reign, a senator named Atilius Titianus. His action is unknown. He might, theoretically, have been an ally of Priscianus. This episode in A.D. 145 is a reminder that all was not quite as happy in the twenty-three year-long reign of Pius as the speech of Aelius Aristides in A.D. 144 might lead one to suppose.[1]

Another death occurred in March of the following year, but of a different kind. The prefect of the city, who was also holding office as consul for the second time, Sex. Erucius Clarus, died suddenly from natural causes. No details are known. He was a link with a bygone era – the younger Pliny had been his friend and patron, and had obtained entry into the senate for him from Trajan. He had distinguished himself in the Parthian war in A.D. 116. He was an eminent patron of letters mentioned by Aulus Gellius as discussing and corresponding with the learned Sulpicius Apollinaris. Clarus may have been the second prefect appointed by Pius (bearing in mind the possibility that Bruttius Praesens was made prefect in or about A.D. 139).[2] His successor is not known. It could well have been the conqueror of the refractory north Britons, Quintus Lollius Urbicus, now certainly back in Rome. He was in office as prefect later in the reign, and may have begun his duties in succession to Clarus.[3]

Meanwhile Marcus' studies with Fronto seem to have been proceeding, perhaps in a slightly desultory fashion. A letter, which seems to be from after his marriage (from the mention of 'my lady' rather than 'my mother') and which carries a hint of discontent gives a good indication of the position. 'To my master. I will have

---

[1] v. Pii, 7, 3–4. Priscianus: PIR 2, C 1418; AE, 1936, 98: 'quod provinciam Hispaniam hostiliter . . . [inq]uietaverit'. Titianus: PIR 2, A 1305. Reinforcements: cf. n. 2, p. 114, also Dessau, ILS, 1362, discussed by Pflaum, op. cit., No. 156.

[2] PIR 2, E. 96.

[3] For Urbicus as prefect, cf. Hüttl, Antoninus Pius, II, 192 (but the close dating there offered is not so certain).

the whole day free. If you have ever loved me, love me today and send me a rich subject, I beseech and ask, and I request and require and implore. For in that law-court subject I found nothing but exclamations. Farewell, best of masters. My Lady salutes you. I want to write something where there should be shouts of acclamation – humour me and look out a "shouting" subject.'[1]

The letter which seems to be Fronto's reply gives him a subject. 'I have slept late. I have sent you a subject: the case is a serious one. A consul of the Roman people, putting aside his toga, has put on the mail tunic and with the people of Rome looking on, at the feast of Minerva, among the young men, has slain a lion. He is denounced before the censors. Shape it up and develop. Farewell, most sweet Lord. Greet your Lady.'[2]

Marcus' reply showed that he was not completely satisfied. For some reason it has no heading, except the word 'Answer', but that may be chance. 'When did it happen and was it at Rome? You don't really mean that affair that happened under Domitian at his palace at Albano, do you? Besides, with this subject it will take longer to make it seem credible than to get angry about it. It seems to me an improbable subject, and I would definitely have preferred the kind I asked for. Write back by return about the date.'[3]

In another letter written probably a little later Fronto does provide another subject. 'I am rather late, my Lord, in replying to you, because I delayed to open your letter on my way to the Forum to plead in court. I am feeling better but the sore is deeper. Farewell my sweetest Lord. Greet my Lady. M. Lucilius, a tribune of the people, has forcibly imprisoned a free Roman citizen when his colleagues had ordered him to be released against their decision. For that action he is "marked" by the Censors. First divide the case, then take either side, as prosecution and defence. Farewell, my Lord, the light of all your friends. Greet your Lady mother.'[4]

Marcus' answer to this letter is not preserved, but he seems by this time to find this kind of intellectual exercise a rather barren occupation. In a fairly long letter written when he was twenty-five,

---

[1] *ad M.C.*, 5, 28=Haines, I, 208.   [2] Ibid., 5, 22=Haines, I, 210.
[3] Ibid., 5, 23=Haines, I, 210.   [4] Ibid., 5, 27=Haines, I, 214.

that is between April 26, 146, and April 26, 147, his reasons are apparent. 'To my master. Gaius Aufidius [Victorinus] gives himself airs, extols his judgment to the skies, denies that a juster man than himself – I must not exaggerate – ever came from Umbria to Rome. What more do you want? He would rather win praise as a judge than as an orator. When I smile, he is disdainful. It is easy to sit yawning next to a judge, he says, but to *be* a judge is noble work. This is a hit at me. Still, the affair has turned out well. It is all right – I am pleased. Your arrival makes me happy but also anxious. No one would ask why it makes me happy. As to why I am anxious, I will tell you, by heaven: although I have had some free time I haven't given a single little bit of it to the task you set me to write. Ariston's books are treating me well at the moment, but also treating me badly. When they teach me better things then certainly they treat me well. But when they show me how far away from these better things my character is, your pupil blushes again and again, and is angry with himself, because at the age of twenty-five my soul still has not drunk in any draught of noble doctrines and purer principles. So I am doing penance, I am angry, I am sad, I am comparing myself with others, I am not eating. Being completely bound up in this disquiet, I have been putting off the duty of writing every day, until the next day. But now I will think up something, and as some Attic orator once warned an assembly of the Athenians, "the laws must be allowed to sleep sometimes" – so I will propitiate Ariston's books and allow them to rest for a little while, and after reading Cicero's minor speeches I will turn my attention fully to that stage poet of yours. But I can only write on one side or the other, for Ariston will certainly never allow me to sleep well enough to defend both sides. Farewell best and most honoured master. My Lady salutes you.'[1]

Ariston, whose books were having such a pronounced effect on Marcus, was a Stoic, a pupil of the founder of the Stoic school and an influential philosopher some four hundred years earlier. He had concentrated on moral issues to the exclusion of the scientific and speculative aspects of Stoicism. This conversion of Marcus to

[1] *ad. M.C.*, 4, 13=Haines, I, 214 ff.

philosophy cannot have been entirely unexpected to Fronto, and it did not, of course, mean the end of his friendship. He remained an honoured and a close friend for the rest of his life. It is perhaps not surprising that Marcus should have felt, at the age of twenty-five, that he had had enough of writing compositions and the other exercises of the art of rhetoric. His marriage may perhaps have had a catalytic effect on him, making him realize that it was time to look carefully at the aims of his life. But his interest in philosophy was not new. It had begun when he was a boy of eleven. At fourteen he had acquired teachers in philosophy, notably the Stoic Apollonius, and in what may have been the first letter, or the first letter of any length, that Fronto wrote to Marcus, he had given him a warning about dabbling in philosophy, although even Fronto must have realized that it was part of a gentleman's education to know something of it. In a later letter Fronto carried the warning further: Marcus had evidently criticized the insincerity of conventional language. Fronto defended the language of oratory. 'I think all speech without these conventions is rough, provincial and uncouth, in fact, unskilful and useless. And I do not think that devices of that kind are any less necessary for philosophers than they are for orators.' Fronto gave the example of Socrates as a philosopher whose command of language was a vital part of his equipment. But at twenty-five Marcus had had enough of taking both sides in imaginary debates.[1]

His formal education was now over. Marcus had enjoyed the best of relations with all his teachers. This would be apparent even without the evidence of his correspondence with Fronto. 'He gave so much honour to his teachers that he kept gold statues of them in his private chapel, and always honoured their tombs by personal visits and offerings of sacrifices and flowers,' the biographer records. His grief at the death of one of his teachers has already been quoted. The biographer adds at this point that 'he devoted so much attention and labour to his studies that it affected his health adversely – the only thing with which fault can be found in his entire boyhood'.[2]

[1] *ad. M.C.*, 4, 3=Haines, I, 2 ff.; ibid., 3, 15=Haines, I, 100 ff. For Ariston, cf. M. Pohlenz, *Die Stoa*, 2nd ed., Göttingen, 1959, 27–8, 123, 163.
[2] *v. Marci*, 3, 5–8.

Apollonius had obviously played an important part in introducing him to Stoic philosophy. But the greatest influence on him was probably Quintus Junius Rusticus. Rusticus was at least twenty years older than Marcus, a little older than Fronto, probably. His very name was almost a political philosophy or programme in itself, for he was a descendant, probably the grandson, of one of the martyrs to the tyranny of Domitian. The 'Stoic opposition' to the bad emperors in the first century, especially to Nero and Domitian, was an important force in shaping the character of the Antonine principate. Apollonius, Rusticus, and a third friend, Claudius Maximus, were the three to whom Marcus must have felt he owed most, since it is for coming to know them that he gives particular thanks to the gods.[1] His tribute to Rusticus is a full one. 'From Rusticus: to acquire the impression that there was need for reform and treatment of character; not to be led astray into enthusiasm for rhetoric, for writing on speculative themes, for discoursing on moralizing texts, for parading in fanciful fashion the ascetic or the philanthropist. To avoid oratory, poetry and "fine writing". Not to parade around at home in elaborate clothes or do things like that. To write letters in a simple style, like the one he himself wrote from Sinuessa to my mother. To be accessible and easy to reconcile to those who provoke or offend, as soon as they are willing to meet me. To read books accurately and not to be satisfied with a general superficial impression or to agree quickly with people who talk round a subject. To have come to know the *Discourses* of Epictetus – of which he let me share his own copy.'[2]

Clearly it was Rusticus who wooed Marcus away from oratory – the implied criticisms of Fronto are more than hints: 'enthusiasm for rhetoric'; 'oratory, poetry and "fine writing" '; 'letters in the simple style'. The contrasts are quite plain. Rusticus' letter to Domitia Lucilla written from Sinuessa has not, of course, survived. But Fronto's two letters to her could be called anything but simple in their style.

In spite of the implied criticisms of Fronto, some years later, at

[1] *Med.*, 1, 17.
[2] Ibid., 1, 7. For Rusticus, cf. *PW*, 10, 1917, 1083 ff.

least, Fronto could speak of the man who had wooed Marcus away from him with respect and affection as 'that friend of mine, the Roman Rusticus, who would gladly give his life for your little finger', in a letter to Marcus. Ironically, however, the occasion for his reference to Rusticus was to mention a disagreement he had had with him over Marcus' natural abilities as an orator. Rusticus gave way, unwillingly and with a frown, when Fronto insisted on the reality of his former pupil's talent.[1]

Fronto himself, years later, put a rather uncharitable interpretation on the conversion to philosophy. 'Then, you seem to me, in the fashion of the young, tired of boring work, to have deserted the pursuit of eloquence and to have turned aside to philosophy, in which there is no introductory section to be carefully elaborated, no account of the facts, bringing them together with concision, clarity and skill. . . .' By contrast, 'you would read a book to your philosopher, listen in silence while your master explained it and nod to show your understanding; would hear again and again: "what is the first premiss? What is the second premiss?" and when the windows were wide open, the point that "If it is day, then it is light" would be laboured. Then you would go away, carefree, with nothing to think over, or to write up at night, nothing to recite to your master, nothing to say by heart, no search for words, no adorning of a single synonym, no translation from Greek to our language.'[2]

Although it was Rusticus who had family connections with the Stoic opposition of previous generations, it was not he but another friend, Claudius Severus, who brought Marcus to a knowledge of what these men had stood for. Severus was probably about eight or nine years older than Marcus. He was from a Greek family of the Paphlagonian city of Pompeiopolis in Asia Minor, and his father had been the first governor of Trajan's new province of Arabia. He had evidently been born there during his father's administration, for he bore the additional name of Arabianus. He was consul in A.D. 146, as colleague of Erucius Clarus. A further witness of his close friendship with Marcus is that his son was to marry Marcus' eldest

---

[1] Fronto, *ad Ant. Imp.*, 1, 2, 2=Haines, II, 36.
[2] Fronto, *de eloquentia*, 3, 4=Haines, II, 74.

daughter. Claudius Severus was not, apparently, a Stoic. He is described by the biographer as being an adherent of the Peripatetic school, in other words an Aristotelian. Marcus' friendship with him, and the influence that he had over Marcus, illustrate that Marcus was not to become a dogmatic Stoic. 'From Severus,' Marcus learned 'love of family, love of truth and love of justice. And through him to have got to know Thrasea, Helvidius, Cato, Dio and Brutus. To form the conception of a balanced constitution, based on equity and freedom of speech and of a monarchy which honours above all else the liberty of the subject. From him too, consistency and uniformity in regard for philosophy. To do good, to be generous to others, to be hopeful. To trust in the love of friends, to be frank and open with those who met with his disapproval, and that his friends did not need to make guesses about his wishes or his dislikes, but he was open with them.' More must be said later about Thrasea and the others whose political ideals Marcus made his own. Even if their application had no long-term effect on the autocratic imperial rule, it was a remarkable thing to find a ruler who professed them and gave every sign of attempting to put them into practice.[1]

The other philosophical friends whose influence Marcus records in the opening book of the *Meditations* are Claudius Maximus, Sextus of Chaeronea, and Cinna Catulus. Claudius Maximus, like Fronto, Rusticus and Claudius Severus, played a part in public life. With Apollonius and Rusticus, he was one of Marcus' three most significant friends in the development of his character. He must have been some years, probably at least ten years, older than Marcus. He was consul in about A.D. 144, and for some five years was governor of the key military province of Upper Pannonia, from A.D. 150–4. In A.D. 158 he was to go to Africa as proconsul, where he had to sit in judgment in a *cause célèbre*, the trial of Apuleius of Madauros, one of the few original writers of the second century A.D. He is thus immortalized by Apuleius, who took good care to propitiate his judge by referring to him in flattering terms. 'You are making a mistake,

---

[1] *Med.*, 1, 14. I regard τοῦ ἀδελφοῦ as a gloss, following Schulz and Farquharson, *Meditations*, II, 457–8. It could mean *consocer* ('co-father-in-law'), however. For the Claudii Severi, cf. *PIR 2*, C 1024 and 1027.

Aemilianus,' said Apuleius, addressing one of his opponents, who had apparently hoped to gain Maximus' support by reproaching the poverty of Apuleius – just because Maximus 'happens to be the owner of an ample estate'. 'You are ill-acquainted with his views if you estimate him according to how Fortune has treated him and not according to the strict rules of philosophy; if you think that a man of strict philosophical principles and such long military service is not more favourably inclined towards moderation rather than to fastidious opulence; if you suppose that he does not approve of riches only on the same principle that he does of some piece of clothing, rather when it fits the person who wears it than when it is unusually long.' Apuleius continually addresses Maximus in person, and credits him with wisdom and learning, in one passage taking it for granted that he is familiar with Aristotle's works *On the generation of animals*, *On the anatomy of animals*, and *On the history of animals*.

Apuleius' favourable language about Maximus might have been regarded as mere flattery, but Marcus' tribute to him is unequivocal. 'From Maximus: mastery of self and in nothing to be hesitant. To be cheerful in all circumstances, especially in illness. A character that was a happy blend of mildness and dignity. Readiness to do what has to be done without fuss. To see in every instance that he said what he really thought and did what he did without any malicious intention. His imperturbability and his ability not be shocked, never to hurry or to hang back, never to be at a loss what to do, not to be downcast or fawningly hypocritical, and again, not to be angry or suspicious. To be generous, forgiving and sincere. To give the impression of being completely straight by nature, not of a forced rectitude. The fact too that no one would ever think that he was looked down on by him but would not venture to regard himself as his superior. And to be agreeable in social life.'[1]

Sextus of Chaeronea was the nephew of the celebrated writer

---

[1] *Med.*, I, 15; Apuleius, *Apol.*, 19 ff.; *PIR 2*, C 933–4. J. Fitz, *Acta Ant. Acad. Sc. Hung.*, 11, 1963, 258 ff., assigns Dessau, *ILS*, 1062, to Claudius Maximus – perhaps rightly, although this creates difficulties. See also A. R. Birley, in forthcoming memorial volume for *E. Swoboda.*

Plutarch. He was a professional philosopher, unlike Maximus, Severus and Rusticus, in the sense that he did not enter on a career in public service, and devoted his life to teaching philosophy. Marcus continued to attend his lectures after becoming emperor, a fact which caused a good deal of surprise and comment. 'From Sextus,' Marcus learned, 'kindliness, how to behave as head of a family, and the meaning of living according to Nature. Dignity without pretence, special consideration for friends, tolerance for amateurs and men whose opinions have no theoretical basis. Readiness to adapt himself to everyone, so that his company was pleasanter than flattery, at the same time commanding the greatest respect among those around him. His sure grasp and method in discovering and systematizing the principles necessary to human life. Never to give the impression of anger or any other emotion but being at one and the same time unemotional and yet full of natural affection. To praise quietly and to be modest about encyclopaedic learning.'[1] The 'natural affection' which Sextus possessed in spite of his philosophical detachment, was a quality which the Roman upper-classes lacked – in fact, as Fronto pointed out to Lucius, there was no word for it in Latin. Marcus remembered Fronto for this observation too.[2]

Marcus' tribute to Cinna Catulus is briefer. 'From Catulus,' Marcus learned, 'not to neglect the rebukes of a friend, even if they happen to be unreasonable, but to try to regain his favour. To praise teachers wholeheartedly, as is recorded of Athenodotus and Domitius, and to have a genuine love for children.'[3] Catulus is totally unknown, but his names suggest that he was of western rather than eastern descent; and the mention of Athenodotus makes it clear that he was a Stoic.[4]

The philosophy of Stoicism takes its name from the public hall, portico, or *Stoa*, in which Zeno, son of Mnaseas, the founder of the

[1] *Med.*, I, 9; cf. Dio, 71, I, 2, and Philostratus, *v. soph.*, 2, I, 9.
[2] Fronto, *ad amicos*, I, 3=Haines, I, 280: 'philostorgus, cuius rei nomen apud Romanos nullum est'; *ad Verum Imp.*, 2, 7, 6=Haines, II, 154. Cf. *Med.*, I, II, and Fronto, *de fer. Als.*, 4=Haines, II, 18.
[3] *Med.*, I, 13. Mentioned only in *v. Marci*, 3, 2.
[4] Athenodotus, a Stoic, was the teacher of Fronto (Haines, I, 204, 270; II, 50).

school, gave his teaching at Athens.[1] Zeno was not an Athenian, and it even seems doubtful if he was Greek. He was from Citium in Cyprus, and was certainly of partly Phoenician origin, like many of the inhabitants of his native island. It may be even that he was of completely Semitic descent. He was born in 333–2 B.C., the year that Alexander the Great ascended the throne of Macedon. He left his home at the age of twenty-two to go to Athens, and, so far as is known, never returned. He was thus ideally fitted, both in time and place, to found a philosophical school which combined elements of Oriental thought with the advanced and disciplined intellectualism of Hellenic culture. He was at first attracted to the teaching of the Cynics, but before long ceased his allegiance to that somewhat perversely eccentric and ascetic sect. He was clearly greatly influenced by the teaching of the Platonic Academy; indeed the life and teaching of Socrates remained an inspiring force throughout the history of Stoicism. After he had begun to work out his own system, the Athenian authorities provided him with rooms in the *Stoa Poikile*, where he began his teaching in 301–300 B.C., attracting numerous followers over a long life as a philosophic theorist and director until his death in 262 B.C.

Marcus does not refer to Zeno, nor to his successor as head of the Stoa, Cleanthes. A good deal of the credit for the originating of Stoic principles went to the third head of the school, Chrysippus, a prolific writer, who evidently did much to systematize the work of his predecessors. Marcus refers once or twice to Chrysippus, as does Fronto in the correspondence, when he wants to give an example of a Stoic.[2] Only a small proportion of the works of the three great initiators of Stoicism has survived, as is the case with most of their successors, so it is not always easy to distinguish between the teachings of individual Stoics at different periods. More

---

[1] The best account of Stoicism is that of M. Pohlenz, *Die Stoa*, 2nd ed., Göttingen, 1959 (2 vols.).

[2] Fronto, *de fer. Als.*, 3,5=Haines, II, 10; *de eloquentia*, 1, 15=Haines, II, 66. *Med.*, 7, 19; 6, 42. Zeno is mentioned by Fronto in *ad Verum Imp.*, 1, 1, 3–4 =Haines, II, 48–50, and *de eloquentia*, 1, 1, 12=Haines, II, 62. Cleanthes is also mentioned in the latter passage. Neither is named in the *Meditations*.

than four hundred years elapsed between the early lectures of Zeno and the birth of Marcus.

There were three main sections into which the Stoic system was divided, logic, physics and ethics. Logic included the theory of knowledge and the study of language, as well as logic in the narrower sense – the study of syllogistic argument and dialectic. Physics included theology and metaphysics as well as all the natural sciences. Ethics, the pursuit of the good life, was the ultimate aim. The relationship between the three branches of the system was illustrated by the Stoics by the use of metaphor. Logic was compared to a wall, physics to the trees protected by the wall, ethics to the fruit borne by the trees. Again, the philosophy as a whole was compared to a body, of which the bones and muscles were logic, the flesh and blood physics, and the soul ethics.

The basis of the Stoics' thought was that knowledge is attainable. They believed the evidence of the senses, and evolved an elaborate explanation of the mode by which the senses and the mind acquire knowledge, which seems now a curiously confused mixture of physiology, psychology and philosophy. Waves of sensation emanate from objects of sense-perception, which strike the sense-organs. This explains the basic acquisition of sense-data. The mind acquires information by the meeting of waves from the mind with waves from the senses. The impact produces a mind-picture – φαντασία. This was, of course, only the starting-point of their theory of knowledge. The crucial point around which it hinged was the 'criterion' for judging the truth of mind-pictures. On this they cannot be said to have made more progress than most other philosophers before and after. Nevertheless their logical theories, such as they were, provided a groundwork from which they could go on to formulate a theory of the universe and a number of fundamental rules of conduct, or rather, one fundamental rule.

The Stoics viewed the universe as a single, unified body, finite, continuous and of spherical shape, existing in an infinite void. Some Stoics toyed with the notion of the sun being the centre of this universe, but rejected this in favour of the earth – unfortunately for the progress of science. The universe is in itself a rational, living being. All its parts are united in a mysterious unity, which make up this indivisible – and divine – whole. In a sense, God is the soul of the universe. The life-force was conceived by Stoics as having the properties of fire: thus fire, heat and motion were the source of all life. It can be seen from this brief summary that the Stoics were, from one point of view, materialists and from another, pantheists. But this would misrepresent their views. They were not materialists in the modern sense, although they believed that everything was made of the same ultimate 'stuff'; and although their God was not separate from the world, their conception of him is nevertheless different from that of the pantheist.

The central concept of the Stoic teaching was the 'rational principle' – *logos* – which, they believed, animated the universe. The aim of the Stoic philosopher was 'to live in harmony with "nature", ' a concept which it is extremely difficult to explain in any other language than Greek. True nature was guided and formed by the *logos*. This was also identified with fate, or divine providence. They believed, with a contradiction which not surprisingly they could never resolve with complete success, both in predestination and in free will. Some Stoics also believed that the universe would come to an end in fire, and that a new universe would then be formed through the action of fire, the life-giving force. But this was subsequently abandoned as being incompatible with the conception of a beneficent providence. The sole good in human life is virtue, the acquisition of which depends on the individual human will. If a man acquires virtue, and lives in harmony with nature, he is thereby freed from dependence on external factors. Desire for external, apparently good things comes only from false judgment, which can be overcome by knowledge. The pursuit of virtue is an end in itself. Nothing else matters. All emotions should be avoided. This may make the doctrine seem cold and selfish. But Stoics also believed in the 'Fatherhood of God and the Brotherhood of Man', and this universalism gives it a more exalted note than the at first sight narrow insistence on *being* virtuous.

By the time of the death of Chrysippus, in the last decade of the third century B.C., the Stoa had acquired a recognized place as one of the leading schools of philosophy. Chrysippus, like Zeno, came from a region (Cilicia in his case) where Semitic and Hellenic elements were intermingled. The father of Chrysippus was from Tarsus, the city of St Paul. Later prominent figures in the Stoic school were also from the eastern Mediterranean. Many commentators have noted similarities between Jewish religious thought and the philosophy of the Stoa. In fact, it may certainly be said that Stoicism was to become, for its adherents, very much of a religion. In the second century B.C. the school grew in influence and in the middle of the century spread to Rome, then the leading Mediterranean power. By the last century of the Roman Republic, chiefly through the direct and indirect teaching of Panaetius and later of Posidonius, its effect on the outlook of numerous leading Romans had become profound. The revolutionary Tiberius Gracchus was influenced by a number of Stoic doctrines, for example, as were his brother-in-law and political antagonist Scipio Aemilianus and Scipio's friend the younger Laelius. The circle of these two men gave Stoicism a considerable following among the Roman nobility. But the imprint of its teaching was to be seen most markedly in Julius Caesar's enemy, the younger Cato, and in Cato's nephew Brutus, the assassin of Caesar. In spite, or perhaps partly because of, the political defeat and deaths of Cato and Brutus, the philosophy which had animated their activity continued to flourish after Caesar Augustus had founded his New Order. Stoicism became the refuge and inspiration of those who found the unashamedly despotic rule of the later Julio-Claudian emperors and of Domitian distasteful and oppressive.

Seneca was the leading expounder of Stoicism in the mid-first century A.D., and although for a time he was the tutor and then the minister of Nero, he was eventually implicated in the unsuccessful conspiracy of A.D. 65 and forced to suicide. But Seneca, although his reputation in his own time and in the Renaissance was enormous, was not thought highly of in the second century A.D. Fronto disapproved of his literary style and the leading Stoics clearly felt that his philosophical teaching had been compromised or tainted by his association with Nero. These criticisms also applied to his nephew, the poet Lucan, whose epic the *Pharsalia* was a glorification of Cato:

victrix causa deis placuit, sed victa Catoni –
The winning side was favoured by the gods,
But the losing by Cato

Lucan's end, at the same time as that of Seneca, had in fact been somewhat inglorious, although his uncle faced death with dignity. The heroes of the second-century Stoics were the political leaders of the Stoic opposition to absolutism, Thrasea Paetus, his son-in-law Helvidius Priscus, and Junius Arulenus Rusticus, probably the grandfather of the teacher of Marcus. These three men lost their lives under Nero, Vespasian and Domitian respectively.[1]

With the assassination of Domitian in September 96, philosophy, and Stoicism in particular, could come out into the open again, and became at first respectable, and before long, fashionable. Its leading teacher was, at the beginning of the second century, Epictetus, a lame ex-slave of Phrygian origin, who had belonged to a freedman of Nero, Epaphroditus. Ironically, it was Epaphroditus who had been mainly responsible for unmasking and suppressing the conspiracy of A.D. 65, in the aftermath of which Seneca, Lucan and Thrasea Paetus lost their lives. Epictetus is said to have been taught by Musonius Rufus. Musonius was no doctrinaire Stoic and the fragments of his teaching and the anecdotes about him that survive give the impression that he remained a typical Roman. His teaching was simple: everyone is capable of goodness; God wants man to be virtuous and superior to pleasure and pain; virtue demands practical training, just like music or medicine – theory is not enough. In his pursuit of the simple, natural life Musonius was a vegetarian, wore simple clothing, did not shave his beard and praised the virtues of working on the land. He insisted on a strict sexual morality – his teaching on marriage, with its emphasis on a true equality and com-

---

[1] Seneca: *PIR 2*, A 617. Lucan: *PIR 2*, A 611. (The quotation is *Pharsalia*, 1, 128.) Thrasea: *PIR 2*, C 1187. Helvidius and his son: *PIR 2*, H 69–70. Rusticus: *PW*, 10, 1917, 1083. G. Boissier, *L'opposition sous les Césars*, Paris, 1875 (and reprints), is still valuable. See also R. Syme, *Tacitus*, Oxford, 1958, II, 558 ff., and for an act of political opposition A. R. Birley, *Class. Rev.*, N.S., 12, 1962, 197 ff.

munity of minds, and on mutual sharing of possessions, was among the most advanced of ancient times. He did not, however, advocate escapism in any form: he preached good citizenship, involving the giving of whatever help was possible to one's fellow-countrymen and fatherland. In his own case this was an impossible aim, as he was exiled by Domitian. In exile he did not compromise: 'Have you ever seen me humble myself before anyone, because I am an exile?' he would say.[1]

Epictetus too was exiled, under Domitian, to Nicopolis on the Adriatic coast of Greece (in modern Albania). After Domitian's murder he was content to remain there, and disciples from many walks of life came to him. He was, like Musonius, far more concerned with the moral side of Stoicism; and Marcus too was to bother very little about Stoic metaphysical or scientific doctrines. The important thing for the Stoic now was freedom to live as one wanted, genuine inner freedom: to be master of one's own soul. It is perhaps not surprising that one who had been a slave should have more to teach about freedom than any other ancient philosopher. The contrast between physical and moral freedom was all the more telling when it came from the lips of one who had experienced both as something new. The emphasis on inner freedom was, also, particularly appropriate under the empire – for Caesar was the common master of all men. But if Caesar too were a Stoic, thinking along the same lines? Epictetus did not know Marcus. But the irony of the fact that the two last great Stoics should have been a lame Phrygian slave and the ruler of the world empire has struck many. Perhaps it should not be emphasized too much. Epictetus had been, as slaves went, in a relatively high grade – an imperial slave at secondhand, so to speak; and he was given his freedom. Still the essential point about slavery was that the slave was the property of his master.[2] Epictetus made light of the condition of slavery, but he could still remind the masters of slaves that slaves were 'kinsmen, your brothers by nature, the offspring of Zeus'. All men are the children of God, with a spark of the

---

[1] M. Pohlenz, op. cit., I, 300 ff.; II, 151 ff. See also M. Charlesworth, *Five Men. Character Studies from the Roman Empire*, Cambridge, Mass., 1936, 33 ff.
[2] *PIR 2*, E 74. Pohlenz, op. cit., 327 ff.

divine fire within them. A master who looks on his slaves as less than that is looking not to the laws of the gods, but 'to the earth, the pit, these wretched laws of ours – the laws of the dead'.[1]

A great deal of Epictetus' teaching has survived, in the form of detailed records of individual periods of teaching with question and answer, longer discourses and short aphorisms. This cannot be summarized briefly, but Arrian, the pupil of Epictetus who recorded his teaching, did make the attempt to do this, and a few key points from that summary may be given here. 'Some things are under our control, others are not. The things under our control are: our mental concepts, choice, desire, aversion, in a word everything that we do. The things not under our control are: our body, property, reputation, public office, in a word everything that is not our own doing. And the things under our control are by nature free, unhindered, unimpeded. The things not under our control are weak, in servitude, subject to hindrance, not our own.'[2] Once this had been recognized, the way was clear. 'Do not seek to have everything happen as you desire, but desire that things happen as they actually do happen, and then you will be well-off.'[3] 'Whoever wants to be free, should not wish for anything or avoid anything that is under the control of others. Otherwise, he has to be a slave.'[4] 'Keep death and exile and all dreadful-seeming things, most of all death, before your eyes day and night; then you will never have any mean thought, or long for something too much.'[5] 'When you have become adjusted to simple living in respect of your body, do not preen yourself about this . . . and if you ever want to train yourself for physical endurance, do it by yourself and not for outsiders.'[6] The summary ends with the famous saying of Socrates, about those responsible for his death: 'Anytus and Meletus can kill me, but they cannot hurt me.'[7] Marcus' Stoic hero Thrasea Paetus, the enemy of Nero, 'used to say: "I would rather be killed today than exiled tomorrow". ' But Musonius told him: 'If you choose death as the heavier of the two, what a

[1] *Discourses*, I, 13.
[2] *Encheiridion*, I, 1–2. For Arrian, cf. *PIR 2*, F 219.
[3] *Ench.*, 8.   [4] Ibid., 14, 2.   [5] Ibid., 21.   [6] Ibid., 47.
[7] Ibid., 53, 4 (Plato, *Apol.*, 30 C–D).

foolish choice. If as the lighter – who gave your the choice? Are you not willing to practise contentment with what you are given.'[1]

The influence of Epictetus is apparent on every page of the *Meditations*. Their character is different from the *Discourses* of Epictetus, more sombre perhaps. But this is not surprising, considering that they were written in the middle of war and death. Marcus had every reason to take to heart the recommendation 'to keep death . . . before your eyes day and night'. The *Meditations*, of course, were written at the end of· his life. But from the age of twenty-five onwards the teaching of Epictetus was one of the mainsprings of Marcus' life.[2]

Several of Marcus' philosopher friends had set him an example in their family lives – Sextus in 'how to behave as head of a family', Severus 'love of family', Cinna Catulus 'to have a genuine love of children'. But he probably did not need these lessons. In A.D. 147 Marcus and Faustina had their first child, a girl, named after her mother – Annia Galeria Aurelia Faustina, by her full names. She was born on November 30, hence more than eighteen months after the marriage. There may have been anxiety about Faustina's capacity to bear children (she had, after all, been ill soon after the marriage). But she was to bear Marcus at least twelve children during the thirty-one years of their marriage. Marcus himself in the *Meditations* thanked the gods that his wife was as she was, 'so obedient, so warm-hearted, so artless'. Faustina acquired a reputation among posterity for being unfaithful, but her eleven or more pregnancies (at least two of the children were to be twins) can have left her little time in thirty-one years for adventures.

The birth of a child was of public importance for Marcus. Pius decided that the time had now come to invest him with some of the imperial powers – in fact the decision must have been taken before the birth, for the powers were proclaimed on the following day, December 1. Marcus received the tribunician power and the *imperium* – the authority over the armies and provinces of the emperor – and the right to bring one measure before the senate after the four

---

[1] *Discourses*, I, I, 26–7.   [2] See Chapter X.

which his father could introduce. Marcus' proper style was now M. Aurelius Caesar, Augusti filius, *trib. pot.* Nine days later, on December 10, his tribunician power was renewed and he became *trib. pot.* II, for this was the day on which his father also renewed his tribunician power. Meanwhile, on December 1, Faustina received the title Augusta.[1]

It is perhaps somewhat surprising that Pius did not consider it necessary after this act of confidence to send Marcus to the provinces and armies, to allow him to gain experience by direct participation. But Pius himself had never had any experience abroad, other than his year as proconsul of the non-military province of Asia; and the reign was a reign of peace. Still, the failure of Pius to give Marcus this experience must be deplored, in the light of future events. Pius himself did not undertake any expeditions in his reign. His expressed reason for this was that 'it was a serious problem for the provincials to support an emperor and his suite, even an economical one'. Marcus was only absent from Pius for two nights during the entire twenty-three years of the reign.[2]

It is remarkable that Marcus was able to fill the role of virtual co-emperor for thirteen-and-a-half years without ever exciting the suspicion that he was impatient to have sole rule for himself. The acid-tongued Valerius Homullus apparently took the opportunity of insinuating to Pius that Domitia Lucilla was eager for her son to come to the throne without delay. He observed her praying in her garden in front of an image of the god Apollo, and commented to Pius: 'That woman is now praying that you may come to your end and her son may rule.' Pius' reply is not recorded,[3] but Homullus was well-known for his barbed tongue. Pius had had to put up with it himself when dining with him. He noticed that his house had some porphyry columns and asked where they had come from – no doubt fully aware that the only source of supply were imperial quarries on the Red Sea. Homullus told him 'When you come to someone else's

---

[1] *PIR* 2, A 714. *v. Marci*, 6, 6. The date of birth and of the new titles are known from *Inscr. It.*, XIII, 1, 207 (they were previously thought to belong to A.D. 146). See *Med.*, 1, 17 *ad fin.*

[2] *v. Pii*, 7, 11; *v. Marci*, 7, 3.   [3] *v. Marci*, 6, 9 – he took no notice, however.

house, be deaf and dumb.' Pius took the joke well enough, and no doubt took the joke about Lucilla too.[1] In fact Marcus' deference to his father was very striking, the biographer reports – but not surprising, in view of the tribute in the *Meditations*. In turn, Pius accepted his advice very readily, no doubt increasingly as the years went on, 'and did not easily promote anyone without consulting him'.[2]

One possible reason why Marcus was not sent abroad is that in A.D. 148 the 900th anniversary of the founding of Rome was celebrated. Pius did not hold Secular Games – too many emperors had already held them, for political reasons, for Pius to stoop to this easy way of gaining popularity. But he did hold magnificent games for the people of Rome, with elephants, giraffes, tigers, rhinoceroses, crocodiles and hippopotami – all to be slaughtered for the pleasure of the Roman populace, one must, regrettably, add. The celebrations of A.D. 148 had been heralded in advance from the start of the reign with allusions on the coinage to the legendary origins of Rome (one of which, the rescue of Anchises from the flames of Troy by Aeneas, has already been mentioned in connection with the name Pius). These reminders of Rome's past fitted in well with the religious aspirations of the age and with Pius' own deep religious sense, which earned for him the comparison with Numa, Rome's semi-mythical second king, who was supposedly responsible for much of the religious ritual of the state. The year A.D. 148 was also the tenth anniversary of Pius' accession, so there was plenty to celebrate.[3] There were, of course, trouble spots. The war in Mauretania was still in progress and in the east a new king had ascended the throne of Parthia. He adopted a threatening posture towards Rome, which Pius eventually managed to pacify by diplomatic means. But it may have been at this time that one of the legionary commanders in the Syrian army, L. Neratius Proculus, took troop reinforcements into Syria in preparation for a 'Parthian War', which, in the end, did

---

[1] *v. Pii*, 11, 8. 　　　　　　　　　　[2] *v. Marci*, 6, 7–8.

[3] For the official recognition in this year rather than A.D. 147 (in which year there is no mention on the Ostia Fasti), cf. *Inscr. It.*, XIII, 1, 207. The games: *v. Pii*, 10, 8–9, recorded on the coinage of A.D. 149 (*BMC*, IV, Antoninus Pius, Nos. 1838 ff., cf. ibid., lv, lxvi).

not break out.[1] It might, perhaps, have been a good thing if Pius had taken decisive military action, for the grievances of the Parthian ruler were merely put into cold storage, until a more favourable opportunity should present itself. The presence of Marcus on either the eastern or the south-western frontiers might well have been profitable for Rome and for the dynasty. But he was not sent.

Marcus kept in close touch with Fronto after his teaching ended, sometimes writing several letters in one day. Fronto was appreciative, but in one letter expressed anxiety in case his own letters and the duty of answering them might have taken up too much of Marcus' time – 'in case I should add to your necessary labours some extra trouble and burden, if in addition to those letters which you write daily, as a necessary duty, to so many people, I too should weary you with having to reply to me'.[2] Thereafter, for some years, the correspondence, as it now survives at least, concerns mainly family news.

Marcus' and Faustina's baby daughter was, it might seem, a sickly infant. At any rate the first mention of the little Faustina in the correspondence with Fronto is to describe an illness. 'Caesar to Fronto. If the gods are willing we seem to have a hope of recovery. The diarrhoea has stopped, the little attacks of fever have been driven away. But the emaciation is still extreme and there is still quite a bit of coughing. You understand, of course, that I am writing this about our little Faustina, for whose sake we have been pretty occupied. Let me know if your health is improving in accordance with my prayers, my master.'[3] Fronto replied that the way Marcus' letter opened had given him a serious shock. 'Fronto to Caesar. Good heavens, how shocked I was when I read the beginning of your letter. The way it was written made me think some danger to *your* health was meant. Then when you made it clear that the danger which I had taken to be yours at the beginning of the note was to your daughter Faustina, how my apprehension was transformed! In

---

[1] Dessau, *ILS*, 1076; cf. *v. Pii*, 9, 6; *v. Marci*, 8, 6
[2] Fronto, *ad M.C.*, 3, 13, 4=Haines, I, 222 ff. Note 3, 13, 1=Haines I, 220: 'tot negotiis, tot officiis, tot rescribendis per provincias litteris'.
[3] *ad M.C.*, 4, 11=Haines, I, 202.

fact not just transformed, but in some way not a little relieved. You may say "Did my daughter's danger seem less important to you than mine. Could it seem so to you, who protest that Faustina is to you a serene light, a festive day, a near hope, a prayer fulfilled, a complete joy, a noble and assured glory?" ' He admits that he does love Marcus more than he loves Marcus' daughter, although he says at first that he does not know why danger to Marcus should shock him more than danger to little Faustina. 'You are more likely to know the cause of this, since you have learned more about the nature and feelings of men than I have, and learned it better.' This is a reference to Marcus' studies in philosophy, which would include psychology, for Fronto goes on to mention his own former teacher in philosophy, the Stoic Athenodotus. He then wrote once more of the nature of his love, two illustrations of which deserve quotation. 'I have sometimes criticized you behind your back in quite strong terms, in front of a very few of my intimate friends. This was in the days when you used to go about in public with too serious a face and used to read books at the theatre or at banquets – I still used to go to the theatre and to banquets myself in those days – and it was on occasions like this that I used to call you a hard and unreasonable person, even a hateful character, when I had been roused to anger. But if anyone else found fault with you in my hearing I could not listen with patience. So it was easier for me to say these things about you myself than to allow others to say them – just as I would find it easier to strike my daughter Gratia myself than to see her struck by anyone else. . . .' He adds another interesting sidelight. 'You know that in all the banks, shops, taverns, eaves, colonnades and windows, everywhere, there are portraits of you exposed to public view, badly painted for the most part and modelled or carved in a plain, not to say worthless, artistic style. Still, all the same, your likeness, however unlike you, never meets my eyes when I am out without making me part my lips in a smile and dream of you.' This little detail is instructive. The likenesses of Marcus which now survive are for the most part expensive and lasting effigies in marble or bronze, or the portraits on the official coinage. But portraits of the prince and the other members of the imperial house, the *domus divina*, 'divine family', must have been as widespread as photographs and portraits of kings and rulers in modern countries, if not more so. Fronto ends his letter with a very human touch. He asks Marcus not to tell Faustina that he loves Marcus more than her – 'for there is a danger that your daughter will be upset by this, as she is a serious and old-fashioned lady, and when I ask to kiss her hands and feet, she may take them away, being annoyed about it, or give them grudgingly. And, the good gods be witness, I shall then kiss her tiny hands and plump little feet with more gladness than your royal neck and honest, merry face.'[1]

A second child came to Marcus and Faustina in A.D. 149, again a daughter, Annia Aurelia Galeria Lucilla, born on March 7.[2] More children came during the A.D. 150s. One or two letters refer to the little girls. 'We are experiencing the summer heat still,' Marcus writes to Fronto, 'but our little girls are, I think I may say, in quite good health, so we think we are enjoying healthy spring temperatures.'[3] A letter of Fronto's asks Marcus 'to give your Faustina a message from me and congratulate her. Kiss our little ladies in my name – and, as I always do, kiss their feet and hands as well.'[4] Another letter, of uncertain date, refers to one of Faustina's pregnancies. It was written when Fronto was ill, and Marcus too had anxieties. 'To my master, greeting. You have increased my anxieties, which I hope you will relieve as soon as possible by the subsidence of the pains and swelling in your knee. As for me the weakness of my Lady mother does not allow me to rest. There is too Faustina's approaching confinement. But we must trust the gods. Farewell, my master, most delightful to me. My mother greets you.'[5] Domitia Lucilla was still living in A.D. 155, but had died before Marcus' accession to the throne in A.D. 161, and, as he says in the *Meditations* that she did not have a long life, she presumably died soon after

---

[1] Ibid., 4, 12=Haines, I, 202 ff.
[2] *PIR* 2, A 707. Her birthday, known from *IGR*, I, 1509, to be March 7, must be assigned to A.D. 149, in view of her elder sister's date of birth (page 135, n. 1). Lucilla may have had a twin brother, who died young, cf. *BMC*, IV, lxvi, and Antoninus Pius, Nos. 678–9. Note also ibid., Nos. 1849, 1858 (one child), 705, 1854 (two children) on the coins of Marcus. See Appendix II.
[3] *ad M.C.*, 5, 19=Haines, I, 224.
[4] Ibid., 5, 42=Haines, I, 244.　　　　[5] Ibid., 5, 45 (60)=Haines, I, 246.

A.D. 155.[1] The pregnancy referred to may have resulted in the birth of another daughter, because a letter placed a little after the one just quoted, in the manuscript, speaks of Fronto's delight at seeing the child. 'I love you ten times as much – I have seen your daughter: I feel I have seen you and Faustina as babies at the same moment, so much that is good in both your faces is blended in hers.' But it is not known which daughter this is.[2]

When Faustina finally bore a son, there was public rejoicing. The Synod of the temple of Dionysus at Smyrna (Izmir) wrote to congratulate Marcus. But by the time he was able to reply, the child was dead. He thanked them for their good wishes, 'even though this turned out otherwise', writing from Lorium on March 28 in an unknown year during the A.D. 150s. Indeed three sons were born to Marcus and Faustina between A.D. 150 and 160, T. Aelius Aurelius, T. Aelius Antoninus and Hadrianus, one of them in A.D. 152. But they, and a daughter Domitia Faustina, died before their father's accession. There were two other daughters who survived, Fadilla and Cornificia, as well as Faustina and Lucilla, although not all the details of the respective ages of these children are known.[3] Two of the boys were certainly buried in the Castel Sant' Angelo, as was Domitia Faustina. It is not known what happened to Hadrianus. He died at the very latest in A.D. 166, but it was fairly clearly some time before this.[4] In one passage in the *Meditations* Marcus thanks the gods that 'my children were not mentally defective or deformed in body'. But on several occasions he speaks of the grief caused by the loss of children. Apollonius had taught him how to bear it, but he refers more than once in other passages to such a loss. 'I see that the child

[1] Still alive in A.D. 155: *CIL*, XV, 1090. Cf. *Med.*, 1, 17 *ad fin.*

[2] *ad M.C.*, 5, 52 (67)=Haines, I, 250. Haines, loc. cit., thinks this may be the short-lived Domitia Faustina, known only from her funerary inscription (Dessau, *ILS*, 385, before the death of Pius). The language would be very suitable to describe a first-born, however.

[3] See Appendix II for details. The dates of birth could be between A.D. 149 and A.D. 160, if the first son was a twin of Lucilla (p. 139, n. 2). Fadilla and Cornificia were probably born at the end of the A.D. 150s (cf. *BMC*, IV, pp. lxxiv–lxxv).

[4] The letter to Smyrna: *IGR*, IV, 1399. A son was definitely born in A.D. 152, cf. *Inscr. It.*, XIII, 1, 207.

is ill. I see it. But I do not see that he is in danger. In this way always stick to your first impressions and add nothing of your own from inside yourself.' This seems to be a reminder that he must not panic when one of his children fell ill. 'One man prays: "How I may not lose my little child", but you must pray: "How I may not be afraid to lose him". ' 'For one who is imbued with true doctrines even the briefest and most familiar saying is sufficient reminder to dispel sorrow and fear, for example:

> . . . leaves –
> The wind scatters some of them on the ground:
> Such are the children of men.

Yes, your children too are "leaves" . . . ' 'Epictetus used to say that as you kissed your child you should say in your heart: "Tomorrow perhaps you will die." "These are ill-omened words." "No," he replied, "nothing that means an act of nature is ill-omened, for otherwise it would be an evil omen to say that the corn has been reaped." ' 'Perhaps you will die' here refers to the parent no doubt, rather than to the child. Whether or not the son born in A.D. 152 died the same year is not known. But Marcus was certainly bereaved of his sister Cornificia in A.D. 152. The cause of her death is not known, but she cannot have been more than thirty. She and her husband Quadratus had two children, a son named Marcus Ummidius Quadratus, aged about seventeen in A.D. 152, and a daughter Ummidia Cornificia Faustina.[1]

In the same year, Lucius, who was to be twenty-two on December 15, was designated quaestor for the next year, before the legal age. In fact as quaestor in his twenty-third year he was only two years under age. Marcus had been quaestor at seventeen. As quaestor in A.D. 153 Lucius gave gladiatorial games, sitting in a place of honour between Pius and Marcus. In A.D. 154 he was consul, with a member of one of the oldest aristocratic families (far older than his own), T. Sextius Lateranus.[2] Thus he received this honour some nine years

---

[1] *Med.*, 1, 8; 8, 44; 9, 40; 10, 34; 11, 34. Cornificia: *Inscr. It.* XIII, 1, 207.
[2] *v. Veri*, 3, 2–3.

earlier than the normal minimum age of thirty-two, and had omitted the praetorship, but again, this privilege was not as great as that received by Marcus, consul at eighteen, and for the second time at twenty-three. Lucius received no other marks of distinction, except, of course, that he was 'son of Augustus'. On official journeys, while Marcus travelled with Pius, Lucius was placed alongside the praetorian prefect Gavius Maximus. He showed loyalty to Pius, rather than affection, according to the biographer. His character was markedly different from that of Marcus, although to a certain extent he was moulded by the example of his adoptive brother, encouraged by Pius, who admired 'the frankness of his nature and his unspoiled way of life'. Lucius was a devotee of sports of all kinds, especially hunting and wrestling, and was something of a pleasure-lover, 'rather too carefree, and a good performer, within bounds, at all kinds of sports, games and fun'. He took an unashamed pleasure in the circus-games and the gladiatorial spectacles, unlike Marcus who used to take a book along to alleviate his boredom. Pius did not entirely approve, but he felt that he had to keep him in the family – without, however, giving him any powers.[1] It is puzzling that Lucius did not marry at this stage. But perhaps he was encouraged to wait until one of Marcus' daughters should be old enough. In A.D. 154 he was already older than Marcus had been at his marriage in A.D. 145; and apparently he was to remain unmarried for a further ten years. Perhaps he married a wife who died young. Alternatively, Pius may have discouraged him marrying, in case dynastic complications should be produced by the birth of a son.

Now that he was in the senate Lucius' training with Fronto had to be put to practical use. The biographer says that he was quite a good speaker, but uncharitably adds the story that the better passages in his speeches were written by his friends. One of his speeches is mentioned in a brief letter of Fronto to Marcus, which also comments on a speech by Pius. 'To my Lord. Whether the merit of the deed enhanced the speech or the speech managed to equal a most

[1] *v. Veri*, 3, 4–7; 2, 9–11. Note *BMC*, IV, Antoninus Pius, No. 239 (pls. 6, 9), however (a coin depicting both Marcus and Lucius in the same *quadriga* as Pius).

noble act, I am uncertain. But certain it is that these words had the same author as those deeds. But your brother's speech also delighted me, for it was polished and judicious – and I am certain that he had very little time to consider it.' Marcus' reply was in agreement. 'Answer. On returning from my father's banquet I got your note, and gathered that the messenger who brought it had already gone. Therefore I am writing this reply quite late in the evening, so that you may read it tomorrow. It is not surprising that my father's speech seemed to you worthy of its subject, my master. But my brother's speech of thanks is, in my opinion, especially praiseworthy, seeing that he had less time to consider it, as you guess. Farewell, my most delightful master. My mother greets you.' There is no clue as to the subject of either speech, but as Lucius' was a speech of thanks, it may be that he was speaking after the grant of the quaestorship in A.D. 153 or the consulship in A.D. 154.[1]

In A.D. 155 Marcus' friend Victorinus was consul. He had probably become Fronto's son-in-law by now. Soon after, Fronto became eligible for the ballot which was held every year for the two senior proconsulships, Asia and Africa (the only two held by former consuls, normally, at this period, between twelve and fifteen years after their consulship). At some time, in, almost certainly, the period A.D. 155–8, Fronto was successful in the ballot and was appointed proconsul of Asia. He began to make preparations. Marcus wrote to him to recommend to his protection when he reached his province a certain Themistocles, made known to Marcus by the son of his philosophy teacher Apollonius. 'For you will, I know, be always very ready to show justice and equity to all the Asians, but your counsel, friendship, and whatever honour and conscience allow a proconsul to extend to his friends, so long as no one else is thereby harmed – these I ask you to extend freely to Themistocles. Farewell, my most delightful master. There is no need to reply.'[2]

---

[1] v. *Veri*, 2, 8; Fronto, *ad M.C.*, 5, 38 (53) and 39 (54)=Haines, I, 240; cf. v. *Pii*, 11, 3, where the question whether Pius composed his own speeches or not is discussed – although Fronto is probably not alluding to this.

[2] *ad M.C.*, 5, 36 (51)=Haines, I, 234. For the normal interval between consulship and proconsulship of Asia and Africa at this time see now B. Thomasson, *Die Statthalter der römischen Provinzen Nordafrikas*, Lund, 1960, I, 30 ff.

But all Fronto's preparations were in vain. His state of health did not permit him to make the journey and undertake the task. He wrote to Pius to explain the position. 'Fronto to Antoninus Pius Augustus. Most reverend Emperor, the facts themselves bear witness that I have made every effort and have been exceedingly eager to fulfil the duties of proconsul. As long as the matter was undecided I claimed my right of balloting. When through having more children another had a prior claim, I was as satisfied with the most splendid province which remained to me, as if I had chosen it myself.' Clearly Fronto had hoped to become proconsul of Africa, the province adjacent to his native Numidia (to which, in fact, Numidia still *de iure*, although not, for the past hundred years and more *de facto*, belonged). Since the time of Augustus, who had legislated with the hope of increasing the birthrate among the upper classes, children were of assistance to senators in increasing the rate of their promotion (and unmarried men older than twenty-four were penalized). Fronto with only one daughter would not be very greatly favoured.

Fronto's preparations had been fairly extensive, and they throw an interesting light on the methods of the Roman administration. 'I made careful preparations to facilitate the transaction of the quantity of business connected with the administration of the province, by enlisting numbers of my friends. I summoned from my home relatives and friends of mine of whose loyalty and integrity I was confident. I wrote to my intimates at Alexandria, instructing them to hurry to Athens, to meet me there, and I handed over the direction of my Greek secretariat to these most learned men. From Cilicia too I urged some distinguished men to come, for having always acted as counsel for the Cilicians in both public and private cases before you, I have a great number of friends in that province. From Mauretania too I summoned to me a man whose love for me is equal to my great affection for him, Julius Senex, in order that I might avail myself not only of his loyalty and diligence, but also of his military effectiveness in the hunting down and keeping in check of brigands.' Fronto's procedure was in fact the normal one for all provincial governors. A governor of a military province would in addition have a number of actual appointments in the armed forces which he could fill by his personal choice. But Fronto was unable to put his plans into practice.[1]

His attack of ill-health may be the one which he describes in a letter to Marcus. 'To my Lord. I have been so seriously afflicted with "cholera"[2] that I lost my voice, gasped and struggled for breath, finally my veins ceased functioning and I lost consciousness and had no apparent pulse. In fact my family gave me up for lost, and I remained insensible for some time. The doctors had no time or chance to revive me with a bath or cold water or food, or of relieving me, except that after nightfall I swallowed a few small pieces of bread soaked in wine. So I was gradually completely resuscitated. For three whole days afterwards I did not recover my voice. But by now, with the help of the gods, I am in pretty comfortable health, I can walk more easily and can speak more clearly. In fact, if the gods will aid me, tomorrow I intend to take a drive. If I find that I can stand up to the flint-paving I will hurry to see you – only when I see you will I live. I will set out from Rome on the seventh day before the Kalends, if the gods will aid me. Farewell, sweetest Lord, most longed for, my best reason for my life. Greet your Lady.' The illness sounds something like a mild stroke, especially as he lost the power of speech for three days. But that is conjecture.[3]

In the second half of the A.D. 150s trouble recurred in Britain. The man chosen to deal with it was Gnaeus Julius Verus, evidently either the son or the nephew of the great Sextus Julius Severus who had governed Britain and suppressed the Jewish revolt under Hadrian. In the middle of the decade references to Britain reappear on the imperial coinage and Pius for a time allowed the title gained by the victory there in A.D. 142, IMP. II, to be included with his other titles once more. Julius Verus seems to have found the new frontier of Lollius Urbicus unsatisfactory, and Hadrian's Wall was

---

[1] Fronto, *ad Ant. Pium*, 8=Haines I, 236. See *Digest.*, 4, 42, on allowances in respect of children; and Mommsen, *Staatsrecht*, I³ (1887), 534 ff.

[2] Not the same as the disease so named today.

[3] *ad M.C.*, 5, 40 (55)=Haines, I, 240 ff.

reoccupied. The Forth-Clyde frontier was destroyed: its immediate fate is uncertain.[1]

At home there was little of moment. In A.D. 156 Lucius' cousin M. Ceionius Silvanus was consul, followed the next year by his uncle, his father's half-brother M. Vettulenus Civica Barbarus. His brother-in-law Plautius Quintillus (probably related in any case to the Ceionii Commodi) was consul in A.D. 159. Quintillus was the husband of Ceionia Fabia, once the betrothed of Marcus.[2]

It is not known whether Pius, Marcus and Lucius ever saw a remarkable document which was addressed to them at this period. 'To the Emperor Titus Aelius Hadrianus Antoninus Pius Augustus Caesar and to Verissimus his son, the philosopher, and to Lucius the philosopher, son of Caesar by nature and of Augustus by adoption, a lover of culture, and to the holy senate and the whole Roman people, on behalf of men of all nations who are unjustly hated and reviled, I, Justinus, son of Priscus and grandson of Bacchius, of Flavia Neapolis in Syria Palestina being one of them myself, have drawn up this plea and petition.' It is the first *Apology* of the future martyr St. Justin. It is perhaps surprising that he calls Lucius 'philosopher and lover of culture' – slightly unexpected attributes. But the fact that he was able to give Marcus the name Verissimus, and that he knew Lucius was the son by birth of (L. Aelius) Caesar, suggests that this description deserves some attention.[3] Justin's *Apology*, which was delivered not much later than A.D. 154,[4] was not the first of its kind – a certain Quadratus had addressed a similar

---

[1] Julius Verus: *PW*, 10, 1917, 857 ff. Degrassi, *I Fasti Consolari*, 43, suggests A.D. 154 for his consulship – perhaps too late, as A.D. 158 was his last year in Britain (*JRS*, 28, 1938, 228), and he had been in Lower Germany before that (Dessau, *ILS*, 1057+8794). The coins: *BMC*, Antoninus Pius, Nos. 1971 ff., 1993 ff. I personally believe that the Antonine Wall was abandoned at this time and not reoccupied until early in the reign of Commodus. For this view see J. P. Gillam, *Trans. Archit. & Archaeol. Soc. of Durham & Northumberland*, 10, 4, 1953, 359 ff., modified slightly by E. Birley, *Research on Hadrian's Wall*, Kendal, 1961, 249–50.

[2] See Appendix II.

[3] Justin, *I Apol.*, *praef.*

[4] In it he alludes to an occurrence in Egypt under the prefect (L. Munatius) Felix who had been replaced by that year.

appeal to Hadrian, of which only a brief fragment is preserved, and early in the reign of Antoninus Aristides of Athens, of whose work a few extracts survive, had done the same.[1] Justin was making an appeal for toleration. But he went further and boldly stated the claims of the Christian faith to pre-eminence, refuting, at the same time, allegations that had been made against Christians. He went dangerously far in attacking the morality implicit in the legends of the deities of the Greco-Roman world, in speaking rather scornfully of the deification of emperors and even in making a slightly derisive reference to the deification by Hadrian of his favourite Antinous – 'whom everybody hastened to worship as a god, through fear, although they knew quite well who he was and where he came from'.

One of those who had attacked the morals of the Christians was Fronto. In one speech he told the familiar tale of the 'incestuous banquets' of the Christians, referring to the ceremony of the *agape*, the 'love-feast' which followed the evening Communion rite in the early Church. The fact that it occurred at night, with both sexes and all ages present, in secret, led to the presumption that it was in fact an orgy. 'After a lot of feasting, when the banquet has warmed up and a passion for incestuous lust and drunkenness has flared up, a dog tied to the lamp is incited to jump and leap by throwa little cake to it beyond the reach of its tether.' When this put the lights out, the guests began their hideous orgies, Fronto proclaimed.[2]

If Fronto had taken up his appointment as proconsul of Asia he would have come across evidence of Christianity of a very different kind. It was probably in early A.D. 156, when the proconsul of Asia was L. Statius Quadratus (who had been consul in A.D. 142, the year before Fronto) that the aged Polycarp was martyred by being burned and then stabbed to death in the arena at Smyrna.[3] But in any case, there were martyrdoms at Rome also, in which the sentences of death were issued by the prefect of the city, Quintus Lollius Urbicus,

---

[1] Justin, *I Apol.*, *praef.*, 1, 29. The dating of the Apologies of Quadratus and Aristides is not settled, but they belong to the period A.D. 128–40, cf. J. Beaujeu, *La religion romaine à l'apogée de l'empire*, I, Paris, 1955, 273.

[2] Minucius Felix, *Octavius*, 9, 8 (printed by Haines, II, 282 ff.).

[3] Eusebius, *Hist. Ecc.*, 4, 15, assigns this event to the reign of Marcus. See Appendix IV.

Fronto's fellow-countryman, the victor in Britain.[1] The *Apology* of Justin probably never reached the emperor and his sons. It would have been handed into one of the imperial secretariats. Nevertheless, Marcus could hardly have remained unaware of Christianity as a young man. During his reign he was to be confronted with the problem which its existence created, and, more important from his point of view, the reaction which it provoked from the common people, on two notable occasions.

In A.D. 156 Pius became 70. He had nearly five more years to live. He was still fit, but being tall found it difficult to keep an upright posture without the use of stays, and he found that he had to nibble some dry bread when he got up, to sustain himself for his morning receptions.[2] As Pius grew older, no doubt Marcus played an increasingly important role.

Some time about A.D. 157 the powerful Gavius Maximus gave up office as praetorian prefect, and was replaced by a young protégé of his own, C. Tattius Maximus. But Tattius Maximus presumably died soon after his appointment, for he was succeeded in A.D. 159 or 160 by two men, the experienced T. Furius Victorinus and a friend of Fronto's named Sextus Cornelius Repentinus, as joint prefects. Repentinus was said to owe his appointment to the influence of the emperor's mistress.[3] But the practice of having two prefects was not exceptional, so this story may be unfounded.

Fronto was involved in an embarrassing affair which concerned Gavius Maximus. A friend of Fronto named Censorius Niger had died, leaving him as heir to five-twelfths of his estate. In the will he used intemperate, unrestrained and ill-advised language in an attack on Gavius Maximus. Fronto had to write to the emperor, whose favour Censorius Niger had lost before his death, to excuse both his friendship and his late friend's conduct. He wrote to Gavius Maximus

---

[1] Eusebius, *Hist. Ecc.*, 4, 17.
[2] *v. Pii*, 13, 1–2.
[3] *v. Pii*, 8, 7–9. Gavius Maximus: H.-G. Pflaum, op. cit., No. 105 *bis*. Tattius Maximus: ibid., No. 138. Furius Victorinus, ibid., No. 139. Cornelius Repentinus: *PIR 2*, C 1428, cf. *v. Pii*, 8, 9.

too. 'Grief added to anger disturbed the man's mind. His other virtues were poisoned and ruined by anger.' He claimed that he had often seen Niger weeping from being deprived of the friendship of Maximus. He explained the whole position in a letter to Marcus, but briefly. 'I began a long letter to you on the subject, but on thinking everything over I decided not to disturb you or call you away from more important matters.'[1]

Around the end of the reign Herodes Atticus was once more involved in a *cause célèbre*. His wife Regilla had died towards the end of a pregnancy. Her brother Bradua, consul in A.D. 160, accused Herodes of her murder. He had in fact treated Regilla rather harshly, but a charge of murder was excessive. It was provoked, however, by the hostility felt by Regilla's Italian family to the flamboyant millionaire Greek. Herodes was acquitted, and mourned Regilla with an ostentatious display of grief verging on vulgarity.[2]

In A.D. 160 Pius may have been ill, for Marcus and Lucius were designated as joint consuls for the following year, for the third and second times respectively – perhaps a deliberate precaution. He finally succumbed, after a short illness, on March 7, 161, the year known to the Romans as that when his adoptive sons Marcus and Lucius were consuls together.[3] His end was tranquil, as was his life. His death was 'very sweet, and like the softest sleep', says Dio.[4] The biographer adds details. The old emperor had eaten some Alpine cheese at dinner, rather greedily. During the night he vomited and the next day had a fever. The day after, when he saw that he was becoming worse and that the end of his life was near, in the presence of the praetorian prefects Furius Victorinus and Cornelius Repentinus, and of his friends, members of the imperial council, whom he had summoned, he commended the state and his daughter to Marcus, and Marcus to them, and gave orders that the golden statue of

[1] Fronto, *ad Ant. Pium*, 3, 4, 7=Haines, I, 254 ff., 260 ff., 258 ff. Censorius Niger: *PIR* 2, C 658; Pflaum, op. cit., No. 97 *bis*.
[2] Philostratus, *v. soph.*, 2, 1, 8–9. Cf. *PIR* 2, A 636 (Bradua), 720 (Regilla), and P. Graindor, *Hérode Atticus, etc.*, 81 ff.
[3] The exact date is deduced from Dio, 71, 33, 4–5.
[4] Dio, 70, 3, 3.

Fortune, which used to be placed in the bedroom of the emperors, should be transferred to the bedroom of Marcus. Then he gave the watchword to the tribune of the guard: 'Equanimity'. He turned over as if to go to sleep, and breathed his last, at Lorium, on his ancestral estate, in his seventy-fifth year. In his fever, when delirious, he had spoken of nothing else besides the state and those foreign monarchs with whom he was angry.[1]

One of Marcus' tributes to Pius has already been quoted – the one which came from the first book of the *Meditations*. There is a briefer tribute, perhaps written earlier, in the sixth book, in which Marcus reminded himself to behave 'in all things like a pupil of Antoninus; his energy in dealing with what had to be done in accordance with reason, his equability everywhere, his piety, the serenity of his face, his sweetness, his disregard for empty glory, and his determination to grasp his work. Also, how he allowed nothing to pass without first looking into it well and understanding it clearly; how he put up with those who found fault with him unjustly, without finding fault with them in return; how he never hurried; how he never listened to slander; what an exact critic he was of men's characters and actions, not given to reproaching, not disturbed by rumours, not suspicious, not pretending to be clever; how he was content with little, in the way of lodging, bed, clothes, food and service; how he loved work and was long-suffering. What a man he was, too, for remaining in his place until the evening, because of sparing diet not needing even to relieve nature except at the normal time. And his constancy and uniformity in his friendships, his tolerance of outspoken opposition to his views and his delight when anyone proposed something better than he did; and how he revered the gods without superstition. May your last hour find you like him, with a conscience as clear as his.'[2]

These recollections are a remarkable tribute. Perhaps the greatest service of Antoninus Pius, and of Marcus too, was that they provided an example of high character on the throne, in admirable conformity with the aspirations of thinking people, such as Dio of Prusa,[3] who had wanted an ideal ruler. There are certainly defects to

[1] *v. Pii*, 12, 4–8; *v. Marci*, 7, 3.　　[2] *Med.*, 6, 30.　　[3] *PIR* 2, D. 83.

be found in his administration, most particularly that his military policy seems to have been somewhat neglectful, as was to appear almost at once in the reign of his successor. The cause has already been stated: the military inexperience of Pius himself, and his reliance for too long a period on the advice of one man, Gavius Maximus.

VI

THE FIRST YEARS AS EMPEROR

MARCUS WAS NOW sole ruler, lacking only the name Augustus and the appellation Imperator. He waited, of course, for the senate to confer his powers and names on him, for the formal election as *pontifex maximus*, and for any other power which he may have lacked. But at the meeting of the senate Marcus refused to be made emperor unless equal powers were conferred simultaneously on his brother Lucius Commodus.

Marcus had made some show of reluctance to assume the burdens of empire; and the biographer says that 'he was compelled by the senate to assume the direction of the state after the death of Pius'.[1] Expressions of unwillingness to rule had not been unknown. Tiberius, like Marcus the sole and obvious successor to the previous ruler, had also made such protestation – undoubtedly both felt genuine reluctance. In Tiberius' case, his complex character was such that men never knew what his true feelings were, but the tradition of his original family was one which found monarchy repugnant and for such a man to be called on to rule openly as a monarch was a moment of unpleasant torment (and his predecessor was the first of all emperors). Marcus, from a family which owed its fortunes to the existence of monarchical government, had a dilemma of a different kind. His natural inclinations were not to public life, but his training for twenty-three years and his Stoic philosophy had made the path of duty plain. He knew that 'the measureless body of empire' required a director, without which it could not stand, as Galba, another ostensibly unwilling ruler, was alleged to have put it. Marcus obviously had a genuine *horror imperii*, but he knew what

[1] *v. Marci*, 7, 5; *v. Veri*, 3, 8.

he had to do. He must have felt that the presence of an imperial partner would, possibly, lighten his task. But more than that, it would fulfil an obligation to Hadrian, whose intention had been clearly stated, that Marcus and Lucius should rule jointly in succession to Pius. Since Pius had done little to forward these wishes in respect of Lucius, Lucius had 'remained a private citizen in his father's house for twenty-three years'.[1]

Now, however, Lucius became in name and in fact joint emperor. He was granted the tribunician power, the *imperium*, the name Augustus. His own names and those of Marcus were altered. Out of respect for Pius, Marcus assumed the surname Antoninus, becoming Imperator Caesar Marcus Aurelius Antoninus Augustus. Lucius gave up his name Commodus and took instead the name which Marcus had borne from birth, Verus, becoming Imperator Caesar Lucius Aurelius Verus Augustus. The niceties of these variations may not be entirely clear to us. Certainly they completely confused the unfortunate author, authors, compiler or compilers of the imperial biographies a century and a half or more later. In the biographies the alteration of names is recorded, but complication is added by the mistaken belief which recurs constantly that Verus was a name which originally belonged to Lucius in any case, and to his father, Hadrian's first adopted son.[2]

Two emperors thus ruled the Roman world for the first time, an innovation, but like most Roman innovations one for which there was ample precedent. It set an example which was followed with increasing frequency. The continuing existence of the ancient twin magistracy of the consulate was one precedent. Previously too, emperors had had colleagues with powers slightly less wide than their own – as indeed was the case with Marcus and Pius from A.D. 147–61. But rulers other than Hadrian had intended that two should succeed them, only to be frustrated. Thus Augustus' grandsons Gaius and Lucius were destined by Augustus to succeed him jointly. Germanicus and Drusus the younger, sons of Tiberius by

---

[1] Tiberius: Tacitus, *Annals*, 1, 11 ff. Galba: Tacitus, *Histories*, 1, 16. *horroi imperii* (of Pertinax): *v. Pert.*, 13, 1; 15, 7. Lucius: *v. Veri*, 2, 11.

[2] *v. Marci*, 7, 6; *v. Veri*, 4, 1 (cf. *v. Hel., passim*, and Appendix I).

adoption and birth respectively, appeared likely to succeed him together at one time, as did at the end of his life Gaius Caligula and Tiberius Gemellus, their respective sons. Nero and Britannicus were another pair, intended by the deluded Claudius to have equal rank. These succession arrangements of the ill-starred Julio-Claudian family proved abortive. Later, Domitian apparently felt that Titus, his elder brother, had thwarted him of his birthright when he did not make him co-ruler at the death of Vespasian.[1]

Marcus and Lucius were joint rulers then. But Marcus had more *auctoritas* – that intangible, but measurable factor in Roman public life. He had been consul once more than Lucius. He became *pontifex maximus*, the highest priesthood being indivisible; Lucius was only *pontifex*. Most important, he had shared in the imperial powers of Pius for nearly fourteen years – and he was ten years older than Lucius. There was little doubt in men's minds which emperor was the senior. But they were to work together for the good of the state. The coins of A.D. 161 proclaimed the *concordia Augustorum*, the harmony of the emperors.[2]

The first act of the emperors, after the meeting of the senate at which their powers and titles had been granted, was to go to the camp of the praetorian guard on the north-eastern outskirts of the city, beyond the *porta Viminalis*. Here Lucius addressed the troops on behalf of both, and they were hailed as *imperator*, emperor. They promised a bounty, or donative, to the troops, of 20,000 sesterces (5,000 denarii) per man, more to officers. This expensive ceremony was now a necessary opening to every reign, as it had been since the stormy and opposed accession of Claudius in A.D. 41. The enormous size of the donative – equivalent to several years' pay for the guardsmen – was not perhaps immediately necessary, considering the peaceful circumstances of their accession. It was emperors who desperately needed military support who had to make promises of

---

[1] See E. Kornemann, *Doppelprinzipat und Reichsteilung im Imperium Romanum*, Leipzig-Berlin, 1930 (who slightly overstates his argument).

[2] Cf. *v. Veri*, 4, 2: 'Lucius quidem Marco vicem reddens si quid susciperet obsecutus, etc.' The coins: *BMC*, IV, M. Aurelius and L. Verus, Nos. 1 ff., 25 ff., etc.

this kind. But a double accession naturally required exceptional celebration – and this generosity was a useful insurance for the future. In return the soldiers would swear allegiance, binding themselves with a military oath – *sacramentum* – no doubt similar in content to extant examples of oaths of allegiance to other emperors.[1]

The next public action was to arrange for the funeral and deification of Antoninus Pius. No opposition to the deification came from the senate, such as Pius himself had experienced in A.D. 138. The remains were laid to rest, after elaborate funeral ceremonies, in the massive mausoleum of Hadrian, which now housed the ashes of several prematurely deceased members of the imperial house, for example children of Pius and Marcus, as well as those of its builder.[2]

No detailed account of the funeral ceremonies is preserved, but presumably it followed the lines of other imperial obsequies – a funeral pyre on the Campus Martius, on which the body was burned in the presence of the leading dignitaries of the state. From the pyre an eagle would fly aloft, released when the flames began to burn, symbolizing the translation of the dead emperor's spirit to the abode of the gods whom he was now joining. It is not recorded whether it was still regarded as necessary for someone to claim that they had witnessed the actual translation to heaven, as had been the case after the funeral of Augustus. A public holiday had been proclaimed, and the funeral procession transported the ashes across the Pons Aelius through, no doubt, festive but solemn crowds. Marcus and Lucius addressed the people in funeral orations in praise of their father, who now became known as 'Divus Antoninus', and, by the same token, his sons now each became 'Divi Antonini filius'. A *flamen* was appointed to minister to the new deity, and a college of priests was chosen from among the closest friends of the imperial family,whose duty it would be to meet on appointed days to sacrifice and feast in honour of Antoninus – on his birthday, for example, and the other days particularly associated with his memory. The temple which Antoninus had dedicated above the Forum to his own wife, to Diva

---

[1] *v. Marci*, 7, 9; *v. Veri*, 4, 3. On the praetorian barracks, cf. G. Zanghieri, *Castro Pretorio*, Roma, 1948. An oath: Dessau, *ILS*, 190 (to Caligula in A.D. 37).
[2] *v. Marci*, 7, 10–11. I follow E. Hohl, *Klio*, 31, 1938, 169 ff.

Faustina, now became the temple of Antoninus and Faustina. It survives as the church of San Lorenzo in Miranda.[1]

At this early stage in the reign came another announcement portending future benefit to the dynasty and the state. Marcus' second daughter, Annia Lucilla, now a girl of just twelve, was formally betrothed to Lucius, her uncle by adoption. Lucius was now thirty. Marcus had married at twenty-four, by no means early for a Roman. Perhaps the marriage of Lucius and Lucilla had been long intended. But if this were so, one wonders why the eldest daughter of Marcus, Faustina, the third of that name, was not chosen. She was now thirteen, perhaps already betrothed, and soon to be married, to Cn. Claudius Severus, son of the close friend of Marcus of the same name. Possibly some simple family agreement underlies the story of these marriages. Marcus would be one to honour a promise, and he might have promised his eldest daughter to the son of his friend. Alternatively, it could be that when Lucius reached the age of marriage he or another member of the family suggested that he should wait until the tiny Lucilla was old enough. Maybe Lucius had always preferred Lucilla to Faustina, and did not mind waiting an extra year and three months. Even so, the situation was slightly paradoxical, for Lucius had once as a boy of seven or eight been betrothed to Faustina, the mother of the two girls. At any rate the match was arranged, and in public commemoration new provision was made for the support of poor children, on the lines of the institution created by Pius in memory of his wife and earlier imperial foundations.[2]

Faustina had been the chief beneficiary in the will of Pius' private fortune, which had been very large at his accession and was probably not much smaller at his death. Marcus had no need of her wealth, of

[1] *v. Marci*, 7, 11; *v. Pii*, 13, 3–4; see also W. Hüttl, *Antoninus Pius*, I, 347 ff., and E. Hohl, op. cit. For accounts of deifications: Dio, 74, 4–5 (Pertinax); Herodian, 4, 1–2 (Severus). Funeral games for Pius are mentioned in *v. Marci*, 8, 2 (misplaced).

[2] *v. Marci*, 7, 7. On the *alimenta* (for poor children in general, rather than just for orphans), cf. R. Duncan-Jones, *Papers of the Brit. School at Rome*, 32, 1964, 123 ff. On Lucilla and her sisters, cf. H.-G. Pflaum, *J. des Savants*, 1961, 29 ff.

course – in fact, at his accession he transferred part of his mother's estate to his nephew Ummidius Quadratus, as his sister Cornificia was now dead. Faustina was three months gone in another pregnancy when her husband ascended the throne. During her pregnancy she dreamed that she was giving birth to two serpents, and that one of them was fiercer than the other. On August 31 she gave birth at Lanuvium to twin sons, who received the names of T. Aurelius Fulvus Antoninus and Lucius Aurelius Commodus, in honour of Pius and Lucius. Antoninus was probably the elder twin, to judge from these names. The astrologers cast favourable horoscopes for both of them. The event was appropriately celebrated on the imperial coinage. The omens were favourable – except that their birthday was the same as that of the unbalanced emperor Caligula, assassinated 120 years previously.[1]

The new emperors were popular with the people of Rome, the normal index of favour. What was especially approved of was their lack of pomp. They conducted themselves *civiliter*. An example of this was the freedom of speech permitted. A writer of comedies named Marullus criticized Marcus and Lucius openly in a new work – and got away with it. In other times, under another emperor, such behaviour would have meant death. But the times were easy. 'No one missed the lenient ways of Pius.'[2]

Fronto was, not surprisingly, overjoyed to see his pupils wearing the purple, and expressed himself in his usual humorous and flattering style. Marcus had told him that he had been re-reading the speech written by Fronto nearly twenty years before, when he became consul, in A.D. 143, in which he delivered a eulogy of Antoninus, and at the same time added praises of the youthful heir-apparent. 'That you have been reading with pleasure the praises of your father which were spoken by myself in the senate as consul designate and on entering office, does not surprise me at all. . . . It was not my speech but your father's merits that you admired, not the

---

[1] *v. Pii*, 12, 8; *v. Marci*, 7, 4; *v. Comm.*, 1, 1–4; 10, 2 (cf. Suetonius, *Caligula*, 8, 1). The story in *v. Marci*, 19, is invented. See Chapter XI and Appendices I and II. The coinage: *BMC*, IV, M. Aurelius and L. Verus, Nos. 155 ff. (pl. 56, 4), 949 ff.   [2] *v. Marci*, 8, 1.

language of the praiser but the actions of the praised that you found praiseworthy. As for my praises of yourself, delivered in the senate that same day – I want you to think of them in this way. There was then an outstanding natural ability in you; there is now perfected excellence. There was then a crop of growing corn; there is now a ripe, gathered harvest. What I was hoping for then, I have now. The hope has become a reality.'[1]

Lucius too wrote to his former tutor several times soon after his accession. He 'complained seriously' in his first letter – as he phrased it with good humour – that he had not been given the chance of embracing or speaking to Fronto when he visited the palace 'after so long an interval'. (Fronto had been away for four months.) Fronto had called at the palace just as Lucius had gone out. He had talked to Marcus alone and neither Fronto nor Marcus had thought of calling Lucius back. Fronto replied at once, apologizing and letting his pen run grandiloquently as he expressed the measure of his indebtedness to Marcus and Lucius. 'For indeed since you and your brother, placed amid such powerful resources, surrounded by such a multitude of men of all sorts and all ranks, on whom you strew your love, since you bestow on me also some portion of your love, what should I do – whose every hope, and all my fortune, are centred in you alone.'[2]

Fronto had returned to his town house in Rome at dawn on March 28, exactly three weeks after the death of Pius, from his country estate, after four months' absence. It may be that he had been on a visit to his home town Cirta in Africa, and that he had set off as soon as the news had reached him. On returning to the city he wrote a brief note in Greek to an imperial freedman, Charilas, asking if it would be convenient for him to call on the emperors. He had not dared, he explained later, to write direct to Lucius or Marcus.[3]

Fronto never gave, in his letters at least, any indication which of

---

[1] *ad Ant. Imp.*, 2, 2=Haines, I, 302 ff.

[2] *ad Verum Imp.*, 1, 3=Haines, I, 294 ff.; ibid., 1, 4=Haines, I, 296 ff.

[3] Ibid., 1, 4, 2=Haines, I, 298 ff. I see no cogent reason why this letter should belong to A.D. 162 rather than to A.D. 161 (as J. Schwendemann, *Der historische Wert der vita Marci, etc.*, Heidelberg, 1923, 143, followed by P. Lambrechts, *Ant. Class.*, 3, 1934, 194).

his imperial pupils he preferred. But one might guess from the fact that he and Marcus made no attempt to send for Lucius on that occasion, that Lucius occupied second place. Lucius' interests remained on a lower plane than those of Marcus. At about this time he was writing to Fronto asking him to adjudicate in a dispute he and a friend named Calpurnius had had over the merits of two actors. Marcus by contrast wrote to Fronto of his reading – the classics, Coelius and a little Cicero – and of his family. His daughters were in Rome, staying with their great-great-aunt Matidia, because the evening air in the country, where Marcus was (at Lanuvium) was too cold for them, it was thought. (Perhaps also it was thought advisable to give their mother Faustina a rest from them as her confinement approached.) Marcus added a request for 'some particularly eloquent reading matter, something of your own, or Cato, or Cicero, or Sallust or Gracchus – or some poet, for I need distraction, especially in this kind of way, by reading something that will uplift and diffuse my pressing anxieties'.[1]

We do not know at what precise moment after his accession he wrote that letter. But he soon had plenty of cares. He had begun his reign 'by giving himself wholly to philosophy, and seeking the affection of the citizens'. He continued to attend public lectures, notably those of Sextus of Chaeronea, which he did not regard as now being beneath his dignity. 'If you had both a mother and a step-mother,' he was to write later, 'you would wait upon your step-mother but would still constantly return to your mother. This is now what philosophy and the palace are to you.' But troubles soon came thick and fast to disturb 'that happiness and freedom from care of his', that *felicitas temporum* proclaimed on his coinage in A.D. 161.[2]

There was a severe flood of the River Tiber, which destroyed many buildings in the city, drowned a great number of animals and left a serious famine in its wake. This was presumably in the autumn of A.D. 161. 'All these disasters Marcus and Lucius dealt

[1] *ad Verum Imp.*, 12, 2=Haines, I, 304 ff.

[2] *v. Marci*, 8, 3-4; Dio, 71, 1, 2. A certain sophist named Lucius mocked Marcus for attending the lectures of Sextus 'at his age': Philostratus, *v. soph.*, 2, 1, 9. *Med.*, 6, 12; *BMC*, IV, M. Aurelius and L. Verus, Nos. 841, 845 (pl. 71, 4; 72, 7).

with by their personal attention.' Italian communities that had been hit by famine were relieved by use of the city's grain supply.[1] Since the year A.D. 15 there had been a Tiber Conservancy Board headed by a senator chosen from the recent consuls, with a staff of permanent officials. Some of the senators may have taken their duties seriously. Pliny had been *curator alvei Tiberis et riparum et cloacarum urbis* some sixty years before, but although one can hardly imagine him not performing the duties of the office with almost excessive conscientiousness, he gives no hint in his letters that it took up much of his time.[2] The *curator* in A.D. 161 was A. Platorius Nepos, probably son or grandson of the builder of Hadrian's Wall of the same name, but one cannot particularly blame him for inefficiency. His probable predecessor was M. Statius Priscus, consul in A.D. 159. Military men like Statius Priscus perhaps looked on urban appointments, like Tiber Conservator, as not much more than paid leave.

Still, Statius Priscus was probably justified, for he had done more than his fair share of hard work in the frontier provinces, work for which the ordinary consulate of A.D. 159 had been very belated recognition. In A.D. 160 or 161 he went to Singidunum (Belgrade), to govern Upper Moesia. He can only have been there a few months when he was transferred to Britain, an indication that the trouble with which Gnaeus Julius Verus had had to deal a few years before was still not under control.[3]

But the most disturbing news was from the eastern frontier. The foreign kings with whom Pius had been angry on his deathbed were clearly the king of Parthia and the rulers of the other independent states on Rome's eastern borders. The troop concentrations which Pius had ordered some years before had only temporarily delayed the crisis. The change of rulers at Rome no doubt emboldened the Parthian king Vologases III, to act quickly. He entered the Roman-protected kingdom of Armenia, expelled its ruler and installed his

[1] *v. Marci*, 8, 4–6; 11, 3.
[2] Pliny, *Epp.*, 5, 14, 2 (3, 6, 6); Dessau, *ILS*, 2927. See R. Syme, *Tacitus*, Oxford, 1958, I, 79.
[3] Dessau, *ILS*, 5932 (Nepos – he had already been at work in early A.D. 161); ibid., 1092 (Priscus).

own nominee, Pacorus, a member of the Parthian royal family (the Arsacids). Trouble had obviously been expected by Rome. The senior Roman officer in the eastern provinces, the governor of Syria L. Attidius Cornelianus, had been due for replacement by A.D. 161, but he had been left at his post, no doubt to avoid giving the Parthians the opportunity of catching a new man on the wrong foot.[1] But the responsibility for dealing with trouble in Armenia always lay in the first instance with the governor of Cappadocia. In A.D. 161 this was a certain M. Sedatius Severianus, a Gaul or Rhinelander. Severianus had had plenty of military experience and was clearly not incompetent. But it sounds as though the effect of the Greek East on him was unfortunate. He was taken in by an itinerant vendor of oracles, of high pretensions, one Alexander of Abonuteichos, a practitioner of mumbo-jumbo on a grandiose scale, with friends in high places – he had become father-in-law of a highly respected senator, P. Mummius Sisenna Rutilianus, who was proconsul of Asia, probably at this very time, and thus he had a powerful protector. Alexander led Severianus to suppose that he could deal easily with the situation and that he would win himself military glory. Severianus accordingly took one of his legions into Armenia, clearly hoping to restore the situation himself, with a show of force. But the force he took was not enough. He was trapped by the leading Parthian general, Chosroes, at Elegeia beyond the frontiers of his province, high up by the headwaters of the Euphrates. After a short attempt to fight back, he realized that further resistance was futile, and committed suicide. His legion[2] was massacred. Various romantic stories were soon in circulation, according to Lucian, concerning the death of Severianus – that 'foolish Celt'. He was said to have fasted to death during a relatively lengthy siege, and a centurion named Afranius Silo was said to have delivered a funeral oration over his tomb in the high tragic manner, and then to have killed himself on

[1] v. Pii, 12, 7; v. Marci, 8, 6; Dio, 71, 2, 1; PIR 2, A 1341 (Cornelianus).
[2] The nearest legion to Elegeia was XV Apollinaris at Satala, but this legion does not disappear from the records, and nor does the other known Cappodocian legion, XII Fulminata. It may be that the famous, and ill-starred Ninth legion, which served so long in Britain, and is often supposed to have met its end there under Hadrian, in fact met its final catastrophe in Armenia.

the spot. The truth was harsher. The affair had been brought to its ignominious end in about three days.[1]

Meanwhile trouble was brewing on other frontiers. War threatened in Britain, and on another northern frontier the Chatti of the Taunus mountains had crossed the *limes*, invading Upper Germany and Raetia. Again, enemy peoples, or potential enemies, had benefited from the change of ruler, hoping to find the new rulers lacking in vigilance, or unprepared.[2] Marcus and Lucius had many rapid decisions to make, but military matters were a sphere for which their previous experience had given them no training. They had never seen an army – other than the praetorian guard – let alone any military action. Antoninus Pius must be held responsible for this serious deficiency in their education. Marcus himself had less experience of war than virtually all his predecessors – but the equally unmilitary Pius perhaps never realized that this mattered. Of all his predecessors, only Nero had never been outside Italy at his accession – even Caligula had lived with the Rhine armies as a boy; Claudius had been born in Gaul; Pius had been proconsul of Asia. Hadrian could hardly have approved, had he foreseen this. He had after all taken immediate steps to give his first choice as heir, the father of Lucius, some experience of armies, frontiers and provincial government, by dispatching him to Pannonia.

One decision had to be made at once. Some improvement was obviously required in the machinery of choosing officers, perhaps even generals and governors. One of the imperial secretaries of state was dismissed, the *ab epistulis* Sextus Caecilius Crescens Volusianus. Volusianus was, no doubt, an amiable figure of literary inclinations

---

[1] *PW*, 2A, 1921, 1006 ff.; A. Stein, *Die Reichsbeamten von Daxien*, Diss. Pann., I, 12, Budapest, 1944, 24 ff.; Lucian, *Alexander*, 27; *id.*, *quom. hist. conscr.*, 21, 24, 25. On Rutilianus cf. *id. Alexander*, 4, 30 ff.; and *PW*, 16, 1933, 533. The Ninth legion: E. Birley, *Roman Britain and the Roman Army*, Kendal, 1953, 25 ff., makes a good case for the view that the Ninth survived at least till the A.D. 130s if not longer, and suggests (27–8) occasions when it might have been transferred to the east. It was certainly out of existence early in the reign of Marcus as its name does not appear on the army list recorded by Dessau, *ILS*, 2288. Recent discoveries suggest that it may have spent some time at Nijmegen in Lower Germany, cf. J. Bogaers, *Numaga*, 12, 1965, 10 ff.

[2] *v. Marci*, 8, 7.

(he was a fellow-countryman of Fronto). Pius had presumably chosen him as *ab epistulis*, quite reasonably, in the way that his predecessors had been chosen, on the basis of his literary talents, for the bureau, as its name indicates, handled imperial correspondence. But as the tenth book of Pliny's letters demonstrates, a large proportion of this correspondence was with provincial governors, and it had to be on the basis of material in the files of this bureau that the talents of officers and administrators were assessed. Marcus replaced Volusianus with T. Varius Clemens, a man from the province of Noricum, who had had a long military career, which included active service in the war in Mauretania; and latterly he had been procurator in five provinces, two of them provinces where the procurator was also the governor and commander in chief, Mauretania Caesariensis and Raetia. Such a man was better suited than Volusianus to advise the emperors on the choice of men to meet a military crisis.[1] Another important change in the administration was the appointment as prefect of the city of Q. Junius Rusticus, the Stoic. The exact date of the appointment is not known, but he was certainly in office by the beginning of A.D. 162, when he was consul for the second time. Rusticus would be an invaluable support to Marcus in his civil administration. The honour which Marcus publicly showed him demonstrated his high importance.[2]

L. Volusius Maecianus was governing Egypt as prefect at the accession, succeeding Furius Victorinus. By A.D. 162 he had been recalled, and made a senator. The only further promotion open to him in the equestrian order was the prefecture of the praetorian guard, but this office had just been filled. Maecianus was appointed prefect of the senatorial treasury (*aerarium Saturni*) and soon after designated consul. Thus Marcus was able to keep this eminent lawyer, his former tutor, by his side.[3]

[1] H.-G. Pflaum, *Les carrières procuratoriennes, etc.*, Nos. 142 (Volusianus) and 156 (Clemens). For this view of the functions of the *ab epistulis* cf. E. Birley, op. cit., 142 ff., 151 ff: It is worth noting here that it was in the A.D. 160s that the bureau of the *ab epistulis* was permanently divided into Greek and Latin sections, cf. G. Townend, *Historia*, 10, 1961, 377.

[2] *v. Marci*, 3, 3-5.

[3] H.-G. Pflaum, op. cit., No. 141.

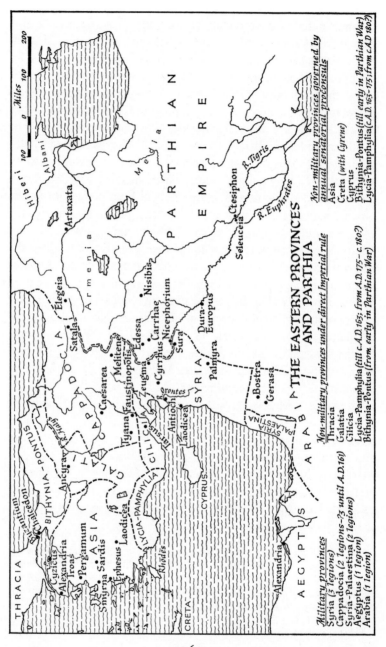

THE EASTERN PROVINCES AND PARTHIA

Military provinces
Syria (3 legions)
Cappadocia (2 legions—3 until A.D.161)
Syria-Palaestina (2 legions)
Aegyptus (1 legion)
Arabia (1 legion)

Non-military provinces under direct Imperial rule
Thracia
Galatia
Cilicia
Lycia-Pamphylia (till c.A.D.165; from A.D.175—c.180?)
Bithynia-Pontus (from early in Parthian War)

Non-military provinces governed by annual senatorial proconsuls
Asia
Creta (with Cyrene)
Cyprus
Bithynia-Pontus (till early in Parthian War)
Lycia-Pamphylia (c.A.D. 163-175; from c.A.D 180?)

164

The replacement of the fallen Severianus was crucial. Surprisingly the choice fell on Statius Priscus, at that time as far away from Cappadocia as he could possibly have been, in Britain. It shows that care was taken to find the right man. To Britain in Priscus' place, to meet an active enemy, was sent one Sextus Calpurnius Agricola. To deal with the trouble from the Germans, Marcus' friend Aufidius Victorinus, Fronto's son-in-law, was chosen, with the appointment as governor of Upper Germany.[1]

Meanwhile reinforcements for the eastern armies were under way. An African senator, P. Julius Geminius Marcianus, perhaps a friend of Fronto, certainly a fellow-Cirtensian, who had been commanding the Tenth legion at Vindobona (Vienna), took detachments of the Danubian legions to Cappadocia. Besides this, three entire legions were ordered to the east, I Minervia from Bonn in Lower Germany, II Adiutrix from Aquincum (Budapest) in Lower Pannonia and V Macedonica from Troesmis on the Danube, in Lower Moesia. The northern frontiers were thus weakened at strategically placed intervals. But the governors of the northern provinces were instructed to avoid hostilities and deal with disturbances by diplomacy wherever possible. Unmistakable signs of future turmoil in central Europe had been noted, but for the time being a solution had to wait on events in the east.[2] Before long further bad news came. Attidius Cornelianus had been defeated and put to flight in an engagement with the Parthian forces. The situation was clearly becoming desperate.[3]

At some stage in the winter of A.D. 161–2, when the news from the east was bad, with the Syrians in a rebellious mood, Marcus and Lucius decided that one of them must go to the war in person. The frontier armies had not fought a full-scale war under direct imperial direction for forty-five years, since Trajan's death in A.D. 117. It was

[1] Dessau, *ILS*, 1092; *v. Marci*, 8, 8. On Calpurnius Agricola's activity in Britain, cf the article by J. P. Gillam cited in n. 1, p. 146, above.

[2] *CIL*, VIII, 7050–1 (Marcianus); Dessau, *ILS*, 2311 (V Macedonica); 1091 (II Adiutrix); 1097–8 (I Minervia). In general, see *PW*, 12, 1924, 1298 ff. On the northern threat: *v. Marci*, 12, 13, and W. Zwikker, *Studien zur Markussäule*, I, Amsterdam, 1941, 35 ff.

[3] *v. Marci*, 8, 6. Cornelianus' defeat may not have been until A.D. 162 (he was still governor in that year: *CIL*, III, 129=6658).

decided that Lucius should go, 'because he was physically robust and younger than Marcus, and better suited to military activity', Dio says. The senate consented. Marcus himself was to remain at Rome, because affairs in the city demanded the presence of an emperor. This is sufficient explanation of the chosen course of action. In the biography of Lucius play is made with other motives. Marcus sent Lucius to the Parthian war, it is asserted, 'either so that his immorality could not be carried on in the city, under the eyes of all, or so that he would learn thriftiness by travel abroad, or so that he would return as a reformed character through the fear inspired by warfare, or so that he might realize that he was an emperor – *imperator*'. There is probably some truth in this, but the biographer has made the spirit behind it seem hard and calculating, when it was probably warm and friendly.[1]

It was realized that Lucius would need a full and experienced staff. One of the praetorian prefects had to go, taking some of the guard. Furius Victorinus was selected. He had served in the eastern provinces before, as procurator of Galatia. Besides this, he had served in Britain, on the Danube, in Spain, as prefect of the Italian fleets and as prefect of Egypt, in addition to occupying various posts in Rome.[2] It was thought advisable to have some senators of wide experience, as well as the prefect. First and foremost they selected M. Pontius Laelianus Larcius Sabinus. He was getting on in years now – his son was to be consul in A.D. 163 – but his military experience was unrivalled. He had begun his career as a young man as tribune of the legion VI Victrix in Germany and was transferred with it from Lower Germany to Britain in A.D. 122, when Platorius Nepos went to build Hadrian's Wall. He had governed both the Pannonian provinces, and then, nine years before, in A.D. 153, he had been governor of Syria. Hence he knew at first hand the major army of the east and the problems of the frontiers. Laelianus was given the honorific rank and title of *comes Augustorum*, 'companion of the Emperors'. Previous emperors had had *comites* with them on travels and campaigns. From now on they seem to have played a more

---

[1] Dio, 71, 1, 3; *v. Marci*, 8, 9; *v. Veri*, 5, 8.
[2] H.-G. Pflaum, op. cit., No. 139; *PIR 2*, F 584.

important role: certainly, an exceptional number are recorded in the reign of Marcus, all of consular rank. Laelianus was described by Fronto a little later as 'a serious man and an old-fashioned disciplinarian'.[1] Meanwhile, M. Iallius Bassus, who had recently been appointed governor of Lower Moesia, was directed to go to the east as another *comes*. Marcus' cousin, Annius Libo, was to go as well, to replace Attidius Cornelianus as governor of Syria. Lucius took his favourite freedmen too, of whom Geminus, Agaclytus, Coedes and Eclectus are named. Another freedman, his old foster-father Nicomedes, now (most exceptionally for a freedman), a procurator and a knight, gave up his duties as head of the posting-service (*praefectus vehiculorum*) in Rome, to take charge of the commissariat for the expeditionary force, retaining his old rank. Thus Lucius could keep his faithful old friend by his side. The Misenum fleet was to convey the emperor and to act as a means of communication and transport.[2]

Lucius set off in the spring of A.D. 162, to take ship from Brundisium (Brindisi). Marcus accompanied him as far as Capua. Lucius went on towards the east coast, feasting in the country houses on his route, and hunting in Apulia. At Canusium (Canossa) he fell ill and Marcus hurried south to see him again, after undertaking vows to the gods for his safety in the senate. Three days fasting and a bloodletting apparently cured him. But it might have been a mild stroke. Fronto was most upset to hear the news, but a letter from Lucius describing his treatment and recovery reassured him. In his reply he recommended a quiet convalescence, and urged that 'as suits your outstanding character you should be moderate in all your desires, which are bound to be keener and more importunate than usual after this enforced abstinence'. Lucius finally embarked, and

---

[1] *PW*, 22, 1953, 39 ff. Dessau, *ILS*, 1094+1100; Fronto, *ad Verum Imp.* 2, 1, 14=Haines, II, 148. On the new role of the *comites*, cf. *PW*, 4, 1900, 626 ff. (but the view there put forward of the role of *comites* under previous emperors is unsatisfactory).

[2] *CIL*, XII, 2718–19 (Bassus); *v. Veri*, 9, 2 (Libo, cf. *PIR* 2, A 668); ibid., 9, 3–5 (the freedmen, not stated explicitly to have gone to the east); H.-G. Pflaum, op. cit., No. 163 (Nicomedes); C. G. Starr, *The Roman Imperial Navy*, Ithaca, 1941, 188 ff.

Marcus fulfilled his vows to the gods. The journey east was by way of Corinth and Athens. It was a true royal progress, accompanied by musicians and singers (uncomfortably reminiscent of Nero, whose birthday, and, to a certain extent, tastes, Lucius shared). At Athens he stayed with Herodes Atticus, and was initiated into the Mysteries of Eleusis, as Hadrian had been a generation before. While he was performing a sacrifice a shooting-star or meteor was observed crossing the heavens from west to east. He then took ship across the Aegean and finally arrived at Antioch, the Syrian provincial capital, by way of the coastal towns of Asia, Pamphylia and Cilicia, dallying particularly in those that were renowned as pleasure resorts, the biographer takes care to record. It is not known how long this journey took.[1]

In the meantime Statius Priscus must have arrived to take command in Cappadocia, having probably travelled rapidly up the Rhine and down the Danube, and through Thrace, Bithynia and Galatia. In the course of A.D. 163 his vigorous generalship gained success for Roman arms. Priscus became something of a legend – it was rumoured that on one occasion the general's bellowing cry had caused twenty-seven enemy soldiers to drop dead.[2]

Marcus found life full of anxiety at this time. He spent a four-day public holiday at Alsium on the Etrurian coast, a famous holiday resort. But he was unable to relax. Apart from anything else one of his daughters had a fever. He wrote briefly to Fronto, saying that he would not describe his activities at Alsium in detail, because he knew that he would be reprimanded. Fronto replied with good humour: 'What? Do I not know that you went to Alsium with the intention of devoting yourself to games, joking and complete leisure for four

[1] *BMC*, IV, M. Aurelius and L. Verus, Nos. 200 ff., 1029 ff.; *v. Veri*, 6, 7–9; Fronto, *ad Verum Imp.*, 2, 6=Haines, II, 84 ff. Eleusis: Dittenberger, *Syll. Inscr. Gr.*, I, 409, 411; *v. Had.*, 13, 1. For the date, cf. J. Schwendemann, op. cit., 145. The shooting-star is recorded by Cassiodorus Senator under the year A.D. 162. Fronto later took the chance of telling Lucius that he was now on the best of terms with Herodes: 'Herodes summus nunc meus, quamquam extet oratio' (*ad Verum Imp.*, 2, 9=Haines, II, 232 ff.).

[2] *v. Veri*, 7, 1; Dio, 71, 3, 1; Lucian, *quom. hist. conscr.*, 20 (the story of the twenty-seven enemy – a joke, no doubt).

whole days?' he wrote ironically. Marcus must relax, he insisted. His ancestors could do it, even though they were occupied with extending the frontiers of the empire. His father, he reminded Marcus, for all his supreme personal qualities, had been keen on exercise in the *palaestra*, and fishing, and had appreciated comedians. He went on to give more examples – 'even your own Chrysippus [the Stoic] used to have his drink every day, they say. . . . Yet, if you have declared war on games, relaxation and pleasure, at least have as much sleep as a free man needs.' He went on to relate an elaborate fable of the appointed boundaries of Morning and Evening. Marcus was evidently devoting much of the night to his judicial business. 'So, Marcus,' Fronto concluded, 'if you need a dream hereafter, I recommend you to sleep freely, until the time comes when your desires are fulfilled, in the way you would wish, in your waking hours.'

Marcus' reply showed that he found the advice difficult. He dictated a hasty acknowledgement: 'I have just received your letter, which I will enjoy properly later. For just now I have duties hanging over me, tasks which cannot be begged off. Meanwhile I will tell you, briefly, as I am busy, what you want to hear, that our little girl is in better health and is running about her room.' Later he continued the letter, while the others were having dinner. He himself had had a light snack. 'That is all the notice you have taken of my advice, you will say,' he wrote after telling this to Fronto. 'But I have taken a lot of notice of it, for I have rested, as your letter suggests, and I will re-read it the oftener, so that I may rest the oftener. But – this devotion to duty! Who knows better than you how demanding it is!' He ends by inquiring solicitously after Fronto's health – he had a pain in his hand. 'Farewell, my best master, man of warm heart.'[1]

The war was proving a strain on Marcus. Some time after it began Fronto wrote a long and carefully composed letter, full of historical analogies, to show Marcus how initial reverses in war could turn into splendid victories. 'Mars has spoken of the Romans often, and in many wars, in this strain. . . . But always and everywhere he has changed our troubles into successes and our terrors into triumphs.' He spoke of reverses under Trajan, Hadrian and

[1] *de feriis Als.*, 1, 3, 4=Haines, II, 2, 4 ff.

Pius. He recalled Herodotus' story of Polycrates of Samos, the man with too much good fortune. 'But you may soon hope for victory, for always in her history has Rome experienced frequent changes of her fortunes.' He had earlier sent Marcus suitable reading matter, including especially a speech of Cicero's, the *pro lege Manilia*, in which Cicero recommended the appointment of Pompey to take supreme command in the war against Mithridates. 'You will find in it many chapters aptly suited to your present counsels, concerning the choice of army commanders, the interests of allies, the protection of provinces, the discipline of the soldiers, the qualifications required for commanders in the field and elsewhere.' The speech emphasized in particular that there was only one man who could lead Rome in the war, only one man that Rome's allies demanded, and so on. This advice may have been a factor in the decision to send Lucius out as supreme commander. The parallel was indeed apt – for Pompey had had to campaign in Armenia.[1]

For all the cares of state and for all his increasing ill-health, Fronto had probably never been happier. 'I have had my fill of life,' he said, replying to Marcus' good wishes for his birthday, 'I see you, Antoninus, as excellent an emperor as I hoped, as just and as free from fault as I guaranteed, as popular and as welcome to the Roman people as I desired, as fond of me as I could wish and as eloquent as you yourself could wish.' The last point naturally gave Fronto enormous pleasure. Marcus, as a result of his increased public duties, now had to put into practice all Fronto's old lessons in public speaking as never before, in a way that he had once thought he would never be able to do with any pleasure. He was 'beginning to feel the wish to be eloquent once more, in spite of having for a time lost interest in eloquence' – since his conversion to philosophy some fifteen or more years before, in fact. Fronto was especially gratified by Marcus' speech in the Senate after an earthquake at Cyzicus in Asia Minor. Marcus had captured the dramatic nature of the event in his language and his audience had been impressed and moved.[2]

---

[1] *de bello Parthico*, esp. 10=Haines, II, 20 ff. (esp. 30).
[2] *ad Ant. Imp.*, 1, 1=Haines, II, 30 ff.; ibid., 1, 2, 2=Haines, II, 34 ff. Cyzicus: ibid., 1, 2, 4 and 7=Haines, II, 34 ff.

Fronto addressed a number of letters to him in which he reminded him at length of the lessons on eloquence inculcated twenty years before. In a telling passage he reminded Marcus of his position. 'Suppose, Caesar, that you can attain to the wisdom of Cleanthes and Zeno, yet, against your will, you must put on the purple imperial cloak, not the philosopher's woollen cape.' He repeated the message of twenty years before, that even philosophers had to command language to express their teaching forcefully: 'Philosophy will tell you what to say, eloquence will tell you how to say it.'[1]

At this time we gain another glimpse into the emperor's family life. One of the twins, Antoninus, had been ill with a cough, but was on the mend. Fronto had not then seen them. When he did so, he was delighted: 'I have seen your little chickens, the most welcome sight in my life. They are just like you in appearance, so much so that nothing could be more alike.' Going to see them was like taking a short cut to Lorium, where Marcus was at the time, he wrote, for 'I saw you not only opposite me but in more places than one, whether I turned to the right or to the left. They have quite a healthy colour, the gods be praised, and strong lungs. One was holding a piece of white bread, like a royal child, the other a piece of black bread – clearly the offspring of a philosopher! . . . So now you must take care that you don't find me somewhat prouder – for I have those that I can love instead of you, not only with my eyes but with my ears'. Marcus was touched by this letter: 'I saw my little sons when you saw them, and I saw you when I was reading your letter. I beg you, my master, love me as you love me, and love me too as you love those little ones of ours. . . . Write often to my lord brother', he added, 'for he especially wants me to gain this request from you. His desires, indeed, certainly make me unreasonable and violent. Farewell, most delightful of masters. Give my love to your grandson.' In the meantime, Faustina was again pregnant. Before the end of A.D. 162 she bore Marcus another son, who was given his father's original names, Marcus Annius Verus.[2]

---

[1] *de eloquentia*, I, 12 and 18=Haines, II, 62 ff., 70.

[2] *ad Ant. Imp.*, I, 1=Haines, 1132; ibid., I, 3=Haines, II, 118 ff.; ibid., I, 4 =Haines, II, 120 ff. M. Annius Verus: *v. Marci*, 21, 3 (aged 7 in A.D. 169), cf. *PIR* 2, A 698, also J. M. C. Toynbee, *JRS*, 49, 1959, 39 ff.

As Fronto had predicted, the fortunes of war had swung to Rome, with the successes of Statius Priscus, who had stormed and taken the Armenian capital Artaxata in A.D. 163. By the end of the year Lucius, as Roman supreme commander, for all that he had not participated actively in the fighting, took the title 'Armeniacus', 'conqueror of the Armenians', and was hailed as *Imperator* by the troops, which allowed him and Marcus to style themselves 'Imp. II' in their official titulature. Lucius had stayed at Antioch for the most part, but spent part of the winter at Laodicea and the summer months at Daphne, a resort on the outskirts of Antioch. Critics claimed that he was spending his time in riotous living of various kinds. Certainly he had become fond of gambling with dice and he had sent to Rome for actors, which Fronto later justified on his behalf by allusion to Juvenal's satirical remark that the people needed 'bread and circuses' (*panem et circenses*): 'knowing that two things especially hold fast the Roman people, the corn-dole and public spectacles' (as he somewhat pompously paraphrased it). Lucius' passion for the sporting life had to be assuaged by dispatches from home conveying the latest news about the fortunes of his favourite chariot team, the Greens, and he had with him a golden statue of the Green horse Volucer as a reminder.[1]

In Syria Lucius also acquired a mistress, no ordinary 'low-born mistress', as his biographer unkindly described her. The lady in question was named Panthea, portrayed by the normally biting satirist Lucian in the most rapturous terms. She was 'a woman of perfect beauty', from Smyrna, one of the Ionian Greek cities of the coast, more beautiful than any statue by Phidias or Praxiteles. Her voice was 'soft, delicious and winning'. She sang wonderfully well to the lyre. She spoke pure Ionic Greek, flavoured with a classical Attic wit. She possessed the gifts of all the Muses, had a shrewd understanding of public affairs, and a gracious, loving and modest nature. Lucian wrote this panegyric in the form of a dialogue between two friends. It had a sequel – Panthea read it, and reproached the author for being too flattering, especially in comparing her to the goddesses,

[1] *BMC*, IV, M. Aurelius and L. Verus, Nos. 233 ff.; *v. Veri*, 4, 6 ff.; 6, 1–5; 7, 1–6.

which frightened her. She had power over Lucius, who even shaved off his luxurious beard to please her, provoking a lot of comment from the Syrians.[1]

Lucius had plenty of work to do as well, particularly in the training of troops, for the Syrian army had apparently become slack from long years of peace. The soldiers stationed at Antioch used to spend more time lounging at tables in open-air cafés than with their units. Pontius Laelianus undertook some formidable kit inspections, ordering the troopers' padded saddles to be slit open, for example; and he jumped heavily on gambling and drinking in the camp. Training was stepped up. Lucius was said by Fronto later to have taken things in hand in person, 'marching on foot at the head of his men as often as he rode on horseback, putting up with the blazing sun and choking dust, leaving his head exposed to sun and shower, hail and snow – and missiles, sweating unconcernedly as if playing games. He inspected soldiers in the field and their quarters in camp, including the sick-bay. He observed casually but keenly the dandified Syrians and the unsophisticated Pannonians. He took a belated bath after his work was done, and ate simple camp-food, drank local wine. Often he slept on leaves or the turf.' He was nevertheless lenient. 'Through so many provinces, so many open dangers of sieges, battles, citadels, posts and forts stormed, he lavished his care and his advice.' The language is suitably ambiguous, for it is fairly certain that Lucius saw little actual fighting himself. Fronto wrote this at the end of the war. In the early stages he heard little from Lucius directly, and after a long interval received an apology for the silence. 'I was unwilling to describe in detail plans which were liable to be altered daily,' Lucius explained, 'and I did not wish to make you . . . a partner in my anxieties, which have made me completely miserable day and night, and almost made me despair of success.'[2] One reason for Lucius' despondency may have been the failure of his attempt at negotiation with Vologases after

---

[1] v. Veri, 7, 10 ('amicae vulgaris'); Lucian, Imagines; pro Imaginibus.

[2] Fronto, ad Verum Imp., 2, 1, esp. 19–20=Haines, II, 128 ff., esp. 148 ff.; ad Verum Imp., 2, 2=Haines, II, 116 ff.; Principia Historiae, 12 ff.=Haines, II, 208 ff.

the successes in Armenia, an attempt which was obviously regarded as an admission of weakness or cowardice.[1]

Meanwhile Marcus' cousin Libo had died, after quarrelling with Lucius, which also no doubt caused him – and Marcus – distress. Libo had taken a high-handed attitude, holding that he was responsible only to Marcus, and no doubt criticizing Lucius' actions. Perhaps not surprisingly his death was the subject of malicious rumour: Lucius was said to have had him poisoned. He was succeeded as governor of Syria by the experienced Gnaeus Julius Verus. Later, when back at Rome, Lucius antagonized conservative opinion by marrying off Libo's widow to his own freedman Agaclytus, against the wishes of Marcus, who some years afterwards made such marriages (between persons of senatorial and freedman status) illegal by decree of the senate.[2]

Another marriage was planned for A.D. 164, that between Lucius himself and Lucilla. Stories of the incomparable Panthea had possibly decided Marcus to advance the date of the wedding. But Lucilla was now of marriageable age in any case (her fifteenth birthday was on March 7, 164). Marcus escorted her as far as Brundisium from where she took ship, accompanied by the bridegroom's uncle M. Vettulenus Civica Barbarus (the very much younger half-brother of Lucius' father), who was made a *comes Augusti* and was perhaps intended to play the role of a family watchdog on Lucius' behaviour (the task in which Libo had failed). Marcus in fact apparently told the senate that he would conduct his daughter to Syria himself. If this was the case, he must have changed his mind later. At any rate he returned to Rome, having sent despatches to the proconsuls of the provinces on her route not to provide any official reception. Ordinarily, the empress Faustina might have accompanied Lucilla, as mother of the bride, but she had her younger children to look after, the twins, now two-and-a-half, and Annius Verus, just over a year old. Another member of the family did go with Lucilla, as well as Civica Barbarus, a lady described as 'his

---

[1] *Princ. Hist.*, 14=Haines, II, 212; Nazarius, *Paneg.*, 24, 6–7 (on which see P. Lambrechts, *Ant. Class.*, 3, 1934, 197 ff.).

[2] *v. Veri*, 4, 2–3; *CIL*, III, 199 (Julius Verus); *Digest.*, 23, 2, 16.

sister', meaning the sister of Marcus. As Cornificia had been dead for twelve years this must be a slip of the pen, and one cannot say who this person was – it might have been Lucilla's own elder sister Faustina, who would now be married and a suitable companion, or one of Lucius' sisters, Ceionia Fabia and Ceionia Plautia. Lucius travelled west from Syria to meet the bridal party at Ephesus, chief city of the province of Asia, where the wedding was celebrated. On becoming junior empress, Lucilla was granted the title Augusta.[1]

The year A.D. 164 saw something of a lull in military operations, and it was mainly to be spent on preparation for the assault on the Parthian homeland – this was probably the reason why the moment was chosen for the wedding, rather than *vice versa*. Armenia was now firmly under Roman control. A new capital was built to replace the destroyed Artaxata. It was called simply Kaine Polis – 'New City' – and it was sited more strategically some thirty miles closer to the borders of Roman territory. Lucius crowned as king of Armenia a pro-Roman Arsacid prince, Sohaemus – not merely pro-Roman, in fact: he was a senator and had even been made consul, so he must have been in exile with Rome for some time, being held in readiness for just such an occasion as this. The event was celebrated on coinage of the year, which bore the legend *rex Armeniis datus*, and depicted Lucius sitting on a platform surrounded by his officers, while Sohaemus standing in front of him saluted. In this year Marcus was finally persuaded by Lucius to share the title of victory Armeniacus.[2]

The means chosen to persuade him was to include the request in

[1] *v. Marci*, 9, 4–6; Civica Barbarus: *AE*, 1958, 15. The husband of Lucilla's sister Faustina, Claudius Severus, was of eastern origin. The husband of Ceionia Plautia, Q. Servilius Pudens, may have been due to set off for the east at this time as proconsul of Lycia-Pamphylia, so it might have been a convenient arrangement if he and Plautia went with Lucilla. See *AE*, 1927, 88; 1929, 85; and D. Magie, *Roman Rule in Asia Minor*, Princeton, 1950, II, 1598; also below, p. 191, n. 1. An alternative is to suppose that the text of *v. Marci*, 9, 4, is now faulty and originally read 'sororis suae filio' rather than 'sorori suae' – meaning M. Ummidius Quadratus, son of Cornificia, and Lucilla's first cousin. Lucilla Augusta: *BMC*, IV, M. Aurelius and L. Verus, Nos. 303 ff.

[2] Dio, 71, 3, 1. On Sohaemus: *PW*, 3A, 1927, 798 ff. *BMC*, IV, M. Aurelius and L. Verus, Nos. 261 ff., 300 ff.; P. Lambrechts, op. cit., 196 ff., asserts (*contra* Dodds and Mattingly) that Lucius performed the coronation in person. It need not have taken place in Armenia.

an official despatch to the senate in A.D. 164. Fronto was not well enough to be in the senate to hear this, but he read the official record, from which he derived enormous pleasure – especially from the successful 'assault on that fortified and unconquered and impregnable citadel which is planted in your brother's heart against the name *Armeniacus* which he had refused'. He pretended that he rated this achievement higher than anything done in the war, when he wrote to Lucius to congratulate him on the despatch: 'eloquent, as befits an orator's letter, vigorous, as befits a general, dignified, as befits a letter to the senate, not too excessive, as befits a letter on military affairs'. As he found Marcus' official reply wonderfully eloquent also, Fronto's cup was full to overflowing.[1]

The expeditionary force had been able to leave Armenia, in readiness for the invasion of Parthia. The main body was led south by Marcus Claudius Fronto, a man of Greek-speaking family, a native of the province of Asia, probably a first generation senator, although his family were of the local aristocracy. Fronto had been in the opening campaign, commanding the Bonn legion I Minervia – the second legion he had commanded – which he had led to the front, then taking command of an army corps of legionary and auxiliary troops under Statius Priscus. Another general becoming prominent was a coeval of Fronto, P. Martius Verus, a westerner, perhaps from Toulouse, and a man of winning personality, who had brought the legion V Macedonica to the war. But the key figure in the new campaign was to be C. Avidius Cassius, a Syrian from Cyrrhus. His father Heliodorus had not been a senator, although he was the descendant of Seleucid kings, but he had enjoyed considerable power and influence under Hadrian, not only as a leading literary figure, but in important government posts, ending up as prefect of Egypt at Hadrian's death, a position in which Pius retained him for several years. His son Cassius clearly had no difficulty in entering the senate, but his early career is unknown. He had recently been consul and was thus a little senior to Martius Verus and Claudius Fronto. Lucius had gone to the Euphrates himself, before his wedding, at the insistence of his *comites*. Initial skirmish-

[1] *ad Verum Imp.*, 2, 1, 3–4 and 15=Haines, II, 130 ff., 144.

ing resulted in the capture of Dausara, well inside Mesopotamia, and Nicephorium down the Euphrates.[1]

Back in Rome Marcus had had a troublesome family matter to deal with. His great-aunt Matidia had died and there was a legal squabble about her will. She had been enormously wealthy and like most rich, childless old women in Rome had attracted a horde of parasites, who at one time had persuaded her to include them in codicils to her will. These had never been confirmed, but as she lay unconscious some of her would-be heirs had taken the opportunity of sealing them up, making them valid. But this created a complication, as it meant that more than three-quarters of her estate was now willed outside the family – contrary to the provisions of the *lex Falcidia*. Marcus was in an embarrassing position. Fronto urged him to press the claims of the family: 'That famous string of pearls which everyone knows about and the rest of those pieces of jewellery of such value – who will buy them? If your wife buys them, people will say she has pounced on the spoil and snapped them up for a minimal price, to make sure the legatees get as little as possible. But Faustina won't buy them, you say. Who then will buy these pearls – which were, after all, left to your family?' Marcus replied that he had considered the matter carefully and was going to write to his brother and make him give the decision.[2]

Meanwhile Fronto sent an account to his son-in-law Victorinus in Germany: 'I have not been free from apprehension that philosophy might persuade him to some perverse decision', he concluded. Victorinus had his wife with him in Germany and she had borne him a son there whom Fronto had not yet seen. Their other children, also boys, named Victorinus and Fronto, had stayed behind with their grandparents.[3] The situation in the north was far from reassuring.

[1] Claudius Fronto: *PIR 2*, C 874. Martius Verus: *PW*, 14, 1930, 2024 ff. Avidius Cassius: *PIR 2*, A 1402. Heliodorus: *PIR 2*, A 1405. Lucius on the Euphrates: *v. Veri*, 7, 6–7. Dausara and Nicephorium: Fronto, *ad Verum Imp.*, 2, 1, 3= Haines, II, 132. This letter belongs to A.D. 164, in view of the references to the title Armeniacus (see previous note).   [2] *ad M. Caes.*, 2, 16–17=Haines, II, 94 ff.

[3] *ad amicos*, 1, 14=Haines, II, 98. The death of Matidia must be after A.D. 161 (still alive in *ad Ant. Imp.*, 2, 1 =Haines, I, 300). Fronto's grandchildren: *ad amicos*, 1, 12=Haines, II, 172; *de nepote amisso*, 2=Haines, II, 222 ff.; *ad Verum Imp.*, 2, 9–10=Haines, II, 232 ff.

Germans had destroyed at least one Roman frontier post in the invasion, and the signs were that all the barbarian peoples of northern and central Europe were in turmoil. It would only be a matter of time before they came into conflict with Rome all along the northern frontier. Another problem that Victorinus had to face was corruption among his officers: a legionary legate who had been taking bribes eventually had to be asked to resign his command.

Another sign of the seriousness of the situation is provided by the presence on the Rhine of a prefect of the guard – a new prefect, T. Flavius Constans, who must have succeeded Cornelius Repentinus in A.D. 163 or a little later. Constans was at Cologne. The legion from nearby Bonn (I Minervia) was, of course, with the eastern armies, its absence weakening the garrison of Lower Germany. The governors of all the northern provinces had a difficult task. In Upper Pannonia, the key province, L. Dasumius Tullius Tuscus, a distant connection of Hadrian's family, was succeeded by the experienced M. Nonius Macrinus. Lower Pannonia, with no legion at all in the absence of II Adiutrix, was under the little-known Ti. Haterius Saturninus. Upper Moesia was being governed by M. Servilius Fabianus Maximus, one of Fronto's friends. He had moved from the Lower Moesian province which he had taken over from Iallius Bassus when the latter joined Lucius' staff; and he was followed in Lower Moesia by the son of Pontius Laelianus. The Dacian provinces were still administered in three separate sections, under a senator of praetorian rank and two procurators.[1]

In Rome Marcus had legal business of a more pressing and public nature than had been provided by his great-aunt's will. His attention to the theory and practice of legislation and the administration of justice were intensive, and it is notable that he was described by professional lawyers as 'an emperor most skilled in the law', and (by the great Papinian) as 'a most prudent and conscientiously just emperor'. The badly-informed and muddled epitomator Aurelius Victor, writing in the fourth century, expressed the opinion that under Marcus 'the ambiguities of the law were wonderfully well

[1] The fort: H. Schönberger, *Quintus Congressus*, *etc.*, Zagreb, 1963, 151. Corruption: Dio, 72, 11, 3–4. Constans: *PIR 2*, F 247 (cf. H.-G. Pflaum, op. cit.,

5. Bronze equestrian statue of Marcus Aurelius as Emperor. Originally on the Lateran Hill in Rome, it was moved to its present striking position, in the Piazza del Campidoglio, by Michelangelo

6a. Coins showing (*top*) 'Th
Harmony of the Emperors',
AD 161; (*left* and *right*) Marc
and Lucius respectively at tl
accession; (*centre*) Faustina I
after the birth of her first ch
(*left*) 'The Happiness of our
times' proclaimed after the
birth of twins to Faustina, a
(*right*) Faustina after the bir
of the twins; (*bottom*) Lucilla
after her marriage to Lucius

6b. Bust of Annius Verus Ca
youngest son of Marcus
Aurelius. (Identification
suggested by J. M. C. Toyn
JRS, 1959, p. 39 ff.)

clarified'.[1] The biography in the Augustan History, in a passage based on a detailed and accurate source, provides a good deal of useful information about Marcus' legal and administrative activity, and this is confirmed and amplified by the citations in legal sources and by inscriptions.

In all the legislation preserved three major interests are apparent. The first is the question of the 'manumission' – liberation – of slaves; the second is the appointment of guardians for orphans and minors; the third is the selection of councillors (*decuriones*) to run the affairs of local communities throughout the provinces. That the liberation of slaves should particularly concern Marcus is not surprising, and the special interest shown in the appointment of trustees and guardians may to some extent be explained by the fact that he had himself lost his father at an early age. The concern with local government is less personal: it was an attempt to combat the growing apathy that was coming over the empire – well-to-do people in the provinces were becoming increasingly anxious to avoid playing their part in local life, partly because this automatically involved them in a heavy financial burden.

The biographer's account of Marcus' administrative and legal activity (which comes after the mention of the marriage of Lucius and Lucilla and before recording the end of the Parthian war) is worth quoting in full here, omitting only the parts which describe activity from later in the reign. 'In the meantime he made safeguards for lawsuits concerning personal freedom, laying down – the first to do so – that every citizen should give names to freeborn children within thirty days of birth and declare them to the

---

[1] *Cod. Just.*, 7, 2, 6; *Digest.*, 31, 67, 10 (cf. *Cod. Just.*, 6, 35, 11); Aur. Victor, *de Caes.*, 16, 11. In general, cf. P. Noyen, *Rev. Int. de Droit de l'Antiq.*, 3rd ser., I, 1954, 349 ff.; ibid., *Ant. Class.*, 24, 1955, 372 ff.,

No. 149). Repentinus: *PIR 2*, C 1428. Tuscus: *PIR 2*, D 16. Macrinus: Dessau, *ILS*, 8830 (cf. R. Syme, *Gnomon*, 29, 1957, 523). Saturninus: *PIR 2*, H 32, Maximus: Dessau, *ILS*, 1080. Bassus: *CIL*, XII, 2718–19. Laelianus: *CIL*. III, 6182=774. I follow W. Zwikker, op. cit., 79 ff., 82 ff., against A. Stein, *Die Legaten von Moesien*, Diss. Pann., I, 11, Budapest, 1940, 45 and 76, in dating the commands of Maximus and Bassus. In general, cf. Zwikker, 35 ff., and *PW*, Supp. 9, 1962, 555.

prefects of the treasury of Saturn'. This was the senate's treasury. One of its prefects in the early A.D. 160s was the lawyer Volusius Maecianus, and he may well have been the originator of the proposal – which was admittedly a step towards increasing the powers of the bureaucracy, but nevertheless ensured that it would be difficult in the future for anyone's status as a free man and a citizen to be called in question. Similar measures were taken for the provinces: 'In the provinces also he established the use of Public Registries, where entries of births were to be made, in the same way as with the prefects of the Treasury of Saturn at Rome, so that if anyone born in the provinces should have to bring an action at law to prove his status as a free man, he could produce this as evidence. He also strengthened the whole of the law dealing with suits to prove freedom; and he enacted other laws to deal with money-lenders and auctions.

'He gave singular attention to the administration of justice: he added a number of court-days to the legal calendar, finally allotting 230 days in the year to the pleading of cases and judgment of suits. He was the first to appoint a *praetor tutelaris* (for previously the appointment of trustees had been the duty of the consuls), so that greater care might be exercised in their appointment. As regards guardians, whereas previously they had only been appointed under the Praetorian Law, or in cases of prodigality or madness, he decreed that all youths might have them appointed – without specific reasons being given.' By a fortunate chance the first man given the new post of praetor to deal with the appointment of trustees has left epigraphic record of this. He was Gaius Arrius Antoninus (no relative of the imperial family, in spite of his names, but a fellow-countryman and friend of Fronto). It was always difficult to find suitable persons to act as trustees or guardians and most of the references to decisions of Marcus in this connection in the legal codes involve the adjudication of claims to exemption – poverty was one valid excuse, as were state service and the tenure of local magistracies above the office of aedile.

'He made the senate the judge in many judicial enquiries, even in those which belonged to his own jurisdiction. None of the emperors showed such respect to the senate as he did. To do honour to the senate, moreover, he delegated the settling of disputes to many senators of praetorian and consular rank who held no magistracy at the time, so that their prestige might be enhanced through their administration of the law. . . . He granted senators the further privilege that when any of them was to be tried on a capital charge, he would examine the evidence in secret and only afterwards bring the case to a public hearing; and he would not allow members of the equestrian order to attend such investigations. He always attended sessions of the senate when he was in Rome, even if there was no measure to be proposed, and if he wished to make any proposal himself, he even came from Campania in person. Besides this, when elections were being held he often stayed in the Senate House until night, and never left the building until the consul had said: "we detain you no further, Conscript Fathers". Further, he made the senate the court to hear appeals from the decision of the consuls.' This deference to the highest order in the land may perhaps seem slightly reactionary now, but it was the only basis in the imperial system for the continuance of orderly government. Emperors who despised and ignored the senate had to rely entirely on naked military rule.

'He was careful in his public expenditure and prohibited libellous accusations, placing a mark of public disgrace on false accusers. He treated with scorn accusations that might profit the imperial treasury.' This refers to accusations of treason, which were at many periods the bane of men of standing: a cheap way of gaining profit and advancement was to be a public informer, and under emperors such as Tiberius, Nero and Domitian the informers had been rampant. 'He made many prudent new arrangements for the support of poor children under state care (*de alimentis publicis*). He appointed supervisors from the senate for many communities, so that he might give wider scope to the exercise of authority by senators. To the Italian communities in time of famine he provided food from the city of Rome, and in general made careful provision for the supply of corn. . . . He maintained the streets of the city and the public highways most diligently. He appointed legal officers for Italy on the example of the consulars that Hadrian had appointed to administer the law.' This last measure was against the policy of Antoninus, and, in contrast to his other actions, might have been unwelcome to the senate. On the other hand it created further civilian posts in the administration, and this may have been well received. The appointment of supervisors for the cities meant, of course, increased centralization of control. But with the unwillingness of well-to-do people to serve on local councils, it was to become increasingly necessary to cope with the resultant inefficiency and corruption by direct governmental interference in local authorities' affairs. At the same time efforts were made to fill the local councils. In reply to an inquiry by Lollianus Avitus, the governor of Bithynia (a province where the local town-councils were notoriously corrupt and inefficient), it was stated that even persons of illegitimate birth could serve on the councils, provided that they were in other respects eligible. Other legislation from the period deals with similar problems.

Summarizing his activity, the biographer says that Marcus 're-stored the old laws rather than introduced new ones. He always kept by him prefects, with whose authority and responsibility he framed his laws. He made use of Scaevola also, a particularly skilled lawyer.

'Towards the people he behaved at all times as in a free state. He was at all times extremely reasonable in restraining people from bad actions and urging them to good ones, generous in rewarding, quick to forgive, thus making bad men good, and good men very good, and he even took insults, which he had to put up with from some people, with equanimity. For when a certain Vetrasinus, a man of deplorable reputation, was standing for office and Marcus advised him to stop the public talk about himself, and he replied that many who had fought with him in the arena were now praetors, he took it with good grace. Again, to avoid taking an easy revenge on anyone, instead of making a praetor who had handled some cases very badly resign his office, he merely handed over the man's legal business to his colleague. The imperial treasury never affected his judgment in any lawsuits involving money. Finally, if he was firm, he was also reasonable.'[1]

---

[1] *v. Marci*, 9, 7-12, 6. The scope of the present work does not permit detailed discussion of the implications of these measures. They are dealt with fully by J. Schwendemann, op. cit. Volusius Maecianus: H.-G. Pflaum, op. cit., No. 141.

A number of cases in private law with which Marcus had to deal, during the first eight years of his reign, concerned family affairs. In reply to a lady named Flavia Tertulla, who had evidently been reported to the authorities as having contracted an illegal marriage, the official reply, in the name of both Marcus and Lucius, stated: 'We are moved by the length of time during which you have been married to your uncle in ignorance of the law; and because you were given in marriage by your grandmother; and because of the number of your children; taking all things together, we confirm the status of your children in this marriage, because it was contracted forty years ago, so that they should be regarded just as if they were conceived legitimately.' In another case a dispute between husband and wife reached the highest court. 'It is a new thing that Rutilius Severus seems to desire, that his wife, who is separated from him, and says that she is not pregnant, should be placed under surveillance. Hence no one will be surprised if we for our part suggest a new plan and a new remedy. Therefore, if he persists in the same demand, the most suitable possible house should be chosen, belonging to a thoroughly respectable woman, to which Domitia may come. There, three mid-wives, approved both for their professional qualifications and for their trustworthiness, who have been chosen by yourself [the magistrate Valerius Priscus, to whom the judgment was addressed], shall inspect her. If all of them, or two out of three, declare that she is pregnant, then the woman must be persuaded to accept being put under surveillance, just as if she had requested it herself. But if she does not in fact have a child, the husband may know that, as far as any odium he incurs and his reputation in general are concerned, he cannot be regarded as having sought this, to do injury to the woman without just cause. But if all, or more than one, declare that she is not pregnant, there will be no reason to have her placed under surveil-lance.'[1] The background to this glimpse into the social history of the time is unfortunately unknown. But reliable tests for pregnancy are of

[1] *Digest.*, 23, 2, 57a; 25, 4, 1, *pr.*

Arrius Antoninus: *PIR 2*, A 1088. The *alimenta:* R. Duncan-Jones, *Papers of the British School at Rome*, 32, 1964, 123 ff. Lollianus Avitus: *PIR 2*, H 40; *Digest.*, 50, 2, 3, 2. Scaevola: *PIR 2*, C 681; H.-G. Pflaum, op. cit., No. 168a.

course a relatively modern invention, and the action taken in this case must be regarded as reasonable in the circumstances.

Inheritance cases were a continuing source of litigation. Apart from other considerations, the imperial treasury (*fiscus*) had an interest, as death duties had to be paid, and the property of persons who died intestate could go to the treasury. A knotty problem arose when it was not completely clear whether a man had died intestate or not, in other words, whether or not his will was valid. The case is reported by the distinguished jurist Ulpius Marcellus. It belonged to the year A.D. 166. 'Recently at the emperor's court, when a certain man had crossed out the names of his heirs and his property, having no owner, was claimed by the imperial treasury, there was for a long time doubt about the legacies, especially about the ones of which the drawing up had been crossed out. For the most part, also, it was thought that the legatees should be excluded, which I certainly thought was the course to be followed, if the man had cancelled all that was written in the will. Some adjudged that what he had crossed out was void by law, all the rest was valid. What then? Can it not also be believed sometimes that a man who had crossed out the names of the heirs should have thought that he had done enough to die the death of an intestate? But in a doubtful case it is not only juster but also safer to follow the more liberal interpretation.' With this preamble Marcellus introduces his account of the proceedings of the imperial council. 'Marcus said: "When Valerius Nepos changed his mind, cut open his will and crossed out the names of his heirs, his inheritance, according to the decision of my Divine Father, does not appear to belong to those whose names had been written down", and he [Marcus] said to the treasury counsel (*advocatus fisci*): "You have your judges." Vibius Zeno said: "I ask, Lord Emperor, that you hear me patiently. What is your decision about the legacies?" Antoninus Caesar [Marcus] said: "Does it seem to you that a man who crossed out the names of the heirs wanted the will to be valid?" Cornelius Priscianus, the counsel for Leon, said: "He only crossed out the names of the heirs." Calpurnius Longinus, the treasury counsel, said: "No will can be valid that does not have an heir." Priscianus said: "He manumitted certain (slaves) as well as giving legacies." Antoninus Caesar dismissed everyone. When he had weighed the matter up, and had ordered them to be admitted again, he said: "The present case seems to admit of the more humane interpretation, so that we may at least consider that Nepos wanted what he had crossed out to be void." He crossed out the name of a slave whom he had ordered to be free. Antoninus in his official reply decided that he should be free none the less. This decision he certainly made from a partiality for freedom.'[1]

This interest in giving any slave the maximum possible chance of attaining his freedom, if there had ever been any question of his master wishing to grant it, was a matter which Marcus was concerned with throughout his reign, and towards the end of it, a decision he made, in a case involving manumission brought to his attention by his friend Aufidius Victorinus, was to be constantly cited by the jurists as the decisive precedent. Not surprisingly, it was a verdict in favour of the slave, as were virtually all his verdicts in cases involving slaves. Two such cases came up at this period of the reign. In one, he was asked by a senator named Voconius Saxa, who was holding some official post, for advice on how to deal with a slave named Primitivus who had gone to remarkable lengths to avoid being sent back to the master from whom he had run away. The slave had confessed to murder. Under torture, to which he was submitted to learn further details about his alleged accomplices, he admitted that the 'confession' was a put-up job, and that no murder had been committed. The imperial reply to Voconius Saxa recommended that the slave should be sold by Saxa's staff, with the condition that he should never be returned to his former master's power. The master should receive the money paid for the slave.

Another case involved the decision whether slaves who had been given their freedom by their master's will were ineligible to receive it if they had been serving a term of imprisonment. The reply to this was that if their sentence had been completed, they could qualify; if they were still serving it, they could not. The position of slaves was gradually being improved throughout the second century. It had been a notable advance when Antoninus Pius had made a master

[1] *Digest.*, 28, 4, 3.

liable to trial for the murder of his own slave, which previously had not been the case, as the slave was simply regarded as a chattel; and Marcus' 'partiality for freedom', noted by Marcellus, operated in their favour.[1]

A case which came up in February 169 illustrates Marcus' continuing concern for slaves. In a will the slaves had been made heirs to an estate, and were described as 'freedmen', although there was no explicit mention of their being set free. Marcus decided that 'the favourable interpretation' should be put on it: they were to be free and to inherit. A number of other cases from the middle period of the reign show Marcus following the same principles. A particular difficulty always arose when no one would accept an inheritance because of the debts that went with it. Marcus did his best to make sure that slaves freed under such wills did in fact achieve their freedom, and added an interesting rider to a judgment in one such case: 'In case the benefit afforded by this rescript is rendered ineffectual in another way, by the Imperial Treasury (*Fiscus*) laying claim to the property, let it be hereby known to those engaged in our service that the cause of liberty is to be preferred to pecuniary advantage. . . .' The same attitude is expressed in another case involving the award of freedom to a slave who was to be called to present a financial statement of his stewardship: 'It seems fairer that liberty should be awarded to Trophimus on the basis of the testamentary request (*fideicommissum*), as it was agreed that it was given without the condition of rendering the accounts, and it is not humane that delay should be made in a question of liberty because of a money matter. An arbitrator must, however, be appointed by the praetor, before whom he must render the account which he appears to have administered.' A great many cases illustrate continuing concern over trustees and guardians. One particularly interesting case reveals Marcus' attitude on an important general principle. 'There is extant a decree of the deified Marcus in these words: "The best course for you if you think that you have any legal demand is to bring it to the test of a legal action." Marcianus replied that he had used no violence. The emperor replied: "Do you think that there is no violence except

[1] *Digest.*, 48, 18, 27; 48, 19, 33.

where people are wounded? It is just as much a case of violence whenever a man who thinks that he has a right to something demands to have it given up to him without going to the courts. So if anyone is shown to me to be in possession of or to have taken, recklessly or without judicial authority, anything belonging to his debtor, or money which was owing to him, and so to have laid down the law for himself – he shall lose his rights as a creditor." [1]

A straightforward case which came before Marcus throws an interesting light on a rather distasteful development in Roman law. A housebreaker who happened to have the rank of knight was punished by being banished from his native province of Africa, from the city of Rome and from Italy, for five years; and it is added here that the penalty for *honestiores* (literally 'the more honourable ones') must not exceed five years' banishment. The term *honestiores* is used for the upper classes, as opposed to the *humiliores* (literally 'more humble ones'). By the second century A.D. it really had become the case that there was 'one law for the rich and one law for the poor', at least so far as punishment went. Even in capital cases penalties or sentences varied strictly according to the rank of the convicted person – and rank depended in the long run on wealth. These scales of rank were becoming gradually more stratified, and it is in fact just during the reign of Marcus that various titles of rank hitherto used unofficially and informally, such as *vir clarissimus* (meaning roughly 'right honourable') for senators and corresponding titles for various grades of knight, first seem to have become official. Imperial procurators began at this period to describe their rank in terms of the salary which went with it.[2]

It might be wondered how much attention the emperor in person would give to legal decision, particularly in relatively trifling cases of private or criminal law. He had, after all, eminent legal advisers. The case of Valerius Nepos indicates however that Marcus did make a personal effort – with the revealing description of the emperor withdrawing to ponder his decision in privacy. But the administration of

---

[1] *Cod. Just.*, 6, 27, 2; *Inst.*, 3, 11, 1; *Digest.*, 40, 5, 37; 4, 2, 13.

[2] *Digest.*, 48, 18, 1, *pr.* On the appearance of class distinctions in Roman law, cf. G. Cardascia, *Revue hist. de droit français et étranger*, 28, 1950, 305 ff., 461 ff.

the provinces must have occupied most of his time; although the war in the east was nominally under the direction of Lucius, the two emperors were joint commanders-in-chief and Marcus contributed close and detailed attention to its conduct.[1]

[1] *Digest.*, 37, 14, 17: The consultation of Volusius Maecianus and Salvius Julianus is specifically mentioned. Scaevola is mentioned by the biographer. On the lawyers, cf. esp. W. Kunkel, *Herkunft und soziale Stellung der römischen Juristen*, Weimar, 1952, esp. 157 ff. (on Julianus).

VII

TRIUMPH AND CRISIS

IN A.D. 165 the Romans thrust into Mesopotamia. Cassius forced the crossing of the Euphrates at Zeugma, took his army across on a bridge of boats, and passed on into the principality of Osrhoene. Meanwhile, another force, probably under Martius Verus, crossed the river further south, then proceeded on down the left bank aiming for Dura-Europos, an originally Greek city re-fortified by the Parthians, with a flourishing commercial and agricultural life. Here there was a bloody encounter, with much loss of life. Further north the main Parthian forces under Vologases opposed Cassius' advance, but he managed to press on, taking Edessa and Nisibis. When one or both of the Roman armies reached the Tigris the Parthian general Chosrhoes only escaped by swimming the river and taking refuge in a cave. The two invading columns united for an assault on the twin Parthian capitals, Seleuceia and Ctesiphon. Seleuceia was occupied and later sacked. At Ctesiphon the royal palace was destroyed.[1]

Cassius' army was suffering from shortage of supplies and from disease – some men had contracted the plague at Seleuceia – but he led the united force back in good order. Laurelled dispatches were sent to Rome announcing the victory. Lucius took the title Parthicus Maximus – 'greatest conqueror of Parthia' – and he and Marcus became Imperator III.[2]

A number of changes had, inevitably, taken place in the administration of the eastern provinces as a result of the war. Pontus-

[1] Suidas, *s.v.* ζεῦγμα (from Dio); Dio, 71, 2; Lucian, *quom. hist. conscr.*, 19, 20, 28, 30; *v. Veri*, 7, 1; Dessau, *ILS*, 1097–8 (Fronto).
[2] *v. Veri*, 8, 2–4; *BMC*, IV, M. Aurelius and L. Verus, Nos. 384 ff., 1248 ff., 1271 ff.

Bithynia in the north of Asia Minor was governed at the opening of the reign by annual proconsuls of praetorian rank, chosen directly by the senate. Its importance as a supply base and line of communications with the west made it essential to place it under direct imperial rule. The people of Pontus, in the north, were wild and somewhat intractable, and a young regimental commander from Upper Pannonia, named Marcus Valerius Maximianus, was placed on the Black Sea coast to supervise difficult areas which might have been susceptible to brigandage and piracy in time of war. The Bithynians were a sophisticated and volatile people. Their rich cities were continually engaged in rivalry over precedence and status, and frequently ran into debt through over-ambitious civic development projects. The joint province was therefore placed under a governor of consular rank, appointed by, and responsible to, the emperors. The governor in A.D. 165 – who may well have been appointed at the opening of the war – was L. Lollianus Avitus, consul nearly twenty years before, in A.D. 144. He had already been proconsul of Africa and came from a noble family. The choice of such a distinguished man might perhaps have compensated the provincials for any fancied indignity at being returned to direct governmental rule. But they were no doubt quite glad, as there was less chance of corruption in the administration. The real reason for the choice of so senior a man was probably simply the shortage of suitably qualified men nearer the normal age. The resources of the senate were at full stretch with the extra needs created by the war. For this very reason the province of Nearer Spain (Tarraconensis) was also governed by some rather senior men at this time. The younger men were needed in more active roles. In Bithynia-Pontus Lollianus Avitus had some trouble from Alexander the 'prophet', but the influence of Alexander's distinguished son-in-law Rutilianus made it impossible for any action to be taken against him.[1]

To compensate the senate for the loss of a province, the emperors transferred Lycia-Pamphylia to proconsuls, thus maintaining the

[1] Avitus: *PIR 2*, H 40. Maximianus: *AE*, 1956, 128. Spain: note especially Salvius Julianus (Dessau, *ILS*, 8973). Changes of status: *v. Marci*, 22, 9, on which cf. A. R. Birley, *A. Ant. Philip.*, 1963, 109 ff.

balance neatly. One other administrative change may belong to this period. The great trading city of Palmyra on the eastern frontiers of the province of Syria, which still retained a great deal of independence and organized most of the overland trade between Babylonia and Syria, was placed under the administration of a *logistes*, Fulvius Titianus, who could be the same Titianus mentioned by Lucian as one of the men who played a role in the eastern war.[1]

By late A.D. 165 the end of the war was in sight. Lucius was jubilant and was making arrangements for Fronto to write the official history. He directed Avidius Cassius and Martius Verus to draw up memoranda for him, which he promised to send to Fronto, and asked whether he should prepare material himself. He showed his vanity plainly when he asked Fronto 'to dwell at length on the causes and the opening stages of the war, and especially on our lack of success in my absence. Take your time to come to my share. Further, I think it necessary to make crystal clear how greatly superior the Parthians were before my arrival, so that the scale of my achievement will be apparent. . . . In conclusion – my achievements are no greater than they actually are. But they can be made to seem as great as you would have them seem.'[2] Statius Priscus is not mentioned in this correspondence, and, indeed, is not heard of again after his successes in Armenia, so it seems likely that he had died, or retired. This would not be surprising, considering that he had seen active service as a young man in the Jewish war of Hadrian. Not every Roman general could be so robust as Pontius Laelianus and Julius Verus.

Avidius Cassius sent one of his tribunes, Junius Maximus, to see Fronto. Maximus was full of Cassius' achievements. Writing to Cassius, Fronto told him of the meeting: 'he appeared in every sphere a tireless eulogist of your labours, your plans, your hard

---

[1] Titianus: *AE*, 1947, 146; cf. Lucian, *quom. hist. conscr.*, 21 (there are alternatives, cf. *PIR* 2, C 1043-4, and *CIL*, III, 537). Lycia-Pamphylia: *AE*, 1927, 88; 1929, 85 (Pudens, a proconsul, dated by D. Magie, *Roman Rule in Asia Minor*, Princeton, 1950, II, 1598, to this period, rightly in my opinion. I regard the legate of the year A.D. 178, recorded in *CIL*, XVI, 128, as having been sent there for a special purpose, see below, p. 266. For a different view, cf. G. Barbieri, *Riv. di Fil.*, 66, 1938, 365 ff.).

[2] Fronto, *ad Verum Imp.*, 2, 3=Haines, II, 194 ff.

work and your sleepless care. In fact, when he came to see me – when I was far from well – in my country house just outside the city, he did not cease till nightfall from telling tale after tale of your expeditionary marches and the discipline which you had restored and kept up to the ancient standard; then your most strenuous vigour in leading the column and your deliberate care in choosing the right moment to join battle. . . . He spoke of you with love and the utmost loyalty', he concluded, 'and he deserves your affection and to profit from your patronage.'[1]

In the autumn or winter Marcus suffered a blow in the loss of one of the twins, Antoninus, who died at the age of four. Marcus had learned from Apollonius 'to be always the same, even at the loss of a child', and obviously he will have borne this in accordance with his Stoic creed. It was harder for Faustina, and as Lucilla was pregnant, it was decided to let her go out to the east to be with her daughter, taking some of the other children. (This seems the probable order of events, but it may be that she went out before the death of Antoninus.)[2]

At about the same time Fronto too was bereaved, by the loss of his three-year-old grandson (whom he had never seen) following a few months after the death of his wife, Gratia. The old man was desperately upset, and unlike his Stoic pupil showed his distress openly. Marcus wrote him a brief letter of consolation: 'I have just learnt of your loss. Since I always suffer torment when a single joint of yours is aching, my master, what do you think I feel when it is your heart that is aching? I am so upset that I can only think of asking you to keep safe for me my sweetest of masters, in whom I have greater solace for this life than you can find sorrow from any source. I have not written this with my own hand, because this evening after my bath even my hand is trembling.'

Fronto's letter of reply was full of bitterness at his fate. He had lost five children himself. Each was an only child, so that he never had a child born except while bereaved of another. Yet somehow he

[1] *ad amicos*, 1, 6=Haines, II, 190 ff.
[2] *v. Comm.*, 1, 4 (the sole mention); Fronto, *ad Verum Imp.*, 2, 4=Haines, II, 236 ('socrum et liberos vestros') records the presence of Faustina in the east.

had borne these afflictions. Now – 'as my Victorinus weeps, I waste and melt away. Often I even make protest to the immortal gods and reproach the fates. For Victorinus, a man of loyalty, gentleness, sincerity and complete innocence of life, a man of conspicuous accomplishments in all the noblest arts, to be thus afflicted by the most cruel death of his son – was this in any sense fair or just?' He questioned the meaning of 'Providence' and 'Fate'. But he could reflect a little further: 'Unless perhaps quite another error misleads us, and through ignorance of the truth we are coveting what is evil as though it were good, turning away from what is good as though it were harmful – and death itself, which seems to everyone a thing of grief, which brings pause to our labours, our anxieties, our troubles, in fact transports us, freed from the miserable chains of the body, to calm and pleasant assemblies of souls, supplied with all good things. That this is the case I would rather believe, than that all human affairs are governed by no providence – or by an unfair one.'

Thus he attempted to console himself. But the presence with him of another grandson, instead of helping him, tormented him more – 'for in his features I see the one that was lost, I imagine I see a copy of his face, I fancy I hear the same sound of his voice in my mind. . . . Not knowing the real appearance of the dead child I torture myself trying to imagine what he was like.' He knew that his daughter would get over the loss. As for himself – 'it would have been more fitting if I had died first myself. . . . But I console myself with the thought that my life is now almost complete and death is near.' He felt that he had lived honourably and well and reflected on his life. At the end of the letter the grief broke in again: 'I have suffered much and seriously from ill-health, my dearest Marcus. Then, afflicted with the most miserable disasters, I have lost my wife, I have lost my grandson in Germany. . . . If I were of iron, I could not write you any more at this time. I have sent you a book which you can take as representing my thoughts.'[1]

Fronto wrote to Lucius at this time as well: 'Worn out as I am with long drawn out and more than usually serious ill-health, and

---

[1] *de nepote amisso*, 1–2=Haines, II, 232 ff.

afflicted too with the most distressing sorrows which have come almost continuously – for in the space of a very few months I have lost both my dearest wife and my three-year-old grandson – in spite of all these blows, still I confess I am a little restored to know that you are remembering me and have been wanting something of mine.' He sent him a copy of one of his speeches, chosen by Marcus, and added: 'Your brother also earnestly discussed with me the thing that I am still more earnestly anxious to undertake, and as soon as you send me your memoranda I will get down to work with the best will in the world.' He was referring, of course, to the projected history.[1]

At the end of A.D. 165 or the beginning of A.D. 166 the relaxation of urgency in the war, with Rome now clearly superior, allowed the return to other duties in the west of a number of the generals. Julius Verus, the governor of Syria, and Claudius Fronto, the successful army commander, returned to Italy with an urgent mission, the recruitment of two new legions, intended for service in the forth-coming northern campaigns, which Marcus realized could not be delayed much longer. In the past – and in the future – the raising of new legions, which was generally done in Italy itself (although the regular recruitment for existing units was by now mostly done in their province of garrison), was generally a prelude to new conquests, the inclusion of new territory within the empire. The raising of a new Second and Third legion was clearly no exception. Marcus must have had far-reaching plans. Iallius Bassus, *comes* of Lucius, was also released from his duties, and was sent to the Danube with a new assignment, the governorship of the most important province along the whole northern frontier, Upper Pannonia. He had already governed Lower Pannonia, which was sometimes considered suffi-cient preliminary training in provincial government for governors of the Upper province. But Bassus had also governed Lower Moesia and had been in the eastern wars. At about the same time, or shortly afterwards, another experienced man, like Avidius Cassius of Syrian origin, was sent to govern Lower Pannonia. This was Tiberius Claudius Pompeianus, son of a knight from Antioch.

[1] *ad Verum Imp.*, 2, 9=Haines, II, 232 ff.

He was to play an important role in the years to come.[1]

In A.D. 166 came the final demonstration of Roman might when the Parthian kingdom was invaded again. This time an assault was made across the northern Tigris, into Media, homeland of the ancient rulers of the east. The new victories of Cassius' armies led Lucius to take a further title, Medicus; meanwhile Marcus accepted the title won in A.D. 165, Parthicus Maximus, and both became Imperator IV. Cassius' victories in the far-off lands beyond the Tigris set people in the east talking. It was rumoured that he had crossed the Indus with one of the Syrian legions, the Third, and some German and Moorish auxiliaries. According to Lucian, one of the many writers who had cashed in on the war by producing histories of it actually included such an episode.

As a matter of fact, in this year, A.D. 166, some Romans did penetrate to the east, in fact very much further than to the Indus – to the court of the Celestial Emperor. Chinese annals record that in this year ambassadors from 'Ngan-touen', or 'An-toun', i.e. Marcus Antoninus, ruler of T'a-ts'in' (one of the Chinese names for the Roman empire), brought gifts for the emperor: ivory, rhinoceros horn and tortoise shell. They had come by 'Ji-nam', i.e. Annam, not by the northern route. (A gold medallion of Marcus has been found near Saigon.) Clearly the 'ambassadors' were freelance traders, probably from Alexandria, who had acquired their gifts on their journey, rather than official envoys. But the episode is interesting, for all that. There is no mention of it in Roman sources.[2]

Fronto wrote to congratulate Lucius: 'although it has for a long time now been wearying and painful for me to go on living, with this ill-health of mine, yet when I see you return with such great glory gained by your own excellence, I will not have lived in vain, and will

---

[1] Julius Verus: *AE*, 1956, 123. Claudius Fronto: *PIR 2*, C 874. Pompeianus: *PIR 2*, C 973. Bassus: Dio, 71, 3, 1a (cf. W. Zwikker, *Studien zur Markussäule*, Amsterdam, 1941, 77, 81, 87, 160). The new legions: see now J. C. Mann, *Hermes*, 91, 1963, 483 ff.

[2] *BMC*, IV, M. Aurelius and L. Verus, Nos. 401 ff. The title Medicus is not much found on the coinage (*BMC*, IV, p. 597), but is recorded on many inscriptions. India: Lucian, *quom, hist. conscr.*, 31. China: see J. O. Thomson, *A History of Ancient Geography*, Cambridge, 1948, 312.

not be unwilling to live on for as long as life is granted to me. Farewell, my Lord, whom I long for so much.' He added greetings to Faustina, and to the children of both of them. Lucilla must have borne Lucius a child before he returned. As some sixteen years later Lucilla evidently had a son-in-law, it was probably a daughter.[1]

The date of Lucius' return and the exact circumstances of the conclusion of hostilities are not recorded. But the Misenum fleet was still lying off the mouth of the Orontes at the end of May 166, so it was later than this. In any case, Lucius could not well have returned until the Median campaign was over and peace had been made. Rome could now have annexed Mesopotamia, as Severus was to do thirty years later. But Severus placed two newly raised legions there as a garrison, and the legions that were being formed at this moment in Italy were intended to serve elsewhere. Two individual cities, Dura-Europos and Carrhae, became Roman colonies. Otherwise native rulers were installed who recognized Roman overlordship. The most important result of the campaign was the securing of Roman authority in Armenia, always the prime Roman interest in the east. The invasion of the Parthian kingdom had been intended to teach the Parthians this lesson, after Vologases had refused to negotiate.[2]

The European legions could now return to their bases. I Minervia returned to Bonn and II Adiutrix to Budapest, where it came under Claudius Pompeianus. But V Macedonica did not return to its old base at Troesmis in Lower Moesia. It was sent instead across the Danube to Dacia, to be stationed at Potaissa. The three Dacian provinces were now reunited, and as the combined province now had two legions as its garrison (XIII Gemina was at Apulum in western Dacia), it was assigned to a governor of consular rank. The first governor was Sextus Calpurnius Agricola, fresh from his experience in Britain.[3]

[1] ad Verum Imp., 2, 4=Haines, II, 236; cf. H.-G. Pflaum, J. des Savants, 1961, 33 ff.

[2] C. G. Starr, The Roman Imperial Navy, Ithaca, 1941, 188 ff. In general, cf. D. Magie, op. cit., I, 659 ff.

[3] PW, 12, 1924, 1297 ff. (art. legio). PIR 2, C 249. I find unsatisfactory the suggestion by H.-G. Pflaum, CRAI, 1956, 189 ff., that the first governor of the reunited Dacia was Aufidius Victorinus.

Avidius Cassius was now made governor of Syria (he may also well have succeeded Julius Verus when the latter left the east), and Martius Verus, who had received the consulate in the spring of A.D. 166, became governor of Cappadocia. When these dispositions had been made, Lucius could return. He did so with reluctance. Although the Syrians had made fun of him, and jokes about him had been heard at the stage performances which he patronized so avidly, he felt he was leaving his own kingdom when he had to return to Rome.[1]

Fronto, of course, was awaiting his arrival eagerly, and this pleased Lucius: 'why should I not picture to myself your joy, my dearest master. Indeed I seem to myself to see you hugging me tightly and kissing me many times,' he wrote. When he finally arrived, the favour shown to Fronto created a certain amount of ill-feeling, in spite of careful effort to avoid causing anyone jealousy. Everyone was eager to greet the conquering hero. Still, Fronto was gratified: 'this honour which you reserved for me I regard as far outweighing everything. Many a time besides this have I noted the special honour which you have shown me by what you have done and said. I value in the highest possible way the many times you have supported me with your hands, lifted me up when I could hardly walk through my weakness; your ever cheerful and friendly look when you speak to me, your readiness to talk to me and your readiness to continue our conversation so long, your unwillingness to end it. . . . Therefore whatever favours I have had to ask from my Lord your brother I have preferred to ask and obtain through you.'[2] This is the last surviving letter of Fronto to either of his imperial pupils, and he must have died soon after this. There are a few further letters from him, to some of his friends – commending one friend, Sardius Saturninus, to another, Caelius Optatus (then governing Fronto's native province); commending Saturninus' son Lupus to Petronius Mamertinus; a friendly letter to the young man he had met recently, Junius Maximus; a letter to his friend Squilla Gallicanus,

---

[1] v. *Veri*, 7, 8–9; *PIR* 2, A 1402 (Cassius); *PW*, 14, 1930, 2024 ff. (Martius Verus).
[2] Fronto, *ad Verum Imp.*, 2, 5=Haines, II, 236; 2, 8=Haines, II, 238 ff.

congratulating him on the successful oratorical debut of his son, Fronto's pupil.[1] Fronto did not complete his history of the Parthian war. Only a Preface survives. He may not even have survived to see the triumph celebrated.[2]

Fronto and his contemporaries might have been piqued had they suspected the unfavourable modern verdict on his style. But Fronto would perhaps have been content to have been remembered as the imperial tutor, praised by Marcus for his insistence on sincerity and humanity, praised by Lucius who was glad to say that he had learned from his master 'sincerity and the love of truth far before the discipline of polite speaking'. It is not known who was responsible for the preservation and publication of the correspondence, but Fronto's memory and name survived with Victorinus, and some fifty years after his death his grandson, Marcus Aufidius Fronto, commemorating a son who died young, proudly described him as 'greatgrandson of Cornelius Fronto, consul, master of the emperors Lucius and Antoninus'. So it was probably the family of Fronto that preserved this record of an attractive friendship, and thus revealed intimate details of the family life of Marcus.[3]

The triumph for the eastern victories was held on October 12. On this day the young prince Commodus, now aged five, and his brother Annius Verus, aged three, were given the name or title of Caesar at the request of Lucius. They and some of Marcus' daughters rode in the triumphal procession. At the same time Marcus and Lucius were awarded the 'civic crown' of oak leaves, presumably by the senate. This was given 'for saving the lives of fellow-citizens' – in their case, clearly, by their wise conduct of the campaigns. They also each received the title 'pater patriae', 'father of the fatherland', which had been offered to Marcus during the war; but he had

---

[1] *ad amicos*, I, 9; I, 10; I, 20; I, 24; I, 25=Haines, II, 240 ff. The dating of these letters is hypothetical.

[2] The date suggested in *PIR* 2, C 1364 (not before the end of A.D. 176) is based solely on an unusually perverse interpretation of *de orationibus*, 12= Haines, II, 114 (line 1).

[3] *Med.*, I, 11. See Haines, I, ix ff., for the fame of Fronto, also p. 19 above; Dessau, *ILS*, 1129.

deferred acceptance of it until his brother's return. The successful generals and others who had participated in the campaigns were decorated appropriately, according to their rank. Furius Victorinus, the prefect of the guard, received 'three Crowns, four headless spears and four siege standards'. Pontius Laelianus, as a consular, received the same decorations, as did Claudius Fronto, for he had become consul between his returning to Italy and the triumph.[1]

Rome had not seen a triumphal procession for nearly fifty years, not since the slightly bizarre triumph celebrated by Hadrian in honour of the dead Trajan, when Trajan's effigy was paraded through the streets. The arrangements were presumably those by now standard, of which the most celebrated illustration comes from the Arch of Titus in Rome, depicting the destroyer of Jerusalem riding in triumph through the streets of Rome, while the seven-branched candlestick and the table of the shewbread are carried before him with the other spoils. In the procession of Marcus and Lucius, without doubt, the senate and magistrates walked. There would be trumpeters, white oxen to be sacrificed, the spoils taken from the enemy laden on wagons, and perhaps pictures illustrating exciting moments in the war, captives in chains, and lictors, behind which came the chariot of the *triumphatores*, dressed in a special costume, carrying sceptres, with crowns on their heads and their faces painted red. Behind them marched their armies (or representatives of their armies). If tradition were followed, a slave stood immediately behind the *triumphator*, whispering 'remember that thou art a mortal', while the army and the people cried out 'Io, Triumphe!' The route followed by the procession began outside the city, beyond the Vatican, at the Porta Triumphalis, went down the Via Triumphalis and across the Tiber, passed the Circus Flaminius, into the Forum, and along the Sacred Way, where the emperors would descend from their four-horse chariot to deposit the laurels of victory in the lap of the statue of Jupiter on the Capitol.[2]

---

[1] *v. Marci*, 12, 7–9, with *v. Comm.*, 11, 13, gives the date. *PIR* 2, F 584 (Victorinus). Dessau, *ILS*, 1094+1100 (Laelianus). *PIR* 2, C 874 (Claudius Fronto).

[2] *v. Had.*, 6, 3. Mommsen, *Staatsrecht*, I², 412.

In spite of the lavish public celebration of the eastern victories, Marcus must have realized that the four-year-long war had been an expensive and ultimately unnecessary interlude. Had it not been for the rash action of Sedatius Severianus, 'that foolish Celt', diplomacy and a vigorous show of force might have produced the results which had been obtained by bitter and lengthy fighting. Admittedly, Rome's relations with her dangerous but unwieldy eastern neighbour seem always to have followed a consistent pattern, with Rome engaged in serious hostilities at fairly regular intervals to maintain her influence in the vital client-states of which Armenia was the largest. There may too have been hidden factors, such as the need by Rome to keep trade-routes with Central Asia and the Far East free from Parthian interference – such causes are generally not mentioned in Roman sources, but they may have influenced the emperors. The shock to Roman prestige at Elegeia had made a war in the east inevitable. As it turned out it was conducted with some success and it provided officers and men with valuable fighting experience for what was to come in the north. But it delayed Rome's response to the situation building up in Central Europe for a shade too long.

After the triumph, more entertainment was provided for the urban populace at Rome, in the shape of games in the Circus. Marcus had perhaps mastered his boredom and dislike of these occasions. The biographer records that 'among other illustrations of his consideration for others this too must be mentioned: after a boy tight-rope walker had fallen, he ordered that safety mattresses should be spread out – this is the reason why safety nets are stretched out today'. Dio also records something of Marcus' attitude to public spectacles. 'So averse was he to bloodshed that he even used to watch the gladiators at Rome contend, like athletes, without endangering their lives – for he never gave any of them a sharp weapon, but they all fought with blunted weapons, like buttoned foils. And so far from allowing bloodshed was he that although he did give orders, at the request of the people, that a certain lion, which had been trained to eat people, should be brought on, he did not look at it and would not give the trainer his freedom, in spite of the persistent demands of the spectators. Instead he ordered a proclamation to be made that the man had not done anything which deserved to win him his freedom.'[1]

When the festivities were over there was pressing public business to attend to. The situation in the north was finally reaching the predicted breaking point. The tribes bordering the empire were being subjected to unbearable pressure from their wilder neighbours in the far north. Big movements of population had begun, including, probably, that which was to take the Goths from Scandinavia to southern Russia. The tribes immediately beyond the Rhine and Danube had been submitted to a Roman protectorate for a century and a half. There had been moments when it had broken down, and on occasion serious warfare, but for the most part the system worked well. An illustration of its smooth operation had been seen early in the reign of Pius, that master of Roman diplomacy. To a certain extent this had forced on these barbarian peoples a degree of peaceful behaviour to which they were ill adapted. Their population had clearly expanded beyond the means of their primitive agricultural techniques. Now the pressure from beyond was forcing them out of their own lands. They were ready to invade – and they wanted land. They wanted to settle, not merely to raid and plunder.

Some time in late A.D. 166 or early 167 the first invasion came. Six thousand Langobardi and Obii burst into Pannonia. A rapid Roman combined operation, under a young cavalry officer named Macrinius Avitus Catonius Vindex and an infantry force under a certain Candidus, swept them out again. Eleven tribes sent envoys to Iallius Bassus, governor of Upper Pannonia, sueing for peace, choosing as their spokesman the king of the Marcomanni, Ballomarius. The envoys made peace, which they ratified with oaths, and returned home. The situation was apparently in hand. The victorious troops had hailed Marcus and Lucius as Imperator for the fifth time, it would seem, but the title Imp. V did not appear regularly in their official titulature until A.D. 168. Possibly there was

---

[1] *v. Marci*, 12, 9–12 (note 15, 1 – jokes about his dealing with documents while at the games). Dio. 71, 29, 4.

hesitation at accepting it for a comparatively minor success; possibly subsequent reverses were to make it seem, at first, a hollow victory.[1] Without doubt Marcus intended to set off for the north in person in A.D. 167. But he was prevented from doing so by a new and particularly pressing threat – the plague. This had been caught first by the army in Mesopotamia, and the returning troops spread it all over the empire. 'It was his fate', the biographer says of Lucius, 'to bring the plague with him to those provinces through which he made his return journey, right up to Rome.' Wild stories circulated about the pestilence as its effect was felt further and further afield. It was believed that a soldier had accidentally cut open a golden casket containing the dread vapour in the temple of Apollo at Seleuceia. Cassius too was blamed: he had sacked Seleuceia in violation of an agreement, after the city had received the Roman soldiers as friends. The plague was a punishment sent by the city's protecting deity. Alexander the 'prophet' cashed in again on the public anxiety, selling magic apotropaic charms to pin to doorposts – 'guaranteed to keep out the plague'. But they had no effect. 'From the frontiers of the Persians as far as to the Rhine and Gaul,' wrote Ammianus Marcellinus two centuries later, 'the foul touch of plague polluted everything with contagion and death.' Orosius, the fifth-century cataloguer of pagan misfortunes (who may therefore have had cause to exaggerate a little), is even more graphic: 'such great pestilence devastated all Italy that everywhere estates, fields, and towns were left deserted, without cultivators or inhabitants, and relapsed into ruins and woodland.'[2]

The effect and scale of this epidemic are a matter of dispute; and it is not even known for certain what disease it was – smallpox, exanthematous typhus, and bubonic plague have been suggested in modern times. Certainly the sources are unanimous in describing it as

[1] Dio, 71, 3, 1a (cf. Dessau, *ILS*, 1107). IMP V: *CIL*, XVI, 123 (167); *BMC*, IV, M. Aurelius and L. Verus, Nos. 458, etc. (168). In general, see W. Zwikker, op. cit., 35 ff., and P. Oliva, *Pannonia and the Onset of Crisis in the Roman Empire*, Praha, 1962, 259 ff.

[2] *v. Marci*, 13, 3–6; 17, 2; 21, 6–7; *v. Veri*, 8, 1–4; Lucian, *Alexander*, 36; Amm. Marc., 31, 6, 24; Orosius, 7, 15, 5–6; 27, 7. For further references and a very detailed discussion, see J. F. Gilliam, *AJPh*, 82, 1961, 225 ff.

exceptionally destructive of human life. One of those sources is the great doctor Galen, who was in Rome in A.D. 166, and left soon to return to his native Pergamum, fairly certainly to avoid the plague. But it has been modern scholars who have concluded that it was the most serious plague in the whole of antiquity, and a major factor in the decline of Rome. This view is probably exaggerated. But of course the effect of the plague was startling and severe, especially in its effect in the capital, by far the most densely populated place in the empire, and on the army, which, living in barracks, was particularly susceptible. The loss of life there was very serious. Marcus was later able to look more calmly on the plague: 'the corruption of the mind is a pestilence, much more indeed than any such corruption and change of the air which surrounds us. For this corruption [i.e. the plague] is a pestilence of animals in so far as they are animals; corruption of the mind is a pestilence to men as human beings,' he wrote in his *Meditations*. But the plague was troubling him on his deathbed thirteen years later, and in Rome in A.D. 167 it must have been his foremost consideration.[1]

The biographer gives a confused but graphic description of the situation in the city at the time. 'The dead were carried away on carts and wagons. At this time, moreover, the emperors enacted the most stringent laws on burying the dead and on tombs; no one was permitted to build a tomb at his country villa (a law still in force today). And indeed the plague carried off many thousands, including many prominent figures. Antoninus erected statues to the most eminent of these. Such too was his kindliness of heart that he ordered funeral ceremonies for the common people to be carried on, even at public expense. There was one foolish person who, with a number of accomplices, was trying to create the opportunity for wholesale burglary. He stood by the wild fig-tree in the Campus Martius, making speeches all the time to the effect that fire was going to come down from heaven and the end of the world would

[1] Gilliam, op. cit., gives the references in Galen. He argues that the effect and scale of the outbreak has been greatly exaggerated (but see F. Millar, *A Study of Cassius Dio*, Oxford, 13, n. 4, for a weakness in one of G.'s arguments). For the various theories as to its nature, cf. Gilliam, 227, n. 8. Marcus on the plague: *Med.*, 9, 2 (cf. *v. Marci*, 28, 4).

come if he were to fall down from the tree and turn into a stork. Of course at the appointed time he fell down and let a stork out from a fold in his clothes. He was hauled off to the emperor, and confessed to the whole business. But the emperor pardoned him.'

Naturally a good deal of the legal activity of this time was concerned with the plague and its effect. It was normally prohibited to carry a body through towns, but when Marcus was asked to adjudicate in a case where this had been infringed he replied that 'those who have transported the body of a man who died on a journey through villages or a town do not deserve punishment, although such things ought not to be done without the permission of the relevant authorities'. The cemeteries were obviously becoming overcrowded, and Marcus and Lucius had to issue an edict to prevent unlawful appropriation of other people's graves: 'a body which had been delivered to a lawful sepulchre, that is, has been covered with earth, must not be disturbed'. In a rescript Marcus declared that 'the heir who prohibits the man chosen by the testator to conduct the funeral from doing so, is not acting rightly'. But he added that there was no statutory penalty for this. Quite what was involved is not clear. But it is possible that the price of funerals and tombs had enormously increased and that those who had been left money preferred to make their own arrangements to deal with the remains of their benefactors, realizing that the carrying out of the full testamentary instructions would greatly diminish the value of the bequest. Another rescript of Marcus and Lucius illustrates the shortage of burial space. It was illegal to buy and sell sepulchres, but it was ruled that 'if the monument has not yet been used (i.e. for burial), anyone may sell it or give it away; or if it is a cenotaph it can be sold, for this is not religiously consecrated'. This was contrary to a previous ruling. Another by-product of the increased death-rate was a rescript excusing those who were attending funeral ceremonies from answering a summons to court.[1]

The man who made his ridiculous speech of warning in the Campus Martius for his own ends had rightly gauged the hysterical temper of the urban populace; and wild stories had, of course,

[1] *v. Marci*, 13, 3-6; *Digest.*, 1, 8, 6, 5; 1, 8, 7; 2, 4, 3.

been circulating about the plague being some form of retribution from the gods. To satisfy this feeling in the obvious way Marcus 'summoned priests from all sides', the biographer records, 'performed foreign religious rites and purified the city in every way. The Roman ceremony of the feast of the gods' – the *lectisternium*, an ancient ceremony at which statues of the gods were placed on banqueting-couches in public places and offerings were placed on a table before them – 'was celebrated for seven days'. The religious ceremonies of A.D. 167 necessitated the presence of the emperor, who was, apart from anything else, the *pontifex maximus*. Also, his presence was an important factor in maintaining public morale. But the measures necessary in A.D. 166 and 167 delayed Marcus' departure for the northern front.[1] An *expeditio Germanica* had been prepared, but the *profectio* of the emperors had to be postponed.

The pressure had shifted a little in the north in A.D. 167. During the summer the gold mines in western Dacia (Rosia Montana in Transylvania) were attacked. Local records ceased there with an inscription of May 29. Calpurnius Agricola clearly had fighting to do. V Macedonica saw action under his command and so, no doubt, did XIII Gemina, the legion nearer to the disturbances. Meanwhile in Pannonia the situation had eased. On May 5 Claudius Pompeianus was able to discharge time-expired veterans of some of the auxiliary units under his command. One of the discharge certificates issued then has survived, and on it Marcus and Lucius bear for the first recorded time the new title Imp. V. The situation was sufficiently well in hand for legionaries of the newly returned II Adiutrix to be able to concentrate on road-repair projects.[2]

Lucius had opened the year A.D. 167 as consul for the third time, an honour which made him equal in one respect to Marcus. His colleague was M. Ummidius Quadratus, Marcus' nephew. But his official duties only occupied him for a few months of the winter at

---

[1] *v. Marci*, 13, 1–2 (cf. W. Zwikker, op. cit., 63 ff.).
[2] *CIL*, III, pp. 921–60 (the gold-mines); Dessau, *ILS*, 2311 (V Macedonica); *CIL*, XVI, 123 (Pompeianus); *CIL*, III, 10615, 10632, 10638 (Aquincum-Sirmium road: a useful preparatory measure for a Roman offensive).

the most. After his return from the war he was eager to relax, and 'behaved with less regard for his brother', according to the biographer, 'for he indulged his freedmen in a rather shameful manner and settled many matters without consulting his brother'. His behaviour left a great deal to be desired – to judge from the biographer's account: 'He brought home actors out of Syria as proudly as if he were bringing foreign monarchs to his triumph. The chief of these was Maximinus, on whom he bestowed the name of Paris' – the name of a favourite actor of Nero. 'Besides this he built a villa on the *via Clodia*, where he indulged with enormous extravagance in orgies for many days, in company with his freedmen and friends of inferior rank in whose presence he felt no shame. In fact he even invited Marcus, who came, to show his brother his own way of life as worthy of respect and imitation. He stayed for five days in that same villa and devoted himself for the entire time to judicial business, while his brother was either banqueting or getting ready for a banquet. Lucius had brought home with him another actor, Agrippus, surnamed Memphius, like a trophy of the Parthian war, to whom he gave the name Apolaustus' – which means 'Enjoyable'; he was manumitted by Lucius, took the names L. Aelius Aurelius Apolaustus Memphius, and had a successful and prosperous career for many years before meeting a sticky end in A.D. 190. Lucius 'had also brought with him harpists and flautists, actors and jesters from the mime-shows, jugglers and all types of slaves whose entertainment Syria and Alexandria feeds on – all in such numbers that he seemed to have won a war not against the Parthians but against the stage profession'.[1] Marcus had to cope with the anxiety of the people of Rome single-handed.

A by-product of the public feeling of the time was probably a spate of accusations against Christians. The 'atheists', renowned, or notorious, for their 'hatred of the human race', might well have been supposed by the superstitious man in the street to be in some way responsible for the wrath of the gods, and, hence, for the plague.

---

[1] *v. Veri*, 8, 6–11. *PIR* 2, A 148 (Apolaustus).

Among the Christians who were martyred at about this time, at any rate, was Justin. In a second *Apology* written later in the A.D. 150's under the impact of death sentences on fellow-Christians by the city prefect Lollius Urbicus, his appeal for clemency had been perhaps more impassioned, and, most interestingly, contained a good deal of reference to Stoicism. St Justin, like other Christian writers of the early period of the Church, found remarkable similarities between Stoicism and Christianity, not least between the Christian Logos, the 'Word' of the opening of St John's Gospel, and the Stoic Logos, the rational principle which governed the universe. Justin and his fellow-martyrs were, ironically, brought for trial before the prefect of the city, the emperor's own instructor in Stoicism, Quintus Junius Rusticus.[1]

Apparently Justin was arrested at the instigation of a Cynic philosopher named Crescens, smarting under the impact of frequent – and public – dialectical defeats at the hands of Justin. What appears to be a verbatim record of the trial has survived. The date is not absolutely certain, but, as argued there are strong *a priori* grounds for assigning it to A.D. 167.

'At the time of the lawless defenders of idolatry, unholy edicts were issued against the holy Christians in the cities and countryside, to compel them to pour libation to the empty idols. The saints were arrested and brought before the prefect of the city of Rome, named Rusticus. When they had been brought before his seat of judgement, Rusticus said: "First, believe in the gods and obey the emperors."

'Justin said: "To believe in the commandments of our Saviour Jesus Christ is not worthy of accusation or reproof."

'Rusticus the prefect said: "What doctrines do you profess?"

'Justin said: "I have tried to study all doctrines and I have adhered to the true doctrines of the Christians, even if they are not pleasing to those who labour under delusions."

'Rusticus the prefect said: "Are those then the doctrines which you find pleasing, you most wretched man?"

'Justin said: "Yes, since I follow them with right belief."

'Rusticus the prefect said: "What is that belief?"

[1] See M. Spanneut, *Le stoïcisme des pères de l'église*, Paris, 1957.

'Justin said: "We worship the God of the Christians, who we believe to be the one creator from the beginning and constructor of all things, visible and invisible, and the Lord Jesus Christ the Son of God, of whom also it was foretold by the prophets, that he would come as the herald of salvation to the race of men, and as the teacher of good pupils. And I, being a man, realize that what I am saying is something tiny in comparison with his boundless divinity. But it was prophesied concerning him whom I now say is the Son of God. For I know that the prophets once prophesied about his coming among men."

'Rusticus the prefect said: "Where do you meet?"

'Justin said: "Where each chooses and is able. Do you think that we all meet together in the same place? No indeed. Because the God of the Christians is not bound by place, but since he is invisible, he fills the heavens and earth and everywhere is worshipped and glorified."

'Rusticus the prefect said: "Tell me, where do you meet, or what place do you collect your pupils together in?"

'Justin said: "I live above the house of one Martin, near the Baths of Timotinus, and during all this time (for this is my second period of residence in Rome) I have not known any other meeting-place than this. And if anyone wanted to come to me, I shared with them the doctrines of the truth."

'Rusticus said: "For the rest, are you not a Christian?"

'Justin said: "Yes, I am a Christian." '

The preliminary examination of Justin over, the prefect questioned Charito, Euelpistus (an imperial slave), Hierax, Paeon and Liberianus. All confessed that they were Christians. Rusticus then turned to Justin again.

'"Listen to me, you are educated, to judge from what you say, and you think that you know what the true doctrines are. If you are flogged and decapitated, do you believe that you will ascend to the heavens?"

'Justin said: "I hope that I will keep my faith in this, if this happens to me. For I know that the divine grace awaits all those who have lived in this way, until the end of the world."

'Rusticus the prefect said: "Do you suspect that you will go up into the heavens and receive some reward?"

'Justin said: "I do not suspect it: I know it, and am most certain of it."

'Rusticus the prefect said: "Well, it now remains to come to the business before us, which is urgent. Come together, and unanimously offer sacrifice to the gods."

'Justin said: "No one in his right mind falls from piety into impiety."

'Rusticus the prefect said: "If you will not obey, you will be punished mercilessly."

'Justin said: "We pray, through our Lord Jesus Christ, that we may be punished, and saved, because this will provide us with salvation and freedom of speech before the most fearful and universal tribunal of our Lord and Saviour." The other martyrs said the same: "Do what you wish, for we are Christians and we do not sacrifice to idols."

'Rusticus the prefect pronounced sentence: "Those who are unwilling to sacrifice to the gods and to obey the command of the Emperor shall be led away and flogged, to suffer capital punishment in accordance with the law."

'The holy martyrs, glorifying God, went out to the accustomed place, and were beheaded, and fulfilled their martyrdom in the confession of their Saviour. And some of the faithful secretly took their bodies away and buried them in a convenient place, with the help of the grace of our Lord Jesus Christ, to whom be glory for age upon age, Amen.'[1]

The pattern followed by the prefect in his interrogation is discernible. First, he establishes that Justin is a Christian. Then, after allowing Justin to enlarge on his belief, he abruptly checks him, and asks where he and his followers meet. This was a question of some importance to the government of any autocratic state. Rome was always particularly suspicious of any clubs and societies, as

---

[1] Eusebius, *Hist. Ecc.*, 4, 16. J. C. T. Otto, *Corp. Apol. Christ. saec. secund.*, III, 262 ff. More recently in R. Knopf-G. Krüger, *Ausgewählte Märtyerakten*, Tübingen, 3rd ed., 1929.

possible breeding-grounds for sedition. After establishing that the others too were Christians, the prefect's intellectual curiosity returns for a moment. He wants to know if the prisoners really believe in life after death, in fact, in the reality of heaven. Again the prefect cuts Justin short – 'to the business before us, which is urgent'. He gives a final warning of the punishment, and when it is rejected he passes sentence. The trial is over. Rusticus had done his duty. If Christians were accused, they had a remarkable privilege, in that they were allowed the opportunity of a free pardon if they recanted. No other crime against the State was pardoned in this way, in return for repentance. But refusal of sacrifice to the gods was a capital offence, and there was no way out. One wonders what the grave Rusticus thought at the time, and afterwards. One wonders what the compassionate emperor thought. It was perhaps at the time of the condemnation of Justin that he first formed the only opinion about the Christians that he expresses in the *Meditations*: 'How wonderful is that soul which is ready, if it must be at this very moment released from the body, either to be extinguished, or to be scattered, or to survive. This readiness must come from an individual decision, and not out of a sheer spirit of resistance like the Christians.' The word translated here as 'spirit of resistance', *parataxis*, is one that is used elsewhere to describe the drawing up of troops in battle and the marshalling of a political party. This describes something a little different from the *mera obstinatio*, 'sheer obstinacy', that others imputed to Christians. It implies rather that Marcus felt that they were not expressing an individual choice by their willingness to suffer death by martyrdom, but were expressing a choice that had been instilled into them: that they were *trained* to die. This would then be a similar opinion to that of Marcus' Stoic preceptor Epictetus, who remarked that the 'Galilaeans' (as he called Christians) were fearless 'by habit'.

Marcus was to have to deal again with an outcry against the Christians (probably motivated by even less creditable impulses) ten years later, this time in Gaul, at Lyons. Again, the law was to take its course. It is tragic – and seemed so to Christians a little later, who tried to alter the historical record – that an emperor such as Marcus

7. Two Aurelian Reliefs; (a) Marcus, on campaign, is met by barbarians asking for mercy. The emperor's bare-headed companion is probably his son-in-law Claudius Pompeianus

b) The emperor, his head covered by a fold of his toga, prepares to perform an official sacrifice

8*a*. Commodus in his early teens

8*b*. Commodus portrayed as the 'Roman Hercules' towards the end of his reign, when he had shaken off all restraints and was devoting himself exclusively to the gladiatorial arena should nevertheless have been a persecutor of the Christian Church.[1]

Meanwhile, Marcus had even more pressing preoccupations than the plague and the hysteria of the people of Rome – the danger to the northern frontiers of the empire. On January 6, 168, Marcus went to the barracks of the praetorian guard, where he addressed the men. No doubt the principal subject of his speech was the forthcoming campaign. All that has survived is concerned with another matter. Veterans of the praetorian guard had evidently been having some difficulty in finding wives for themselves (it is just possible that this too was a by-product of the plague – the praetorians might have become unpopular as responsible for bringing it back from the east). To assist their task as suitors Marcus announced that prospective fathers-in-law of veteran guardsmen would gain the same privileges from the birth of a grandson that they would receive at the birth of a son of their own.[2]

When the emperors finally 'departed, clad in the military cloak', in the spring of A.D. 168, for the north, they were certainly accompanied by an experienced officer, Furius Victorinus, who may have been sole prefect. A number of *comites* were attached to the general staff, including Aufidius Victorinus, Vitrasius Pollio (husband of Marcus' cousin Fundania Faustina), along with the redoubtable Pontius Laelianus and Dasumius Tullius Tuscus. The experience of these two former governors of Upper Pannonia would be invaluable. Lucius chose as *comes* his former subordinate Claudius Fronto. The reports from the north were discouraging. The Marcomanni and another tribe called Victuali were creating trouble on the frontier, together with other tribes who had been driven on by the more distant peoples to the north. They threatened to invade unless they were peaceably admitted. Nevertheless, negotiation produced some success and several tribes sent ambassadors to the governors of the

---

[1] *Med.*, 11, 3. Pliny, *Epp.*, 10, 46, 3. See F. Martinazzoli, *Parataxeis*, Firenze, 1953. There were other martyrdoms at this period in the provinces: for further discussion cf. Appendix IV.

[2] *Frag. Vat.*, 195.

frontier provinces asking pardon for their treaty-breaking. Lucius felt that this was enough and had been unwilling to set off. By the time the imperial party reached Aquileia (the ancient predecessor of Venice) the situation seemed well under control. The Quadi, always one of the most important peoples, had been defeated. Their king lost his life and they were anxious that Rome should approve the choice of successor, as in the old days. Other peoples retreated and their kings put to death the tribesmen responsible for the incidents.[1]

Lucius now felt, again, that the personal participation of himself and Marcus was unnecessary, a feeling heightened by a new development. 'The prefect Furius Victorinus was lost and part of the army had perished.' No details are given to elucidate this cryptic statement in the biography of Marcus. As a result it has been often assumed that the prefect and the troops had been killed in battle. But the context of the biographer's information gives no indication that any fighting which involved the guard had taken place at this juncture. On the other hand the other sources paint a consistent picture of enormous losses from plague among the armies of Rome: 'whole Roman armies perished', says Eutropius; 'the Roman army was destroyed, almost annihilated' by it, according to St Jerome, who is followed by Orosius; and the biography itself, already quoted earlier as describing the thousands wiped out by the plague, in a later passage is more explicit, speaking of 'many thousands of civilians and soldiers'.[2]

Victorinus was replaced by M. Bassaeus Rufus, a tough soldier who had risen from humble Italian peasant origins. Rufus had not long before been appointed prefect of the city police, the *vigiles* – he was still in office on March 10, 168 – not a usual position for a man of his strictly army background to fill, and a sign that Marcus had been determined to keep the situation in the city under firm control in the difficult period after the triumph. But in the spring of A.D. 168 Rufus had been sent out as prefect of Egypt and was there

[1] *v. Marci*, 14, 1–4. Furius Victorinus (see next note). Aufidius Victorinus: H.-G. Pflaum, *CRAI*, 1956, 189 ff. Pollio: Dessau, *ILS*, 1112–13. Laelianus: ibid., 1094+1100. Tuscus: ibid., 1081. Fronto: ibid., 1098.

[2] *v. Marci*, 14, 5 (on which see W. Zwikker, op. cit., 66); Eutrop., 8, 12; Jerome, *Chron.*, pp. 206 f. Helm (cf. Orosius, 7, 15, 5–6); *v. Marci*, 17, 2.

when news of his further promotion reached him. His urgent recall indicates that it was still thought worth while to wait for the right man for the job. Before long it was going to be increasingly difficult to find the right men at all. Rufus was soon given a colleague, M. Macrinius Vindex, perhaps the father of the dashing cavalry officer whose action in Pannonia had stemmed the first barbarian onslaught. The Macrinii, their names reveal, were clearly Celts in origin, perhaps from Cologne, or even from Colchester in Britain.[1]

In spite of Lucius' reluctance – he had settled in for a season's hunting and banqueting, while he hoped to persuade Marcus to return to Rome – Marcus was adamant, and both emperors crossed the Alps to inspect the frontier provinces. Marcus maintained that it was essential to carry out the intended programme, for the retreat of the barbarian people appeared to him to be a deliberate manoeuvre to gain time. Realizing that the vast expeditionary force could overwhelm them they hoped to lull the Romans into a false sense of security. Marcus and Lucius 'dealt with everything relevant to the protection of Italy and Illyricum' (the old name for the Pannonian provinces). These measures included the setting up of a new command, the *praetentura Italiae et Alpium* – 'the Italian and Alpine front'. The man appointed to take command of this was an African senator, Quintus Antistius Adventus, who had served with distinction in the eastern wars, at the outset of which he had been in command of the Palestine legion VI Ferrata. He had been transferred to the Lower Pannonian legion II Adiutrix when it came to the east with Geminius Marcianus, and at the end of the war had governed Arabia in succession to Marcianus. He had returned to become consul and curator of public works in Rome.[2]

Servilius Fabianus Maximus, who had given faithful service in the north for seven years, governing Lower and Upper Moesia successively, was replaced in Upper Moesia by Claudius Fronto, and evidently came to Aquileia himself, presumably as *comes* of the

---

[1] Rufus: PIR 2, B 69; H.-G. Pflaum, *Les carrières procuratoriennes, etc.*, No. 162+*add*. Vindex: Pflaum, op. cit., No. 161.

[2] *v. Marci*, 14, 5-6; *v. Veri*, 9, 7-8. Adventus: PIR 2, A 754 (see also Appendix III).

emperors. He brought his personal doctor with him, which was a wise precaution; but the doctor himself died. Marcus had persuaded Galen to join the imperial staff at Aquileia, no doubt hoping that he could do something about the plague. Another expert present at imperial headquarters was an Egyptian priest, Harnouphis, presumably one of those whose aid had been invoked in the previous year, to combat the plague with religious rites. At Aquileia he dedicated an altar to Isis.[1]

Other measures were taken to reorganize the administration of northern Italy on a war footing. The experienced legal expert Arrius Antoninus, who had already had service in the north as one of the new *iuridici*, was made curator of Ariminum (Rimini), a normally straightforward post which must have acquired enhanced importance now as the town was the roadhead of the *via Flaminia*, the main arterial route from Rome to the north-east. A procurator who had served as a regimental officer in the Parthian war, and in Britain with Calpurnius Agricola, among other appointments, Publius Helvius Pertinax, was given a procuratorship to deal with the *alimenta* along the *via Aemilia*, the main east-west route of northern Italy, an area he knew well, for his freedman father had settled in Liguria. Pertinax had two powerful patrons, Lollianus Avitus and Claudius Pompeianus. This normally minor post may have had an increased salary and additional duties on account of the war. Another procurator, Vehilius Gratus Julianus, was given a special task force.[2]

The emperors settled down to spend the winter of A.D. 168-9 at Aquileia. They must have determined to launch an offensive in the following spring. But the position was grim. The cold and the ever-present plague caused a large number of deaths, as Galen records. He recommended that the emperors should return to Rome. In midwinter they finally set off, at Lucius' insistence, having sent a letter to the senate announcing their intentions. After only two days'

---

[1] Dessau, *ILS*, 1080; *IG*, XIV, 2343; Galen, 19, 18=*script. min.*, 2, 98-9. Harnouphis: J. Guey, *Rev. de Phil.*, 22, 1948, 19 ff.

[2] Antoninus: *PIR* 2, A 1088. Pertinax: *PIR* 2, H 73, and more recently H.-G. Pflaum, op. cit., No. 179 (and cf. also *AE*, 1963, 52). Julianus: Pflaum, op. cit., No. 180.

journey Lucius took a stroke in the carriage, near Altinum, where he died three days later. Marcus returned to Rome with the body.[1]

The biographer in the Augustan History has various sordid rumours to retail about the death of Lucius. It is said that Marcus had, in effect, murdered him, either by cutting a piece of pork with a knife smeared on one side with poison and handing the poisoned piece to Lucius, eating the other one himself; or by getting a doctor named Posidippus to perform a bloodletting at the wrong time. It was alleged, alternatively, that his mother-in-law Faustina had murdered him by sprinkling poison on some oysters, 'because he had betrayed to Lucilla the fact that they (Lucius and Faustina) had had sexual intimacy'. It was said, again, that Lucilla was responsible, because of her jealousy of the influence that Lucius' sister Ceionia Fabia had over him. Fabia had even begun a conspiracy with Lucius, it was said, which was revealed to Marcus by the freedman Agaclytus and it was supposed to be then that Faustina did away with Lucius. Even Cassius Dio recorded the story that Lucius perished for plotting against Marcus.[2]

The story that Lucius was murdered is of the kind dear to the heart of the biographer and can hardly be credited, as the biographer himself admits. Marcus may, in the long run, have been relieved to be free of Lucius. But in the short run it left him with a number of problems, and meant that his strategy had to be emended.

The character of Lucius as given in the Augustan History is clearly something of a travesty. His faults were emphasized, to highlight the good qualities of Marcus, possibly with some ulterior motive, such as an allusion to contemporary figures at the time of writing; but perhaps simply for literary effect. It was a stroke of luck for the biographer to have discovered the fascinating detail that Lucius' birthday was the same as that of Nero, and he made full play with this. If the account given by the biographer is ignored, a different picture emerges. The testimony of Marcus himself in the *Meditations* and of Fronto must be set aside too, perhaps, as biased in favour of Lucius. What is left – Dio, Aelius Aristides, Lucian, an

[1] *v. Marci*, 14, 7–8; *v. Veri*, 9, 10–11.
[2] *v. Veri*, 10, 1–5; 11, 2–3; *v. Marci*, 15, 5; Dio, 71, 3, 1.

anonymous panegyrist of Constantine, and the emperor Julian –
gives little ground for upholding the verdict that Lucius was a worthless libertine, or even a dull and indolent fellow. He quite clearly had
faults, which Marcus may have attempted to cover up. But the
atmosphere of the time would not have made it possible for him to
be a second Nero.[1]

---

[1] For a slightly exaggerated but salutary effort to redress the balance, see
P. Lambrechts, *Ant. Class.*, 3, 1934, 173 ff., who quotes all the evidence. In
v. Marci, 20, 3-4, it is stated that Marcus promised to make a fresh start in
governing the State now that the somewhat unconscientious Lucius was gone;
and that he claimed the credit for planning the victory over Parthia. There
may be some truth in this, although it may be doubted whether Marcus
phrased it quite as the biographer records.

VIII

THE NORTHERN WARS

THE FUNERAL ceremonies of Lucius had to be performed immediately Marcus returned to Rome. Marcus made generous provision for the support of Lucius' sisters, aunts, other relatives and freedmen. Lucius himself was deified under the name of Divus Verus. The worship of the new god in the Roman pantheon was conducted by the priesthood of Antoninus Pius, whose members (or some of them) now became *sodales Antoniniani Veriani*. This emphasized the unity of the family. It also saved trouble and expense. No separate temple is known to have been built for Divus Verus. The rites of commemoration in his honour were no doubt conducted in the temple of Antoninus and Faustina. Inscriptions record several men, who, already priests of Antoninus, became priests of Verus too. One was the friend of Marcus, Aufidius Victorinus. Another was M. Nonius Macrinus, who describes himself as 'chosen out of the closest friends'. He was from northern Italy, as were the Ceionii, Lucius' original family, and he had been consul in A.D. 154, the same year as the much younger Lucius. The following year, A.D. 170, Macrinus was to go to Asia as proconsul, but he was probably present at the deification ceremonies at Rome in early A.D. 169.[1]

Once the family business had been transacted, Marcus turned his attention to a financial crisis. A major cause of this was the plague, since it would have greatly diminished the governmental revenues from taxes and imperial estates. But the raising of new legions at the

---

[1] *v. Marci*, 15, 3–4; 20, 1–5; *AE*, 1957, 121 (Victorinus); Dessau, *ILS*, 8830 (Macrinus). After a year in Asia, Macrinus went to the front as *comes. BMC*, IV, M. Aurelius and L. Verus, Nos. 503 ff., 1359 ff.

same time meant a vast increase in capital expenditure; and more troops still had to be raised, to plug the gaps revealed in the northern defences. The plague had also created vast gaps in the ranks of existing units. In the case of one legion, VII Claudia, stationed in Upper Moesia at Viminacium on the Danube, a record is preserved. At least twice the normal annual intake of recruits was necessary in A.D. 169. Only the number of those from this intake who survived the wars and the succeeding years to be demobilized in A.D. 195 is known: but this is more than 240 men. Besides replenishing existing legions and recruiting new ones, fresh auxiliary units were enrolled. Slaves were accepted as volunteers for military service and received their freedom on enrolment. Gladiators were formed into special units. Bandits were conscripted as well, especially the wild hillmen of Dalmatia and Dardania – a country which has always bred ideal guerrilla fighters. Where possible, mercenaries were hired from Germanic peoples. The police forces maintained by the Greek cities of the east were brought under direct governmental orders.[1]

Not all these measures necessarily belong to the year A.D. 169. But the event of which they were the cause certainly took place in this year – the famous auction of imperial property in the Forum of Trajan. 'So that this [the recruitment] should not be a burden to the provinces he held an auction of palace property in the Forum of the Deified Trajan, as we have related, in which, apart from clothes and drinking cups and gold vases he also sold statues and paintings by great artists.' The biographer had already included a reference to this auction in a passage borrowed from another late writer, Eutropius (or from a source common to both), which gives more details and a less specific, but more acceptable cause. 'When he had drained the whole treasury for this war, and could not induce himself to impose any extraordinary taxes on the provincials, he held an auction in the Forum of the Deified Trajan of imperial furnishings, and sold gold, crystal and myrrhine drinking vessels, even royal vases, his wife's silk and gold-embroidered clothing, even certain jewels in fact, which he had discovered in some quantity in an inner sanctum of Hadrian's. Indeed, the sale went on for two months, and such a

[1] *CIL*, III, 8097; *v. Marci*, 21, 6–8 (cf. W. Zwikker, op. cit., 105 ff.).

quantity of gold was acquired that after he had carried through the remainder of the Marcomannic war in accordance with his intentions, he gave permission to buyers to return their purchases and get their money back, if they wanted. He did not cause trouble to anyone, whether he returned what he had bought or not.'[1]

Marcus must have realized that new taxation would be extremely unpopular and not very productive. A gesture like the palace auction had more than a practical benefit – it demonstrated that the emperor was willing to make sacrifices. As a Stoic, Marcus cannot have found it any great hardship to get rid of some of the trappings of power. (Faustina may have resented losing some of her jewels and dresses.) This auction was not the only measure taken. C. Vettius Sabinianus, an experienced senator of modest origin (he had been promoted from the equestrian order), who had already commanded one of the two new legions, the Third Italica, was sent to Gaul 'to examine the accounts' in the three Gallic provinces under direct imperial rule. This meant in effect that the taxation assessment would be radically reviewed, clearly with the hope of obtaining higher revenues. This was a more effective way than new taxes to raise the necessary finances. But in spite of these emergency measures the currency was debased in the reign of Marcus – an ominous sign.[2]

Marcus was clearly determined to return to the front in A.D. 169. The precise chronology of events in this year, as in others in the war, is very obscure, but there seems little doubt that heavy fighting was going on, concentrated in the Hungarian plain, the re-entrant of barbarian territory crossed by the valley of the river Theiss, surrounded on the west by Lower Pannonia, on the south by Upper Moesia and on the east by Dacia. In the course of A.D. 169 – if not before – the governor of Dacia, Calpurnius Agricola, gave up his command hurriedly. Possibly he died in action, or from the plague. Claudius Fronto, governor of neighbouring Upper Moesia, was ordered to take over part of Agricola's province, namely Dacia Apulensis, the central sub-province. One of the other two Dacian

---

[1] v. Marci, 21, 9; 17, 4–5.
[2] AE, 1920, 45. See G. Mickwitz, Geld und Wirtschaft, etc., Helsingfors, 1932, 33 ff.

sub-provinces, Malvensis, was at this time probably assigned to the command of its procurator, Macrinius Avitus, the man who had been decorated for his spectacular defeat of the Langobardi and Obii two years before, when he had been a cavalry commander. Another man evidently in Dacia as procurator at this time was the future emperor Pertinax, but his exact position is unknown. The conduct of Pertinax in Dacia won him unpopularity in some quarters, and his dismissal from office was brought about. Not long after this, although it is unknown whether it was in A.D. 169 or 170, Claudius Fronto took over the whole province of Dacia, the united 'Three Dacias'. He was succeeded, it seems possible, in Upper Moesia, by the commander of one of the Dacian legions, V Macedonica, Calpurnius Julianus (perhaps a relative of Calpurnius Agricola). Julianus had not been consul, a normal pre-requisite for governors of Upper Moesia and for all provinces with more than one legion. One of the legions must have moved out with Claudius Fronto (an indication that the major threat was shifting eastwards). Marcus had to make a considerable number of changes of this kind in the administrative hierarchy, for military reasons.[1]

There is thus every reason why Marcus should have been anxious to get back to the front. But he had first to consider the problem of what to do with his daughter Lucilla, the widow of Lucius. A young widow with the title Augusta (and with an infant daughter) was in need of protection. Not only that, however. She might be used by some unscrupulous and ambitious person for his own ends. Marcus solved the problem in a radical way. 'Although the period of mourning [for Lucius] had not expired, he gave his daughter in marriage to Claudius Pompeianus, the son of a Roman knight, of advanced age, a native of Antioch and of not sufficiently noble birth.' Faustina was opposed to the marriage – and so was Lucilla. The obligatory period of mourning of a Roman widow at this period is not certain. It is likely that it was twelve months, and this marriage took place by September or October at the latest, just before Marcus was setting

---

[1] *PIR* 2, C 249 (Agricola), 874 (Fronto), 270 (Julianus); H 73 (Pertinax); Dessau, *ILS*, 1107 (Avitus). Cf. A. R. Birley, *A. Ant. Philip.*, 1963, 109 ff., and H.-G. Kolbe, *Bonn. Jahrb.*, 162, 1962, 407 ff.; and note the statement in *v. Marci*, 22, 9.

out for the war. The biographer may exaggerate the age of Pompeianus somewhat (the word used is *grandaevo*), for he was still alive twenty-four years later. But he was a good deal older than Lucius, perhaps over fifty. To Lucilla, who was twenty, this may have seemed disagreeably elderly. But what was worse was his origin. His father had not even been a senator, and he was a Syrian. In fact, the only other senator from Syria known at this period is the victorious general of Lucius, Avidius Cassius. But Cassius' father had been an intimate in court circles, and if not a senator, had been prefect of Egypt. Besides which, the family of Cassius was descended from kings of the east. There is no suggestion of anything romantic of this kind in the ancestry of Pompeianus. But Pompeianus had served in the north – he had been governor of Lower Pannonia in A.D. 167 – and Marcus had decided to make him his chief military adviser. His very origin was an advantage in the long view: it would not give him any dangerous ambitions, of the kind which men of nobler origin married to an Augusta might acquire.[1] The marriage therefore took place.

Immediately before his departure for the war, Marcus withdrew from the late summer heat of Rome to Praeneste (Palestrina). Here he suffered a family tragedy. His younger son, Annius Verus, had a tumour below the ear. He had an operation, but did not recover, and died, at the age of seven. Now only one son, Commodus, and four daughters remained. Marcus' conduct showed that he was fully imbued with Stoic self-discipline. He mourned his son for five days only, during which time he gave some attention to public business. The games of Jupiter Best and Greatest were then in progress – which indicates a date in September or October. 'Because he did not want to have them interrupted by public mourning he merely ordered that statues of his son should be decreed, that a golden image of him should be carried in procession at the Circus games and that his name should be inserted in the hymn of the Salii.'[2]

[1]. *v. Marci*, 21, 6; cf. *PW*, 13, 1927, 1700 (*art.* luctus). *PIR* 2, C 973 (Pompeianus), A 1402 (Cassius), A 1405 (Heliodorus). Cf. J. Keil, *Klio*, 31, 1938, 296 ff., and H.-G. Pflaum, *J. des Savants*, 1961, 39 ff.

[2] *v. Marci*, 21, 3–5; *PW*, Supp. 5, 1931, 617 ff. (*art.* ludi). The death of Annius Verus was selected by Walter Pater as the subject of one of the most intensely felt passages of his *Marius the Epicurean*.

After this private grief Marcus was perhaps grateful for the prospect of action. But it was almost autumn when he left Rome for the front, accompanied by a picked staff, and the campaigning season was virtually over. Pompeianus certainly went with him, probably Lucilla too. Faustina was at the front with Marcus at a later stage, but it is probable that she remained in Rome now. She may have been pregnant again. Her last child, another daughter, was born about A.D. 170. She was named Vibia Aurelia Sabina. Another, or an additional, reason may have been that there was anxiety about the health of Commodus.

Other advisers as well as Pompeianus accompanied Marcus again, such as the veteran Pontius Laelianus and Dasumius Tullius Tuscus, both ex-governors of Upper Pannonia. The son of old Pompeius Falco, Q. Sosius Priscus, apparently also came. Julius Verus may have been called on to give Marcus the benefit of his wide experience. He had not served on the Danube, but his family was from the Dalmatian hill-country and he must have had a good personal knowledge of the terrain and conditions in which the Roman armies would have to operate (during their deployment within the empire, that is, for an offensive campaign was planned, to carry Roman arms beyond the Danube).[1]

The location of Marcus' headquarters for the winter of A.D. 169–70 is unknown. A likely base would have been Sirmium on the river Save, a tributary of the Danube (modern Sremska Mitrovica in Yugoslavia), possibly even Singidunum (Belgrade), at the confluence of the Save and Danube. The main fighting was presumably in the area where Claudius Fronto was in command. Marcus' base a few years later, when there was further fighting in the same region, was Sirmium, so it is a strong possibility for the winter of A.D. 169–70.

The campaigning season of A.D. 170 was to open with a massive Roman offensive across the Danube. The raising of new legions had generally in the past been the prelude to conquest and annexation of

---

[1] On the birth of Sabina, cf. Appendix II. Dessau, *ILS*, 1094+1100 (Laelianus); ibid., 1081 (Tuscus); ibid., 1057+8794; *AE*, 1956, 123 (Julius Verus, cf. H.-G. Pflaum, *Les carrières procuratoriennes, etc.*, pp. 401 ff.); *CIL*, VI, 31753 (Priscus, cf. W. Zwikker, op. cit., 182).

new territory for the empire, and there seems little doubt that Marcus felt that the policy implied by the raising of two legions must be carried out. How he occupied himself in the winter of A.D. 169–70 is not recorded. Much of his time would be spent in the normal round of legal and administrative duties and decision-making, which would have followed him to the camp. In addition to this he would have had to supervise the maintenance of good health, discipline and training in the vast force under his personal command. It was his first full season in winter-quarters. It may well have been at this time that he began keeping the philosophical notebook which he left behind him at his death.

The events of A.D. 170 and the years of warfare that followed are nowhere fully recorded, and any account that can be pieced together must inevitably be in considerable part hypothetical.[1] The imperial coinage of the year A.D. 170 gives some assistance. The *profectio* of Marcus from Rome, the official departure for the expedition in the previous autumn, is announced. Another issue depicts the emperor addressing troops and bears the legend *adlocutio*, the normal sign of the opening of a campaign. Other coins herald Roman victories, but these must be regarded as aspirations of future success, or at best as general statements of confidence arising out of some successes won by Claudius Fronto. It must be doubted whether the offensive directed by Marcus was successful. On the contrary, there is every suggestion that it met with disaster. The only clear statement of this is found in the satirist Lucian's attack on Alexander the false prophet of Abonuteichos. This curious figure apparently provided the armies of Rome with an oracle, which forecast success if they began their offensive by casting two lions into the Danube. The advice was adopted. The beasts swam across to the enemy side and were dealt with by the barbarians without difficulty. They were taken for an unusual kind of dog or wolf and despatched with clubs. 'Immediately our side incurred its greatest blow, with the loss of almost 20,000 men. Then followed what happened with Aquileia, and the city's narrow escape from capture.' There is no need to believe Lucian's

---

[1] See Appendix III.

implication that the disastrous Roman defeat would not have occurred if it had not been for Alexander's oracle. But the conclusion that a Roman offensive met a disastrous setback, and was followed soon after by a barbarian invasion of Italy, is inescapable.[1]

The siege of Aquileia is also referred to by the late fourth-century historian Ammianus Marcellinus.[2] Speaking of the Quadi in his own time, he goes on to recall their former strength, demonstrated by 'plundering raids once carried out with headlong speed, and Aquileia besieged by the same people, with the Marcomanni, and Opitergium wiped out, and many bloody deeds carried out in extremely swift military engagements, against which, when the Julian Alps had been breached, the earnest emperor Marcus could hardly make any resistance. . . .' The breaching of the Julian (i.e. Carnic) Alps by the invaders must therefore have occurred before Marcus could cut them off. The Marcomanni and Quadi with their allies, coming from Bohemia and Slovakia, had used the Amber Route. Antistius Adventus, if he was still in the Alpine zone as commander of the *praetentura*, failed to stem their advance. He may have moved elsewhere by now, and as Marcus had been attempting to launch an offensive into the barbarian lands across the Danube, northern Italy may no longer have been strongly garrisoned. The invaders had at any rate been able to slip through a gap, while the main Roman forces were facing in the opposite direction. Marcus must have made a desperate effort to get up the valley of the Save, but the invaders managed to enter Italy.[3]

The province of Upper Moesia was also in trouble at this time, for Claudius Fronto, governor of the Three Dacias, was obliged before the end of A.D. 170 to take Upper Moesia under his command again, combining the governorship of both provinces simultaneously. This can only mean that the governor of Upper Moesia was put out of action suddenly, with no time to replace him in the normal way. It was perhaps at this time also (though this is less certain) that the

---

[1] *BMC*, IV, M. Aurelius, Nos. 1371 ff., 531 ff. Lucian, *Alexander*, 48.

[2] Amm. Marc., 29, 6, 1.

[3] Adventus: *PIR* 2, A 754, and see Appendix III, where the date of the invasion here given is supported.

legate of the legion IV Flavia, normally based at Belgrade, had to be replaced at short notice. The only man that could be found was the young senatorial tribune of the neighbouring VII Claudia, M. Roscius Lupus Murena. Before the end of A.D. 170 Claudius Fronto himself was dead. The inscription on his monument, which provides much of the information about the vicissitudes of the provinces under his command, recorded that 'after several successful battles against Germans and Jazyges, he fell, fighting for the republic to the last'. His successor in the Dacias was Sextus Cornelius Clemens. To Upper Moesia came the governor of neighbouring Thrace, Caerellius.[1]

Whether or not Italy was invaded in A.D. 170, it is clear that in this year barbarian forces burst into the Balkans, overrunning the frontier provinces, Thrace and Macedonia and even reaching Achaea, coming as far as Eleusis. Athens was lucky to escape. The tribe named as entering Macedonia and Achaea is the Costoboci, a people of uncertain origin who lived to the north or north-east of Dacia. Once the frontiers had been breached they met with virtually no opposition. The cities – the cities which Aristides had depicted in such glowing terms – were unwalled and ungarrisoned. In one or two places vigorous resistance was hurriedly organized by local levies, but the general picture was one of pillage, burning and slaughter. Claudius Fronto had tried in vain to stem the tide which came on after the disastrous failure of Marcus' offensive. Marcus had been caught in the middle, somewhere on the middle Danube, while two tides of invasion flowed into the Empire.[2]

To meet the crisis Pompeianus was chosen to deal with the invasion of Italy and the Alpine region. He made Pertinax one of his principal assistants, thus vindicating his recently tarnished reputation. Another procurator, Vehilius Gratus Julianus was sent with a task force to clear Macedonia and Achaea. Valerius Maximianus was given a task force composed of marines from various fleets, with

---

[1] *PIR 2*, C 874 (Fronto); 1340 (Clemens); 160 (Caerellius, on whom cf. A. R. Birley, *A. Ant. Philip.*, 1963, 109 ff.); Dessau, *ILS*, 8834+*AE*, 1933, 198 (Murena).

[2] W. Zwikker, op. cit., 167 ff.

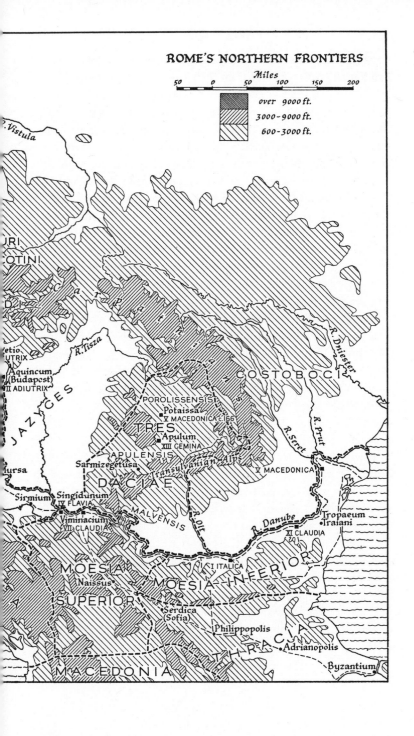

ROME'S NORTHERN FRONTIERS

Miles
50   0   50   100   150   200

over 9000 ft.
3000-9000 ft.
600-3000 ft.

R. Vistula

URI
OTINI
D

Ca   r   p

etio
UTRIX
Aquincum
(Budapest)
II ADIUTRIX

R. Tisza

COSTOBOCI

R. Dniester

JAZYGES

POROLISSENSIS
Potaissa
V MACEDONICA c.166

TRES

Apulum
XIII GEMINA

APULENSIS

R. Serret

R. Prut

Sarmizegetusa

DACIAE

Transylvanian Alps

V MACEDONICA

ursa

Sirmium   Singidunum
IV FLAVIA

MALVENSIS

Oltu

Danube

Tropaeum
Traiani

Viminacium
VII CLAUDIA

R. Danube

XI CLAUDIA

MOESIA

I ITALICA

MOESIA-INFERIOR

Naissus

SUPERIOR

Serdica
(Sofia)

Philippopolis

THRACIA

Adrianopolis

MACEDONIA

Byzantium

strong cavalry support, to conduct supplies down the Danube to the Pannonian armies, cut off from their supplies to the south.[1]

The raid of the Costoboci was not so serious as the invasion of Italy. The invaders of Greece were too far from their homeland, in difficult country, and by the time they reached Attica much of their force must have been spent. The dislodgement of the Marcomanni and Quadi and their allies from northern Italy and the Alpine provinces was more difficult, however, and must have been a protracted task. Communications between Marcus' headquarters and Rome by the land route would have been extremely tenuous for some months, and it is therefore not surprising to find evidence that in A.D. 170 the port of Salona, chief city of the province of Dalmatia, was fortified by detachments of the new Second legion. It was essential to maintain the alternative sea-link with Italy: the crossing from Split to Ancona is a short one.[2]

Many of the towns in the empire, uneasy after what had happened, must have begun to want walls for themselves. Many towns and forts had been destroyed. During this period Marcus found it necessary to lay down that towns which wanted walls should seek the emperor's permission. This would discourage panic measures in areas where they were unnecessary. But in the danger zone steps were taken, as at Philippopolis (Plovdiv) in Thrace.[3]

Marcus probably spent the winter of A.D. 170–1 moving from place to place. But in A.D. 171 he moved his headquarters to Carnuntum on the Danube. He had clearly realized that the Marcomanni and their allies were the chief enemy. In the course of A.D. 171 the last invaders were trapped at the river crossing as they attempted to make their escape, laden with booty. Their force was destroyed, and the booty was returned to the provincials. Marcus was hailed by the troops as Imperator for the sixth time. This salutation is recorded on the coinage in late A.D. 171, together with a 'German victory', i.e., over the Germans, but for most of the year the coinage bore no claims of Roman victory. On the contrary, appeals were made to the loyalty and unity of the armies, fighting under extremely

[1] Dio, 71, 3, 1–2; v. Pert., 2, 4; Dessau, ILS, 1327; AE, 1956, 124.
[2] Dessau, ILS, 2616–17. [3] Digest., 50, 10, 6; CIL, III, 6121, 7409.

difficult conditions. This suggests that the victory came late in the year – and that the armies' morale was low.[1]

This reconstruction of events is not the only possible one. The invasion of the Costoboci reaching far into Greece clearly occurred in A.D. 170, as did the death of Claudius Fronto. What is not certain is how long after the failure of Marcus' offensive the Marcomanni invaded Italy. It may not have been until early in A.D. 171. But the fact that Marcus did not record any victory on the coinage until late in A.D. 171 suggests that the operations of Pompeianus and Pertinax in clearing the invaded areas cannot have been completed until then.

Italy had not been invaded by a foreign enemy for hundreds of years. Nevertheless Marcus regarded it as essential to press on with his plans for an offensive, an offensive which was to be not merely a punitive campaign, but a campaign of conquest. Meanwhile, in A.D. 171 there was disquieting news from another part of the empire. The Iberian peninsula had been invaded by Moorish rebels who had crossed the Straits of Gibraltar. The area which met the full brunt of their assault was Baetica, one of the senatorial provinces, governed by a proconsul, and with no garrison to defend it. Marcus despatched his friend Aufidius Victorinus to Spain, to govern both Tarraconensis and Baetica simultaneously. This deprived the senate of a province, and to compensate it, Marcus assigned Sardinia to its sphere. A young man who had been going out to Baetica to serve as quaestor, after a term as quaestor in Rome (this double service being another sign of the shortage of personnel), L. Septimius Severus the future emperor, went to Sardinia instead. Aufidius Victorinus had only one legion, the Seventh Gemina based at Legio (Leon) in the north of the peninsula. To strengthen his army, Marcus sent the procurator Gratus Julianus there from Greece. He must by now have completed his task of clearing out the remnants of the Costoboci, and his men would have become highly experienced in this kind of warfare.[2]

[1] Eutrop., 8, 13, 1; *v. Marci*, 21, 10; *BMC*, IV, M. Aurelius, Nos. 540–1, 1388, etc. (IMP VI); 1394, etc., 1395 ff. (*concordia* and *fides exercituum*).

[2] H.-G. Pflaum, *CRAI*, 1956, 189 ff.; *v. Sev.*, 2, 3–4 (cf. J. Guey, *Bull. Soc. Nat. Ant. de France*, 1956, 33); Dessau, *ILS*, 1327 (on which cf. H.-G. Pflaum, *Les carrières procuratoriennes, etc.*, No. 180).

Fragments of Cassius Dio's account of the war have been preserved. One describes briefly the invasion of Italy, and its repulse by Pompeianus and Pertinax. It adds an interesting comment: 'Among the barbarian dead were found even the bodies of women wearing armour.' This indicates that the enemy peoples were on the move in a serious way. If they had their womenfolk with them – they wanted land. This detail, with its implications, is confirmed by the biographer of Marcus, who recorded that before Marcus and Lucius set off together (A.D. 168) the Marcomanni and Victuali had been demanding to be allowed to enter the empire. In a later passage, describing the great invasion, the biographer says that 'all the peoples from the frontier of Illyricum right as far as Gaul had conspired together'. This common policy had indeed already been seen in A.D. 166 or 167 when ten tribes chose Ballomarius the king of the Marcomanni as their spokesman in negotiations with Iallius Bassus. Taken together, with the background of archaeological evidence to illuminate them further, these items of evidence help to explain why Marcus thought it necessary to depart in a radical way from the policy of his predecessors over the German question. He was faced with quite new problems.[1]

After the first victory he had won in person, although he accepted the salutation as Imperator, he refused the troops' request for a donative, 'saying that whatever they got from him over and above their regular pay would be wrung from the blood of their parents and families; as for the fate of the sovereignty, God alone could determine that. So temperately and firmly did he rule that even when engaged in so many and so great wars, he never did anything unworthy by way of flattery or as the result of fear.' The biographer gives a slightly less dramatic picture of Marcus as commander-in-chief: 'Always, before he did anything, both in military and civil affairs, he consulted with the foremost men. This was an especially frequent saying of his: "It is fairer that I should give way to the advice of so many friends – and such friends – than that so many of these friends should follow my advice, the advice of one man." Certainly, because he seemed hard, from his devotion to philosophy,

[1] Dio, 71, 3, 2; v. Marci, 14, 1; 22, 1.

both in his military discipline and in his whole way of life, he was bitterly criticized. But he answered all his critics in speeches or pamphlets.' The biographer adds, however, that because many noblemen had lost their lives in the war, Marcus' friends urged him to abandon it and return to Rome. But this advice he disregarded.[1]

In late A.D. 171 a period of intense diplomatic activity began. Marcus, probably at Carnuntum, met envoys from the barbarian peoples. He was aiming to detach some of the members of the barbarian 'conspiracy', so that the most dangerous members of it could be isolated. In this he was partly successful. Shortened extracts of some of Dio's account of the negotiations have survived. 'Marcus Antoninus remained in Pannonia to receive the barbarian embassies. For many of them came to him at that time, some of which, led by a twelve-year-old boy named Battarius, promised alliance. They were given money, and succeeded in restraining Tarbus, chieftain of a neighbouring people, who had entered Dacia, demanding money and threatening war if he was not given it. Others asked for peace, like the Quadi. It was granted them, first, in the hope that they could be detached from the Marcomanni, second, because they gave Marcus many horses and cattle, and promised to surrender all deserters and captives as well – 13,000 at first, the rest later. But they were not given the right to attend markets, because it was feared that the Jazyges and the Marcomanni, whom they had sworn not to receive and not to allow to pass through their country, would mingle with them, pretend to be Quadi themselves, spy out Roman positions and buy provisions. As well as those that came to Marcus, many others sent envoys, some by tribes and some by nations, offering to surrender. Some of them were sent on campaigns elsewhere, as also were the captives and deserters who were fit; others received land in Dacia, Pannonia, Moesia, Germany and Italy itself. Some of the ones settled at Ravenna revolted and even dared to try seizing the city. For this reason Marcus did not bring any barbarians into Italy again, but even banished those who had come there previously.'[2]

[1] *BMC*, IV, M. Aurelius, No. 540, cf. 541, 1388 (VIC GER); Dio, 71, 3, 3-4; *v. Marci*, 22, 3-8.
[2] Dio, 71, 11; Dessau, *ILS*, 8830.

Some of the statements about land settlement in this passage are anticipatory, but it is probable that some barbarian settlers were accepted at this time. Marcus has been severely criticized for this step. It is regarded as the beginning of the barbarization of the empire. But if the statement of Orosius concerning the depopulation of the countryside can be accepted, there was some justification. It could even be argued that depopulation of the countryside, especially in Italy, had been beginning before the plague, to an alarming extent. Besides this, if the settlers were from peoples which Marcus intended to incorporate within the empire, the criticism has less point in any case. They were to be romanized sooner or later, by one means or another.

Diplomatic activity also went on in Dacia, conducted by Claudius Fronto's successor as governor, Cornelius Clemens. Another extract from Dio describes this. 'The Astingi, led by their chieftains Raüs and Raptus, entered Dacia with their entire households, in the hope of obtaining money and land in return for their alliance. They failed to obtain what they asked for, and left their wives and children under the protection of Clemens, while they went to take possession by force of the land of the Costoboci. But when they had defeated that people, they continued to inflict damage on Dacia. The Lacringes were afraid that Clemens, through fear of the Astingi, might bring them into the land which they inhabited. So they attacked them while they were off their guard and achieved a decisive victory. As a result, the Astingi undertook no further military action against the Romans, but in response to urgent appeals to Marcus obtained money and the promise of land in return for any damage they might inflict on his enemies.' The Astingi and Lacringes were both branches of the people whose name was later to become notorious – the Vandals. Their exact location at this time is unknown. The choice of the lands of the Costoboci by the Astingi suggests that this attack came after that people had been weakened by their great raid of A.D. 170. The acquisition of these two tribes as allies was valuable to Rome, enabling Marcus to concentrate with more confidence on the subjugation of Bohemia.

'This tribe [the Astingi] did in fact fulfil some of its promises,' the extract from Dio continues, 'whereas the Cotini, although they made similar offers, on deceiving Tarrutenius Paternus, the secretary in charge of the emperor's Latin correspondence, with the pretence that they were willing to make a campaign with him against the Marcomanni, not only failed to do this, but handled Paternus very roughly, thereby bringing about their own destruction later.' The Cotini were neighbours of the Marcomanni and Quadi, a people with strong Celtic elements. Their adhesion to Rome would have provided a valuable base. Besides this, they controlled iron mines which may have been an important source of raw materials for weapon making among the barbarian peoples of the region. Tarrutenus [as the name is more correctly rendered] Paternus was later to play an important military role as praetorian prefect at the end of the reign. He was also a jurist, who wrote on military law. The choice of a man of this type for the vital post of *ab epistulis Latinis* shows that Marcus still preferred to fill this post with military men rather than with the literary figures who had occupied it in the past. In spite of the failure with the Cotini, the neutralization of the Quadi meant that Rome had knocked out one of the three major enemies, and had driven a wedge between the other two.[1]

In A.D. 172 the offensive into enemy territory, which had been so many times postponed by the turn of events, at last took place. The coins of the year show another *adlocutio* scene, marking the opening of a new campaign; and a coin bearing the inscription *virtus Aug.* – 'the valour of the emperor' – depicts Roman troops crossing a bridge. This is the scene shown at the beginning of the column of Marcus Aurelius in the Piazza Colonna at Rome. The benign personified figure of Father Danube looks on while a Roman army marches across a bridge of boats. The fighting was not all in Rome's favour. It may have been in this campaign (unless it occurred in the fighting on Roman soil in the previous year) that 'the Marcomanni were successful in a certain battle and killed Marcus [Macrinius] Vindex the [praetorian] prefect'. Marcus found it difficult to replace Vindex. He would have liked to appoint Pertinax, but Pertinax had only recently been promoted to the senate for his outstanding achieve-

[1] Dio, 71, 12, 1–3; cf. 71, 11, 6; *PW*, 4A, 1932, 2405 ff. (Paternus).

ments with Claudius Pompeianus, and was now commanding the legion First Adiutrix. The prefect of Egypt, Calvisius Statianus, who would have been a normal selection in other circumstances, was too far away and in any case had problems of his own to face. Marcus may have left the post vacant and have continued with one prefect only, the tough if somewhat illiterate Bassaeus Rufus.[1]

One other episode recorded seems to belong to this campaign. Marcus is said by the biographer to have 'summoned a thunderbolt from heaven by his prayers and destroyed an enemy military engine'. This episode is depicted in an early scene on the Column; and a remarkable series of coins of A.D. 172 shows Marcus, in full general's uniform, being crowned by the goddess Victory – and carrying, in addition to his lance, the thunderbolt of Jupiter, which seems a clear allusion to the occurrence. It is not hard to reconstruct what happened. Marcus may indeed have prayed during a thunderstorm, for lightning to strike the enemy. (This was only the first of two such instances of divine intervention, the second of which – the battle of the Rain Miracle – was to achieve wider acclaim, and is particularly difficult to date, although here it is assigned to the following year.) By the end of the campaigning season of A.D. 172, Marcus had achieved victory over the Marcomanni and took the title Germanicus, presumably at the request of the senate. The title was awarded to his son Commodus on October 15. The coins of A.D. 172 did not carry the title, but they announced the 'subjugation of Germany' – *Germania subacta* – and also advertised the clemency of the emperor in his treatment of the conquered enemy: a female figure, carrying a hexagonal shield (the personified figure of Germany), is portrayed kneeling before the emperor. The Marcomanni accepted a treaty imposing severe restrictions on them.[2]

The award of the title Germanicus to Commodus might suggest that he was with Marcus during A.D. 172. This possibility appears to gain confirmation from an inscription set up by a private individual

[1] *BMC*, IV, M. Aurelius, Nos. 1425–7; Dio, 71, 3, 5; *v. Pert.*, 2, 6 and 9; *PIR* 2, C 356 (Statianus – the dating of whose prefecture is now clarified by *SB*, VI, 9393); *PIR* 2, B 69 (Rufus).

[2] *v. Marci*, 24, 4; *v. Comm.*, 11, 14; Dio, 71, 3, 5; 71, 15; *BMC*, IV, M. Aurelius, Nos. 566–7, cf. 1412 (*Clementia*); 1413 (*Germania subacta*).

at Marsala in Sicily, which prays for the safety and return of Marcus 'and of his children'. This can only be dated approximately – it belongs to the early period of Marcus' campaigning, after the death of Lucius, and before he was awarded the title Germanicus. But the children who were with Marcus may have been daughters only. Lucilla was almost certainly with the armies, with her father and her new husband Pompeianus. Her elder sister Faustina, with her husband Claudius Severus, may also have been there. The third sister Fadilla, had probably only recently married. Her husband was M. Peducaeus Plautius Quintillus, nephew of Lucius. This couple may also have been at the front with Marcus. Commodus' ill-health has already been mentioned. Its nature is unknown, but he was cured by Galen, whom Marcus had failed to persuade to accompany him to the war. Commodus' restoration to health is recalled on an engraved jewel, bearing the words: 'salvo Commodo, felix Faustina' – 'when Commodus is well, Faustina is happy'.[1]

The year A.D. 172 saw problems in the east. In Egypt there was rebellion, recorded in an extract from Cassius Dio. 'The so-called Bucoli [i.e., 'herdsmen', the population of a district of the Delta of the Nile], under the leadership of a certain priest, Isidorus, began a disturbance in Egypt, and caused the rest of the Egyptians to revolt. First, dressed in women's clothes, they had deceived the Roman centurion into believing that they were going to give him gold as ransom for their husbands, and then struck him down when he came near. They sacrificed his companion too, and after swearing an oath over his intestines, ate them. Isidorus surpassed all his followers in bravery. Then, having defeated the Romans in a pitched battle, they nearly captured Alexandria – and would have succeeded if Cassius had not been sent against them from Syria. His strategy was to destroy their mutual harmony and to split them up, for because of their desperation as well as their numbers he had not dared to attack them while they were united. Thus, when they began quarrelling, he defeated them.' Cassius' entry into Egypt required special authority, for as a senator he was automatically excluded from Egypt

[1] G. Barbieri, *Kokalos*, 7, 1961, 15 ff.; Galen, 14, 651 ff.; *Rev. arch.*, 39, 1901, 121.

by a regulation of Augustus. He received special powers over all the eastern provinces, placing him on a footing similar to that which Lucius had held during the Parthian war.[1]

There was also trouble in Armenia. Sohaemus, the philoroman king installed by Lucius in A.D. 164, was expelled by elements favourable to Parthia. He was restored by P. Martius Verus, governor of Cappadocia. The man responsible for the trouble may have been a certain Tiridates who, according to Dio, 'stirred up trouble in Armenia and killed the king of the Heniochi, and then thrust his sword in Verus' [i.e. Martius Verus] face, when he rebuked him for it'. Tiridates' punishment was not severe, 'Marcus did not put him to death, but only sent him to Britain' – which makes it sound as if Britain was then the Roman equivalent of Siberia. However, it was chosen merely as a conveniently distant place from Armenia. Dio took the opportunity, when recording the restoration of Sohaemus, to give a character sketch of Martius Verus: 'Martius not only had the ability to overcome his opponents by force of arms, to be a move ahead of them by his speed or to outwit them by surprise action, which is the true strength of a general, he could also persuade them by plausible promises, conciliate them by magnificent gifts and tempt them by bright hopes. There was a grace about all his actions and words, a charm that soothed the annoyance and anger of everyone, while raising their hopes even more. He knew the proper time for flattery and presents and for entertaining people with his hospitality. Since in addition to these talents he showed perseverance in his undertakings and energy coupled with speed in his dealings with the enemy, he made it clear to the barbarians that it was worth more to aim for his friendship than his enmity.' When he arrived in Armenia, Martius Verus found that the garrison of Roman soldiers left in the New City (the new capital which replaced the destroyed

[1] Dio, 71, 4; cf. 71, 3, and Philostratus, *v. soph.*, 2, 1, 13. Some believe that he was given these powers at the end of the Parthian war, but it is more likely that they were first conferred only when a specific need arose – although it is conceivable that they were conferred in A.D. 170, when the invasions made it seem imperative that the east should be ruled with a strong hand. I am glad to see that J. Schwartz, *Historia-Augusta-Colloquium*, Bonn, 1964, 163 ff., takes the same view on the date at which Cassius received his special powers.

Artaxata) by Statius Priscus were in a mutinous state, and he took steps to remedy the situation.[1]

Marcus may well have hoped to return to Rome in A.D. 173, after his victory over the Marcomanni. In fact, his return is even announced on a medallion of the year. His two sons-in-law, Claudius Severus and Claudius Pompeianus, were the consuls for the year, both for the second time, and he may have hoped that he could be present in Rome to lend his prestige to their holding of office. As it turned out, even Pompeianus is unlikely to have returned to Rome. During the campaign against the Marcomanni, the Quadi had not kept to their promises: they had harboured fugitive Marcomanni. This was not surprising, as the two peoples were closely related, both being branches of the Suebic Germans. It was perhaps more surprising that Marcus had been able to secure any kind of promise from them. Now they had to be dealt with. The main war against the Quadi should be assigned to the year A.D. 173.[2]

Only one incident is recorded from the war against the Quadi. A detailed account of a most unusual battle is given in an extract from Dio, which his epitomator the Byzantine monk Xiphilinus felt gave an inadequate record, and therefore supplemented with observations of his own. Various chroniclers also give a few details. This is the famous battle of the Rain Miracle. 'A great war against the people called Quadi also fell to his lot, and it was his good fortune to win an unexpected victory – or rather, victory was granted by God. For when the Romans were in danger in the course of the battle, the divine power saved them in a most unexpected way. The Quadi had surrounded them in a place favourable to themselves, and the Romans were fighting bravely with their shields fitted close together. The barbarians held back from fighting, expecting that they would easily overcome the Romans, who were worn out by the heat and by thirst. They hemmed them in on all sides, so that they could not obtain water from anywhere. For they themselves were far superior in numbers. Consequently the Romans were in a bad

---

[1] Dio, 71, 3; cf. *PW*, 3A, 1927, 798 ff.

[2] Gnecchi, II, p. 27, M. Aurelio, No. 2; cf. W. Zwikker, op. cit., 135 ff.; Dio, 71, 13, 2. See further Appendix III.

way, from their exhaustion, wounds, the sun and their thirst, and
could neither fight nor retreat, but were standing in line and in their
positions, scorched by the heat, when suddenly a great many clouds
rolled up and a great downpour burst over them – not without the
assistance of the gods. In fact, there is even a story to the effect that
Arnouphis, an Egyptian magician, who was a companion of Marcus,
had invoked by enchantments various deities, in particular Hermes
Aërios [Mercury, the god of the air], and by these means brought on
the rain. . . . When the rain poured down, at first all turned their
faces upwards and let the rain fall into their mouths, then some held
out their shields and helmets to catch it, and not only took great
gulps of it themselves, but gave it to their horses to drink. When the
barbarians charged them, they drank and fought at the same time.
Some, already wounded, actually gulped down the blood that
poured into their helmets, along with the water. In fact, most of
them were so eager to drink that they would have suffered seriously
from the enemy's onslaught, if a violent hailstorm and several
thunderbolts had not fallen on the enemy. . . .' Dio continues with a
purple passage describing the effect of this utter confusion in the
barbarian ranks. 'Marcus was saluted as Imperator by the soldiers
for the seventh time,' Dio adds, 'and accepted the title without consulting the senate, contrary to his normal practice, regarding it as a
gift from heaven.' In addition, Faustina was given the title 'Mother
of the Camp'. The former title appears on the coinage in A.D. 174.
The title for Faustina makes it practically certain that she was now
with Marcus, probably to compensate for the cancelled visit of
Marcus to Rome – he would not have seen Faustina for three years,
unless meetings had been arranged that are not recorded, and he had
probably not yet seen his youngest daughter at all.[1]

Xiphilinus, as mentioned, found Dio's account unsatisfactory.
The reason for this was that within a very few years of the incident a
firm tradition had been established that it had been the prayers of
Christian soldiers of the Twelfth Legion that had brought the rain,
not the efforts of the Egyptian priest Harnouphis. Xiphilinus gives
the Christian version. Unfortunately, one of the items of evidence

[1] Dio, 71, 8–10; *BMC*, IV, M. Aurelius, Nos. 609 ff., 1483 ff.

which he cites is valueless. The Twelfth legion had the name 'Fulminata', 'bearer of thunder', probably because its emblem was the thunderbolts of Jupiter. The legion had been called this for well over a century, but Xiphilinus and other Christian writers allege that it was awarded the title 'Thundering' because of this battle. That is false. The Twelfth Fulminata was in fact a legion of Cappadocia, and it is not absolutely certain that it was fighting in the northern wars (although this is quite possible – in fact, it might explain why there had been trouble in Armenia, if part of the Cappadocian garrison was away). Besides this, eastern legionaries were likelier than any others to have been Christian at this time. There may therefore have been some Christian soldiers involved in the battle.[1]

Unfortunately there is no reason to suppose that they were given any credit for the victory by Marcus, as is also alleged. On the contrary, coins of the year A.D. 173 portray the god Hermes, and it seems likely that Marcus built a temple to this god in gratitude. A medallion shows Jupiter in a four-horse chariot destroying barbarians with his thunderbolts.[2] On the Aurelian Column, the event is depicted in graphic detail. The weary Romans are exhibited in marching order. A legionary points at the sky and immediately to the right rain is seen falling. One man waters his horse, another drinks, some hold up their shields to collect the water. The downpour is personified as a frightening and semi-human figure, with gloomy face and long beard, whose hair melts into descending streams of water. The rain-spirit rushes forward over men and animals, while beneath him appears a prospect of dead barbarians and stricken horses. If the personification had a name, it can only have been the name of one of the gods whose aid was acknowledged on the coinage – presumably Hermes Aërios, although the grim and frightening figure is very unlike the normal youthful winged-footed Hermes or Mercury. The god described by Dio as 'Hermes Aërios' is apparently a native Egyptian deity, Thoth-Shou, whose aid was invoked by the exotic

[1] See Appendix IV.
[2] *BMC*, IV, M. Aurelius, Nos. 1441 ff.; Gnecchi, II, p. 28, M. Aurelio, No. 11.

Egyptian priest Harnouphis. In any case, Marcus recognized the assistance only of the pagan gods. Unfortunately, even the exact date of the battle remains uncertain. The only clear indication is provided by Dio's information that after it Marcus accepted the title of Imperator VII, which appears on the coinage in A.D. 174. But the title could have been accepted in A.D. 173 or even earlier and not announced on the coinage immediately (as was the case with IMP. V in the year A.D. 167). None, except Dio, by implication, dates it to A.D. 174. An important piece of information is also given by certain sources: the Roman commander was not the emperor in person, but Pertinax. Another, very late and unreliable, source seems to state that the event occurred in the land of the Cotini, not that of the Quadi. The biographer of Marcus is unfortunately very brief, and he recounts both the lightning miracle and the rain miracle in the same sentence, clearly regarding them both as events which happened in the presence and by the agency of Marcus himself, possibly (although this is not obvious) more or less simultaneously. Argument on these questions might be lengthy, tedious and, probably, inconclusive. But some conclusions should be stated. It seems likelier that it was Pertinax who was with the Roman army at the time of the Rain Miracle, for this is not the kind of story that would have been invented. It is understandable that some versions assert that Marcus was present, but it should be noted that Dio does not say so – although it could be assumed by an incautious reader that he meant this. In view of the profusion of coins of A.D. 173 celebrating the *Religio* of Marcus, it might seem justifiable to assert that Marcus had been there. But it must be remembered that he had certainly already been credited with a 'lightning miracle' in A.D. 172. In A.D. 173 Pertinax was a very subordinate senator, and further miraculous intervention would be better alluded to by references to the piety of the emperor. The fact that there were two 'miracles' caused by similar phenomena explains why they were conflated in most sources and the composite occurrence assigned to Marcus. It may, incidentally, be noted that the despised source which assigns the rain miracle to the territory of the Cotini may in fact be providing the location of the lightning miracle. In A.D. 172 the Cotini would have been due for attack after their treatment of Tarrutenus Paternus.[1]

Divine assistance was seconded by Roman valour. The tough Pannonian cavalry officer Valerius Maximianus slew with his own hands Valao, the chieftain of the Naristae, a smaller neighbour and ally of the Quadi. The lengthy inscription set up in his honour some ten years later by the councillors of the city of Diana Veteranorum (Zana) in Numidia gives full details, with which Maximianus was no doubt only too willing to supply them: he was 'publicly praised by the emperor Antoninus Augustus and presented with a horse, *phalerae* and arms'. This native of Poetovio (modern Ptuj in Yugoslavia) in the province of Upper Pannonia had already given and was to give more vital service in this war against an enemy that directly threatened his own homeland. In addition to this decoration, he was promoted to command the crack double strength cavalry regiment (*ala milliaria* – a unit of which there were at most twelve in the entire army, less than half as many as there were legions), the *ala I Ulpia contariorum* stationed at Arrabona (modern Györ in Hungary), which had done good service in the war from the very start, when under Macrinius Avitus it repulsed the invasion of the Langobardi and Obii in A.D. 166 or 167.[2]

The war that Marcus and the Roman armies were fighting was a desultory affair, as the visual record of it on the Aurelian column illustrates. Apart from the great Rain Miracle battle, there were scarcely any pitched battles, but a succession of minor engagements against an enemy that had to be fought section by section. As a result, new methods of deploying the troops had to be worked out. Instead of fighting as a legion, the legionary troops were split up into special detachments (*vexillationes*). The chance record of inscriptions has preserved details of some of the special commands necessary in the war and of careers of outstanding generals. Vettius Sabinianus was now legate of XIV Gemina, but his real task was to

---

[1] Harnouphis and Hermes Aërios: see the remarkable article by J. Guey, *Rev. de Phil.*, 22, 1948, 16 ff. I confess I still find the chronology of these events baffling, in spite of the arguments of Guey (in *Mél. d'arch. et d'hist.*, 60, 1948, 105 ff. and 61, 1949, 93 ff.). See Appendix III.

[2] *AE*, 1956, 124. On Maximianus cf. H.-G. Pflaum, op. cit., No. 181 *bis* and add.

be acting governor of Upper Pannonia while the governor was fighting beyond the frontiers with Marcus. A young senator named Julius Pompilius Piso was given a task force composed of the First Italica and Fourth Flavia, legions of Lower and Upper Moesia respectively, with their auxiliary units. He was given the powers of a governor. This may have been to administer newly conquered territory. But it is not possible to date this most unusual command very precisely – it might even have been held at the time of crisis in A.D. 170–1. Macrinius Avitus had gone on from the outwardly civilian post of curator of Ariminum (Rimini) where he succeeded Arrius Antoninus, to govern Upper Moesia in succession to Caerellius, who moved to Raetia. In about A.D. 173 Macrinius Avitus was made consul and went on to govern Lower Moesia, being followed in the upper province by Pertinax.[1]

The year A.D. 173 was the third year in succession that Marcus had spent at Carnuntum. The second book of his *Meditations* is headed 'at Carnuntum'. The third is headed 'On the Granua'. The Granua, the modern Hrón or Gran, is one of the northern tributaries of the Danube, and flows through Slovakia, the confluence being a little to the west of the great southward bend of the Danube, just within the

[1] *AE*, 1920, 45 (Sabinianus); Dessau, *ILS*, 1111 (Piso); ibid., 1107 (Avitus). Cf. A. R. Birley, *A. Ant. Philip.*, 1963, 109 ff.

PLATES 9–16: Eight scenes from the Aurelian column, Rome

9 (*opposite*). The personified figure of the river-god Father Danube watches as the Roman army marches over a bridge of boats into enemy territory (*Left-hand part of Scene III*).

10. The Roman army, led by the emperor and his staff, cross the bridge of boats into enemy territory across the Danube (*Right-hand part of Scene III*).

11. An enemy siege engine is destroyed by lightning, as the emperor looks on (*Left-hand part of Scene IX*).

12. The Rain Miracle: the mysterious rain-god spreads out his arms over dying barbarians and their horses and grateful Romans (*Scene XVI*).

13. Enemy prisoners are decapitated—presumably captured rebels or treaty-breakers from the Quadi (*Scene LXI*).

14. The heads of decapitated enemy are displayed to Marcus Aurelius by his soldiers (*Scene LXVI*).

15. The emperor sacrifices at an altar on the field (*Scene LXXV*).

16. Marcus Aurelius with some of his staff outside a fort (*Scene LXXX*).

10. The Roman army, led by the emperor and his staff, cross the bridge of boats into enemy territory across the Danube

11. An enemy siege engine is destroyed by lightning, as the emperor looks on

12. The Rain Miracle: the mysterious rain-god spreads out his arms over dying barbarians and their horses and grateful Romans

13. Enemy prisoners are decapitated—presumably captured rebels or treaty-breakers from the Quadi

14. The heads of decapitated enemy are displayed to Marcus Aurelius by his soldiers

15. The emperor sacrifices at an altar on the field

16. Marcus Aurelius with some of his staff outside a fort

confines of Upper Pannonia. If Marcus came near the source of the Hrón, he would have been close to the headwaters of the northward-flowing River Vistula – which he might even have seen, for the Vistula rises in the lands of the Cotini. The River Hrón flows near the boundaries of the Quadi and the Sarmatian Jazyges, the fierce horse-men of the Hungarian Plain. These were to be Marcus' next antagonists.

The Quadi had had the same terms imposed upon them as the Marcomanni (full details are not recorded). In the course of A.D. 174 they broke their word again, by giving assistance to the Jazyges. In addition to this, they were not returning all the captives and deserters as promised – 'only a few,' according to Dio – those that they could neither sell nor usefully employ for any work. Or, if they ever did hand over any of those who were in good physical condition, they kept back relatives of these men, 'so that the men handed over would desert again in order to rejoin them'. This situation in itself argues a severe lowering of morale on the Roman side, and the men-tion of deserters goes a long way to explain why coins were issued in A.D. 171 appealing to the loyalty and harmony of the armies. It had always been a principle of Roman law that a captive regained his legal status as a Roman citizen when he returned from captivity. But this meant that there was no obligation on him to repay the ransom money. It seems to have been the case that, as a result of the enor-mous numbers who fell into enemy hands by one means or another at the beginning of the A.D. 170s, Marcus enacted that ransomed captives did not regain their rights until they had repaid their ran-som money. This somewhat inhumane enactment was probably designed to encourage private individuals to undertake the ransom-ing of captives as a business proposition, as the only means of getting substantial numbers back.

Another development caused further anxiety. The Quadi ex-pelled their philoroman ruler Furtius and the anti-Roman Ario-gaesus took power. Marcus refused to recognize Ariogaesus – in fact set a price on his head, alive or dead – and rejected the conciliatory offer of the surrender of 50,000 captives in return for renewal of the peace treaty. (All Roman treaties were made with individuals, and the Quadic treaty would require renewal on the change of ruler.)

However, when Ariogaesus was captured, Marcus treated him mildly. His punishment was exile in Alexandria. On the same principle that had been followed when Britain was made the place of exile of an Armenian dissident, somewhere as far away as possible was selected. Ariogaesus' subsequent fate is not recorded.[1]

Details of the Roman campaigning against the Jazyges are not recorded, except for one incident. Mention is made of a Roman victory against them. As the title IMP. VII was not announced on the coinage of A.D. 174 until some way through the year, it may be that this victory was regarded as confirming the salutation accepted under extraordinary circumstances for the Rain Miracle victory. It has been noted that the title Germanicus disappears from the coinage at the end of A.D. 173, and it has been suggested that this was caused by the revolt of the Quadi. If a German people was again in arms against Rome, retention of a title which claimed conquest and victory over that people would seem, particularly to the scrupulous Marcus, somewhat presumptuous, and he may have given orders for it to be dropped. In that case, the campaign against the Jazyges with which the Quadic revolt is associated by Dio may have also begun in late A.D. 173. The incident from the campaign against the Jazyges recorded by Dio refers to a winter battle on the frozen Danube, which he regarded as something of a military curiosity. The Jazyges had obviously attempted a surprise attack. The Romans reacted vigorously and pursued them back over the ice. The enemy expected that the Romans could easily be outmanoeuvred in a battle under such conditions, as their own horses had been trained to go well even on ice. 'The Romans on observing this were not worried, but formed together in a compact body, facing the enemy all at once. Most of them laid down their shields and supported one foot on them, so that they would not slip.' With their superior discipline they were able to get the better of the Jazyges. This battle belongs to the winter of A.D. 173–4 or 174–5.[2]

At some stage in the fighting of A.D. 174 the Jazyges sued for peace, but it was refused them. After his experience with the Quadi,

---

[1] Dio, 71, 16; 71, 13, 2–4; cf. E. Levy, *Class. Phil.*, 38, 1943, 159 ff.
[2] Ibid., 71, 7, 1; *BMC*, IV, M. Aurelius, Nos. 609 ff., 1483 ff.

Marcus was unwilling to take chances. It would seem, in fact, that the Jazygian envoys had represented only part of their people, the supporters of one of their kings, Banadaspus, who was imprisoned by his own people for making overtures to Marcus. It may have been in A.D. 174 that the Marcomanni appealed for a relaxation of the terms imposed on them. 'In view of the fact that they had fulfilled all the conditions that had been imposed on them, even if grudgingly and unwillingly, Marcus restored to them half of the neutral zone along their borders, allowing them to settle up to five miles from the Danube; and he fixed places and days for mutual trade (which had not been settled before), and exchanged hostages with them.'[1]

Dio records two incidents from the German war – he himself was doubtful about their historical importance, but they do convey something of the atmosphere of the wars. 'A boy who had been taken prisoner was questioned by Marcus. "I cannot give you a reply," he said, "because of the cold. So if you want to gain any information give orders for a coat to be given me, if you have one." A soldier who was on watch one night on the Danube heard a shout from his fellow soldiers who were prisoners on the other side. He at once swam across just as he was, set them free, and came back.'

The Column of Marcus provides the best commentary on the wars. It may never be possible to use it as a guide to the exact chronology of events, but it portrays the actuality of the fighting in a far more vivid way than any written description ever could. There is a change of atmosphere from the aggressive martial confidence of the Column of Trajan, which extolled the disciplined achievement of the armies of Rome. There is a note of pathos that is only too clear, when the burning and destruction of enemy villages, the execution of rebels and the remorseless onset of battle are displayed, carved on the winding panels. The only unity that it possesses is the ever present figure of Marcus, generally accompanied by a faithful counsellor who is surely Claudius Pompeianus. The war was a grim and sordid necessity. Marcus knew it, and the artists of the column clearly felt it.[2]

Marcus carried on his judicial business as uninterruptedly as

---

[1] Dio, 71, 15–16.   [2] Dio, 71, 5, 1–2; on the spirit of the column see especially P. G. Hamberg, *Studies in Roman Imperial Art*, Uppsala-Copenhagen, 1945.

possible during the war. 'Whenever he had spare time from the war he held court.' Dio states, 'he used to order that an abundant supply of water should be measured out for the speakers on the water-clocks used in court, and he went into the preliminary inquiries and examinations at great length, so as to administer strict justice from every point of view. As a result, he often spent as many as eleven or twelve days trying the same case, in spite of holding sessions at night sometimes. For he was hard-working and applied himself with detailed care to all the responsibilities of his office. He never said, wrote or did anything as if it were an unimportant matter, but would sometimes spend whole days over some tiny point of detail, thinking that it was right that an emperor should never do anything hurriedly. For he believed that, if he should overlook even the smallest detail, it would result in criticism of all his other actions. Yet he was so weak physically that at first he could not endure the cold and, even after the soldiers had assembled at his command, would withdraw without addressing a word to them. He ate very little food, and that always at night. He could not take anything in the daytime, except some of the medicine called *theriac*. This he took not so much because he was afraid of anything, but because he was suffering from a chest and stomach condition. It is said that the practice of taking this drug enabled him to endure both this and other illnesses.' The point of Dio's remark about *theriac* is that the word means literally 'anti-dote', and emperors and other rulers in antiquity not infrequently took some form of antidote to give them immunity from poison. The medicine which Marcus took was prescribed for him by Galen. It contained opium. Galen records that Marcus tried to give up taking the drug, but found that he could not do without it – he could not sleep, and had to take a regular dose again. This *may* indicate that he had become an opium addict. But Marcus did not become a helpless addict like Thomas de Quincey, and the attempt to dis-cover traces of the opium eater's confused and distorted imagination in the *Meditations* has not been very convincing.[1] It is reasonable to

[1] Dio, 71, 6. Cf. T. W. Africa, *J. Hist. Ideas*, 1961, 97 ff. (unconvincing), and for another 'diagnosis', R. Dailly-H. van Effenterre, *Rev. Ét. Anc.*, 56, 1954, 347 ff.

suppose that he took the opium as a pain-killer and as a sleeping-draught. The illness he suffered from sounds like some form of ulcer, which would not be surprising.

Since Dio introduces Marcus' close attention to his legal business at this stage of his narrative, this is an appropriate point to mention one or two cases which required his attention at this time. But first a statement of administrative interest from the biographer may be mentioned. 'Marcus enrolled many of his friends in the senate, with the rank of aedile or praetor. He bestowed the rank of aedile or praetor on many senators who were poor but undeserving of blame – and he did not appoint anyone as a senator whom he did not know personally.'[1] His law-tutor Maecianus had of course been enrolled in the senate at an early stage in the reign. But it was during the heavy fighting which led to severe loss of life in all ranks that he was obliged to make men like Pertinax and Macrinius Avitus senators and give them immediate positions of high military responsibility. There was indeed a severe shortage of suitably qualified men for high command. In the reign of Pius men like Statius Priscus who had been promoted to the senate had to serve a long apprenticeship in junior posts before attaining to the responsibilities which their talents deserved. The crisis of the Marcomannic or northern wars made such procedure inadvisable. Marcus was no respecter of persons – as his choice of Claudius Pompeianus as son-in-law indicates. He judged strictly on merit.

An interesting case came up during this period involving the family life of a senator. 'A certain Brasidas, a Spartan senator of praetorian rank, had emancipated his sons from his control when a legacy had been left to them by his divorced wife (which they could receive only on condition that they were *sui iuris* by their father's death). Therefore, Scaevola recalls, the deified Marcus decreed that the legacy must be handed over to them, having understood the wishes of their mother, who had put off their receiving the legacy until their father's death because she did not believe that their father would emancipate them. But she would have done so if she

[1] *v. Marci*, 10, 4–5.

had hoped that he would emancipate them. Scaevola heard Marcus adjudicating on such a case in his audience hall (*auditorium*).' One may wonder whether Brasidas had made some arrangement with his sons, to share some of their mother's inheritance with them, on condition that he emancipated them from his authority so that they could obtain it in the first place. But Marcus evidently felt that the action was reasonable.[1]

Scaevola, one of Marcus' main advisers on legal questions, does not reveal where the hearing took place. It may have taken place at Marcus' headquarters, at Carnuntum or at Sirmium, as did another celebrated case involving a Greek senator, which although of insufficient legal interest to have been recorded by the lawyers, is reported in some detail by Philostratus in his *Lives of the Sophists*. The senator was Marcus' former tutor Herodes Atticus. The exact background to the case is somewhat obscure, in spite of the details given by Philostratus in his biography of Herodes. It had its origin, apparently, in the hostility shown to Herodes by the Quintilii brothers, who had been acting as special commissioners in the province of Achaea. The family of the Quintilii was from Alexandria Troas, a Roman colony in the province of Asia near the site of Troy – and therefore Latin in origin. They had risen to some prominence by the reign of Pius, and the brothers Maximus and Condianus achieved the exceptional honour of being consuls together for the year A.D. 151. Their sons were also in high favour. Maximus, the son of Condianus, was consul in A.D. 172, and his cousin the younger Condianus was also obviously having a successful career. Herodes disliked the two brothers and indulged in the luxury of calling them 'Trojans', which for a Greek may have been a pleasant private joke. But the Quintilii encouraged Herodes' enemies, and hostility to him at Athens grew. Herodes brought a charge of 'conspiracy to set the people against him' before the proconsul. But his adversaries, Demostratus, Praxagoras and Mamertinus, appealed to Marcus. They hoped to find him favourable to their side, Philostratus says, because Marcus suspected Herodes of having intrigued treasonably with Lucius against him. This assertion may be somewhat

[1] *Digest.*, 36, 1, 23 (22), *pr.*

exaggerated. 'Now the emperor was based among the peoples of Pannonia, with his headquarters at Sirmium, and Demostratus and his friends lodged near the imperial residence. Marcus provided them with supplies and often asked them if they needed anything. He was in any case disposed to treat them favourably, and his wife and his little daughter, who still could not speak properly, urged him to do so. His little daughter especially used to fall at her father's knees and implore him with many blandishments to save the Athenians for her.' This must be Vibia Aurelia Sabina, Marcus' and Faustina's youngest child, as is apparent from a later reference to the daughter being three years old.

Herodes had brought with him to Sirmium two twin girls whom he had brought up from childhood (they were the daughters of his freedman Alcimedon) and had made his cupbearers and cooks. Shortly before the tribunal met, they were killed by lightning while they were asleep in the tower where Herodes and his party were lodging in the suburbs of the town. The emotional Herodes was driven frantic with grief, and when he appeared before the emperor all his usual eloquence deserted him. Instead he attacked Marcus violently. 'This is all I get in return for my hospitality to Lucius – though it was you who sent him to me! These are the reasons on the basis of which you judge me – and you are sacrificing me to the whim of a woman and a three-year-old child!' The praetorian prefect Bassaeus Rufus felt that only one conclusion was possible: Herodes obviously wanted to die. 'Herodes replied: "My good fellow, an old man fears little" ', and swept out of the court before his allotted time was up. Marcus 'did not frown or change his expression', but told the other side to make their defence, ' "even though Herodes does not give you leave" '. Marcus listened for some time without showing his feelings, but eventually the whole attack on Herodes moved him to open tears. However, the attack was not only on Herodes personally, but also on his freedmen. These Marcus punished, although mildly, and Alcimedon was pardoned, on the grounds that the loss of his daughters had already caused him sufficient suffering. Philostratus could not be absolutely certain what happened to Herodes, but concludes that a suggestion that he was exiled was unfounded. He did in fact live for a while after the trial, at Oricum in Epirus, a city that had benefited from his generosity, but this was not exile, says Philostratus. It is probable that Marcus advised Herodes to live away from Athens for a time.[1]

The biographer records a number of administrative measures which Marcus took in his absence from Rome. 'He left forceful instructions while absent that the entertainment of the Roman people should be provided by the richest givers of public spectacles. For there had been popular rumours that he intended to deprive them of their entertainments after he had taken the gladiators away to the war – and to drive them to take up philosophy. He had in fact ordered that the ballet-dancers (*pantomimi*) should start their performances nine days later than usual, so that business should not be disrupted. There was talk, as we mentioned earlier, about his wife's love-affairs with ballet-dancers, but he cleared her of these charges in his letters.' The effect of the calling-up of the gladiators for military service was in fact, it appears, to bring an enormous increase in the prices demanded by the *lanistae*, the trainers and promoters. This price-increase was intensely unpopular, and was to have tragic effects – as a by-product – a few years later. Faustina's alleged dalliance with undesirable lovers was the subject of a good deal of malicious gossip. She was also rumoured to have a fancy for gladiators. Her only opportunity for indulging such fancies must have been at the beginning of the A.D. 170s, and it may have been partly to put a stop to the gossip, however much truth or otherwise there was in it, that Marcus summoned her to the front with their youngest child.

'He prohibited riding and driving within the city boundaries. He abolished mixed bathing. He reformed the morals of married women and young nobles, which were growing lax. He separated the sacred rites of Serapis from the miscellaneous ceremonies of the Pelusia. There was a rumour, as a matter of fact, that certain persons masquerading as philosophers had been making trouble both for the state and for private citizens, but Marcus refuted this charge. It was his custom to give lighter sentences for all offences than those usually inflicted by the laws, although on occasion he showed himself

[1] *PIR 2*, C 681 (Scaevola); Philostratus, *v. soph.*, 2, 1, 11–12.

implacable towards those who were clearly guilty of serious crimes. He himself conducted trials of distinguished men for capital offences, and with complete fairness. Once he rebuked a praetor who had heard the pleas of the defendants in a hurry, and ordered him to hold a retrial, saying that it was a matter of honour for the accused that they should be tried by a judge who judged on behalf of the people. Marcus always acted with equity, even in his dealings with enemy prisoners of war. He settled an immense number of foreigners on Roman soil.' With the brief mention of the two miracles that follows, this miscellaneous summary by the biographer of his activity in the years A.D. 169–75 is almost concluded.[1]

The campaigning season of A.D. 175 brought a renewed assault on the Sarmatians. Marcus was now determined to make their territory and that of the Marcomanni and Quadi into a province. He is in fact credited with the wish to exterminate the Sarmatians utterly. It is not quite clear how literally this statement (in Cassius Dio) should be taken. But the territory of the Marcomanni was already partially occupied, by a detachment of troops from the African legion Third Augusta, and it may well be that Julius Pompilius Piso with his special force and special powers was occupying part of the Sarmatian lands. But the campaign can barely have been under way for a few weeks, in early spring, when news was brought to Marcus that Avidius Cassius, the governor of Syria and by Marcus' order virtual ruler of the whole east, had raised the standard of rebellion, and had been recognized as emperor in most of the eastern provinces, including Egypt.[2]

---

[1] v. Marci, 23, 4–24, 4.

[2] Dessau, ILS, 2747 (III Augusta, cf. H.-G. Pflaum, Les carrières procuratoriennes, etc., No. 198); ibid., 1111 (Piso); Dio, 71, 16, 1; v. Marci, 24, 5–6.

IX

THE LAST YEARS

THE NEWS of Cassius' rebellion apparently reached Marcus like a
bolt from the blue.[1] He ought to have had some warning of it, for
example through the head of the Greek Secretariat, the *ab epistulis
Graecis*. For a time during the wars this post was held by an expert
on Plato named Alexander, from whom, Marcus records in the
Meditations, he learned 'not often and only from necessity to say to
anyone and to write in a letter that "I am too busy", and not to get
out of the duties involved in our relationship with those who live
with us by some expression like that, with the excuse of "pressure of
business" .' Alexander is said to have died at his post.[2] Criticism of
him would be unfair. But it seems a little surprising that such a man
was chosen by Marcus, considering his choice for the Joint Secretariat or the Latin Secretariat of tough men with a military background such as T. Varius Clemens and Tarrutenus Paternus. But
the functions of the head of the Greek Secretariat at the time of the
northern wars had no doubt been expected to be, more or less, concerned with peaceful matters. In any case, other holders of the post
are known from this period. One of them, Ti. Claudius Vibianus
Tertullus, was in office at some time in the period A.D. 172–5. He
received promotion, as well, so fault was not found with him. Another,
T. Aius Sanctus, was later made Commodus' tutor in oratory.[3]

---

[1] Dio, 71, 17 (ἐξεπλάγη); 71, 23, 3.
[2] *PIR* 2, A 503. *Med.*, 1, 12 (probably not a teacher of Marcus as maintained
by J. Schwendemann, op. cit., 11 ff.).
[3] H.-G. Pflaum, *Les carrières procuratoriennes*, etc., Nos. 156 (Clemens), 172
(Paternus), 252+*add*. (Tertullus), 178 *bis* (Sanctus). On the office, see Pflaum,
II, p. 684, n. 1.

Whatever the cause, Marcus was totally unprepared, and extremely disturbed by the news, which reached him in the form of a despatch from P. Martius Verus, governor of Cappadocia, who had remained loyal. The rebellion is a highly puzzling episode. Both Dio and the biographer assert that Cassius proclaimed himself emperor at the wish of Faustina. With more convincing detail it is explained that she had expected Marcus to die – 'she was in despair over her husband's health'[1] – or that 'seeing that her husband had fallen ill and expecting that he would die at any moment, she was afraid that the empire would fall to someone else as Commodus was young and rather naïve – and that she would be reduced to a private station. Therefore she secretly persuaded Cassius to make his preparations, so that if anything should happen to Antoninus, he might take over both her and the empire. So, while he was considering this, a message came that Marcus was dead (in such circumstances rumours always make things out to be worse than they actually are). At once, without waiting for confirmation, he laid claim to the empire, on the grounds that he had been elected by the soldiers then in Pannonia. In spite of the fact that he not long after learned the truth, nevertheless, having once made a beginning, he did not change course, but within a short time took control of all the region south of the Taurus, and began preparations to seize the throne by war.'[2] The biographer springs into the breach to defend Faustina's reputation in his largely fictitious biography of Cassius, but his advocacy is tarnished by the bogus letters which he produces to support his case.[3] Cassius Dio and the biographer's source for the anti-Faustina version which he records, Marius Maximus, were both young men at the time of the event they described, and must be given some credence, even if, it must be admitted, very few persons can have had the opportunity of learning the truth.[4]

Marcus had certainly been unwell, as Cassius Dio himself records.[5] Some at least of his *Meditations* had been composed

---

[1] *v. Marci*, 24, 6, repeated with more details in *v. Av. Cass.*, 7, 1.
[2] Dio, 71, 22, 3.
[3] *v. Av. Cass.*, 9, 5–11, 8. See Appendix I.
[4] See Appendix I.   [5] 71, 1, 2; 71, 6, 3–4; 71, 24, 4; 71, 36, 2–3.

already. That work is full of references to the nearness of death. Marcus clearly did not expect to live long. Avidius Cassius can hardly have been able to know that a short while before his emperor had written of himself in his private notebook as 'one already on the threshold of death', had thought of suicide, and had then calmly resolved to 'wait for death with a good grace'.[1] But Marcus' ill-health and weakness must have been common knowledge. Faustina was with Marcus. Commodus was in Rome. If Marcus had in fact died when he was thought to have, with Commodus a boy of thirteen who had not yet assumed the toga of manhood, it is clear that some other person would have needed to take on the role of his protector. Even Nero had been older (nearly seventeen) at the death of Claudius – not that he was a likely choice as a precedent.[2] The days of child-emperors were yet to come. If Marcus died in A.D. 175, one man was in a stronger position than any, his son-in-law Tiberius Claudius Pompeianus, twice consul, husband of the junior Augusta, popular with the senate, and, having been with Marcus and the armies throughout the four previous campaigning seasons, well known, at the least, to the most powerful armies in the empire. But Faustina – and Lucilla – felt an antipathy to Pompeianus.[3] Avidius Cassius was the only available counterweight to him. There is no need, however, to suppose any personal relationship between the empress and the rebellious general. If they had ever met, which is not unlikely, it must have been at least nine years previously, when Faustina joined Lucilla in the east at the end of the Parthian war.

Cassius was declared a public enemy by the senate as soon as the news reached it, and it ordered his property to be confiscated.[4] His position was not strong, but neither was it hopeless. He had a strong personal following in his native Syria and in much of the east, due partly to his royal origin, partly to his successes in the Parthian wars and in suppressing the revolt of the Boucoli. He had powerful

---

[1] *Med.*, 2, 2; 2, 11; 2, 17 (written 'Among the Quadi').

[2] On Nero, see *PIR* 2, D 129.

[3] *PIR* 2, C 973. See H.-G. Pflaum, *J. des Savants*, 1961, 33 ff., on this marriage.

[4] *v. Marci*, 24, 4; *v. Av. Cass.*, 7, 6–7.

marriage connections with an extremely rich and extensive family group of Lycian notables through his son-in-law, Claudius Dryantianus.[1] In terms of actual power he could count on, at most, seven legions, his own three in Syria, two in Palestine, one in Arabia, and one in Egypt – for Calvisius Statianus, the friend of Fronto (who could not 'find sufficient praise for him'), had acceded to him. Statianus may, of course, have had little choice. It must be remembered however that Cassius had been in Egypt in A.D. 172, and the two men may have had the opportunity of speculating together about possible future action. Statianus had been *ab epistulis Latinis* during the early years of the reign, and therefore may have had a great deal of highly valuable intimate knowledge about the previous behaviour of men whose support might be sought. Statianus' freedom of action must have been increased by the fact that his family was, probably, with him. At any rate his son Faustinianus, the same for whom Fronto, who 'loved him like a son', had obtained a military commission in Lower Germany some fifteen years before, now held an important post in the Egyptian administration, as *idiologus* at Alexandria.[2]

With Egypt in his power Cassius controlled the main granary of Rome, and the opportunity to exert economic blackmail existed. But he had failed to win over Martius Verus, his former associate in the Parthian War and governor of Cappadocia, to his cause. Verus should have had two legions under his command, although both of these were probably depleted by the demands of the Danubian front. Cassius may at first have hoped for some support from the Danube armies, especially if some of the eastern legionaries were there, and some of the men in northern legions must have served under him against the Parthians. But his strict discipline may not have endeared him to them. At any rate, no support for him seems to have been forthcoming from any of the European provinces.

---

[1] Dryantianus: *PIR 2*, C 879. The members of the family are recorded on the inscription, *IGR*, III, 500 (Cassius is omitted).

[2] Fronto, *ad amicos*, 1, 5=Haines, I, 290 ff. Cf. *PIR 2*, C 346 and 356, and H.-G. Pflaum, *Les carrières procuratoriennes*, etc., Nos. 166 and 177. But note also *SB*, VI, 9393, from which it can be deduced that his prefecture of Egypt ran without a break from A.D. 170–5.

Herodes Atticus is reported to have sent him a letter celebrated for its brevity. It contained one word: ἐμάνης ('you are mad').[1]

At Rome there was panic. It was thought that Cassius would arrive during Marcus' absence and that he would ravage the city 'like a tyrant' in revenge for his having been declared a public enemy. Marcus took immediate steps. Vettius Sabinianus, at the time serving as governor of Lower Pannonia, was sent with a special force 'to protect the city' (*ad tutelam urbis*). Marcus also summoned Commodus to his side.[2] Commodus had taken a step towards entering public life a few months earlier. On January 20, 175, he had been admitted to the colleges of priests. Before his departure for Pannonia, still wearing the *toga praetexta* of boyhood, he distributed bounty to the people in the Basilica of Trajan. The event was commemorated on coins, which symbolically depict the event: the seated Commodus holds out his right hand; the personified figure of Liberalitas stands before him holding an *abacus* and cornucopiae, while a citizen holds up a fold of his toga to catch the falling coins; behind Commodus stands a figure who may· be the prefect of the city (probably T. Vitrasius Pollio at this time, husband of the emperor's cousin). This giving of bounty was probably not so much to commemorate the entry into the priesthood of the young prince, as to celebrate in advance his assumption of the *toga virilis*. Marcus had decided that this should take place at once, at the front, instead of waiting for the traditional date, the Liberalia of March 17. Thus the giving of largesse to the people probably came immediately after the summons from Marcus and before Commodus' departure. The benefaction was in any case a useful insurance of public support among the volatile urban populace. At the same time, the coins somewhat anxiously proclaimed the loyalty and unity of the armies.[3]

[1] Philostratus,·*v. soph.*, 2, 1, 13. On the disposition of legions see the convenient survey by A. Betz, *Carnuntina*, ed. E. Swoboda, Graz-Köln, 1956, 17 ff.

[2] *v. Marci*, 25, 2; *v. Av. Cass.*, 7, 7; *AE*, 1920, 45; Dio, 71, 22, 2.

[3] *v. Comm.*, 1, 10; 2, 1; 12, 1–3. *BMC*, IV, M. Aurelius and Commodus, Nos. 1517 ff. (*liberalitas*), 1495 ff. (*concord. exerc.*), cf. 625 (*securitas publica*). See J. M. Heer, *Philologus*, Supp. 9, 1901, 14 ff. Vitrasius Pollio is named as prefect only in a forged letter tacked on to Justin's *Second Apology* (for a convenient text see Haines, II, 300 ff.); but the inscription, Dessau, *ILS*, 1112, could have recorded this in its original state.

At first Marcus tried to keep the news of the uprising secret, but when he could conceal it from the army no longer – 'the troops were strongly disturbed by the rumour and were talking a lot' – he addressed a speech to them, Dio records.[1] As Dio had the opportunity of knowing something of the events of A.D. 175 from personal experience and from eye-witness accounts, there may be some echoes in his version of an actual speech of the emperor.

'It is not to express anger, fellow soldiers, but to lament my fate, that I have come before you. For why become angry at the deity, to whom all power belongs?' He lamented the horrors of war, and the greatest horrors of civil war, and the discovery of disloyalty 'by a dearest friend'. This last expression may be technically accurate. Cassius may well have been one of those co-opted into the priesthood of the *sodales Veriani*, 'ex amicissimis'. Marcus said, Dio continues, that if the danger had been his personal danger alone, he would have been willing to set before the army or the senate the issue between himself and Cassius, and would gladly have yielded the empire to him without fighting, 'if this had seemed to be for the common good. For it is for the common good that I continue to labour and undergo danger, and have spent so much time here outside Italy, although I am already old and weak, and unable to take food without pain or sleep undisturbed.' This has the ring of truth. One may wonder, however, what issue there was between Marcus and Cassius which either might have considered susceptible to public debate. It can only have been the question of peace or war. There was, as the biographer records, a peace party among the emperor's advisers which was reluctant to continue the war. In the eastern provinces, there must by now have been considerable opposition to its continuance. Cassius might well have won support on a promise to end for good a war against northern barbarians to whom the eastern empire was indifferent, a war which can only have seemed unproductive and was an actual drain on their resources. Marcus was still bent on expanding the empire in the north.

Marcus' speech went on, according to Dio, with an appeal to the

<hr />

[1] Dio, 71, 23, 3.

loyalty and fighting spirit of the Danubian armies. Cassius' armies of the east were fewer in number than their own forces, he said, but even had they been greater by thousands, they never had and never would prove superior. He reminded them that the loyal Martius Verus had been as successful as Cassius against the Parthians, if not more so. Cassius was likely to change his mind when he heard that he (Marcus) was in fact alive. However that might be, he hoped that Cassius would not kill himself or be killed on learning that he was coming against him, for that would deprive him (Marcus) of the opportunity of giving an example of mercifulness 'for surely goodness has not completely perished among men, but a fragment of the ancient virtue remains'. Marcus wrote to the senate in similar terms, 'never abusing Cassius in any way, except that he constantly referred to him as ungrateful. Nor did Cassius say or write anything insulting to Marcus.'[1]

The biographer of Cassius includes in his unconvincing farrago the statement that Cassius proclaimed at the outset, when he still believed, or wanted it to be believed, that the emperor was dead, the deification of Marcus. But the temptation to the biographer to insert 'documentary evidence' at other points, to pad out his scanty information, was too great, and 'letters of Cassius' are produced, which include derisive comment about Marcus. These are quite worthless. Marcus was clearly in a much stronger position than Cassius. The armies of the Rhine and Danube now possessed a combined strength of sixteen legions, and with Britain, Spain and Numidia, Marcus had another five on which he could count, not to mention the élite corps of the praetorian guard. On the other hand his troops were perhaps battle-weary, and he could only take a proportion of them with him.[2]

Commodus left Rome on May 19. It cannot have taken him much more than two or three weeks at the most to reach his father at

---

[1] Dio, 71, 24, 1–4; 71, 25–71, 27, 1. Cf. Dessau, *ILS*, 8830, and *v. Marci*, 7, 11 (*sodales Veriani*). Ibid., 22, 8 (peace-party – somewhat exaggerated by J. Morris, *J. Ctld. Wbg. Inst.*, 15, 1952, 37).

[2] *v. Av. Cass.*, 7, 1–3; cf. 1, 1–7; 14, 2–8 (more plausible but equally valueless, cf. Appendix I). On the legions, see A. Betz, op. cit. (p. 256, n. 1).

Sirmium. The ceremony of the *tirocinium fori* obviously did not take place at once. A suitable day had to be chosen. July 7 was selected – 'the Nones of July, the day that Romulus disappeared from the earth'. Thus Commodus entered the ranks of the *cives Romani* under the protection of Rome's founder. Marcus commended his son to the army. At the same time he became *princeps iuventutis*, leader of the knights – and, by the same token, his position of heir-apparent was publicly proclaimed. The ceremony was a demonstration to Cassius and to Rome that Commodus was, after all, ready to take the purple if Marcus should die.[1]

The news that Marcus was facing civil war in the east inspired various barbarian tribes to offer assistance. This Marcus declined, declaring that 'the barbarians ought not to know of any trouble arising between the Romans'. During his preparations for departure, news was brought him that Cassius was dead, slain by a centurion named Antonius, after 'a dream of empire lasting three months and six days'. His head was sent to Marcus who refused to see it and had it buried. Martius Verus had taken control of Syria. One of his first acts was to burn the correspondence of Cassius, containing, no doubt, material which could incriminate many in high position (not least, perhaps, Faustina).[2]

In spite of the abrupt downfall of his adversary, Marcus still felt that it was necessary to go to the east in person, to inspect the eastern provinces and to try to restore their loyalty to the dynasty. It was therefore necessary to conclude peace with the Jazyges. As it is recorded that news of Cassius' death came to Marcus 'at the same time as news of many victories over different barbarians', it would seem that peace was made after Cassius' death. Marcus was recognized once more as emperor in Egypt by July 28. It was probably in July or August that he received the title Sarmaticus, 'conqueror of the Sarmatians', and the eighth salutation as Imperator. Curiously, however, it is reported that because of his alarm he made peace with

---

[1] *v. Comm.*, 1, 11; 2, 2; 12, 2–3. Cf. J. M. Heer, op. cit., 17 ff., for an excellent analysis.
[2] Offers of aid: Dio, 71, 27, 1a. Death of Cassius, ibid., 71, 27, 2–28, 1; *v. Av. Cass.*, 8, 1. Martius Verus: Dio, 71, 29, 2.

the enemy, most exceptionally for him, without consulting the senate over the terms.[1]

'The Jazyges were defeated and came to terms', wrote Cassius Dio. 'Zanticus himself came as a suppliant. Previously they had imprisoned Banadaspus, their second king, for making overtures to Marcus, but now all their leading men came with Zanticus and accepted the same terms as the Quadi and Marcomanni had been given, except that they were required to live twice as far away from the Danube. The emperor, in fact, had wanted to exterminate them utterly. It was obvious that they were still strong at this time and that they had caused the Romans great damage, from the fact that they surrendered 100,000 captives that were still in their hands, even after the many who had been sold, had died or had escaped; also from the fact that they at once provided as their contribution to the alliance 8,000 cavalry, 5,500 of which Marcus sent to Britain.'[2]

Although it is obvious that sending the Sarmatians to Britain was a convenient means of placing them far from home where they would not be dangerous, at the same time, the mere fact that the already enormous garrison of that province was reinforced with soldiers (probably mainly cavalry) equal in numbers to a legion or to eleven normal sized auxiliary cohorts or *alae*, must indicate that the trouble in Britain which began in A.D. 162 was not yet over. The governor at this time was probably Q. Antistius Adventus, soon to be succeeded by Caerellius, a veteran of the Danubian wars.[3] Other parts of the empire were also in a disturbed state. Aufidius Victorinus and Vehilius Gratus Julianus had evidently dealt with the Moorish invasion of Baetica – Julianus had been back from Spain in two other posts before peace was concluded on the Danube in A.D. 175. But there was more trouble to come in Spain.[4]

There had been danger in northern Gaul also: disturbances of an

---

[1] Dio, 71, 27, 2. See R. Rémondon, *Chron. d'Égypte*, 26, 1951, 364 ff. New titles: *BMC*, IV, M. Aurelius and Commodus, Nos. 1513, 1523. Peace: Dio, 71, 17.

[2] Dio, 71, 16.   [3] Adventus: *PIR 2*, A 754. Caerellius: *PIR 2*, C. 160.

[4] Victorinus: H.-G. Pflaum, *CRAI*, 1956, 189 ff. Julianus: ibid., *Les carrières procuratoriennes*, etc., No. 180 (cf. No. 221+*add*. and v. *Marci*, 22, 10, for trouble later on).

unknown nature among the Sequani in the Jura, and an invasion of
Belgica presumably near the coast, by the North Sea German tribe
of the Chauci. They were repulsed by the governor of Belgica, Didius
Julianus, with hastily raised local levies. Didius became consul in
A.D. 175 at the age of forty-two, by no means early for one who had
been brought up for a time by the emperor's mother Domitia
Lucilla. He went on to be governor of Dalmatia, not a province of
the first importance by now; but he had some fighting to do in the
suppression of brigandage in the wild hinterland.[1] Julianus' colleague as consul was Helvius Pertinax, now aged forty-nine and at
the height of his powers. Marcus had become extraordinarily impressed with this freedman's son from Liguria, who had once tried
to make a career as a centurion. After his worth had become apparent when Pompeianus had rescued him from disgrace, he went
from strength to strength. According to his biographer, Marius
Maximus preserved a eulogy of him by Marcus on the occasion of
his appointment as consul. The speech related 'all that he had done
and had suffered'. Some however expressed their distaste that a
man of such origin should hold the *fasces* (not that he in fact went to
Rome to perform the duties of his office – he did not enter the senate-
house until some ten years after becoming a senator). The line of
Euripides was quoted: 'Such things are forced on us by wretched
war.'[2] However, Marcus chose him as his *comes* to accompany him to
the east.

Another officer chosen to accompany Marcus was M. Valerius
Maximianus, who, with the rank of procurator, was put in charge
of a special force of Marcomanni, Quadi and Naristi – the latter
being the people whose chief he had killed in battle not long before – 'to punish the Oriental rising'. This description of Cassius'
revolt, revealed by the inscription in honour of Maximianus at
Diana Veteranorum, appears to indicate that it really was a

---

[1] *PIR* 2, D 77. *v. Didii*, 1, 7–8 (on which cf. R. Syme, *Gnomon*, 31, 1959, 514).
v. Marci, 22, 10.

[2] Ibid., H 73; H.-G. Pflaum, op. cit., No. 179; H.-G. Kolbe, *Bonn Jahrb.*,
162, 1962, 407 ff. The details are mostly known from the *vita*. Dio, 71, 22, 1
(Euripides, *Supp.*, 119). See also A. R. Birley, *A. Ant. Philip.*, 1963, 109 ff.

widespread rebellion. The information that Marcomannic and other barbarian troops were taken to the east appears to contradict Dio's statement that Marcus refused barbarian offers of assistance. But the Marcomanni and their neighbours probably did not offer this assistance. Tribes allied to Rome by choice, such as the Astingi and Lacringes, might have done so. The Marcomanni and the others named here were, like the Sarmatae, providing men under the terms of an agreement dictated by Rome, as much by way of hostages as anything else.[1]

Marcus set out for the eastern provinces probably in August 175, accompanied by Faustina and Commodus and other members of his family. In addition to Pertinax and Valerius Maximianus, others known to have been on the staff were the Quintilii brothers. Their home being in the Troad, they were especially suitable companions. Their sons, in the meantime, were evidently left in high command on the Danube, holding the posts, as has been plausibly suggested, of governors of the two Pannonian provinces. Another to go to the east was the North African senator C. Arrius Antoninus, who took over Cappadocia from Martius Verus, and had probably therefore been sent ahead of the imperial party. The praetorian prefect Bassaeus Rufus certainly accompanied Marcus, presumably with a strong force of guardsmen.[2] Marcus' exact route and its timetable is uncertain. He passed through Syria, avoiding Antioch, the rebel seat of government, and Cyrrhus, the birthplace of Cassius, and went through Palestine to Egypt. He seems to have spent the winter of A.D. 175–6 at Alexandria. During his stay there Palestine and part, at least, of Syria were placed under the special military rule of a second praetorian prefect, whose name is not known. If the fragmentary inscription from Capua referring to this man has been correctly interpreted, he was promoted prefect from the relatively very junior position of praetorian tribune. Several of the men who

---

[1] H.-G. Pflaum, op. cit., No. 181 *bis+add.*; *AE*, 1956, 124.

[2] The elder Quintilii: Philostratus, *v. soph.*, 2, 9, 2; cf. *PW*, 24, 1963, 983 ff. Their sons: Dio, 71, 33, 1 (cf. W. Reidinger, *Die Statthalter des ungeteilten Pannoniens und Oberpannoniens, etc.*, Bonn, 1956, 88). Arrius Antoninus: *PIR* 2, A 1088. Bassaeus Rufus: *PIR 2*, B 69; H.-G. Pflaum, op. cit., No. 161.

might otherwise have filled the post, such as Pertinax, were now ineligible, being in the senate.[1]

Marcus punished the unfortunate Calvisius Statianus lightly. His punishment was only banishment to an island, and the records of the case were burned. His associates were released from custody. In spite of the city of Alexandria's fervent adherence to Cassius' cause, Marcus treated it with moderation. 'While in Egypt he conducted himself like a private citizen and a philosopher at all the schools and temples, in fact everywhere.' It seems that it was while he was at Alexandria that 'he conducted much negotiation and ratified peace with all the kings and ambassadors of the Persians (i.e. Parthians), when they came to meet him'.[2]

In the spring he left Egypt to tour the Asian provinces. He left one of his daughters at Alexandria, which may have been a token of his forgiveness. It is not known whether he went to Syria by land, going through Palestine again. He might have gone by sea from Alexandria to the mouth of the Orontes. On his journey through Palestine to Egypt in the autumn he had been struck, according to Ammianus Marcellinus, by some characteristics of the Jewish inhabitants of the province. As the text stands, he made a comment on their 'sluggishness' or 'idleness'. On more than one occasion he apparently found the riotous behaviour and lack of concern with hygiene of the inhabitants something of a trial. Once he is said to have exclaimed with a groan: 'O, Marcomanni, O Quadi, O Sarmatians! At last I have found people idler (*inertiores*) than you!' It is not clear with what application this judgment should be understood, in the case either of the Jews or of Marcus' northern enemies. It may well be that some other word was originally written by Ammianus (e.g., *incertiores*), but the story is probably apocryphal in any case.[3]

However this may be, a kernel of truth in another story of Marcus

[1] *v. Marci*, 25, 11–26, 3. The prefect: *EE*, VIII, 478, as interpreted by H.-G. Pflaum, op. cit., No. 165 (but see the retraction, on grounds which I regard as insufficient, in the *addenda*, p. 980. But it remains hypothetical, at least). Cf. *v. Pert.*, 2, 9.

[2] Dio, 71, 28, 2–4; *v. Marci*, 25, 4 ff.; 26, 1–3 and 10 ff.

[3] *v. Marci*, 26, 4; *Amm. Marc.*, 22, 5, 5.

and the Jews may have originated from a meeting in Palestine at this time. A Roman emperor named 'Antoninus son of Asverus', who is more plausibly identified with Marcus than with any other candidates ('Asverus' probably refers to Marcus' father Annius Verus), is said to have been on terms of great intimacy with the celebrated Rabbi Juda I. The Jewish sources assign the origin of this intimacy to the infancy of both men; and, subsequently, they are said to have carried on a lengthy correspondence, and to have discussed such matters as the nature of the soul. The details given in the Talmud may be suspicious, but they are probably no more than embroiderings of an account of an actual meeting. It would accord well with the character of an emperor who conducted himself in Egypt 'like a private citizen and a philosopher' and who 'left many traces of his philosophy behind him in the east' to engage in philosophical discussion with the most learned man in Palestine.[1]

No details of Marcus visit to Antioch are recorded. From there he went on into Cilicia. He stopped in Tarsus, for the special purpose, according to Philostratus, of hearing the boy prodigy Hermogenes, the fifteen-year-old sophist, declaim. The boy's powers as an orator delighted Marcus, who gave him splendid presents.[2]

From Tarsus the road led towards the Taurus mountains. In a village in the foothills, named Halala, Faustina died. Cassius Dio takes the opportunity of making various insinuations about the cause of her death. Suicide is suggested, the motive being to avoid the penalty for having made an 'agreement' with Cassius. Suicide, at this belated stage, is an implausible story. The expectation of life for a woman of however exalted rank in ancient times, particularly for one who had borne twelve children, was low. Death at about forty-six was not unusually early (her mother had also died young). Dio gives gout as an alternative cause of death. But, whatever the precise cause, the long and tiring journeys she had undertaken in

---

[1] The 'Antoninus' in the Talmud is widely regarded as being Caracalla, cf. *Jewish Encyclopaedia*, I, 1901, 656 ff. But see L. Wallach, *Jewish Quarterly Review*, 31, 1940, 259 ff., and J. Schwartz, *Historia-Augusta-Colloquium*, Bonn, 1964, 146 ff. The internal evidence seems inconclusive, but Marcus is likelier on general grounds.

[2] Philostratus, *v. soph.*, 2, 7, 1.

the previous six to nine months cannot have done her health much good, and she had been with the army for some time before that.

She was deified by the senate. Marcus renamed the place of her death Faustinopolis. A relief now in the Museo del Campidoglio in Rome depicts Marcus watching Faustina's ascent to heaven. A large number of coins were issued in honour of her memory, and various other commemorative measures were taken. Marcus must have been aware of some at least of the stories about his wife, and it seems that the measures which he took were a deliberate vindication of her reputation.[1] He was certainly very distressed at her death, as Dio himself records.

Shortly after this bereavement he had occasion to write to the senate on the question of the treatment of Cassius' supporters. One of Cassius' sons, Maecianus, had been killed soon after the rising had ended. The other, Heliodorus, was banished. His daughter Alexandria, and son-in-law Dryantianus, were given freedom of movement, and 'entrusted to the protection of their uncle by marriage' presumably the wealthy Lycian senator Claudius Titianus. Marcus emphasized with great vigour in his despatch to the senate that he wanted to keep his reign 'unstained by the blood of any senator'. Dio places this request immediately after the death of Faustina, and adds, somewhat enigmatically, 'as if from this alone he might be able to gain some consolation for losing her'. In fact, this principle was established over a century before, probably through the efforts of the Stoic senators Helvidius Priscus and Junius Mauricus; and Nerva and his successors, if not the Flavians as well, swore an oath that they would not put any senator to death, on their accession. Marcus must have become anxious that this principle might now be in jeopardy. A practical step was now taken in the form of a decree forbidding a man to govern the province of his

---

[1] v. *Marci*, 26, 4–9; Dio, 71, 29, 1; 31, 1–2. On the expectation of life in antiquity, cf. A. R. Burn, *Past and Present*, 1953, 2 ff. The site of Faustinopolis has now been securely identified with Basmakçi, between the Cilician Gates and Tyana, cf. M. H. Ballance, *Anatol. Studies*, 14, 1964, 139 ff. (pl. xxvii). The coins: *BMC*, IV, M. Aurelius and Commodus, Nos. 698 ff., 1550 ff., on which see H. Mattingly, *Harv. Theol. Rev.*, 41, 1948, 147 ff.

origin. This had had a dangerous effect on Cassius.[1] At this time also Lycia was probably transferred, temporarily, from the annual proconsul to the direct imperial rule of a *legatus Augusti pro praetore*.[2] Cassius may well have had considerable support in that province. Marcus' journey through the Asian provinces ended at Smyrna, where he stayed for some time. Philostratus records the story of his meeting there with Aelius Aristides, who, Marcus was surprised to find, allowed three days to pass without calling. The Quintilii brothers arranged for him to come the next day, when he explained that he had been engaged in such deep meditation that he had been unable to allow himself any interruption. Marcus liked this answer, and he asked when he could hear the great orator declaim. 'Give me my subject today, and hear me speak tomorrow', was the reply. Aristides explained that he was not one of those extempore orators who 'vomit up their speeches'. He asked Marcus to allow his pupils to be present in the audience as well, a request which Marcus granted – 'for that is democratic'. Aristides then asked that the pupils should be permitted to shout and applaud as loud as they could. 'The emperor smiled, and replied: "That depends on you".'[3]

From Smyrna Marcus and Commodus and their party crossed to Athens on their way back to Rome. Marcus must have had many motives for wanting to visit the intellectual capital of the empire, the home of philosophy, including his own Stoicism, and of all the liberal arts. If Philostratus may be believed, he had another specific motive – he wished to be initiated into the Eleusinian mysteries: the mysteries of Demeter and Persephone took place at Eleusis each September. With their notions of a happy after-life in the Underworld, they may have had some particular appeal to Marcus now, when his thoughts were constantly on death.

After the trial at Sirmium, Herodes had finally returned to Attica,

---

[1] Dio, 71, 30, 1–31, 2; *v. Marci*, 26, 10–13; cf. S. J. de Laet, *Ant. Class.*, 13, 1944, 127 ff.; A. R. Birley, *Class. Rev.*, N.S. 12, 1962, 197 ff.

[2] *CIL*, XVI, 128. For the problems concerning this province, see above, p. 191, and p. 175, n. 1.

[3] Philostratus, *v. soph.*, 2, 9, 2; cf. R. Pack, *Class. Phil.*, 42, 1947, 17 ff. See also Appendix IV on possible activity by Christians at this time.

and had written to Marcus complaining that he no longer received letters from him, 'although once Marcus had written so often that three couriers had on one occasion arrived at his house in a single day, treading in one another's footsteps'. Marcus then began to write to Herodes once more, according to Philostratus, who quotes one letter written when Marcus 'was mourning his wife who had recently died', from 'his military winter quarters'. The latter term gives the impression that Marcus was on the Danube, but although it was not in fact winter, the letter must have been written from his headquarters in Asia. Even if there was no actual war going on, Marcus' activities in the east, where he had a considerable force of men, were certainly military enough. After lamenting Faustina's death and remarking on his own poor health (Marcus was now fifty-five), he went on: 'For you I wish good health, and that you should regard me as well-disposed towards you. Do not regard yourself as unjustly treated because I punished some of your household – with the mildest possible punishment – after I had found out their crimes. So do not be angry with me for this – but if I have annoyed you in any way, or am still annoying you, ask reparation from me in the temple of Athena at the time of the Mysteries. For I made a vow, when the war was blazing at its fiercest, that I too would be initiated, and I could wish that you yourself would perform the initiation.'[1]

Marcus, together with Commodus, was duly initiated. There is no record of Herodes having taken a part in the ceremony, although he was no doubt present. The initiator of Marcus and Commodus was the same L. Memmius who had initiated Lucius fourteen years previously. The biographer mentions Marcus' initiation and states that he had himself initiated 'to demonstrate his innocence of wrong-doing' – an essential prerequisite for admission – 'and he entered the sanctuary unattended'.[2]

Cassius Dio records an important action of Marcus at Athens.

---

[1] v. Marci, 27, 1; Dio, 71, 31, 3; Philostratus, v. soph., 2, 1, 12. The vow was probably made when Eleusis was ravaged by the Costoboci; Marcus later restored the temple (cf. W. Zwikker, op. cit., 166 ff.).

[2] v. Marci, 27, 1; Dittenberger, Syll. Inscr. Gr., I, 411.

'He bestowed honours on the Athenians, and he established teachers at Athens in every academic discipline, for the benefit of mankind, and he granted them an annual salary.' Philostratus relates that Marcus asked the advice of Herodes for several of the appointments, namely the four chairs of philosophy for a Platonist, an Aristotelian, a Stoic and an Epicurean. But he appointed one, Theodotus, to a chair of rhetoric on his own initiative. This man had been involved in the 'conspiracy' against Herodes, so advice from that quarter would have been heavily biased. Philostratus elsewhere mentions another professor of rhetoric at Athens at the time, Adrianus of Tyre, a pupil of Herodes. Adrianus had been appointed to his chair by Marcus before his arrival in Athens, on the strength of his reputation alone. 'The consular Severus' (who must be Marcus' son-in-law Cn. Claudius Severus) had made some severe criticisms of Adrianus' style, so Marcus went to hear for himself; Adrianus was to speak on a theme which the emperor had set for him. Marcus was impressed, and the sophist received a number of gifts and privileges. The criticism of Claudius Severus had probably been made in a friendly spirit, as he was the patron of Adrianus, and together they had attended Galen's anatomical demonstrations in Rome some twelve or more years before, along with Vettulenus Civica Barbarus and other distinguished personages of intellectual inclinations.[1]

After this refreshing interlude, Marcus and Commodus took ship to Italy. The voyage was eventful – there was a violent storm – and the coins later issued to commemorate their safe crossing had a more than conventional meaning. On reaching Brundisium, Marcus exchanged his general's uniform for the toga, and his soldiers were likewise instructed to don civilian clothes.[2]

Back in Rome, in the late autumn, Marcus addressed the people. He referred to his many years of absence, and some of his audience called out 'eight' (that is, A.D. 169–76 inclusive), and held up all four fingers of both hands – to indicate that they should be given

---

[1] Dio, 71, 31, 3; Philostratus, *v. soph.*, 2, 2, 1; 2, 10, 4. *PIR 2*, C 1024 (Claudius Severus). *PIR 2*, H 4 (Adrianus).

[2] *v. Marci*, 27, 2–3. *BMC*, IV, M. Aurelius and Commodus, Nos. 1615–16, 1618 ff.

eight gold pieces. Marcus smiled and said 'eight'; and they did later receive this sum.[1] Preparations were made for the triumph. Marcus was determined that Commodus should participate in it with him, so on November 27 the young prince, who had as yet no other official position, was granted *imperium*, which gave him the necessary status. At the same time Marcus requested that he should be excused from the provisions of the *lex annaria*, which governed the minimum age at which magistracies might be held. Obviously it had been intended for some months that Commodus should take office as consul in January 177 – probably from the previous spring. In January Commodus was fifteen, younger even than Nero had been when consul for the first time in A.D. 55, and was, in fact, the youngest consul of the Romans hitherto.[2] His colleague was to be his brother-in-law, Fadilla's husband, the nephew of Lucius, M. Peducaeus Plautius Quintillus.

The mother of Quintillus, Ceionia Fabia, apparently tried at this time to interest Marcus in a second marriage, to herself. But Marcus rejected the overtures of his former fiancée. He was unwilling to marry again and 'give so many children a stepmother', the biographer records. But he took a mistress instead, the daughter of one of Faustina's procurators. Her name is unknown. Pius had done likewise after his wife had died. In fact, the excuse was not very plausible if it was made. Only two of the surviving six children now remained unmarried, Commodus and Vibia Aurelia Sabina, the two youngest. Cornificia must have been married by now, her husband being Petronius Sura Mamertinus, son of one of Pius' first praetorian prefects.[3]

The triumph was celebrated on December 23. Only one detail is recorded. Marcus ran beside the triumphal chariot in which his son sat, in the Circus Flaminius. This was to do honour to the spectators, and Commodus presumably had to stay in the chariot to control the horses. Still, some clearly found the scene rather striking. Marcus had been voted a triumphal arch by the senate the previous month,

---

[1] 'Eight': Dio, 71, 32, 1.
[2] v. *Marci*, 27, 5; v. *Comm.*, 2, 3–5; 12, 5.
[3] v. *Marci*, 29, 10. See Appendix II for details.

in honour of his victories: 'because, surpassing all the glories of all the greatest *imperatores* before him, having wiped out or subjugated the most warlike peoples' – and here the record breaks off. The arch has not survived, although some of the reliefs which adorned it seem to have. (It may have been at this time also that the senate voted for the erection of the Column to commemorate his achievements, but some doubt attaches to this.) Coins were issued in honour of the triumph – 'De Germanis, De Sarmatis'. Members of Marcus' staff received decorations for the part that they had played. Such are recorded for Bassaeus Rufus and Pontius Laelianus, for example, both of whom had come to the end of their service, and Julius Verus and Sosius Priscus were probably honoured as well. Pertinax was back on active service and could not attend, but he, Maximianus and others also received their marks of honour.[1]

After the triumph Marcus went to Lavinium to rest. However he was back in Rome for Commodus' entry into his consulship on New Year's Day. On the same day, evidently, Commodus was granted the tribunician power, and later in the year, the name Augustus and all the other titles, honours and powers of an emperor (except the office of *pontifex maximus*). He was now joint ruler, in the same position that Lucius had been from A.D. 161 to 169. If Marcus died, Commodus would need no further powers. His succession was now completely assured – he would merely continue to rule. Largesse – the 'eight gold pieces' – and 'wonderful spectacles' were provided in honour of the occasion.[2]

Commodus was still receiving education. Only three of his teachers are named in the biography, the Greek and Latin elementary teachers Onesicrates and Antistius Capella, otherwise unknown, and T. Aius Sanctus the orator (whose name is given incorrectly as 'Ateius' Sanctus). The name of his *educator* or τροφεύς, Pitholaus, is recorded

[1] *v. Comm.*, 2, 4; *v. Marci*, 16, 2; cf. J. M. Heer, op. cit., 23 ff. Dessau, *ILS*, 374. On the column, see Appendix I. Laelianus: Dessau, *ILS*, 1094+1100. Maximianus: *AE*, 1956, 124. Sosius Priscus: *CIL*, VI, 31753 (on which cf. W. Zwikker, op. cit., 182). The coins: *BMC*, IV, M. Aurelius and Commodus, Nos. 736 ff., 740 ff., etc.

[2] The discussion of these matters by J. M. Heer, op. cit., 20 ff., esp. 28–9, remains the most satisfactory.

by Galen. But he must have finished with the attentions of Onesi-crates, Capella and Pitholaus long since, and have begun oratory with Sanctus by A.D. 176. It is not known what *grammatici* instructed him in the interim. Marcus himself had given Commodus some instruction, in the best old tradition, and had procured for him the best available teachers. In fact in the *Meditations* Marcus records his gratitude that he had been able to find such good teachers for his children. Aius Sanctus was probably from Campania, and hence could have been an Italian of Greek origin and culture, a possibility to which some support is given by his having held the post of *ab epistulis Graecis*. It may well be that he held this post during the tour of the east when the head of the Greek Secretariat would need to be with Marcus, and his tuition of Commodus thus could have begun very soon after Commodus assumed the *toga virilis*. Back in Rome Sanctus served successively as the head of two of the financial departments, as procurator of the *ratio privata* and as *a rationibus*. It may reasonably be supposed that he was able to continue his in-struction of the prince at the same time.[1]

Various unfavourable criticisms of Commodus' character as a boy are retailed in the Augustan History. The faults criticized are described mostly in a general way, and the specific habits listed are not particularly discreditable – an interest in pottery-making, danc-ing, singing and whistling might in certain circumstances be re-garded as positively commendable. An early fondness for vulgar jokes and for performing as a gladiator may have been unfortunate tastes, but not necessarily disastrous. One detailed story is given, of a piece of boyish fury at the age of eleven: he ordered a bathkeeper, who had let the bath at Centumcellae go lukewarm, to be thrown into the furnace. The slave to whom the order was given burned a sheep-skin instead. The story might be true: Marcus would then be away, for it belonged to the period August 172–August 173, when Com-modus might well have got out of hand. But it is the type of story that the biographer and some of his sources were particularly fond of inventing. If it were true, it would not be revealing of a sensationally

---

[1] *v. Comm.*, 1, 6. Sanctus: *AE*, 1961, 280, on which cf. H.-G. Pflaum, op. cit., No. 178 *bis*, whose dating differs slightly from that suggested in the text.

evil and odious character, merely of impetuous bad temper. After all, the order was not carried out, and was probably only shouted out in a tantrum. Dio's statement should be preferred, that Commodus was not naturally wicked. Still, the contrast with the grave eleven-year-old Marcus, who tried to live the philosopher's life, is very striking.[1]

Fighting was evidently still going on in the north in A.D. 177, or at any rate broke out again in that year. There was a Roman victory, presumably gained by the Quintilii cousins. Marcus was saluted as Imperator for the ninth time and Commodus for the second time. What was equally serious was the amount of brigandage that was going on still. Before Marcus' return to Rome he had despatched Valerius Maximianus on a new special mission. His salary was increased, and he was given the post of procurator of Lower Moesia, and the task of 'capturing a band of Brisean bandits on the borders of Macedonia and Thrace' – that area where the boundaries of Bulgaria, Greece and Yugoslavia now meet, through which the rivers Axios or Vardar and Strymon flow, on the western fringes of the Balkan mountains. Meanwhile Didius Julianus, as governor of Dalmatia, was facing similar problems. The bandits he was fighting were probably based in Albania or Montenegro. However, by A.D. 177 he had been promoted to Lower Germany, and was succeeded by Vettius Sabinianus, who had at long last been made consul.[2]

In Rome Marcus now turned his attention to the civilian administration; and a considerable number of his legal decisions from the period of his joint rule with Commodus (A.D. 177–80) have been preserved. Interesting cases of murder came up. In a reply to Scapula Tertullus, Marcus and Commodus wrote: 'If you have ascertained that Aelius Priscus is so insane that he is permanently mad and thus that he was incapable of reasoning when he killed his

---

[1] v. Comm., 1, 7–9; v. Marci, 2, 6; Dio, 72, 1, 1.
[2] Dio, 71, 33, 1. IMP. IX: BMC, IV, M. Aurelius and Commodus, Nos. 1632 ff. Maximianus: H.-G. Pflaum, op. cit., No. 181 bis. Didius: v. Didii, 1, 9 (cf. p. 261, n. 1). Sabinianus: AE, 1920, 45, cf, PW, 8A, 1958, 1861 ff.

mother, and did not kill her with the pretence of being mad, you need not concern yourself with the question how he should be punished, as insanity itself is punishment enough. At the same time he should be kept in close custody, and, if you think it advisable, even kept in chains. This need not be done by way of punishment so much as for his own and his neighbours' security. If however, as often happens, he has intervals of sanity, you must investigate whether he committed his crime on one of these occasions and thus has no claim to mercy on the grounds of mental infirmity. If this is so, refer the case to us, so that we may consider whether he should be punished in accordance with the enormity of the crime – if he did in fact commit it in a rational interval. But since we learn by letter from you that his position in respect of place and treatment is such that he is in the hands of friends, even, in fact, confined to his own house, your proper course is to summon those in charge of him at the time and to enquire how they were so remiss, and then to pronounce on each case separately, according as to whether there is any excuse or aggravation for their negligence. The object of keepers for the insane is not merely to stop them from harming themselves, but from destroying others; and if this happens, there is some justification for casting the blame for it on those who were somewhat negligent in their duties.'[1]

Two decisions concern *crimes passionels*. A father had killed the lover of his married daughter, but the daughter herself had survived his attack. The *lex Cornelia* laid down that homicide in such a situation was justifiable only if both members of the adulterous couple were killed. But as the woman was seriously injured, the emperors granted the father a pardon, as he had clearly acted under provocation, and had not spared his daughter deliberately. In another case a husband who was found to have killed his wife when he caught her in the act of adultery was adjudged not guilty of capital murder.[2]

A rescript of general application issued at this time is very significant of the prevailing social conditions. It was expressly laid down

[1] *Digest.*, I, 18, 14.
[2] Ibid., 47, 5, 33 (32), *pr.*; 48, 5, 39 (38), 8.

that 'governors and magistrates and police are bound to assist slave-owners in searching for their runaway slaves and that they are bound to give them up if they find them. Also that persons on whose land slaves are in hiding are to be punished if any unlawful behaviour can be brought home to them. Anyone whatever who apprehends a runaway slave must bring him forward publicly. Magistrates are enjoined to keep any such slaves carefully in custody so as to prevent their escape.' This illustrates the growing seriousness of a problem which developed into full-scale war within a few years, and was to continue almost indefinitely until the fall of the western empire. Another rescript of Marcus and Commodus, to Piso, mentioning a particular case, again illustrates the atmosphere of the times. 'Since it is established by you, dearest Piso, that Julius Donatus, after being terrified by the arrival of brigands, had fled to his villa, and was wounded, and then, soon afterwards, making his will, repaid the services of his slaves, neither the family loyalty of his wife's grand-mother nor the anxiety of the heir ought to have the effect of sum-moning to punishment those whom their master himself absolved.' The details of the case are slightly obscure (the text needs emenda-tion and it is not clear quite what happened after Donatus' death), but the picture of the country landowner fleeing in panic to his villa, and his slaves rushing to tend his wounds, is vividly present.[1]

An important decision was made at this time affecting the position of slaves. In reply to an official query put to him by his old friend Aufidius Victorinus, now perhaps occupying the post of prefect of the city of Rome, Marcus, with Commodus, gave a ruling concern-ing the manumission of slaves, which is cited nearly twenty times in the legal collections (mostly naming Marcus only and not Com-modus, and only naming Aufidius Victorinus on a few occasions). The most frequent citation includes the words: 'He attains his liberty in accordance with the ruling of the Deified Marcus' (*ex constitutione divi Marci venit ad libertatem*). This *constitutio*, also referred to as 'the so-called law of liberty', is nowhere quoted in full, but from the cases where it is cited as the basis of a judgment, it seems that it was designed to make sure that slaves did obtain their

---

[1] *Digest.*, 11, 4, 1, 2; 29, 5, 2.

freedom if their masters had intended that they should have it, whatever legal obstacles might be put in their way by third parties. This had particular application to the case of slaves sold on the understanding that they would be set free after a stated period. This provision was, quite obviously, often evaded by buyers of slaves. Although the general rescript concerning runaway slaves quoted earlier reveals the harsh realities of the situation in which an economy based on slave-labour was liable to find itself, it is fair to say that Marcus' attitude, as revealed not only by the much-quoted reply to Victorinus, but by other decisions made earlier in his reign, was one of deep compassion for the position of individual slaves, and that he did take some steps to improve their position.[1]

In the course of the year A.D. 177, Marcus initiated a piece of legislation in the senate involving a matter for which he had always felt some distaste, namely gladiatorial spectacles. Probably largely as a result of his own action in conscripting gladiators into the armed forces some years previously, the costs of putting on public performances had soared enormously. The shortage of trained gladiators meant that the professional promoters (*lanistae*) had raised their prices to a prohibitive level. This development affected the pockets of the upper classes throughout the empire, for on them fell the duty of providing entertainment for the masses. Some time in the summer of A.D. 176 an appeal went to Marcus from the council of the Three Gauls. Here it was the duty of one of the council, chosen in annual rotation, as High Priest of the three Gallic provinces, to provide public entertainment at the annual festival at Lugdunum (Lyons) beginning on August 1, in honour of Rome and Augustus.

The priest appointed for the following year, A.D. 177, had already resigned himself to squandering his entire fortune, when news of the proposed legislation arrived. Marcus had decided to allow his procurator in the Gallic provinces to supply criminals condemned to death, at a cheap price, for use as gladiators. This special concession was made, it seems, not only because of the economic crisis in the world of mass entertainment, but because some archaic religious ritual in the Gallic provinces had involved the use of human

---

[1] *Cod. Just.*, 4, 57, 2; cf. *Digest.*, 4, 4, 11, 1; 26, 4, 3, 2; 40, 1, 20, *pr.*

sacrificial victims, known as *trinqui*. The state was now in effect to supply *trinqui* at six gold pieces a head.

The Gallic priest was overjoyed that his financial burden was to be lightened, and declared that he now positively welcomed the duty of putting on a spectacle, which he had previously repudiated. In the course of that year Marcus and Commodus brought in a decree in the senate to fix prices for gladiators throughout the empire, and the special provision for the Gallic provinces was embodied in it. The provisions of the senatorial decree which was passed are known from two inscriptions, at Sardis in Asia Minor and at Italica in the Spanish province of Baetica. That at Sardis, inscribed on marble, is only preserved in part, but it can be supplemented by the bronze tablet from Italica containing much of a speech by an unknown senator. This senator not only quotes extensively from the imperial proposals, but describes the grateful reception which they had received in the Gallic provinces. It is of course very rare to have a verbatim record of a speech by a senator. In particular, although the speech does not represent anything approaching modern concepts of free debate, it nevertheless demonstrates considerable latitude in the amount of expression of opinion allowed. The senator himself presumably had some connection with Gaul. The fact that the minutes of this senatorial business were set on record in two places at opposite ends of the empire, neither of them in Gaul, where there was particular interest in the proposals, indicates that this was done on governmental instructions. Marcus must have decided that it would be valuable to make widely known the fact that he had taken steps to lighten the burdens of the wealthy classes, whose support, at a time when the empire was in difficulties, was more than ever essential.[1]

The effect which this legislation had in Gaul and upon the Christians cannot, however, have been anticipated. For, if there were a shortage of criminals condemned to death, there was no easier way of increasing the supply than by bringing in accusations against Christians. Public confession of Christianity and refusal to recant

---

[1] I follow here the interpretation of J. H. Oliver and R. E. A. Palmer, *Hesperia*, 24, 1955, 320 ff., which revolutionizes our understanding of the decree. See also, on the *trinqui*, A. Piganiol, *Rev. Ét. Anc.*, 20, 1922, 283 ff.

was still a capital offence. 'It was the seventeenth year of the emperor Antoninus Verus [i.e. A.D. 177]', Eusebius records. 'In that year, in certain parts of the world, persecution of us was rekindled more violently by popular violence in the cities and tens of thousands were distinguished by martyrdom, as one may judge from what happened in one nation. . . . Gaul was the country in which the arena for these manifestations was prepared.' Eusebius goes on to quote from a letter sent by the Christian churches in Gaul to their brothers in the faith in Asia and Phrygia. It is an appalling document. A full-scale persecution of Christians had broken out. They were hounded by the mob in Lyons, and dragged into the town forum by the tribune commanding the cohort of police and by the civic authorities. They were then accused, and, on confession, were placed in custody until the governor of Lugdunensis arrived. A Christian named Vettius Epagathus, 'a man of position', tried to intervene on behalf of the accused when the governor arrived, but was howled down by the mob. The governor ignored his appeal and asked him if he were a Christian. When Epagathus confessed 'in a clear voice', he was placed under arrest himself. The governor then ordered all the Christians to be prosecuted, and the testimony of pagan slaves belonging to some of them was accepted, accusing them of cannibalism and incest. This increased public frenzy against them. They were subjected to torture of the most brutal kind. Some died before the spectacle was put on, including Pothinus the Bishop, a man of over ninety, who died in prison from the effects of the beating he had received from the crowd after his interrogation.

Finally the executions by ordeal in the arena began. 'Maturus and Sanctus and Blandina and Attalus were led out to the wild beasts as a spectacle of inhumanity for the public and for the council of the provinces [κοινὸν τῶν ἐθνῶν, i.e. the *concilium Galliarum*], the day of fighting against wild beasts having been specially appointed for our people.' Maturus and Sanctus met their deaths heroically: after a day of 'being made a spectacle to the world as a substitute for all the variations of gladiatorial combats', they were finally 'sacrificed' – precisely as the *trinqui* were in the barbarous Gallic ritual. Blandina had been hung on a stake for the beasts to attack, but none would touch her, and she was finally taken down for use on a later occasion. Attalus was then brought into the amphitheatre and was led round with a placard bearing, in Latin, the words, 'This is Attalus, the Christian'. But the governor was informed that he was a Roman citizen, and ordered him to be sent back to jail. He was awaiting instructions from the emperor as to how Roman citizens should be treated.

In the meantime the resolution of the surviving Christians had been strengthened, and some of those who had at first denied the faith were spurred on to confess themselves Christians. They were led out for interrogation by the governor, 'at the beginning of the festival there, at which there is a heavy attendance as all the [Gallic] provinces gather together for it'. Marcus had apparently written back to the governor with the instructions that any Roman citizens who recanted should be released, but that the rest should be beheaded. A few recanted, but most stayed firm, and the governor had the sentence carried out. Beheading was the death that St Paul had suffered under Nero, for it was a Roman citizen's privilege to die in this way. The non-citizens were sent to the wild beasts. In order to please the mob the governor included Attalus in their number, which was a definite breach of the law. The people wanted to watch him being tormented in the amphitheatre, which duly happened. He was finally burnt to death. Then Blandina and a boy of about fifteen named Ponticus, both of whom had been led in every day to watch the others being tortured, were sacrificed.

No burial was permitted for the mangled remains. The authorities must have known that Christians attached great importance to burial, and attempts made by surviving Christians were thwarted. After six days the remains were burned and the ashes thrown into the Rhône.[1]

There had already been persecution of Christians under Marcus. Indeed Eusebius appears to state that Polycarp of Smyrna was martyred under Marcus, although most modern scholars date this to the year A.D. 156. However, Justin and others were certainly martyred in Rome in or about A.D. 167. In the reign of Marcus, protest

[1] Eusebius, *Hist. Ecc.*, 5, *pref.* and 1.

was made by a bishop named Meliton, who spoke of 'new decrees' which were resulting in persecution throughout Asia. It is a striking coincidence that Meliton was Bishop of Sardis, precisely the city where the copy of the *senatus consultum* on reducing gladiatorial expenses has been found. It may be that local magistrates in other provinces had been applying, successfully, to have extended to them the privilege granted to the Gallic *concilium*, of purchasing condemned criminals from the procurator at six gold pieces a head.

There is no doubt that the persecution at Lyons was deliberately fomented to fill the amphitheatre on the cheap. Since nothing like it recurred in Gaul, it is logical to suppose that steps were taken to prevent this odious abuse happening again. Alternatively, the Gallic authorities may have been so revolted by what they had unleashed that they did not repeat their actions.

The bitter paradox that an emperor of such noble personal aspirations as Marcus Aurelius was the persecutor of the Christians has never ceased to cause surprise and sadness. Eusebius was even confused enough to distinguish between 'Antoninus Verus', the persecutor of A.D. 177, and 'Marcus Aurelius Caesar, his brother', who was alleged to have been impressed by the piety of the Christians at the battle of the Rain Miracle. Elsewhere he quotes the letter of Meliton to 'the emperor', meaning Marcus, and describes him as 'far more of a philanthropist and a philosopher' than Hadrian and Pius.

Marcus' personal attitude to the fate of the Christians must remain largely undiscoverable: the *Meditations* may provide a clue, but this is uncertain. What he knew of them may have been seriously distorted by the excesses of heresies such as Montanism. But as a Stoic, who by his training and by the necessity of his position believed profoundly in the duty of the individual towards the state, he cannot have viewed kindly the activities of people who professed complete lack of concern with worldly life. Also hostility to Christianity was growing. It is no coincidence that the first written attack on the faith of which much is preserved, that of Celsus, dates from just this moment of history. There is no need to suppose that

Marcus actively approved of persecution any more than had Trajan, for example. But the precedent had already been established, that to be a Christian was in itself a capital crime. Marcus clearly did not initiate the persecutions personally. But equally he would have seen no reason to obstruct the course of law. What remains an enigma is that, in spite of the existence of this fixed legal attitude, Christianity still survived and flourished. There was never any legal obstacle to persecution, yet it was only when times were hard, and scapegoats were wanted, that it broke out.[1]

Another important legal measure was taken in the following year, A.D. 178. This was the *Senatusconsultum Orfitianum*, named after one of the consuls of the year. This gave preference to a woman's children as to her inheritance, over her brothers, sisters and other relatives of her own family (*agnati*). This may seem of relatively minor significance, but it was in fact a great step forward in the recognition of a woman's individual existence apart from her family.[2]

It may also have been at this time that Marcus made a decision arising out of Cassius' rebellion and its aftermath. The property of a certain 'Depitianus, a senator, who had participated in the Cassian frenzy' was ordered to be seized by the *fiscus* after his death, according to the Severan jurist, Paulus. 'Depitianus' is generally identified with Cassius' son-in-law Dryantianus, who had been liberally treated at first. The reasons behind this decision are not stated, and no hint is given as to the cause or manner of his death – which might have been from natural causes.[3]

Whatever the motives for this treatment of a pardoned traitor's estate, they cannot have been fiscal, for the economy had now been placed on a securer basis. In this year Marcus cancelled all debts incurred to the treasury and *fiscus* over the past forty-six years reckoned inclusively, that is from the year A.D. 133. Hadrian had likewise cancelled debts in A.D. 118, but it is not known why the

---

[1] Meliton: id., ibid., 4, 26, 3 ff. See further Appendix IV.

[2] *Digest.*, 38, 17; *Inst.*, 3, 4; *Cod. Just.*, 6, 57. At this point in the narrative some mention of the *tabula Banasitana* would have been desirable. But as the full text of that document remains – regrettably – unpublished, discussion here would be unprofitable, cf. Appendix I.

[3] *Cod. Just.*, 9, 8, 6, *pr.* ; cf. *PIR 2*, C 859.

interim period was not included. Perhaps the years A.D. 118–33 had already been dealt with. Documents concerning the years A.D. 133–78 were publicly burnt in the Forum.[1]

In this year there was a disastrous earthquake at Smyrna. An appeal went from the ruined city to ask for assistance from the emperor. The eloquent Aelius Aristides composed their plea, and he bewailed Smyrna's fate so movingly that Marcus 'groaned on many occasions at passages in his "lament", but when he came to the words: "She is a desert and the west winds blow through her," he shed tears over the letter.' Inspired by Aristides he consented to rebuild Smyrna. Cassius Dio, more prosaic than Philostratus, does not mention Aristides, but includes the detail that a senator of praetorian rank was appointed to supervise the work. This generosity towards Smyrna, Dio states, was only one example of 'the gifts of money that he made to various cities. . . . Therefore I am surprised that even now [i.e., about A.D. 218] people criticize him on the grounds that he was not open-handed. For although, in general, he was very economical, yet he never avoided a single necessary expenditure – in spite of the fact that he did not burden anyone by financial levies and that he had of necessity to pay out very large sums beyond the normal regular expenses.' In fact the *congiaria* in Marcus' reign were very liberal.[2]

Unfortunately, at the same time as the economic position was showing signs of recovery, the situation on the Danube was deteriorating. It is noticeable that the titles of victory *Germanicus* and *Sarmaticus* disappear from the coinage of this year. Dio records that 'the Quintilii had been unable to bring the war to an end, although the two of them possessed much shrewdness, courage and experience'. By the middle of the year Marcus must have realized that his own presence was required once again, to give a new impetus to the armies. Meanwhile the Moors had invaded Spain again, and the

---

[1] Dio, 71, 32, 2.

[2] Ibid,, 71, 32, 3; Philostratus, *v. soph.*, 2, 9, 2. It is interesting to reflect that when Dio wrote the words quoted (from the abridgement of Xiphilinus) he was probably at Smyrna himself: he had been appointed special commissioner for Pergamum and Smyrna by Macrinus (Dio, 79, 7, 4).

procurator of one of the Mauretanian provinces had to be given special powers.[1]

Commodus was to go north with Marcus, and for this reason it was decided to bring forward the date of his marriage. The chosen bride was Bruttia Crispina, granddaughter of the friend of Hadrian and Pius. Her father Bruttius Praesens had been consul in A.D. 153, and hence was probably a year or two older than Marcus. It was too late in the year for Praesens to be selected as the colleague for his son-in-law in the consulship in A.D. 179. That honour had already been bestowed on Martius Verus, still, no doubt, in Syria at the time. However, Praesens was to be consul for the second time in A.D. 180, instead, with Julius Verus as his colleague. The wedding was a modest occasion. 'The marriage was celebrated in the manner of private citizens.' But largesse was given to the people and the event was commemorated on the coinage. An *epithalamium*, or wedding hymn, for Commodus was written by the sophist Julius Pollux, who had shortly before this dedicated a Lexicon to the young prince. However poor his style, he had a winning voice and Commodus later made him professor of rhetoric at Athens. But the wedding hymn was probably sung by a choir.[2]

The biographer records that before Marcus set off he swore a solemn oath on the Capitol that he had not knowingly been responsible for the death of any senator, and that he would even have preserved the rebels if he had known in time. Aurelius Victor describes another remarkable scene. Marcus was 'so outstanding for his wisdom, lenience, innocence of character and literary attainments that when he was about to set off against the Marcomanni with his son Commodus, whom he had made Caesar, he was surrounded by a crowd of philosophers, who were protesting that he should not commit himself to the expedition and to battle, before he had expounded the difficulties and obscurities of the philosophical schools. Thus it was feared, from zeal for philosophy, that the uncertainties

---

[1] *BMC*, IV, pp. cxxx, cxliii; Dio, 71, 33, 1; cf. H.-G. Pflaum, op. cit., No. 221+*add*.

[2] Dio, 71, 33, 1; *v. Marci*, 27, 8; Suidas, *s.v.* Πολυδεύκης; Philostratus, *v. soph.*, 2, 12, 2. Praesens: *PIR 2*, B 165. Crispina, ibid., 170. For Julius Verus, cf. A. Degrassi, *I Fasti Consolari*, etc., Roma, 1952, 50.

of war would affect his safety. And so greatly did the liberal arts flourish in his reign that I would think it the glory of the times.'[1]

A third event immediately preceding the departure is noted by Cassius Dio. Marcus had asked the senate for funds from the treasury, as a mark of formal deference, because these funds were always at his disposal in any case. ' "As for us," he said, speaking to the senate, "we are so far from having any possessions of our own that even the house we live in is yours." After this speech, he threw the bloody spear kept in the Temple of Bellona into ground symbolically regarded as enemy territory (as I have heard from people who were there), and set off.' This latter action would have been taken by Marcus in his capacity as one of the *fetiales*. This priesthood in fact had had the regular duty of declaring war from the earliest days of Rome's existence. Marcus had probably only continued, rather than revived, a traditional practice. If the statement about his 'possessions' is genuine, then Marcus was certainly exaggerating, in view of his considerable inherited wealth. But it probably represents fairly his attitude to the imperial property.[2]

Marcus and Commodus finally left Rome on August 3, 178, on the *expeditio Germanica secunda*, as it was officially named. Among those who accompanied them were Claudius Pompeianus, Vitrasius Pollio and Bruttius Praesens from those related by marriage to the Antonine house. The new praetorian prefect was Tarrutenus Paternus, the authority on military law who had been on the first expedition, for Bassaeus Rufus was now dead or in retirement. Marcus had appointed a colleague for Paternus by A.D. 180, namely Tigidius Perennis. Some of Marcus' best generals were certainly in the north already, with the Quintilii, for example Helvius Pertinax,

---

[1] *v. Marci*, 29, 4; Aurelius Victor, *de Caes.*, 16, 9–10. This episode, if it is not invented, may have occurred in A.D. 169, except that Commodus is not known to have accompanied his father then. On the other hand, Commodus was, in A.D. 169, a Caesar of three years standing whereas in A.D. 178 he had been Augustus for a year. If Victor were a more reliable author this passage might be good evidence for Commodus having gone to the front in A.D. 169. As it is, it looks as if the events should be assigned to A.D. 178.
[2] Dio, 71, 33, 2–3.

who had been moved from Lower Moesia to the militarily more vital Dacia.[1]

The imperial headquarters for the winter of A.D. 178-9 is not known (there can have been little time left for campaigning when Marcus reached the front). One significant decision was probably made soon after Marcus arrived. The redoubtable M. Valerius Maximianus was 'chosen by the Most Sacred Emperors to be a member of the Most Honourable Order [*a sacratissimis imperatoribus in amplissimum ordinem allectus*] and straightway appointed legate of the legion First Adiutrix.' Maximianus had held three procuratorships since participating in the expedition to the east. Now he finally entered the senate. This man's career is in many ways even more striking than that of Pertinax. It illustrates once again Marcus' ability and willingness to recognize worth. 'It is impossible to make men exactly as one wishes them to be,' he said once, 'but it is our duty to use them, such as they are, for any service in which they may be useful to the state.'[2]

In the campaigning season of A.D. 179 supreme command in the field was assigned to Tarruntenus Paternus. He brought the enemy to fight and won a victory after a battle which lasted a whole day. Marcus was acclaimed Imperator by the armies for the tenth time (and Commodus for the third time). No further details are given, but the enemy was probably the Quadi.[3]

Marcus' activity during the second expedition seems to be described in various extracts of Cassius Dio which have survived. 'The Jazyges sent envoys and asked to be released from some of the terms that they had agreed to. Some concessions were granted to them so that they should not become completely disaffected. However, neither they nor the Buri were willing to ally themselves to the Romans until they had been given assurances by Marcus that he would definitely carry the war through to its conclusion, for they were afraid that he might make a treaty with the Quadi as he had

---

[1] *v. Comm.*, 12, 6. Paternus: H.-G. Pflaum, op. cit., No. 172. Perennis: *PW*, 6A, 1936, 952 ff. Pollio: Dessau, *ILS*, 1112. Praesens: *PIR* 2, B 165. Pompeianus: *PIR* 2, C 973. Pertinax: *PIR* 2, H 73 (and cf. p. 261, n.2).

[2] *AE*, 1956, 124; Dio, 71, 34, 4.

[3] Dio, 71, 33, 3-4; *BMC*, IV, M. Aurelius and Commodus, Nos. 1695 ff.

done before – and thus leave them with enemies on their borders.'
The conditions granted to the Jazyges are detailed in another
passage. Most of the restrictions imposed in the treaty of A.D. 175
were lifted, except for those concerning their public assemblies and
markets, and, in particular, the ban on the use of boats of their own,
as well as a total prohibition against landing on the islands in the
Danube. He made them one important concession. They were to be
allowed, subject to the approval of the governor of Dacia on the
particular occasions, to pass through Roman territory to the lands of
their Sarmatian cousins the Roxolani, on the Black Sea.[1]

Meanwhile powerful pressure was being exerted on the two most
powerful German tribes, the Quadi and Marcomanni. Twenty
thousand men were stationed in forts in the territories of each of
these tribes. That is the equivalent of more than six legions, but a
large proportion of the troops were undoubtedly auxiliaries and the
legions were in any case operating in detachments (*vexillationes*) at
this time. Whatever the composition of the force it is certain that a
large number of semi-permanent forts were constructed, and eventually remains of some of them may be recovered in Bohemia and
Slovakia. Dio even records that the soldiers stationed in the embryo
province of Marcomannia had 'baths and all the necessities of life in
abundance'. The Romans were in fact now firmly on top. It was they
who were now receiving deserters from the Germans, in contrast to
ten years or so previously, and they were able to recover many of
their own men who had been taken prisoner. The Germans were kept
constantly harassed, unable to pasture their flocks or cultivate the
land. Finally the Quadi attempted to emigrate *en masse* to the north,
hoping to find a home among the Semnones, another Suebic people.
'But Antoninus learned of their intention in advance and prevented
them by blocking the roads. Thus he showed that he wanted not only to
acquire their land but to punish the people as well.' This judgment
by Dio is faulty. To Marcus land without inhabitants would be useless. The empire itself was no longer in need of fresh areas to settle –
rather the reverse, as the settlements of barbarians in Italy itself
and the provinces demonstrate. Indeed, an instance arose at this

[1] Dio, 71, 18–19.

very time. The Naristi, the smaller neighbours of the Marcomanni and Quadi, came over in large numbers (three thousand, according to Dio) and were given land within the empire. Marcus wanted to romanize the Marcomanni, Quadi and Jazyges, not merely to acquire their land.[1]

The occupation of enemy territory went on throughout the winter of A.D. 179–80, as is proved by an inscription carved high on a crag above the River Váh (Waag) at Trenčin in Slovakia, eighty miles north of the Danube frontier, which records the presence there of Valerius Maximianus, now with the Second Adiutrix; and that is confirmed by Maximianus' own inscription from North Africa, describing him as 'commander of the *vexillationes* wintering at Leugaricio' (the Roman version of the native name for Trenčin).[2] During the winter, before the New Year of A.D. 180, Cn. Julius Verus died. His place as consul with Bruttius Praesens was taken by young Quintilius Condianus.[3]

The fulfilment of Marcus' intention to create two new provinces was now in sight, but early in March of A.D. 180, when the campaigning season was about to begin, he fell seriously ill. He was at Vindobona (Vienna) on the Danube, obviously with the intention of completing the wearing into submission of the Suebic Germans.

When Marcus realized that his condition was serious he sent for Commodus, according to the biographer. He asked him not to regard the completion of the war as a task beneath his dignity. If he did this, it would seem like a betrayal of the interests of the state. Commodus replied that his own health was his first consideration. Marcus consented but asked that he should 'wait for a few days and not set off at once'. This can only mean that Commodus had some justification in thinking that his health was in danger. These had been the sentiments of Lucius at Aquileia, when plague was rife in the army. A slightly different version of the conversation is given by another fourth-century writer according to whom Commodus

---

[1] Ibid., 71, 20–1.

[2] *CIL*, III, 13439; *AE*, 1956, 128.

[3] A. Degrassi, op. cit., 50. The news of Julius Verus' death did not reach the eastern provinces in time, for his name went on to some official records.

replied that 'tasks can be completed by a man in good health, even if only gradually. A dead man can complete nothing.'

Marcus 'then began to abstain from eating and drinking in his desire for death, which made his condition worse. On the sixth day he called his friends, and, smiling at the concerns of men and despising death, said to them: "Why do you weep for me instead of thinking rather of the plague and death in general?" And when they wanted to withdraw, he groaned, and said: "If you give me leave to go now, I say farewell to you, as I go on ahead." And when he was asked to whom he commended his son, he replied: "To you, if he prove worthy, and to the immortal gods." ' In another passage, drawn from a different source, the biographer relates that Marcus on this occasion expressed the same sentiments about Commodus that Philip had about Alexander, and that he regretted that he was leaving such a son behind him. But this story is suspect.

When the army learnt of their emperor's serious condition, the men were deeply moved with grief, 'for they loved him as none other'. 'On the seventh day his condition worsened and he allowed only his son to see him. But he sent him away at once, in case the disease should be passed on to him. Having sent his son away, he covered his head, as if he wanted to sleep, but during the night he breathed his last.' Dio gives a different, and briefer, version. At the point of death he is said to have commended Commodus to the protection of the soldiers. 'To the tribune who asked him for the watchword he said: "Go to the rising sun. For I am already setting." '

The exact cause of his death is not known. From his own reported mention of the plague, from his sending Commodus away from his sickbed to avoid the risk of infection, and even from Commodus' pre-occupation with his own health, it sounds as if Marcus had caught the plague. However, Dio states that his death was deliberately brought about by his doctors – 'as I have been plainly told' – to gain favour with Commodus, and implies that Marcus knew his son to be in some way responsible. But Dio also says, when stating his own view of the cause of death, that it was not 'as a result of the disease from which he was still suffering'. This refers to the stomach and chest condition which he had described earlier. It might have been cancer. But speculation is unprofitable. Marcus died on March 17, 180, two days before the traditional date for the opening of the campaigning season, and just over a month before his fifty-ninth birthday.[1]

[1] v. Marci, 27, 11-12; 28; Dio, 71, 33, 4-34; Epit. de Caes., 17, 2. The place of death: Aurelius Victor, de Caes., 16, 14, and Epit. de Caes., 16, 12, give Vindobona (Vienna); Tertullian, Apol., 25, gives Sirmium. The former should be preferred, as Victor, although writing much later, was much more likely to be well informed (and to care) than Tertullian about places in Pannonia. I omit Herodian's death scene (1, 3-4), on the inaccuracy of which see E. Hohl, 'Kaiser Commodus und Herodian', SDAW, Berlin, 1954, 3 ff.

X

THE MEDITATIONS

IT IS REPORTED of Marcus by the biographer that during his last stay in Rome 'the saying of Plato was always on his lips: "States flourish if philosophers rule or if rulers are philosophers".' The story may be apocryphal. If it were true it might seem to provide ammunition for those who find the philosophical thought of Marcus, as it appears in the *Meditations*, little better than the musings of a self-conscious prig. Self-conscious, Marcus certainly always was, and sometimes he recognized that he was in danger of priggishness. But his self-awareness was too vigilant to allow this to become an actuality. If he was quoting Plato's dictum frequently, at Rome in A.D. 177 and 178, it may have been for good reason – to justify to sceptics and critics his continued public preoccupation with philosophy, of which the culmination was the extraordinary scene at the time of his departure for the front in August 178.[1] Marcus knew he had critics, and pictured to himself with wry humour their relief after his death: ' "We shall breathe more easily without this schoolmaster. He wasn't hard on us – but I felt that he was silently condemning us." This is the fate of the virtuous man – as for the rest of us, how many other reasons there are for many to want to be rid of us.'[2]

It is not known how Marcus' *Meditations* were made public. It might be that he entrusted them to a secretary before he died. Or they might have been discovered in his private papers after his death. There is no indication, either, as to how soon they were made

---

[1] *v. Marci*, 27, 7 (Plato, *Republic*, 473 D); *Med.*, 11, 7.
[2] *Med.*, 10, 36.

public. It has been suggested that Bishop Clement of Alexandria was familiar with them. Clement died between thirty and forty years after Marcus and if he had read the *Meditations*, it would suggest that they were available by the end of the second century. Cassius Dio, in the speech he puts in Marcus' mouth, written probably in A.D. 218, a few years after Clement's death, echoes a passage in the *Meditations* very closely. But the same argument could be applied to both, that the passages from the *Meditations* with which they appear to be familiar could have been echoed by Marcus himself elsewhere (e.g. in his speeches or letters) or by contemporaries.[1]

Herodian, writing in about A.D. 240, says of Marcus that 'he was a lover of old-fashioned language . . . as is witnessed by what has come down to us of his sayings and writings'. This may include the *Meditations*. At any rate, by the fourth century the work was undoubtedly well known. The orator Themistius, friend of Marcus' great admirer and imitator Julian, addressing the emperor Valens, told him (flatteringly): 'You have no need of the *Precepts* of Marcus, or of any excellent sayings of any particular emperor.' This was in the year A.D. 364. Quite when the enigmatic author of the life of Avidius Cassius in the Augustan History was writing is less certain. But it was not more than a few years earlier than A.D. 364, at most, and was probably some decades later. At any rate, this author, with his embroidered version of the scene from August 178, shows his familiarity with Marcus' *Meditations*, which he calls *paraeneseos*; and he alleges that Marcus spent three days giving public lectures to interpret them. This is one of the Augustan History's pleasanter inventions. The subsequent history of the *Meditations* is not relevant here. But the letter of Arethas, deacon of Patras, (later Archbishop of Caesarea), to Demetrius, Archbishop of Heracleia, written in the late ninth or early tenth century, deserves partial quotation: 'Marcus the Emperor's most profitable book I have had for some time, an old copy though, not to say completely tattered, which spoils its usefulness to those who want to use it. However, I have been able to have a new copy made and can send it on to

---

[1] Clement: Farquharson, *Meditations*, II, 548. Cf. Dio, 71, 24, 2, with *Med.*, 5, 33. On the *Meditations* in general see Appendix I.

posterity in a new dress.' The deacon charitably passed on his old copy to the Archbishop.[1]

The *Meditations* are now in twelve 'books', although it is by no means certain that this is Marcus' own arrangement. Certainly it does not imply that the *Meditations* were written in chronological order from Book 1 to Book 12. In fact Book 1, in which Marcus summarises the benefits he has received in his life and those to whose example he is grateful, may well have been written last, when he was very near to death, and placed at the beginning by way of preface.[2] The few internal indications of date make it clear that much of the work was written on campaign, hence in the last ten years, or a little more, of his life. There is little doubt that Marcus was really writing 'To Himself' in much of the *Meditations* (not that the title τὰ εἰς ἑαυτόν is the author's own). But equally, in many places, he wrote in a way which suggests that he may have had some other listener in mind. Some passages are like short formal essays. Others are collections of aphoristic quotations or near-quotations. Both these features are regarded as powerful arguments to support the view that 'the larger bulk has a decided literary aim'. This raises a fundamental question: to what extent does a writer write for himself alone? The question as it affects Marcus Aurelius is largely unanswerable. The *Meditations* represent the emperor's private notebooks, in which he wrote while on campaign. He may well have realized that someone else might see what he wrote. But I prefer to believe that he wrote as he did for himself alone, in the first instance. That what he wrote has in many places a decidedly literary cast is the not surprising reflection of his many years of study of classical literature. That some of what he wrote also appears to be directed at others should not be surprising in the case of a man who tried to train himself even to think thoughts that he would never be ashamed to express to anyone who asked him suddenly: 'What are you thinking now?' The incomplete, even incoherent, form in which

---

[1] Herodian, 1, 2, 3; Themistius, *Or. Philadelph.*, 6, p. 81c; v. *Av. Cass.*, 3, 6–7; *Cod. Mosc.*, 315 f., 115 r., ed. Sonny, *Philologus*, 54, 182, for Arethas (quoted in Farquharson, *Meditations*, I, xvii).

[2] This is argued by F. Martinazzoli, *La 'successio' di Marco Aurelio, etc.*, Bari, 1951.

the work is preserved, the abrupt changes of subject, the repetitions, may not be due entirely to the time and manner in which Marcus wrote. Those responsible for publication may have made a poor job of it. But attempts to reconstruct an 'original' arrangement have been unconvincing, even if they are useful as a guide to studying his thought.[1]

It is ironic that Marcus, whose name is most familiar to posterity through the medium of the *Meditations*, dwells frequently in them on the uncertainty of posthumous fame. 'Little then is each man's life and little the corner of the earth he lives in, and little even the longest survival of his fame with posterity, and that too passed on through a succession of poor mortals, each one of them soon to die, with no knowledge of themselves even, let alone of a man who has died long ago.' 'Shall mere fame distract you? Look at the speed of total oblivion of all and the void of endless time on either side of us and the hollowness of applause. . . . For the whole earth is but a point, and of this what a tiny corner is our dwelling-place, and how few and how paltry are those who will praise you.' 'The man whose heart flutters for fame after death does not picture to himself that every one of those that remember him will also very soon die. Then again their successors, until finally the entire remembrance of the man is extinguished. . . . But even supposing that those who are to remember never die and their remembering is thus immortal – what is that to you? To the dead praise means nothing, I need not say – and what is it to the living, except for some practical purpose?' 'In a short space of time will come for you obliviousness of everything – and everything will be oblivious of you.' Further similar passages could be quoted.

⳦ In several other passages he reflects on the transience of human history with specific reference to the past: 'Consider for example the times of Vespasian, and you will see all these things: people marrying, rearing children, falling ill, dying, making war, holding festivals,

---

[1] See Farquharson, *Meditations*, I, lviii ff. M. van den Hout, *Mnemosyne*, 4, 1950, 330 ff., has detected a few echoes of Fronto. The search for sources of Marcus' thought is endless, but is largely ignored in the present work. See Appendix I for a number of examples.

trading, farming, flattering, asserting themselves, suspecting, plotting, praying for other people's death, muttering about present conditions, making love, hoarding money, wanting the consulship, wanting the throne. Now that life of theirs exists no more anywhere. Pass on, again, to the times of Trajan. Again, all the same. That life is dead too.' 'Words familiar once are now obsolete. So too are the names of those once renowned in song, now obsolete in a sense, Camillus, Caeso, Volesus, Dentatus, and a little later Scipio and Cato, then Augustus too, then Hadrian and Antoninus. For everything fades away and quickly becomes a myth; and soon complete oblivion covers them over. And this I say of those who shone in some remarkable way. For the rest, as soon as the breath left their bodies, they were "unnoticed and unwept". ' 'How many a Chrysippus, how many a Socrates, how many an Epictetus has eternity already devoured.'[1]

Although there is no question but that Marcus was writing in the middle of a terrible war, with other external preoccupations such as the plague and the revolt of Cassius, it has struck many how little obvious reference there is to external events. 'Yet here we find no echo of these great struggles. There is only one reference to the Sarmatian War' is the understandable complaint of a modern scholar who has wrestled with the scanty evidence for the history of the northern campaigns.[2] If the literary-minded emperor had had tastes like Julius Caesar, then *Commentaries* on the Marcomannic and Sarmatian Wars might have appeared. It is better not to regret that it happened otherwise. In any case the view that there is 'no echo' of the wars is mistaken. To the reader with some imagination many pages of the *Meditations* can be seen to have an intensity and a special choice of imagery for which the wars were responsible. The wars in fact were the reason for their being written. They are full of thoughts of death. A tranquil Marcus Aurelius, happy in Rome or in the country with his family and his books, living like Pius to a ripe old age, would probably never have put pen to paper, or would have

[1] 3, 10; 4, 3; 4, 19; 7, 21; 4, 31; 4, 32–3; 7, 19.
[2] P. Oliva, *Pannonia and the Onset of Crisis in the Roman Empire*, Praha, 1962, 22.

contented himself with completing his *Deeds of the Ancient Greeks and Romans*.[1]

The second Book of the *Meditations* is headed 'Written among the Quadi on the Granua' and the third 'Written at Carnuntum'. In Book 10 comes the famous sole explicit reference to his wars. 'A spider is proud when it catches a fly, a man when he snares a hare, another when he nets a fish, another wild boars, another bears. another Sarmatians. If you test their principles, aren't they all brigands?' Marcus did not exult in his victories. But some of his men must have taken pride in their personal prowess against the enemy. The artists of the Aurelian Column in Rome have authentically recaptured the resignation and sympathy which motivated Marcus, in their portrayal of the northern wars.[2]

Apart from specific mention of names, there are many places where the influence of personal contact with the grim realities of war is apparent. The sentiments expressed in 'Despise the flesh, gore, and bones and a network, a wickerwork of nerves, veins, arteries', from the beginning of the book written on campaign in enemy territory, may have been polished by attendance at Galen's dissections. But it must have been consciousness of the body heightened by witnessing death and wounding that made him use the word 'gore' (λυθρός). Experience of battle inspires other passages. 'When a man's understanding has been chastened and purified, you will find no trace of a festering wound, gangrene, abscess, beneath the skin.' 'Just as surgeons always keep their instruments and lancets ready to hand for emergency operations, so you too should keep your beliefs ready, for the diagnosis of things divine and human.' 'Even what is closest [to the reason], the body, is cut, cauterised, suppurates, becomes gangrenous – yet let the part which makes judgments about these things be silent: that is, let it judge nothing to be good or bad which can happen equally to a good man or to a bad man.' This is faithfulness to Epictetus' teaching. The vivid language surely reflects personal experience, as another passage certainly does:

---

[1] Cf. *Med.*, 2, 2 and 3 ('put away your books'); 3, 14 (the *Deeds*).

[2] 10, 10. On the spirit of the column, cf. P. G. Hamberg, *Studies in Roman Imperial Art*, Uppsala-Copenhagen, 1945.

'if you've ever seen a dismembered hand or foot or a head cut off, lying apart somewhere from the rest of the body. . . .' The reliefs on the Columns of Trajan and of Marcus spring to mind, depicting soldiers holding up the heads of their decapitated foes; and, likewise (on the Column of Trajan), army surgeons attending to wounded Romans on the battlefield.[1]

In a section reflecting on the common lot of all men, death, he recalls Alexander the Great, Pompey and Caesar, who 'utterly destroyed whole cities so many times, and on the field of battle cut to pieces many tens of thousands of cavalry and infantry – and they themselves one day left the field of life'. The word 'gore' recurs shortly afterwards. Pursuing a philosophical conceit for a while he wonders 'how the earth can contain the bodies of those who have been buried in it, through countless ages'. The thought was one which a man who had seen many of his friends and officers die, and, if Lucian can be believed, 20,000 men from his army fell in one battle, may be excused for indulging in.[2]

The sources do not speak of Marcus being wounded personally. It is unlikely that he was. But Dio speaks of his weakness and of the pain in his chest. It is probably this which was at the back of the jotted comments on pain which occur here and there. 'In the case of every pain, be ready with the thought that it is not dishonourable and doesn't harm the mind that holds the helm. . . . This saying of Epicurus should help you – pain is neither unbearable nor unending, so long as you remember its limitations and don't add to it with your imagination.' 'On pain: what we cannot bear takes us away [from life]; what lasts can be borne.' 'Pain in the hand or foot is not against nature, provided that the foot and hand are fulfilling their own tasks. Hence not even for a man as man is pain contrary to nature. If it's not contrary to nature, it's not evil for him.' Thus he tried to apply the Stoic criteria to his own position.[3]

Sleep was a problem for him, as Dio and Galen record. He found it difficult to pull himself out of bed at dawn, after a disturbed night

---

[1] 2, 1 (cf. 8, 37); 3, 8; 3, 13; 4, 39; 8, 34.
[2] 3, 3; 4, 21; Lucian, *Alexander*, 48; *v. Marci*, 13, 5.
[3] 7, 64; 7, 33; 6, 33.

perhaps, when he had finally used Galen's *theriac* to help him get to sleep. 'At daybreak, when you are getting up with reluctance, let this be before your mind: "I am getting up to man's work".' 'When you are stirred from your sleep with difficulty, recall to mind the thought that acts in the service of the community are part of your constitution, but sleeping is what you have in common with dumb animals.' 'Let it make no difference to you whether you are shivering or warm, so long as you are doing your duty, whether you are drowsy or have had sufficient sleep, whether you are hearing ill or good spoken of yourself, whether you are dying or doing something else – for dying too is one of the actions of life. So in this too it is enough to "make the best use of the present".' His sleep was not always tranquil: 'be sober again and recall yourself, shake off sleep again – and realize that it was dreams that disturbed you, and now that you are fully awake again, look at these things as you looked at those'.[1]

His consciousness of his duties as emperor and commander-in-chief are never far from his mind. 'Each hour decide firmly, like a Roman and a man, to do what is to hand.' 'And let the divinity within you be the master of a being that is manly, and mature in years, a statesman and a Roman and a ruler – who has taken up his post, as would one who is waiting for the retreat to be sounded, from life.' 'Don't be ashamed to be helped. The task in front of you is to carry out your allotted duty, like a soldier in a storming-party. Suppose that you're lame and can't scale the wall by yourself. Yet it is possible with another's help.' He quoted Plato's *Apology* to strengthen his determination. 'Wherever a man takes up his post, either because he thinks it is the best place or because his officer has placed him there, there, I think, he should stay, and face the danger, taking nothing else into account, neither death nor anything else, in comparison with dishonour.'[2]

The military metaphors seem to recur in a passage from the book written 'Among the Quadi.' 'Do things breaking in on you from outside distract you? Well, give yourself some free time to learn some

---

[1] 5, 1; 8, 12; 6, 2; 6, 31 (the conclusions drawn from this by T. W. Africa, *J. Hist. Ideas*, 1961, 97 ff., seem a little too far-reaching).

[2] 2, 5; 3, 5; 7, 7; 7, 45 (Plato, *Apol.*, 28 E).

new good thing, and stop leaving your post. But now you must guard against another sort of wandering off course also: those who are weary of life and have no target at which to aim every impulse, or, in general, every mental impression (φαντασία), are triflers, in their actions as well [as their words].' 'Just as those opposed to you in your progress in agreement with right principle will not be able to divert you from right conduct, so you must not let them divert you from good will towards them. Be equally on your guard in both respects, both in steady judgment and behaviour and in gentleness to those who try to hinder you or are difficult in other ways. For to be hard on them is a weakness, just as much as to abandon your course and surrender from fear – for the man who panics and the man who is alienated from his natural kinsman and friend are both deserters from their post.' 'Always run the short way', he says near the end of the fourth Book, 'and nature's way is short. So do and say everything in the most healthy way, for a determination like this is a release from troubles and warfare and every care and affectation.' His detached attitude in the middle of the fighting, and his reliance on his Stoic creed are powerfully summed up in Book 2. 'Of human life, time is a point, existence is a moving stream, sensation is dim, the whole fabric of the body susceptible to decay, fame uncertain – briefly, all the things of the body are as a river, all the things of the spirit a dream and a tomb, life is like war and a sojourn in a foreign land. What then can escort man? One thing and one alone, philosophy.' Some of these ideas derive ultimately, perhaps, from Heraclitus. They would be impressive in any context. But the fact that they were written during war, during 'a sojourn in a foreign land', adds considerably to their effect on the reader.[1]

The image of the river, first used by Heraclitus, recurs several other times. 'Time is like a river composed of all things that happen, a rushing torrent.' 'In such a fog and filth, in so great a flowing past of being and of time, of movement and of things moved, what can be respected or be pursued with enthusiasm I do not know.' 'All being is like a river in ceaseless flow, its activities in continual change, its causes constantly varying, scarcely anything stable.' 'The world-

[1] 2, 7; 11, 9; 4, 51; 2, 17.

cause is like a river in flood. It carries all before it.'[1] Marcus had seen rivers before he went to Pannonia – and the Tiber in destructive flood. But he had never seen a great river like the Danube, and this must have had its effect on him. The eerie flat landscape of Burgenland, around the Neusiedlersee, in particular, which has had a perceptible effect on great creative artists (Haydn and Liszt), can hardly have failed to impress him, likewise the flat lands of the Marchfeld and the Hungarian plain.

References to other external events occur also, detached as always, but vivid. He talks of 'fleeing from the plague', but applies it to the corruption of the mind, 'far more corrupting' than the plague itself. He has a passing reference to 'treaties and armistices in war', and a little further on reflects on treachery. 'Turn inwards to your own self whenever you blame a traitor or an ungrateful person, for it is clearly your own fault, if you trusted such a man to keep loyal.' Taken together these passages leave an impression, which it is difficult to reject, that they were written with the events of the summer of A.D. 175 in mind, when Avidius Cassius, whom Marcus never publicly abused, beyond his constantly referring to him as 'ungrateful', rebelled, and Marcus made peace with the Sarmatians.[2]

Two further possible echoes of contemporary preoccupations may be mentioned here. 'He who runs away from his master is a runaway slave. But law is a master and the lawbreaker is a runaway slave too.' This recalls the increasing prevalence of slaves running away, and the 'general rescript' concerned with this some time in the years A.D. 177–80. 'Visualize to yourself every man who gives way to pain or discontent at anything at all is like the pig being sacrificed, kicking and squealing.' Marcus had to perform the military sacrifice of the *suovetaurilia* on several occasions during the wars. (It marked the official opening and closing of a campaign.) Marcus is shown performing such a sacrifice on one of the reliefs which were on his triumphal arch.[3]

Marcus is much preoccupied with death in the *Meditations*. The first Book was almost certainly written last. It looks as if it was

[1] 4, 43; 5, 10.   [2] 9, 2; 9, 9; 9, 42; cf. Dio, 71, 27.
[3] 10, 25, cf. *Digest.*, 11, 4, 1, 2; 10, 28.

intended as a kind of spiritual last will and testament. The remaining books are full of thoughts of death. Metaphor after metaphor, simile after simile, are brought in as the emperor struggles to reconcile himself with the prospect that his life was nearing its end. 'The governor of the universe' has 'set a time-limit' on you, he tells himself. 'Do each act as if it were your last.' The concept of his life nearing its close is one that recurs again and again. The 'winding of the threads ordained by providence' or by Clotho, one of the three Goddesses of Fate, was nearing its conclusion.[1]

Sometimes he says, briefly, 'life is short'. On one occasion he puts it to himself that one of the gods might tell him: 'tomorrow you will be dead'. Later he goes beyond this and tells himself to think of himself as already dead, and to regard what remains as a bonus – to be lived 'in accordance with nature'. A man's death is not the same as an actor having to break off in mid-performance. Death must not come as a surprise. It must not be despised either: 'smile at its coming'.[2]

Above all he reminds himself again and again that death is natural. 'Death is like birth, a mystery of nature.' He thinks of the great men of the past who are dead, of men who clung greedily to life, of cities like Pompeii that are, in a sense, now dead. 'Alexander the Great and his stable-boy both met their death in the end.' 'Soon enough you will vanish into nothing, like Hadrian and Augustus.' He quotes Euripides and Plato on death. 'The court of Augustus, his wife, his daughter, his grandsons, stepsons, sister, Agrippa, his kinsmen, his friends, Areius, Maecenas, his doctors and sacrificial attendants, – the whole court is dead. Then pass on to other courts – and the death not of a single man but of a whole family, like that of Pompey. And that epitaph: "The Last of his Line".' He thinks of mourners, such as Lucilla his mother mourning his father Verus, and of Panthea mourning her lover Lucius. 'And if they were still sitting by the tomb, would the dead notice? And if they did notice, would it please them?'[3]

[1] 2, 4; 2, 5 (cf. 7, 69); 2, 3; 4, 34.

[2] 4, 26; 6, 30; 4, 47; 7, 56; 3, 8 (cf. 11, 1); 11, 3 (cf. 3, 7; 7, 69).

[3] 4, 44; 2, 12; 4, 5; 3, 3; 4, 48; 6, 24; 8, 5; 7, 35; and 44-6 (Plato); 7, 50-1 (Euripides); 8, 31; 8, 25; 8, 37.

The simile of the retreat from the battlefield of life, and the idea of the river of time, have already been mentioned; and also his views on posthumous fame. His ideas on life after death were not fixed. He reviews the possibilities as dispassionately as he can. Sometimes he thinks of death in the orthodox Stoic way, as a dissolution of the body's material into the whole from which it came. He tells himself not to speculate. 'Either there is a random interlocking of atoms, and a scattering again, or there is unity, order, providence. If the first, why do I even desire to wear myself out in a world formed by chance, and in such a confusion. . . ? And why am I disturbed? The scattering of the atoms will come upon me whatever I do. But if the alternative be true, I worship and I am calm, I take courage in the governor of all.' 'On death: either dispersal, if we are merely atoms; or if we are a true unity, either extinction or a change of dwelling-place.' In the last book he turns to the question more than once. How can the gods have allowed this, the gods who ordained everything, with love for mankind; that truly good men should be utterly extinguished? But, he tells himself, if it ought to have been ordered differently, 'the gods would have made it so; for if it were just, it would be possible also, and if it were in accordance with nature, nature would have brought it about'. He argues with himself whether there is an inexorable destiny, whose decrees cannot be transgressed, or a divine providence that listens to human prayer, or simply an ungoverned chaos. If it is inexorable destiny, why resist? If a divine providence, he should make himself worthy of assistance. If nothing but random chaos, then he should be glad that amid the flood of waves, he has a mind that can direct. In the last words of the *Meditations* he masters his fears. 'Man, you have been a citizen in this great city. What does it matter to you whether it is for five years or for fifty? For what is in accordance with the laws is equal for every man. Why then is it terrible, if it is not a tyrant nor an unjust judge, but nature herself who brought you in, that sends you away from the city – as if the praetor who engaged an actor were to dismiss him from the stage? "But I have not spoken my five acts yet, only three." "Quite true – but in life three acts are the whole play." For he defines the perfect whole, the cause yesterday of your composition, today of your dissolution; you are the cause of neither. Go away then, gently. For he who releases you, releases you gently.'[1]

Death for Marcus was a release, a 'lying down to rest'. 'Remind yourself that the story of your life is finished and your service is completed.' The theme of service to others was always present. He had no illusions about the character of those around him. 'At dawn say to yourself first: "I shall meet inquisitive, ungrateful, insolent, treacherous, slanderous men".' But he adds that 'all these qualities come from their ignorance of good and evil'. The thought comes again in a later passage: 'next pass on to the characters of those who live around you, even the best of whom it is hard to put up with'. But again he qualifies this with 'not to say that it is hard for a man to put up with himself', and elsewhere he tells himself to 'think of the good qualities of those around you, when you want to cheer yourself up: the energy of one, the modesty of another, the generosity of another, and so on. For there is nothing so cheering as the images of the virtues shining out in the character of one's contemporaries, and meeting as far as possible in a group. So you should keep them ready.'[2]

Sometimes he yearned for the chance to withdraw from it all. 'Men search out retreats for themselves, in the country, by the sea, in the mountains – you yourself, more than most, are in the habit of longing for such things. But all this is most unlike a philosopher – you can retreat inside yourself any hour you like.' His thoughts must have returned wistfully to the quiet days of his youth spent at Lanuvium or Baiae. It may even be that when he told himself never to let anyone 'hear you finding fault with court life again, not even yourself', there was a conscious or unconscious realization that his life in the palace had been, if nothing else, preferable to life in army headquarters. On occasion he told himself that his 'station in life' made his profession of philosophy difficult. But later he says that 'no other calling in life is so fitted for philosophy as this in which you now find yourself'.[3]

A frequent image that Marcus uses is that of the city of the world,

---

[1] 6, 10; 7, 32 (cf. also 4, 14 and 21; 5, 13; 6, 4 and 10; 7, 19, 25 and 32; 8, 5 and 18); 12, 5; 12, 14 (more fully in 2, 11); 12, 36.
[2] 6, 28; 5, 4; 5, 31; 2, 1; 5, 10; 6, 48.   [3] 4, 3; 7, 9; 8, 1; 11, 7.

the universal city of which all men are citizens, 'the most venerable of all cities and constituted societies', obedience to whose laws is the 'aim of all rational beings'. 'Test everything one meets in life', he says, 'in accordance with its "value in reference to the whole, and to man, who is a citizen of the highest city, of which all other cities are like individual houses." A man who "cuts off his own soul from the soul of reasonable creatures" is a fragment cut off from the city, which is a unity.' 'What does not harm the city does not harm the citizens either.' 'What does not benefit the hive does not benefit the bee.' 'The poet sings: "Dear City of Cecrops" – and will you not say "Dear City of God"? '[1]

Marcus had no illusions about himself. 'This too can make you despise vain glory, the fact that you can no longer achieve the aim of having lived your whole life, or at least, your life from manhood, as a philosopher. To many other people as well as to yourself you have plainly fallen far short of philosophy. So you are tainted and it is no longer easy for you to gain the reputation of a philosopher.' 'Will you, my soul, one day be good, simple, single, naked, plainer to see than your surrounding flesh.'[2]

The philosophy of life expressed in the *Meditations* is not orthodox Stoicism. It is the individual attitude to life of a man who has studied and thought for a long time about the problems of conduct and the different teachings of the philosophical schools, and has made his own selection, strongly influenced by his own experiences. Stoic doctrines predominate, as is not unexpected in the case of one so closely associated with Stoics like Junius Rusticus and Claudius Maximus, not to mention his philosophy tutor Apollonius. The idea of the 'city of the world' and the constant effort to 'live in accordance with nature' express the essence of Stoic doctrines. 'Be free', he tells himself, as Epictetus had taught. 'It is what is hidden within you that controls the strings.' 'Keep yourself every hour for freedom, contentedly, simply and reverently.' 'The understanding that is free from passions is a citadel.' 'Bear and forbear', he says, as Epictetus did. His religion is strongly monotheistic, even if he revered the individual deities of the traditional Roman religion of which he was

[1] 4, 3; 2, 16; 3, 11; 4, 29; 5, 22; 6, 54; 4, 23.　　　　[2] 8, 1; 10, 1.

the official head, as aspects of the one God. ' "Live with the gods" –
but the man who continuously presents his soul to them . . . is living
with the gods.' In the same sentence he speaks of 'the deity'
(ὁσαίμων).[1]

The deepest impression left on Marcus by the teaching of any
single Stoic predecessor was that made by Posidonius' concept of
the world as a unified organism, in which the inner tension in everything preserves it as a composite whole. 'Meditate often on the bond
between all things in the universe, and their mutual relationship to
one another. For all things are in a way woven together and all are
because of this dear to one another. For one thing follows on another
in order because of the stress movement and common spirit and the
unity of all being.' This concept was closely related to that of the
world-city, which Posidonius, living in the first century B.C. when
Rome's predominance had at last begun to unify the Mediterranean
peoples, had eloquently expressed.[2]

It is difficult to select any one passage which summarizes Marcus'
philosophy. But in one written at Carnuntum, in the third Book, the
essence of his attitude to life comes out clearly. 'If you do the work
on hand following the rule of right with enthusiasm, manfully and
with kindheartedness, and allow no side issues to interrupt, but
preserve the divinity within you pure and upright, as if you might
even now have to return it to its Giver – if you make this firm, expecting nothing and avoiding nothing, but are content with your
present activity in accordance with nature and with old-fashioned
truthfulness in what you say and speak – you will live a happy life,
and there is no one who can prevent this.'[3] Reading the *Meditations*
for long periods can be conducive of melancholy. The atmosphere is
certainly strongly tinged with darkness, although in many places it is

---

[1] 4, 23; 3, 4; 4, 3; 10, 38; 8, 51; 8, 48; 5, 33 (cf. Epictetus, frag. 10, and
Discourses, 4, 8, 20); 5, 27; 11, 8. C. G. Starr, *Civilization and the Caesars*,
Ithaca, 1954, 250, prefers to regard the *Meditations* as 'stale mumblings'.
Many writers have found it difficult to avoid the use of cliché, particularly
when writing in an acquired language, as was Marcus.

[2] 6, 38 (cf. M. Pohlenz, op. cit., I, 348 ff.; II, 170). The concept of the
world-city occurs again and again. Cf. H. Neuenschwander, *Mark Aurels
Beziehungen zu Seneca und Poseidonius*, Berne, 1951.   [3] 3, 12.

lightened by vivid imagery – figs and olives, the drooping heads of ripe corn, rosebuds and saplings, vines bearing another summer's grapes, scuffling puppies or quarrelsome children.[1] But he was not trying to achieve 'fine writing'. 'Forget your thirst for books, or you will die muttering.'[2]

The *Meditations* are the self-expression of a ruler of a great empire who could see further than his empire. 'Asia and Europe are corners in the Universe. Every sea is a drop in the Universe – Mount Athos is a clod of earth in the Universe. Every instant of time is a mere point in eternity.' 'I have a city and a fatherland. As Antoninus, I am a Roman, as a man, I am a citizen of the Universe.' He wanted his Rome to be as near to his ideal city as he could. He knew it was difficult – 'don't hope for Plato's Utopia, but be content to make a very small step forward and reflect that the result of even this is no trivial success'. But the man whose friends had made him familiar with the lives of Thrasea and Cato, and able to 'conceive the idea of a state based on equity and freedom of speech, and of a monarchy which cherishes above all the liberty of the subject', had aspirations that were capable of realization. His hope was not fulfilled. But the verdict on his reign of Ammianus Marcellinus, admirer in his turn of Marcus' admirer Julian, is one that Marcus deserved: 'after calamitous losses things were restored anew, because the temperance of old had not yet been infected with the irresolution of negligence and laxity . . . with unanimous ardour highest and lowest hastened, as if to a calm and peaceful haven, to an honourable death in the service of the republic'. Cassius Dio, who experienced for himself the reign of Marcus and of his successors, gives explicit credit to the emperor himself. 'He did not have the good fortune that he deserved, for he was not physically strong, and for almost his whole reign was involved in a series of troubles. But I for my part admired him all the more for this very reason, that amid unusual and extraordinary difficulties he both survived himself and preserved the empire.'[3]

[1] 3, 1; 4, 20; 5, 6; 5, 33.   [2] 1, 7; 2, 3.
[3] 6, 36; 9, 29; 1, 14; Amm. Marc., 31, 5, 14; Dio, 71, 36, 3. See also J. O. Thomson, *JRS*, 43, 1953, 47 ff.

XI

EPILOGUE

IN THE JUDGMENT of posterity and of many contemporaries who
survived him, Marcus Aurelius was the perfect emperor. Two
criticisms only are laid against him: that he persecuted the Christians;
and that he permitted, even actively enforced, the choice of a worthless son as his successor. Persecution of the Christians at the hands
of a Stoic emperor may be deplored perhaps, but should not occasion surprise. The conditions prevailing in the reign of Marcus –
plague, war, civil war – made anti-Christian outbursts inevitable.
Those who appeared to be lacking in public spirit in such circumstances were unlikely to be sympathetically regarded. It is surprising
only that more were not martyred. The gulf which separated the
emperor of Rome from that secret, 'external superstition' was still
vast, although it had begun already to narrow – on both sides.
Christianity was aiming at the higher orders of society; and the
higher orders were already becoming diluted with new elements of
many kinds. The old order was changing.

In the light of subsequent events the martyrdoms under Marcus
may appear to have strengthened the Christian Church at a crucial
point in its history, when tolerance would have fostered still further
the growth of heresies and permitted some kind of disintegration.
Persecution produced martyrs – witnesses to the faithful and to the
waverers that their faith was superior to that of the doctrinally suspicious and at the same time less uncompromising followers of
Gnosticism, Montanism and the like. That the Christians recognized
the value of martyrdom is demonstrated by the various outbreaks of
voluntary martyrdom which occurred in periods of tolerance as well
as during the persecutions. By the time that systematic persecution

began, under Decius, the Church was too strong to be stamped out. The sporadic episodes under Marcus were enough to satisfy local pagan hatred of people whose behaviour was incomprehensible but suspect – people who were often of immigrant descent, and therefore liable in any case to be the victims of xenophobia. The persecutions meant much more than this to the Christians, but the government did not know and did not care: the maintenance of law and order was the prime consideration. This is not a justification for Marcus, for justification would be inappropriate.[1]

Less than thirteen years after Marcus died, his son too was dead, at the age of thirty-one; and soon afterwards a civil war began that lasted for four years. The violent shocks which these events gave to the imperial system were the origins, it has seemed to many, of the half-century – or century, even – of chaos which followed, even of the decline and fall of the empire. Supposing that the judgment were correct, can this be blamed on Marcus? It is now realized that it is absurd to believe that any system of 'choosing the best man' as emperor ever existed, except as a pious fiction in the minds and mouths of men like Pliny. It was chance that Nerva, Trajan, Hadrian and Pius had no sons. These emperors did not acquire their position through chance. But neither did they acquire it after rigorous selection from a short list of *capaces imperii*. Marcus is said to have repudiated the advice that he should divorce his wife for infidelity with the reply that if he divorced her, he would 'have to return her dowry as well' – in other words, the empire.[2] But Marcus did not become emperor because he was the son-in-law of Pius, and Marcus knew this.

Marcus' toleration of his wife's infidelity has in fact formed the basis of a further charge against him. But most of the stories about Faustina must be discounted. It was the subsequent behaviour of their son which led men to invent stories that the wife of Marcus had had a liaison with a gladiator. It was the only way that they could explain to themselves the discrepancy in character between Marcus and Commodus. Faustina may have been unfaithful to Marcus later.

[1] See Appendix IV on Marcus and the Christians.
[2] *v. Marci*, 19, 8–9.

In A.D. 160, when she was only thirty (or younger), the mother of four young children (the two youngest born in A.D. 159 and 160), who had lost three others in infancy, it is difficult to believe that she could have been unfaithful. When Marcus was away from her for three years or more (autumn A.D. 169 – autumn A.D. 172, perhaps till 173), until she joined him at the front, things may have been different. There were stories about affairs with ballet-dancers (*pantomimi*) then. She might have met temptation in the east in A.D. 165–6. Lovers of rank are named also, one of whom paid her court when Marcus was at home, it was said.[1] Finally, there was the story of the messages to Cassius – passion combined with treason. This last is probably untrue. But it may be that at some time she had let it be known that if Marcus died before Commodus reached his majority, she would prefer Cassius as her own and Commodus' protector, rather than her uncongenial son-in-law Pompeianus. Although the Stoic emperor could view the act of physical love as a mere process, he remembered his wife with love and gratitude. A few escapades would not have been enough to obliterate the memory of more than twenty years of happily married life.[2]

Commodus ended his life hated – by his own class. The only emperor born in the purple had been ruled by favourites, first the chamberlain Saoterus, then by Tigidius Perennis, as praetorian prefect a coldly efficient Grand Vizier, then by a freedman, Cleander. When these three had gone, Commodus began to break loose (A.D. 190), and to indulge his fantasies to the full. A plot was formed and on New Year's Eve A.D. 192 he was strangled in his bath. The new emperor was Helvius Pertinax, who proclaimed a return to

[1] *v. Marci*, 19; 23, 7; 26, 5; 29, 1–3; *v. Comm.*, 1, 3–9; 8, 1. J. Toutain, *Hommages Bidez-Cumont*, Bruxelles, 1949, 331 ff., and H. Mattingly, *Harv. Theol. Rev.*, 41, 1948, 147 ff., come to differing conclusions about the morals of Faustina. It would be more useful to ask when and where she could have wanted and had the opportunity to commit adultery – the years A.D. 170–3 are likely. On the other hand, the biographer (*v. Marci*, 29, 1–3) asserts that Marcus on one occasion discovered an admirer of Faustina breakfasting with her – and that many found fault with Marcus for his *patientia*. The truth will never be known.

[2] *Med.*, 6, 13; 1, 17 *ad fin.* (both passages probably written after Faustina's death, when Marcus had a mistress, cf. *v. Marci*, 29, 10).

the policies of Marcus.[1] Less than three months later he too was dead, replaced briefly by Didius Julianus, the one-time protégé of Domitia Lucilla. Didius began under a cloud and never had a chance. The men who had backed Pertinax acted, the ultimate victor being Septimius Severus.

Marcus had to allow his son to succeed him. If Commodus had not succeeded in A.D. 180, there would have been civil war then, rather than thirteen years later. Marcus hoped that the influence of men like Pompeianus and Aufidius Victorinus would keep Commodus on the right track, but this was not fulfilled.

The memory of Marcus was kept green, for various reasons. He was deified, as a matter of course, by Commodus. Septimius Severus, for political convenience, proclaimed himself the 'son of the Deified Marcus', and called his son Marcus Aurelius Antoninus to give an air of legitimacy and continuity to his rule. Julian the Apostate paid Marcus the best tribute in his *Caesars*. Although the criticism of his choice of Commodus is repeated (but not, of course, the charge of being a persecutor), the gods give their vote to Marcus at the heavenly contest of merit between the emperors of Rome.[2]

Marcus' reign has been thought to mark 'the end of the ancient world'.[3] Perhaps it did – although a lot of ancient history came after him. The world may have been 'beginning to put on the monk's hood' in his reign – but Marcus himself did not. He longed for a retreat, but he obeyed the call of duty. After his death, his plan to create two new provinces was given up. Had it succeeded, Rome would have had a far better frontier in the north: not a river, but mountain ranges. A river line was a neat and obvious frontier, but mountains are a better barrier. Tacitus, writing some twenty-four

---

[1] F. Grosso, *La Lotta Politica al Tempo di Commodo*, Torino, 1964, is the most recent and most comprehensive survey. It appeared too late to be taken into consideration here.

[2] Julian, *Caesars*.

[3] The title of E. Renan's memorable work, *Marc-Aurèle et la fin du monde antique*, is a programme in itself. The judgment 'le monde . . . s'encapuchine' has some validity, but it hardly applies to Marcus personally. He did not have the opportunity to become a religious recluse, even if he had wanted to (which is another question).

years before the birth of Marcus, expressed the view that 'the freedom of the Germans is a deadlier enemy than the despotism of Arsaces'. He was right. Forty-six years after Marcus' death the Arsacid rulers of Parthia were overthrown and the Persians again ruled on the Tigris (a matter to cause some preoccupation to the aged Cassius Dio).[1] Five hundred and seventy-four years after that (A.D. 800), Constantinople was still the capital of the eastern Roman empire, with six-and-a-half centuries more before her. But a German king was being crowned emperor of the Romans in Rome.[2]

Had the policy of Marcus been carried through, the western empire might have survived, no one can say with what effect. Or it may be that the empire established by Augustus carried in it from the start the seeds of its own decay. Such imponderables need not, however, affect the judgment of Marcus Aurelius.

Tacitus, *Germania*, 37, 3; Dio, 80, 3.
[2] Namely Charlemagne.

APPENDIX I: THE SOURCES

(A) ANCIENT SOURCES

The sources for the life of Marcus, as for any period of ancient history, may be classed as literary, epigraphic, numismatic and archaeological.

Foremost among the ancient literary sources are, naturally, the writings of Marcus himself, notably his correspondence with Fronto and his *Meditations*. The letters of Fronto have recently been re-edited by M. J. van den Hout (Leyden, 1954), who makes an attempt to arrange the individual letters solely on the basis of the order in the MSS. C. R. Haines in the useful Loeb edition (with translation, 2 vols., 1919-20) tried to rearrange them on historical grounds. Haines' dating is in many cases quite hypothetical. Some letters can never be accurately assigned to one year. Others can be re-dated on the basis of new evidence from other sources about persons or events mentioned. But Haines' edition remains extremely useful, and his account in his preface of the rediscovery of the letters by Cardinal Angelo Mai in the early nineteenth century remains a good introduction to the subject. I must here record my indebtedness to Haines' translation.

There is a vast bibliography of works dealing with the *Meditations*. I have relied mainly on the edition by A. S. L. FARQUHARSON[1] and I have found his translation of great assistance. But I have avoided questions of *Quellenforschung*. The works of F. MARTINAZZOLI (*La 'successio'*, etc.) and H. NEUENSCHWANDER, among recent studies, may be mentioned in this connection. The short article by M. J. van den HOUT, in which he examines possible traces of Fronto's influence in the style and content of the *Meditations*, is of interest.

The various legal compilations of ancient times - the Digest, Code of Justinian, etc - are another source which preserve the actual writings of Marcus, in a rather specialized field. An emperor's rescripts were naturally to a large extent stereotyped in form, and the imperial secretariat together with Marcus' legal advisers obviously had a hand in the content also. But

---

[1] Works listed in Appendix V are referred to in the other appendices by author's name in small capitals.

P. NOYEN, in two extremely useful articles, argues the view that Marcus' personality comes across strongly in his legislation or legal responses. NOYEN lists all Marcus' legal pronouncements. I have not been able to consult the works of A. DUMÉRIL and M. SCARLATA FAZIO. I have found the encyclopaedic dictionary of A. BERGER of great assistance. On one specific piece of legislation the article by J. H. OLIVER and R. E. A. PALMER should be mentioned (the *SC de sumptibus gladiatoriis minuendis*).

Two main sources deal with the life and reign of Marcus, the Greek historian Cassius Dio and the biographer whose work forms part of the so-called *Historia Augusta*. Unfortunately, Dio's account of the reign of Pius (A.D. 138–61), and of the first few years of the reign of Marcus, is totally lost, and for the years A.D. 121–38 and 170–80 only excerpts and epitomes are preserved (with one or two isolated fragments referring to the A.D. 160s). In spite of this, Dio is virtually the only reliable narrative source for the period on which his work has survived in any form. But there is a certain amount of disagreement about the order in which the various extracts and epitomes should be placed. The standard edition is that by U. P. Boissevain (5 vols., Berlin, 1895–1931, reprinted 1955). The Loeb edition and translation (by E. Cary; London-Cambridge, Mass., 1927, reprinted 1955: the relevant volumes are 8 and 9) is unfortunately rather unsatisfactory for the reign of Marcus and adopts different numeration from that of Boissevain. F. MILLAR has recently published a work on Cassius Dio, which is a valuable study of his methods, beliefs and background. Dio was born in the reign of Marcus and entered the senate early in the reign of Commodus. His testimony is undoubtedly of high value, although he was greatly biased in favour of Marcus and against Faustina II and Commodus.

The *Scriptores Historiae Augustae* are a source of a very different kind (Teubner edition by E. Hohl, I, 2nd. ed., Leipzig, 1955, II, 1927; Loeb edition and translation by D. Magie, London-Cambridge, Mass., 3 vols., 1921–32, reprinted 1954). The relevant lives in the collection are those of Hadrian, 'Helius Verus', Pius, Marcus, L. Verus, Avidius Cassius, Commodus, Pertinax, Didius Julianus and Severus, with a few items in other lives. It should be stated at the outset that the so-called 'minor lives' – those of 'Helius Verus', L. Verus, Avidius Cassius, Albinus, Niger, of the second-century personages treated – are virtually worthless as independent sources. In particular, the 'documents' which they contain are fictitious (cf. the work of J. HASEBROEK, and the bibliography and discussion by D. Magie in the preface to his Loeb edition, vols. 1 and 2, addenda in vol. 3, where the early history of the controversy provoked by H. Dessau is lucidly surveyed). Since the epoch-making article by Dessau ('Über Zeit und Persönlichkeit der *Scriptores Historiae Augustae*', *Hermes*, 24, 1889, 337 ff.) a great deal of ink has been spilt over this work, and the controversy has not yet been settled. The work was ostensibly composed at the end of the third and beginning of the fourth centuries, by six authors. In spite of the arguments of A. MOMIGLIANO, I am convinced of the truth of Dessau's basic contention, that the work was composed considerably later, probably at the end of the fourth century, and probably by one man. N. H. BAYNES' case that it was composed in the reign of Julian, as propaganda for that emperor, is now not accepted (but Baynes' discussion of the work remains very valuable). For a recent survey of the problem see the article by A. CHASTAGNOL. The question as to when, why and by whom such a work was composed is not strictly germane to the question of its value as a source for the second century. The question remains, what sources did the biographer or biographers use for the second-century lives, and how valuable, or reliable, were those sources? At one time scholars confidently divided the sources of the *S.H.A.* into two main categories: a chronological, factual, narrative source; and a biographical source, rather unreliable. This concept dominates the fundamental studies of the Lives of Marcus and of Commodus by J. SCHWENDE-MANN and J. M. HEER. But such rigid categorization is not particularly helpful and it may seriously be doubted whether it bears much relation to the truth (see the remarks of F. GROSSO, p. 59). It is generally agreed, however, that an important source for the second-century lives was Marius Maximus, frequently cited by the *S.H.A.* (see the index to the editions of Hohl and Magie) as a source for facts of varying importance for the lives of most of the emperors from Trajan to Elagabalus (apparently cited as the author of a Life of Nerva by the Scholiast on Juvenal 4,83). It is generally agreed that Marius Maximus was the author of a second Twelve Caesars, in continuation from Suetonius, and that he was the same as L. Marius Maximus Perpetuus Aurelianus cos. II ord. 223. This man was a leading general of Severus, prominent also under Caracalla, Macrinus and Severus Alexander; and in Alexander's reign the opportunity arose for the first time of writing a second Twelve Caesars (Nerva, Trajan, Hadrian, Pius, Marcus, Commodus, Pertinax, Didius, Severus, Caracalla, Macrinus, Elagabalus). The value of Maximus' lost work has been disputed (cf. G. BARBIERI'S 1954 article, with full references), but I prefer to follow the opinion of E. HOHL (*Kaiser Commodus*, etc., p. 3) in regarding Maximus as the principal source of the *S.H.A.* for the lives of the second-century emperors. Maximus was a contemporary of Cassius Dio, and in a good position to obtain valuable historical material. Even if his work was filled with scandal (see the judgment of the sterner Ammianus Marcellinus, 28,4,14, who classes him with Juvenal) it was undoubtedly copious (cf. *S.H.A., v. Firm.*, 1,2: 'homo omnium verbosissimus'). The *S.H.A.* sometimes tired of Maximus, and turned elsewhere, e.g. to Eutropius or to their own tediously fertile imagination. But much valuable material remains, even if the 'documents' in the minor lives are rejected. The works of J. SCHWENDEMANN and J. M. HEER are still indispensable analyses of this material in spite of the defects mentioned above, in the absence of a modern historical edition of the *S.H.A.*

Another third-century writer, apart from Dio and Maximus, is Herodian, whose work survives *in toto*. But Herodian takes the death of Marcus as the starting-point for his work, which covers the years A.D. 180–240, and, in any case, his value as an independent witness is negligible (cf. E. HOHL, *Kaiser Commodus*, etc. F. GROSSO'S interesting analysis of Herodian on Commodus, p. 30 ff., has not led me to revise this opinion).

Information of varying value is provided by various later writers such as Ammianus Marcellinus, Aurelius Victor, the anonymous author of the *Epitome de Caesaribus*, Eutropius and Orosius, and by various chroniclers. Contemporary non-historical writers such as Apuleius, Aelius Aristides, Galen and Lucian are an indispensable adjunct, and often include facts not recorded elsewhere. Of special importance is Philostratus, a contemporary of Cassius Dio, whose *Lives of the Sophists* is particularly useful on Herodes Atticus. I have made considerable use also of Aulus Gellius' *Attic Nights*. Gellius was a contemporary of Marcus and is very illuminating on the intellectual life of the first half of the second century (see the detailed study by R. MARACHE).

The life of Marcus cannot be properly appreciated without taking into account the first century and early second century, in particular the writings of Martial, Quintilian (on whom see now the article by M. WINTERBOTTOM), Juvenal, Pliny, and Tacitus (on whom see R. SYME'S monumental study published in 1958).

The writings of Marcus' Stoic predecessors also have to be taken into consideration. I have relied mainly on the work of M. POHLENZ, who gives full references, and whose summaries of the life and thought of Musonius, Seneca, Epictetus and Marcus himself (p. 300 ff.) are models of clarity.

Christian writers fall into a special category. The Acts of the martyrs are collected by R. KNOPF and G. KRÜGER. In addition there are the second-century apologists (on whom see now B. Altaner, *Patrology*, tr. H. C. Graef, Freiburg-Edinburgh-London, 1960, p. 114 ff.). There is much of relevance in Origen's attack on Celsus, a contemporary of Marcus who attacked the Christians (see the translation with notes by H. CHADWICK). Finally, there are the later historians and chroniclers, notably Eusebius' *Historia Ecclesiae*. 'Marcus and the Christians' is the subject of Appendix IV, in which further references are given.

The basic collections of epigraphic material are the *CIL*, Dessau's *ILS*, *AE*, and *IGR*. *Inscr. It.* XIII, 1, edited by A. Degrassi, is a vital source of new information for the reign of Pius, publishing the surviving portions of the *Fasti Ostienses* for the period (supplemented by H. NESSELHAUF). A number of important new inscriptions have been made use of in the text. But it is a matter of regret that the *tabula Banasitana* has not yet been adequately published. This document, discovered in 1957, records a decision of Marcus and Commodus and their *consilium* at a meeting of July 6, 177. It concerns the grant of citizenship to a native chieftain, and gives the names of a number of witnesses, including the two praetorian prefects. But the discussion of the document by W. SESTON and M. EUZENNAT is no substitute for an adequate publication, and I have been unable to make any use of it (see the eloquent protests of F. GROSSO, p. 143).

The numismatic evidence may be used in various ways. *B.M.C.* IV, by H. Mattingly, is a most exhaustive examination of the coin-material (slightly in need of emendation on the reign of Marcus, in view of the work of ZWIKKER). G. MICKWITZ has an important brief analysis of the depreciation of the coinage in the reign of Marcus.

Archaeological evidence covers many categories. It can, for example, illuminate the history of the Roman frontiers. On these matters, see the works listed in Appendix V under the names of F. KŘÍŽEK, P. OLIVA, H. SCHÖNBERGER and E. SWOBODA, as well as the comprehensive survey by W. ZWIKKER of the background to the Marcomannic Wars and the archaeological evidence for their course. For the Marcomannic Wars of Marcus there is another type of material which may be classed broadly as archaeological, namely the Aurelian reliefs, especially those of the Column. Unfortunately, in spite of the confidence with which these are sometimes used, agreement on their dating and significance has not really been reached. The recent excellent illustrated edition of the Column by C.

CAPRINO et al. in my opinion avoids several of the difficulties. In particular, the important paper by J. MORRIS is not taken into account. Morris questions one of the basic premises of the accepted dating, namely that the Column represents only the northern wars of A.D. 172–5. His arguments designed to show that the Column depicts, rather, the years A.D. 173–5 and 177–80 may not be, themselves, preferable. But I think that Morris has made a good case for doubting the existing dating, which depends on the assumption that Commodus is not depicted anywhere on the Column. In view of the weathered condition of many of the reliefs (and the fact that some of the details are Renaissance replacements) this confidence seems misplaced. In any case, the *damnatio memoriae* of A.D. 193, coming at a time when the Column may have been only just completed, might well have resulted in representations of Commodus being removed from the Column, as they were from elsewhere. On the whole, I am inclined to follow ZWIKKER, GUEY and others in believing that the reliefs followed a chronological order. On the other hand it would not be surprising if the artists of the Column, or those who gave the orders to the artists, had decided to place the 'Rain Miracle' scene (XVI) low down, so that as many people as possible could see it, whatever its place in the historical order of events. This order of events still remains to be established. On the spirit of the Column, in addition to the works already cited, reference may be made to P. G. HAMBERG.

(B) MODERN WORKS

There is no very recent biography of Marcus (it may be noted that of A. S. L. FARQUHARSON, 2nd. ed., Oxford, 1952, was originally written in 1928, and published postumously) which can really be called comprehensive. Reference may be made to the very full bibliography in A. GARZETTI (esp. p. 696 ff.), covering the years 1936–59.

APPENDIX II:
STEMMATA OF THE ANTONINES

A: Trajan and Hadrian
B: Antoninus Pius
C: Marcus
D: The Children of Marcus
E: Lucius

A: TRAJAN AND HADRIAN

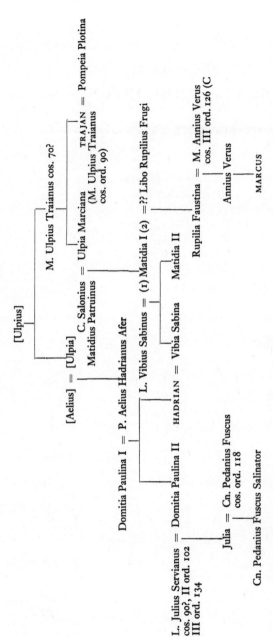

Most of the material for this stemma will be found in R. SYME's *Tacitus*, appendix 87 (pp. 792 ff.). The only point on which there is room for doubt is the marriage of Rupilius with Matidia I. This is accepted by H.-G. PFLAUM in *Historia–Augusta–Colloquium* following J. CARCOPINO and P. GRENADE. For doubts, cf. A. GARZETTI, p. 689. It would certainly explain Dio's assertion (69, 21, 2) that Hadrian and Marcus were kinsmen. But I prefer to follow Syme, pp. 791–2, in regarding the Dasumii as the likely link between the Aelii Hadriani and Marcus (through the Calvisii). In any case, as Syme emphasizes, both the Aelii and the Annii Veri were families long settled in the province of Baetica. The kinship might therefore date back to many generations before the birth of Marcus. It is worth mentioning here that Plotina, Trajan's empress, was from Nemausus, the home of Antoninus Pius' ancestors.

SYME's analysis, in *Tacitus*, *Colonial Elites*, and, most recently, in *JRS* 54, 1964, provides the best commentary on these 'colonial' Romans and on the alliances of the Spanish, Provençal and Italian families which formed the dynasty of the Antonines.

B: ANTONINUS PIUS

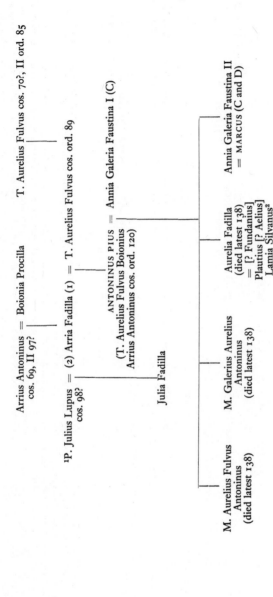

Arrius Antoninus = Boionia Procilla
cos. 69, II 97?

T. Aurelius Fulvus cos. 70?, II ord. 85

[1]P. Julius Lupus = (2) Arria Fadilla (1) = T. Aurelius Fulvus cos. ord. 89
cos. 98?

ANTONINUS PIUS = Annia Galeria Faustina I (C)
(T. Aurelius Fulvus Boionius
Arrius Antoninus cos. ord. 120)

Julia Fadilla

M. Aurelius Fulvus
Antoninus
(died latest 138)

M. Galerius Aurelius
Antoninus
(died latest 138)

Aurelia Fadilla
(died latest 138)
= [? Fundanius]
Plautius [? Aelius]
Lamia Silvanus[2]

Annia Galeria Faustina II
= MARCUS (C and D)

[1] For Julius Lupus (some connection of the Flavian dynasty), see SYME, *Tacitus*, p. 794, and G. TOWNEND, in *JRS*, 1961.
[2] The husband of Pius' daughter Fadilla was perhaps a Fundanius, although clearly linked with the Aelii Lamiae and Plautii Silvani (cf. *AE* 1947, 4, and Chapter II, above, page 31, note 2, and page 32, note 1). Hence a connection is possible with the enigmatic Plautia (E).

C: MARCUS

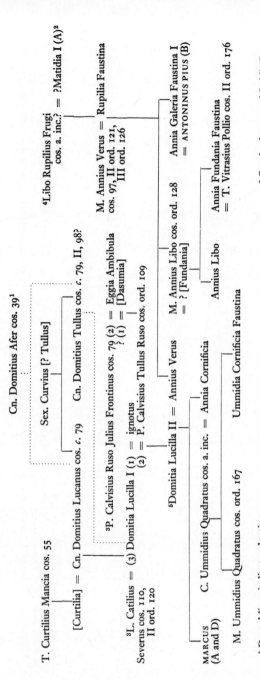

Cn. Domitius Afer cos. 39[1]

T. Curtilius Mancia cos. 55

Sex. Curvius [? Tullus]

⁴Libo Rupilius Frugi cos. a. inc.? = ?Matidia I (A)[2]

[Curtilia] = Cn. Domitius Lucanus cos. c. 79   Cn. Domitius Tullus cos. c. 79, II, 98?

M. Annius Verus = Rupilia Faustina
cos. 97, II ord. 121,
III ord. 126

³P. Calvisius Ruso Julius Frontinus cos. 79 (2) = Eggia Ambibula
? (1) = [Dasumia]

³L. Catilius = (3) Domitia Lucilla I (1) = ignotus
Severus cos. 110,   (2) = P. Calvisius Tullus Ruso cos. ord. 109
II ord. 120

Annia Galeria Faustina I
= ANTONINUS PIUS (B)

M. Annius Libo cos. ord. 128

⁵Domitia Lucilla II = Annius Verus

Annia Fundania Faustina
= T. Vitrasius Pollio cos. II ord. 176

M. Annius Libo cos. ord. 128
= ? [Fundania]

Annius Libo

C. Ummidius Quadratus cos. a. inc. = Annia Cornificia

Ummidia Cornificia Faustina

MARCUS
(A and D)

M. Ummidius Quadratus cos. ord. 167

[1] Dotted lines indicate adoption.

[2] See A, above, on Matidia I.

[3] My father, Professor E. Birley, has drawn my attention to difficulties in the dating and interpretation of the career of P. Calvisius Ruso Julius Frontinus, which he hopes to discuss in print on a future occasion.

[4] The name of the paternal great-grandfather Rupilius is given in *v. Marci*, 1, 4, as 'Rupili Boni'. This must be a scribe's error (haplography) for 'Rupili Libonis'. No senator is otherwise recorded with the *cognomen* Bonus, whereas the names 'Libonis Rupili Frugi' are recorded epigraphically (*AE* 1940, 39). This man is probably the same as the consular 'Libo Frugi' recorded as speaking in a debate in the senate in about 100 (Pliny, *Epp.* 3, 9, 33)—and as the great-grandfather of Marcus. The emendation would explain the appearance of the *cognomen* Libo in the nomenclature of Marcus' uncle, M. Annius Libo. I hope to publish this suggestion in more detail elsewhere in the near future. Here it may suffice to point out that Rupilius Libo, or Libo Rupilius Frugi, was probably a grandson of M. Licinius Crassus Frugi cos. ord. 27 and his wife Scribonia. Thus Marcus would be descended not only from colonial Romans, but from such great figures of Rome's past as Pompey and Crassus, and the Scribonii Libones and Calpurnii Pisones; and the marriage to Rupilia—combined with some link with Hadrian—goes some way to explain the remarkable prominence of Marcus' grandfather, the cos. III ord. of 126.

[5] I follow SYME (*Tacitus*, p. 793) in his suggested emendation of *v. Marci*, 1, 3, to read: 'mater Domitia Lucilla Calvisi Tulli <filia, avia materna Lucilla Domiti Tulli> bis consulis filia'.

D: THE CHILDREN OF MARCUS

MARCUS = Faustina II (B and C)

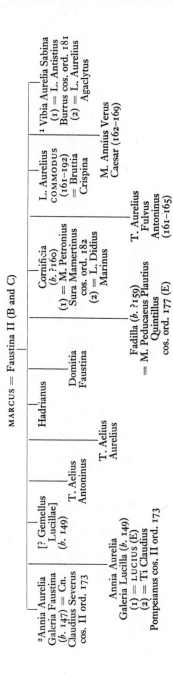

²Annia Aurelia Galeria Faustina (b. 147) = Cn. Claudius Severus cos. II ord. 173

[? Gemellus Lucillae] (b. 149)

T. Aelius Antoninus

T. Aelius Aurelius

Annia Aurelia Galeria Lucilla (b. 149) (1) = LUCIUS (E) (2) = Ti Claudius Pompeianus cos. II ord. 173

Hadrianus

Domitia Faustina

Fadilla (b. ?159) = M. Peducaeus Plautius Quintillus cos. ord. 177 (E)

Cornificia (b. ?160) (1) = M. Petronius Sura Mamertinus cos. ord. 182 (2) = L. Didius Marinus

T. Aurelius Fulvus Antoninus (161–165)

L. Aurelius COMMODUS (161–192) = Bruttia Crispina

M. Annius Verus Caesar (162–169)

¹Vibia Aurelia Sabina (1) = L. Antistius Burrus cos. ord. 181 (2) = L. Aurelius Agaclytus

The best discussion is by H.-G. PFLAUM in *J. des Savants*, whose conclusions I largely follow (the study by J. KEIL is also still useful). It is worth mentioning in particular the detailed and revealing examination by Pflaum of the descendants of Marcus and their vicissitudes (a subject not treated in the present work).

¹ I diverge from Pflaum over the date of birth of Sabina. Philostratus, *v. soph.*, 2, 1, 11, explicitly refers to a 'three-year-old child' of Marcus being at Sirmium with him, hence in 173 or 174. Pflaum for some reason which he does not state describes Sabina as aged between 7 and 11 at this moment, although she was clearly the youngest child and is regarded as such by Pflaum himself.

² Pflaum has apparently overlooked that *Inscr. It.* XIII, 1, 207 reveals that Faustina was born in 147, not 146 as previously thought.

E: LUCIUS

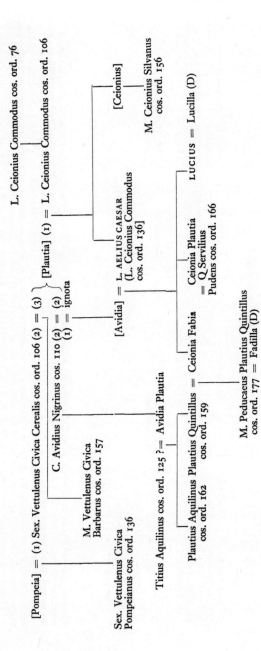

The basis for this stemma is the article by SYME in *Athenaeum*. See also PFLAUM in *J. des Savants* (but his article in *Historia–Augusta-Colloquium* fails to take Syme's discussion fully into account regarding the third marriage of Plautia and the origin of the name Fabia, questions which cannot be dealt with here).

APPENDIX III:

THE MARCOMANNIC WARS

The importance in the history of the Roman Empire of the Marcomannic or Danubian wars of Marcus Aurelius is generally recognized. Rome's armies had to face a kind of Blitzkrieg launched by a vast 'barbarian conspiracy'. Serious weaknesses were exposed. The empire was invaded, and devastated. Marcus fought back. But his radical scheme to solve the problem was not carried out because of his death. One cannot say whether it would have succeeded – perhaps the annexation of new territories would have been too much for Rome (cf. the interesting study by G. WALSER). On the other hand the mountain frontier which it would have given the empire would have been greatly superior, from the military point of view, to the river line of the Danube. The Suebic Germans had become relatively civilized after long years of contact with Noricum and Pannonia. They, and the fierce Sarmatians, would have strengthened Rome's armies immeasurably had they been pacified and subjugated. As it turned out, the determined prosecution of the wars by Marcus ensured peace in the north for many decades. But when trouble broke out again, new groupings had appeared. Caracalla fought the Alemanni in A.D. 213 – their name (*Aller Männer*, all men) reveals their origin. They were a confederation of tribes. The struggle with Rome in the A.D. 170s had brought changes among the northern peoples, making them more able, and more eager, to launch assaults on the wealthy colossus to their south. The wars also affected Rome. The constant fighting made heavy demands on the army at all levels. Changes in the High Command, and in the deployment of armies, necessitated by the urgency of the moment, became, in many cases, permanent. The Marcomannic Wars were a very significant factor in the process which ended the Augustan principate and, after years of chaos, produced a new empire in its place.

Unfortunately, the chronology of these wars is a vexed question, on which agreement has not been, and perhaps never will be, reached. The basic cause lies in the fragmentary nature of the literary records. There exists no ancient narrative history at all of the opening stages of the war, and Cassius Dio's account of the campaigning in the A.D. 170s has only survived in fragmentary excerpts and epitomes. (Further complication – rather than clarification – is caused by the existence of the historical reliefs on the Aurelian Column.) In any case, any writer in ancient times must have had great difficulty in presenting a coherent account of a war fought on a very extended front against a constantly changing enemy. The study of the chronology was revolutionized by w. ZWIKKER, whose work was intended as a preliminary to a study of the reliefs of the Column (this never appeared, on account of Zwikker's death). His work, published in 1941, deals very thoroughly (if sometimes somewhat polemically) with the literature on the subject up to 1940, which for that reason is not discussed here. His work can be improved on in certain respects in the light of new evidence, largely epigraphic; for example, the inscriptions recording the career of M. Valerius Maximianus and revealing the activity in recruitment of Cn. Iulius Verus (*AE* 1956, 123 and 124), and attesting the early career of P. Helvius Pertinax (published by H. G. KOLBE). In other respects his interpretation of careers of senators and equestrians can be improved on, notably in the light of H.-G. PFLAUM's work on the careers of procurators (1960–1). R. Egger, in his review of Zwikker (*Gnomon*, 18, 1942, 329), greatly improved Zwikker's interpretation of the important career of C. Vettius Sabinianus (cf. also *PW* 8A, 1958, 1861 ff.). The most revolutionary aspect of Zwikker's chronology was that he dated the great invasion of Italy to A.D. 170 or 171, rather than to one of the years A.D. 166–9. This has not been universally accepted, but I regard it as the most satisfactory solution (I prefer A.D. 170 to 171, the year favoured by Zwikker).

Zwikker's dating of the invasion of Italy has been criticized, most notably perhaps by A. DEGRASSI (1952). Degrassi's main interest was to determine the moment at which Q. Antistius Adventus was appointed to command the newly created *praetentura Italiae et Alpium*. Rightly, in my opinion, he assigns this to the year A.D. 168 (p. 116 ff.), against Zwikker (p. 162 ff.) who dates it to c. 171. But both Degrassi and Zwikker have as a basic premiss the assumption that Adventus could only have been appointed to such a post *after* the invasion of Italy. First, there is no reason why Adventus should have been the only holder of such a post (although none other is recorded at present – but Ti. Claudius Pompeianus may have been given analogous powers in A.D. 170 or 171). Second, there is no reason why Marcus should not have been capable of creating the *praetentura* even before the invasion. Third, there is no reason to suppose that the

324

existence of the *praetentura* command, of itself, could have prevented the invasion. Fourth, if Adventus was, at the time of the invasion, entrusted with the defence of northern Italy – and, as it turned out, failed in his task, initially at least – that is not a sufficient reason for believing that he would have been disgraced (he in fact went on to govern Lower Germany and Britain – and a close relative, perhaps his son, married the youngest daughter of Marcus). Fifth, it is, in any case, quite possible that by A.D. 170 his command had been, partially, at least, dismantled, and that he had already left northern Italy to govern Lower Germany. Zwikker's effort to date Adventus' consulate and appointment to the *praetentura* to a rather later period (cos. 168, *praetentura* A.D. 171) than generally held (cos. 166–7, *praetentura* A.D. 168) is unconvincing and, I believe, unnecessary.

Zwikker assigned to the year A.D. 170 or 171 another 'special command', that of L. Vitrasius Flamininus (p. 163 ff.), 'leg. pr. pr. Italiae Transpadanae et provinciae Moesiae Superioris et exercitus provinciae Dalmatiae' (*C IL* X, 3870). But I prefer to follow A. STEIN (*Moesien*, p. 41) in regarding Flamininus as the cos. 122, and in any case R. SYME has shown good reason for doubting that the three offices apparently recorded on the now lost inscription of Flamininus could have been held simultaneously, as Zwikker maintained (cf. *Gnomon*, 31, 1959, 514). In the absence of confirmation I have preferred to leave the career of Flamininus out of my account of the wars. I might refer also to my paper in *Acta Antiqua Philippopolitana*, etc., where a number of military careers of the period are discussed (though I must point out that on p. 110 of that paper I still accepted Zwikker's interpretation of the career of Antistius Adventus).

I cannot follow Zwikker in another aspect of his dating. He makes the Roman offensive of A.D. 172 open with the campaign against the Quadi (p. 191 ff.). I accept his arguments that the offensive began in that year, but I do not accept that the fragments of Cassius Dio prove that the Quadi were attacked before the Marcomanni. It may be convenient if I set down my chronology of the years A.D. 170–5 in schematic form:

A.D. 170 Roman offensive fails. Greece, and perhaps Italy also invaded.

A.D. 171 Invaders repulsed from empire (invasion of Italy early in A.D. 171, if not earlier). Marcus negotiates at Carnuntum: Quadi and others make peace.

A.D. 172 Marcomanni attacked by Rome. Quadi break treaty by assisting them. Marcomanni defeated.

A.D. 173 Quadi attacked, defeated, make peace.

A.D. 174 Jazyges attacked, Quadi break treaty again.

A.D. 175 War against Jazyges continues. Armistice in summer.

An important reason why Zwikker proposed the order of events which he did, was the fact that most of the sources record that the 'Rain Miracle' took place in the lands of the Quadi, or in the war against them; and that this event is depicted in a very early scene (XVI) on the Aurelian Column. J. GUEY, in his fundamental (and fascinating) re-examination of the evidence for the 'Rain Miracle' and of the role of the Egyptian priest Harnouphis, opts firmly for the year A.D. 172, following and supporting with new arguments the dating of Zwikker (who, nevertheless, did not exclude entirely the year A.D. 173, see p. 217). I am less convinced than Zwikker and Guey about the dating of the Aurelian Column (see appendix I), but I admit that my account of the episodes in chapter VIII is not entirely satisfactory: the Lightning Miracle (scene XI) is assigned to A.D. 172 and the Rain Miracle (scene XVI) to A.D. 173. It might have been preferable to date the Rain Miracle to the end of A.D. 172 – by which time the Quadi might have broken their treaty, relatively late in the campaigning season. A way out might be to argue that the Rain Miracle took place not among the Quadi but among the Cotini, as the spurious letter of Marcus, forged for Christian purposes, alleges (see Fronto, Haines, II, 303 ff. for a convenient text). GUEY, in his article in *Rev. de Phil.*, p. 17, n.4, explicitly chooses to ignore this source, but I feel that there are elements in it which are genuine (as was argued long ago by A. HARNACK). A difficulty would be solved if both miracles belonged to A.D. 172, the second taking place ἐν κοτίνῳ or ἐν κοτίνοις. Those who follow ZWIKKER and GUEY in making the war against the Quadi precede the war against the Marcomanni have to tackle this difficulty. My account in Chapter VIII is inevitably something of a compromise, to avoid too many pages of tedious argument. The chronology of the later years of the war does not involve comparable difficulties and need not be entered into here.

In view of the immense importance of the wars it may be useful to refer to a number of works which I have found helpful. That of ZWIKKER is the most fundamental. Of more recent work, P. OLIVA gives a useful account of the wars and their effects on Pannonia (esp. pp. 259–310), and E. SWOBODA'S study of the key site of Carnuntum is much more comprehensive on the history and archaeology of the Danubian frontier-zone than its title might suggest, especially in the present context pp. 47–58 and pp. 246–55 (with invaluable bibliography and citations of important passages from the ancient sources). Swoboda and F. HAMPL arrived independently at the conclusion that Marcus did not in fact ever intend to annexe two new provinces. Interesting though their respective analyses of the available material are, I cannot accept this conclusion; for a brief statement, cf. my review of Swoboda in *Gnomon* 37, 1965, 728. This question reflects a general problem with this period: it is for the most part virtually impossible to discover the originators of policy, or even the nature of the policy itself. J. GUEY'S detailed studies of the Rain Miracle have already been mentioned. On traces of Roman activity beyond the Danube the article by F. KŘIŽEK and the volume entitled LIMES-ROMANUS-KONFERENZ-NITRA are useful (more will undoubtedly be learned from excavation and field surveys in Central Europe, about Marcus' campaigns). Finally the article on *Pannonia* in *PW* Supp. 9, 1962, (by A. Mócsy) may be mentioned. This study and the works by OLIVA and SWOBODA between them give almost comprehensive bibliographies of recent work, which I will not attempt to repeat here.

APPENDIX IV:
MARCUS AND THE CHRISTIANS

The reign of Marcus Aurelius undoubtedly marked a turning-point in the relationship between the Roman State and the Christian Church (see, for example, J. BEAUJEU, p. 353 ff.). H. GRÉGOIRE even goes so far as to call Marcus 'en un sens . . . le premier persécuteur' (p. 24 ff.). The literature on the topic is vast (for the Rain Miracle, see appendix III), and I cannot do more here than give a brief summary of the salient points.

The martyrdoms in the reign were numerous, and they fall into two distinct groups: those *circa* A.D. 167 and those *circa* A.D. 177 (see M. SORDI, p. 365 ff.). To the first group belong the martyrdom of Justin and his companions at Rome, those of Carpus, Papilas and Agathonice at Pergamum, and some others. I am doubtful about the date of death of Sagaris, Bishop of Laodicea, condemned under the proconsul 'Servilius Paulus'. This is generally regarded as an error for '*Sergius* Paulus'=L. Sergius Paulus cos. II ord. A.D. 168, who must have been proconsul not later than summer A.D. 167 (so SORDI, p. 365 with n.2). But there were several senatorial *Servilii* in the mid-second century, and Q. Servilius Pudens cos. ord. A.D. 166, for example, might well have become proconsul of Asia (in that case, at the very end of the reign). Hence the emendation of Eusebius, *Hist. Ecc.*, 4,26,3, to read ἐπὶ Σεργίου Παύλου instead of ἐπὶ Σερουιλίου Παύλου seems to me less than certain. Perhaps Παύλου should be emended instead.

The martyrdom of Polycarp is dated by H. GRÉGOIRE (p. 108 ff.), whose arguments have been widely accepted, to A.D. 177, but I still prefer the date of A.D. 155 or 156 (cf. W. HÜTTL, II, p. 33 ff., esp. 52–4, and *PW* 21, 1952, 1673 ff. Mr G. E. M. de Ste. Croix kindly informs me that he hopes to be able to demonstrate that GRÉGOIRE'S arguments (p. 110 ff.) about the date of the origins of Montanism are mistaken, and that the movement began earlier than GRÉGOIRE believes. This would weaken one of his major arguments. W. H. C. FREND, whose outstanding book on the persecutions unfortunately appeared too late to be taken into account here until proof stage, favours a dating to the period A.D. 165–8 (p. 295 n. 1).

I have given, in Chapter IX, an account of the Lyons martyrdoms of A.D. 177 which follows closely the remarkable study by J. H. OLIVER and R. E. A. PALMER. I cannot accept the arguments put forward with much ingenuity and at great length by J. Colin (*L'empire des Antonins et les martyrs gaulois de* 177, Bonn, 1964), attempting to show that the martyrdoms of A.D. 177 described in Eusebius took place not at Lyons but at Sebastopolis in Pontus Galaticus.

The question of the 'new decrees' mentioned by Meliton of Sardis (in Eusebius, *Hist. Ecc.*, 4,26) has been examined repeatedly. See, most recently, the work of M. SORDI, whose attempt to find a trace of 'new decrees' in *Digest.* 1,18,13 and 48,13,4,2, is interesting, if not completely convincing. I certainly do not believe that any 'new decrees' were issued directly and specifically against the Christians. Legislation passed in time of crisis designed to deal firmly with anyone who stirred up public anxiety might possibly have been applied against Christians (e.g. *Digest.* 48,19,30), but this is unlikely (cf. G. E. M. de Ste. CROIX, p. 14). At Lyons in A.D. 177 special factors caused the persecution – special factors created by a piece of imperial legislation, namely the *senatusconsultum de sumptibus gladiatoriis minuendis* (cf. OLIVER and PALMER). It is tempting to wonder whether Meliton and his fellow-Christians in Asia may not have regarded this *senatusconsultum*, granting, as a special concession to provincial councils, the right to purchase criminals condemned to death for use as gladiators, 'on the cheap', as the thin edge of the wedge. Even if the *senatusconsultum* only granted the privilege to the Tres Galliae, lobbying may already have begun, by the time the decree was published, to have it extended elsewhere; and it is possible that the hope of obtaining cheap gladiators might have induced prospective promoters of public spectacles in the province of Asia to incite prosecutions of Christians.

SORDI'S suggestion (p. 368 ff.) that the apology of Meliton may have been composed while Marcus was in the east in A.D. 176, when intellectuals of all descriptions were clamouring for the emperor's attention, is certainly attractive. But I do not think that Eusebius, *Hist. Ecc.*, 4,26,7, can be dated as closely as SORDI argues. It could belong, in fact, to any period from the death of Annius Verus Caesar (autumn A.D. 169) to the death of Marcus. The apology of Athenagoras was probably composed, it may be agreed, in the year A.D. 177.

The martyrdoms at Scilli in the province of Africa, on July 17, 180, four months after the death of Marcus, were really a hangover from the persecutions of his reign (cf. F. GROSSO, p. 669), and indicate merely that

Commodus had done nothing to modify official policy by this date; and that anti-Christian feeling was still widespread.

The basic causes of the persecutions lay in popular hatred and suspicion of Christians, combined often with xenophobia. It is no accident that the majority of the Lyons martyrs mentioned by name in Eusebius bear Greek names: they would be of merchant origin, immigrants who had brought their religion with them from the east. Persons of this type would be liable to unpopularity at any time. In periods of disaster, their practice of a religion which denied the existence of the gods (and therefore would appear to have provoked the wrath of the gods) would render them liable to vicious attacks. Attacks by pagans were never officially encouraged by the Roman government until the third century. The prime concern of the government was always to keep the peace and to discourage riots and outbreaks of religious or race hatred. But if Christians *were* brought to trial, and if they confessed, the Roman magistrates had no alternative but to condemn them to death, for the 'name' alone, under a ruling which may have been made by Nero. Sometimes, as at Lyons, additional charges – of incest, cannibalism, etc. – may have been fabricated, and admitted by the magistrate, but this was unnecessary and unwelcome to the government, although to the anti-Christians it may have provided the satisfaction of creating further hostility to Christians. On these questions the article by G. E. M. de Ste. CROIX is especially valuable.

In the reign of Marcus there were plenty of public disasters – floods, famine, war, plague, invasion, civil war, financial crisis. These were exactly the circumstances to provoke anti-Christian demonstrations, as Tertullian graphically, and sarcastically, put it: 'If the Tiber floods to the walls, if the Nile does not flood the fields, if the sky stands still, if the earth shakes, if there is famine, or plague, at once [the cry goes up]: "The Christians to the lion!".' (*Apol.* 40, 2). The gods were the cause of such phenomena, and the Christians dishonoured the gods. Not only that, but they were not a nation, as were the Jews, who at least had some excuse for their perverse monotheism – it was a national tradition. The Christians were regarded as a polyglot collection of dangerous innovators. It is significant that it is precisely in the reign of Marcus that one of the first reasoned attacks on the Christians appeared, that of Celsus (see the translation with notes of Origen's reply to Celsus by H. CHADWICK). Certain passages are very revealing (e.g. 8,73, where he urges the Christians to 'be fellow-soldiers with the emperor', and 8,75, where he urges them to accept public office). The Christian reply to these charges was to come before long, with Tertullian, notably; and the early appearance of the legend of the Thundering Legion shows that the charge of lack of patriotism had struck home.

The attitude of Marcus himself to the Christians is difficult to discover from any direct evidence. Only in one passage of the *Meditations* (11,3), does he refer to them by name. In Chapter VII I have tried to elucidate this: Marcus seems to have believed that the Christians were ready to die because they had been *trained* to be ready, without exercising any choice as individuals. C. R. Haines, in an appendix to his Loeb edition and translation (London-New York, 1916, 318 ff.) argued that in certain other passages also Marcus had the Christians in mind, without naming them (1,6; 3,16; 7,68; 8,48,51). I follow FARQUHARSON (*Meditations*, II, 440) in rejecting any allusion to Christians in 1,6. But I find plausible the idea that 3,16 does allude to them: 'To have the mind as guide to what seem to be duties is also a characteristic of men who disbelieve in the gods, who betray their country, who do anything they like when they have locked their doors.' But the judgment would be applied to others as well, as FARQUHARSON (op. cit., 587) points out. 7,68 and 8,51, which refer to men preserving their calm while their bodies are being torn by wild beasts, would fit the martyrdom of Christians very well. FARQUHARSON (op. cit., 779) regards this as improbable. 8,48 – 'the governing principle is unconquerable ... even if its opposition is unreasonable', recalls in its language the passage 11,3, as Haines points out. (8,48 is ignored by Farquharson in this context.) I feel that Haines may be justified in concluding from these passages that Marcus felt some kind of admiration for the Christians' obstinate adherence to their principles (although I cannot accept the rest of Haines' discussion of Marcus and the Christians).

There is no doubt that Marcus' general religious attitude was one of extreme piety (cf. FREND, 268–9). Sincere belief in the traditional religion was in fact a characteristic of most of the persecutors of the Church (cf. J. VOGT). The theological beliefs in the *Meditations* are perhaps vague and uncoordinated, but they were deeply held (cf. J. BEAUJEU, 332 ff.). However, the personal attitude of the emperor was really immaterial at this moment. Enough has, I hope, been said to indicate why the persecutions happened in the reign of Marcus. (For ancient sources, cf. appendix I.)

APPENDIX V:
ABBREVIATIONS AND WORKS CITED

(A) ABBREVIATIONS

This list gives modern works cited in the notes in abbreviated form. Other works and articles are given in (B).

AE=L'Année épigraphique. Revue des publications épigraphiques relatives à l'antiquité romaine, Paris, 1888 and following, ed. R. Cagnat–A. Merlin.

BMC, IV=H. Mattingly, *Coins of the Roman Empire in the British Museum, IV, Antoninus Pius to Commodus,* London, 1940.

Cagnat-Merlin, *ILAfr.*=R. Cagnat–A. Merlin-L. Chatelain, Inscriptions Latines d'Afrique, Paris, 1923.

CIL=Corpus Inscriptionum Latinarum, I-XVI, Berlin, 1863 ff.

Dessau, *ILS*=H. Dessau, *Inscriptiones Latinae Selectae,* 3 vols., Berlin, 1892–1916 (reprinted 1960).

Farquharson, *Meditations*=A. S. L. Farqûharson, *The Meditations of Marcus Antoninus,* 2 vols., Oxford, 1944.

Gnecchi=F. Gnecchi, *I Medaglioni Romani descritti e illustrati,* 3 vols., Milano, 1912.

Haines=C. R. Haines, *The Correspondence of Marcus Cornelius Fronto,* 2 vols., London-Cambridge, Mass., 1919 (revised and reprinted, 1928, 1955).

Inscr. It., XIII, 1=*Inscriptiones Italiae,* XIII, 1, ed. A. Degrassi, Roma.

JRS= Journal of Roman Studies.

PIR 2= *Prosopographia Imperii Romani,* saec. I, II, III, 2nd. ed. by E. Groag and A. Stein, I (A-B), Berlin-Leipzig, 1933, II (C), 1936, III (D-F), 1943, IV, 1 (G), Berlin, 1952, IV, 2 (H), 1958.

PW=Realencyclopädie der classischen Altertumswissenschaft, ed. Pauly-Wissowa-Kroll-Mittelhaus-Ziegler, Stuttgart, 1893 ff.

SB, VI=vol. VI of *Sammelbuch Griechischer Urkunden aus Ägypten,* ed. Biliabel-Presigke et al. Berlin-Leipzig, 1926ff.

Articles in PW are not listed.

AFRICA, T. W., 'The opium addiction of Marcus Aurelius', *Journal of the History of Ideas*, 1961, 97.

ALEXANDER, P. J., 'Letters and Speeches of the Emperor Hadrian', *Harvard Studies in Classical Philology*, 49, 1938, 141.

AURIGEMMA, S., *Villa Adriana*, Roma, 1961. [1961, 199.

BALDWIN, B., 'Lucian as a social satirist', *Classical Quarterly*, N.S. 11,

BALLANCE, M. H., 'Derbe and Faustinopolis', *Anatolian Studies*, 14, 1964, 139.

BARADEZ, J., 'Les nouvelles fouilles de Tipasa et les opérations d'Antonin le Pieux en Maurétanie', *Libyca*, 2, 1954, 89.

BARBIERI, G., 'L' Amministrazione delle Province Ponto-Bitinia e Licia-Pamfilia nel II secolo d. Cr.', *Rivista di filologia*, 66, 1938, 365.

— 'Mario Massimo', *Riv. di filologia*, 32, 1954, 36; 262.

— 'Nuovi iscrizioni di Marsala', *Kokalos*, 7, 1961, 15.

BAYNES, N. H., *The Historia Augusta: Its Date and Purpose*, Oxford, 1926.

BEAUJEU, J., *La religion romaine à l'apogée de l'empire*, I: *La politique religieuse des Antonins* (96–192), Paris, 1955.

BÉRANGER, J., 'L'hérédité du Principat', *Revue des Études Latines*, 17, 1939, 171.

BERGER, A., An encyclopaedic dictionary of Roman Law, *Transactions of the American Philosophical Society*, N.S. 43, 2, Philadelphia, 1953, 333.

BETZ, A., 'Zur Dislokation der Legionen in der Zeit vom Tode des Augustus bis zum Ende der Prinzipatsepoche', *Carnuntina, Vorträge beim Internationalen Kongress der Altertumsforscher, Carnuntum*, ed. E. Swoboda, Graz-Köln, 1956, 17.

BIRLEY, A. R., 'The oath not to kill senators', *Classical Review*, N.S. 12, 1962, 197.

— 'The status of Moesia Superior under Marcus Aurelius', *Acta Antiqua Philippopolitana: Studia Historica et Linguistica, Serdicae* (Sofia), 1963, 109.

— 'The duration of provincial commands under Antoninus Pius', memorial volume for E. Swoboda (forthcoming).

BIRLEY, E., *Roman Britain and the Roman Army*, Kendal, 1953.

— 'Senators in the emperors' service', *Proc. British Academy*, 39, 1954, 197.

— 'Hadrianic Frontier Policy', *Carnuntina etc.* (see under BETZ, A.). 25.

— *Research on Hadrian's Wall*, Kendal, 1961.

BLOCH, R., *The Origins of Rome* (Eng. tr., revised), London, 1960.

BOGAERS, J. E., 'Romeins Nijmegen', *Numaga*, 12, 1965, 10.

BOISSIER, G., *L'opposition sous les Césars*, Paris, 1875 and reprints.

BURN, A. R., '*Hic breve vivitur*', *Past and Present*, 16, 1953, 2.

CAPRINO, C. – COLINI, A. M. – GATTI, G. – PALLOTTINO, M. – ROMANELLI, P., *La colonna di Marco Aurelio*, Roma, 1955.

CARCOPINO, J., 'L'hérédité dynastique chez les Antonins', *Revue des Études Anciennes*, 51, 1949, 262.

CARDASCIA, G., 'L'apparition dans le droit des classes d'honestiores et humiliores', *Revue historique de droit français et étranger*, 28, 1950, 305 ff.; 461 ff.

CHADWICK, H., *Origenes: contra Celsum*, Cambridge, 1953.

CHARLESWORTH, M. P., *Five Men: Character Studies from the Roman Empire*, Cambridge, Mass., 1936.

CHASTAGNOL, A., 'Le problème de l'histoire Auguste: État de la question', *Historia-Augusta-Colloquium Bonn 1963*, Bonn, 1964, 43.

COLINI, A. M., 'Storia e Topografia del Celio nell' Antichita', *Memorie Pontif. Accademia di Archeologia*, 7, 1944, 138.

COLLINGWOOD, R. G. – MYRES, J. N. L., *Roman Britain and the English Settlements*, 2nd. ed., Oxford, 1937.

CORBETT, P. E., *The Roman Law of Marriage*, Oxford, 1930.

de Ste. CROIX, G. E. M., 'Why were the Early Christians persecuted?', *Past and Present*, 26, 1936, 6.

CROOK, J., *Consilium Principis*, Cambridge, 1955.

DAICOVICIU, C. – PROTASE, D., 'Un nouveau diplôme militaire de Dacia Porolissensis', *Journ. Roman Studies*, 51, 1961, 63.

DAILLY, R. – van EFFENTERRE, M. H., 'Le cas Marc-Aurèle: Essai de psychosomatique historique', *Revue des Études Anciennes*, 56, 1954, 347.

DEGRASSI, A., *I Fasti Consolari dell' Impero Romano dal 30 av. C. al 613 d. C.*, Roma, 1952.

— *Il confine nord-orientale dell' Italia romana*, Diss. Bern. 1,6, Bern, 1954.

DILL, S., *Roman Society from Nero to Marcus Aurelius*, London, 1904, reprint New York, 1956.

DUDLEY, D. R., *A History of Cynicism from Diogenes to the Sixth Century A.D.*, London, 1937.

DUMÉRIL, A., *De constitutionibus M. Aurelii Antonini* (Thèse Paris), Toulouse, 1882.

DUNCAN-JONES, R., 'The Purpose and Organization of the *Alimenta*', *Papers of the British School at Rome*, 32, 1964, 123.

FARQUHARSON, A. S. L., *The Meditations of Marcus Antoninus*, 2 vols., Oxford, 1944.

— *Marcus Aurelius: His Life and His World*, 2nd. ed., Oxford, 1952.

FITZ, J., 'Legati Augusti Pro Praetore Pannoniae Inferioris', *Acta Antiqua Academiae Scientiarum Hungaricae*, 11, 1963, 245 (in English).

FREND, W. H. C., *Martyrdom and Persecution in the Early Church*, Oxford, 1965.

GARZETTI, A., *L'Impero da Tiberio agli Antonini*, vol. VI of *Storia di Roma*, Bologna, 1960.

GILLAM, J. P., 'Calpurnius Agricola and the Northern Frontier', *Trans. of the Architectural and Archaeological Soc. of Durham and Northumberland*, 10, 4, 1953, 359.

GILLIAM, J. F., 'The plague under Marcus Aurelius', *American Journal of Philology*, 82, 1961, 225.

GRAINDOR, P., *Hérode Atticus, Un milliardaire antique et sa famille*, Le Caire, 1930.

GRÉGOIRE, H., 'Les persecutions dans l'empire romain', *Mem. Acad. Royale de Belgique*, 46, 1950; 2nd. ed., 1964.

GRENADE, P., 'Le réglement successoral d'Hadrien', *Revue des Études Anciennes*, 52, 1950, 258.

GROAG, E., 'Zu neuen Inschriften', *Jahreshefte d. Oest. Arch. Inst.*, 29, 1935, Beibl. 177.

GROSSO, F., *La lotta politica al tempo di Commodo*, Torino, 1964.

GUEY, J., 'La date de la "pluie miraculeuse" (172 après J.-C.) et la colonne Aurelienne', *Mél. d'Archéologie et d'Histoire*, 60, 1948, 105; 61, 194, 93.

— 'Encore la pluie miraculeuse, mage et dieu', *Revue de Philologie*, 22, 1948, 16.

— 'La date de naissance de l'empereur Septime-Sévère d'après son horoscope', *Bull. Soc. Nat. Ant. de France*, 1956, 33.

HAMPL, F., 'Kaiser Marc Aurel und die Völker jenseits der Donaugrenze, Eine quellencritische Studie', *Festschrift R. Heuberger*, Innsbruck, 1960, 33.

HAMBERG, P. G., *Studies in Roman Imperial Art, with special reference to the State Reliefs of the Second Century*, Copenhagen-Uppsala, 1945.

HARNACK, A., 'Die Quelle der Berichte über das Regenwunder im Feldzuge Marc Aurels gegen die Quaden', *Sitzb. Preuss. Akad.* Berlin, 2, 1894, 835.

HASEBROEK, J., *Die Fälschung der Vita Nigri und Vita Albini in den Scriptores Historiae Augustae*, Berlin, 1916.

HEER, J. M., *Der historische Wert der vita Commodi in der Sammlung der Scriptores Historiae Augustae, Philologus*, Supp. Band 9, 1901, 1 (part also published separately, Heidelberg, 1901).

HOHL, E., 'Die angebliche Doppelbestattung des Antoninus Pius', *Klio*, 31, 1938, 169.

— 'Kaiser Commodus und Herodian', *Sitzb. d. Deutsch. Akad. der Wiss.*, Berlin, 1954, 1, 3.

van den HOUT, M. J., 'Reminiscences of Fronto in the Meditations of Marcus Aurelius', *Mnemosyne*, 4, 1950, 33.

HÜTTL, W., *Antoninus Pius*, 2 vols., Prag, 1936 and 1933.

JARRETT, M. G., 'The African contribution to the Imperial Equestrian Service', *Historia*, 12, 1963, 209.

KÄHLER, H., *Hadrian und seine Villa bei Tivoli*, Berlin, 1950.

KEIL, J., 'Kaiser Marcus und die Thronfolge', *Klio*, 31, 1938, 293.

KLOSE, J., *Roms Klientelrandstaaten am Rhein und an der Donau*, Breslau, 1934.

KOLBE, H. G., 'Der Pertinaxstein aus Brühl', *Bonner Jahrbücher*, 162, 1962, 407.

KNOPF, R., – KRÜGER, G., *Ausgewählte Märtyrerakten*, 3rd. ed. Tübingen, 1929.

KORNEMANN, *Doppelprinzipat und Reichsteilung im Imperium Romanum*, Leipzig-Berlin, 1930.

KŘIŽEK, F., 'Neue Ergebnisse der römischen Forschung in der Tschoslowakei', *Limestudien*, ed. R. Laur-Belart, Basel, 1959, 77.

KUNKEL, W., *Herkunft und Soziale Stellung der römischen Juristen*, Weimar, 1952.

de LAET, S. J., 'Note sur deux passages dans l'Histoire Auguste', *Antiquité Classique*, 13, 1944, 127.

LAMBRECHTS, P., 'L'Empereur Lucius Verus: Essai de rehabilitation', *Antiquité Classique*, 3, 1934, 173.

LEVY, E., 'Captivus redemptus ab hoste', *Classical Philology*, 38, 1943, 159.

LIMES-ROMANUS-KONFERENZ NITRA, Bratislava, 1959.

LUGLI, G., *I monumenti Antichi di Roma e suburbio*, III, Roma, 1938.

MAGIE, D., *Roman Rule in Asia Minor*, 2 vols., Princeton, 1950.

MANN, J. C., 'The raising of new legions under the Principate', *Hermes*, 91, 1963, 483.

MARACHE, R., *La critique littéraire de langue latine et le développement du goût archaïsant au IIème siècle*, Rennes, 1952.

MARROU, H.-I., *A History of Education in Antiquity*, Eng. tr., London, 1956.

MARTINAZZOLI, F., *La 'successio' di Marco Aurelio; Struttura e spirito del primo libro dei Pensieri*, Bari, 1951.

— *Parataxeis: Le testimonianze stoiche sul Cristianesimo*, Firenze, 1953.

MATTINGLY, H., 'The consecration of the Elder Faustina and her daughter', *Harvard Theological Review*, 41, 1948, 147.

MICKWITZ, G., *Geld und Wirtschaft im römischen Reich der vierten Jahrhundert nach Christus*, Helsingfors, 1932.

MILLAR, F., *A Study of Cassius Dio*, Oxford, 1964.

MOMIGLIANO, A., 'An unsolved problem of historical forgery', *Journal of the Warburg and Courtauld Institutes*, 17, 1954, 22.

MORRIS, J., 'The dating of the Column of Marcus Aurelius', *Journal of the Warburg and Courtauld Institutes*, 15, 1952, 32.

— 'Leges Annales under the Principate', *Listy Filologické*, 87, 1964, 317.

NESSELHAUF, H., 'Ein neues Fragment der Fasten von Ostia', *Athenaeum*, 36, 1958, 219.

NEUENSCHWANDER, H., *Mark Aurels Beziehungen zu Seneca und Poseidonios*, Bern, 1951.

NOYEN, P., 'Divus Marcus Princeps Prudentissimus et Iuris Religiosissimus', *Revue Internationale du Droit de l' Antiquité*, 3eme ser., 1, 1954, 349 (in Flemish).

— 'Marcus Aurelius the Greatest Practician of Stoicism', *Antiquité Classique*, 24, 1955, 372.

OLIVA, P., *Pannonia and the Onset of Crisis in the Roman Empire*, Eng. tr., Praha, 1962.

OLIVER, J. H., 'The Ruling Power: A Study of the Roman Empire in the Second Century after Christ through the Roman Oration of Aelius Aristides', *Transactions of the American Philosophical Society*, N.S., 43, 4, Philadelphia, 1953, 869.

— and PALMER, R. E. A., 'Minutes of an Act of the Roman Senate', *Hesperia*, 24, 1955, 320.

d' ORGEVAL, B., *L' Empereur Hadrien: Oeuvre législative et administrative*, Paris, 1950.

PACK, R., 'Two Sophists and two Emperors', *Classical Philology*, 42, 1947, 17.

PAOLI, V. E., *Rome, Its People, Life and Customs*, Eng. tr., London, 1963.

PFLAUM, H.-G., *Les procurateurs équestres sous le haut-empire romain*, Paris, 1950.

— 'La carrière de C. Aufidius Victorinus, condisciple de Marc-Aurèle', *Comptes-Rendues de l'Academie des Inscriptions et Belles Lettres*, 1956, 189.

Les carrières procuratoriennes équestres sous le haut-empire romain, 3 vols., Paris, 1960–1.

— 'Les gendres de Marc-Aurèle', *Journal des Savants*, 1961, 28.

— 'Le réglement successoral d'Hadrien', *Historia-Augusta-Colloquium*, Bonn, 1963, Bonn, 1964, 95.

PIGANIOL, A., 'Les trinci gaulois: gladiateurs consacrés', *Revue des Études Anciennes*, 20, 1922, 283.

POHLENZ, M., *Die Stoa: Geschichte einer geistigen Bewegung*, 2nd. ed., Göttingen, 1959.

REIDINGER, W., *Die Statthalter des ungeteilten Pannoniens und Oberpannoniens von Augustus bis Diokletian*, Bonn, 1956.

RÉMONDON, R., ' Les dates de la révolte de C. Avidius Cassius', *Chronique d'Égypte*, 1951, 364.

RENAN, E., *Marc-Aurèle et la fin du monde antique* (*Histoire des Origines de Christianisme*, vol. 7), Paris, 1881 and reprints; Eng. tr. (abbreviated), London, 1903.

SCARLATA-FAZIO, M., *Principi vecchi e nuovi di diritto privato nell' attivita giuridica dei divi fratres*, Catania, 1939.

SCHÖNBERGER, H., 'Das römische Lager in Rödgen und das Numeruskastell in Altenstadt', *Quintus Congressus Internationalis Limitis Romani Studiosorum, Acta et Dissertationes Archaeologica*, III, Zagreb, 1963, 157.

SCHWARTZ, J., 'Avidius Cassius et les sources de l'Histoire Auguste,' *Historia-Augusta-Colloquium Bonn 1963*, Bonn, 1964, 135.

SCHWENDEMANN, J., *Der historische Wert der Vita Marci bei den Scriptores Historiae Augustae*, Heidelberg, 1923.

SESTON, W. – EUZENNAT, M., 'La citoyenneté romaine au temps de Marc-Aurèle et Commode', *Comptes-Rendues de l'Academie des Inscriptions et Belles Lettres*, 1961, 317.

SORDI, M., 'I nuovi decreti di Marco Aurelio contro i Cristiani', *Studi Romani*, 9, 1961, 365.

SPANNEUT, M., *Le stoïcisme des pères de l'église*, Paris, 1957.

STARR, C. G., *The Roman Imperial Navy*, Ithaca, New York, 1941.

— *Civilization and the Caesars*, Ithaca, New York, 1954.

STEIN, A., *Der römische Ritterstand*, München, 1927.

— *Die Legaten von Moesien*, Diss. Pann., I, 11, Budapest, 1940.

— *Die Reichsbeamten von Dazien*, Diss. Pann., I, 12, Budapest, 1944.

— *Die Präfekten von Agypten in der romischen Kaiserzeit*, Diss. Bern, 1,1, Bern, 1950.

SWOBODA, E., *Carnuntum; Seine Geschichte und seine Denkmäler*, 4th ed., Graz-Köln, 1964.

SYME, R., *The Roman Revolution*, Oxford, 1939 (repr. 1952).

— 'Antonine Relatives: Ceionii and Vettuleni', *Athenaeum*, 35, 1957, 306.

— 'Imperator Caesar. A Study in Nomenclature', *Historia*, 7, 1958, 172.

— *Colonial Elites*, London, 1958.

— *Tacitus*, 2 vols., Oxford, 1958.

— 'Missing persons II', *Historia*, 8, 1959, 207.

— 'Pliny's less successful friends', *Historia*, 9, 1960, 362.

— 'The wrong Marcius Turbo', *Journ. Rom. Studies*, 52, 1962, 87.

— 'Hadrian and Italica', *Journ. Rom. Studies*, 54, 1964, 142.

TAYLOR, L. R., *The Divinity of the Roman Emperor*, Middletown, Conn., 1931.

THOMASSON, B., *Die Statthalter der römischen Provinzen Nordafrikas von Augustus bis Diokletian*, 2 vols., Lund, 1960.

THOMSON, J. O., *A History of Ancient Geography*, Cambridge, 1948.

— 'Marcus Aurelius and the small earth', *Journ. Rom. Studies*, 43, 1953, 47.

TOUTAIN, J., 'Réflexions sur une monnaie romaine', *Hommages Bidez-Cumont*, Bruxelles, 1949, 331.

TOWNEND, G., 'Some Flavian Connections , *Journ. Rom. Studies*, 51, 1961, 57.

— 'The post *ab epistulis* in the second century', *Historia*, 10, 1961, 375.

TOYNBEE, J. M. C., 'A Bust of an Antonine Boy', *Journ. Rom. Studies*, 49, 1959, 39.

VOGT, J., *Zur Religiosität der Christenverfolger*, Heidelberg, *Sitzenb. d. Heidelb. Akad. d. Wiss., Phil.-Hist. Klasse*, 1962, 1.

WALLACH, L., 'The colloquy of Marcus Aurelius with the Patriarch Judah I', *Jewish Quarterly Review*, 31, 1940, 259.

WALSER, G., 'Zu den Ursachen der Reichskrise im dritten nachchristlichen Jahrhundert', *Études Suisses d'Histoire Generale*, 18–19, 1960–1, 142.

WINTERBOTTOM, M., 'Quintilian and the Vir Bonus', *Journ. Rom. Studies*, 54, 1964, 90.

WIRSZUBSKI, C., *Libertas as a Political Idea at Rome during the Late Republic and Early Principate*, Cambridge, 1950.

ZANGHIERI, G., *Castro Pretorio: Tomba e Fucina dell' Impero Roman*, Roma, 1948.

ZWIKKER, W., *Studien zur Markussaule*, I Allard Pierson Stichting Universiteit van Amsterdam, *Arch.-Hist. Bydragen*, 8, Amsterdam, 1941.

INDEX

THE
OPEN
DOOR

invites the reader into the mind and
heart of one of the most beloved women
in America. Here for the first time in
one volume is a treasury of Helen
Keller's philosophical reflections —
the beliefs which have given encouragement and joy to those who know her and
to the world. This is a book of profound
wisdom and inspiration, sparkling with
the enjoyment of living.

A special beauty miraculously
springs from the inner vision of this
remarkable woman, who, denied the
ordinary paths to knowledge of the
things of this world, has nevertheless
found her way unerringly to the essences
of life. Her joy in obstacles overcome,
her strong and uplifting faith in God,
her courage and zest will bring to the
reader a fresh appreciation of the
wellsprings of happiness available
to us all.

The Open Door

BY HELEN KELLER

The
Open Door

❧ ☙

❧ BY HELEN KELLER ☙

Doubleday & Company, Inc., Garden City, New York

ACKNOWLEDGMENTS:

The selections on pages 25, 47, 63, 70, 73, 75, 82, 91, 96, 137, are from THE WORLD I LIVE IN, published by The Century Company. Those on pages 19, 26, 43, 49, 66, are from MY KEY OF LIFE, copyright, 1926, 1954, by Helen Keller. Reprinted by permission of the publishers, Thomas Y. Crowell Company, New York. The pieces on pages 11, 32, 34, 61, 69, 80, 89, 95, 97, 101, 113, 126, 127, 131, were taken from WE BEREAVED, published by Leslie Fulenwider, Inc. The remainder of the material was selected as follows from books published by Doubleday & Company, Inc.: THE STORY OF MY LIFE: 23, 51, 72, 90; OUT OF THE DARK: 37, 40, 54, 62, 84, 88, 102, 122; MY RELIGION: 12, 20, 22, 24, 28, 29, 35, 39, 44, 55, 57, 65, 100, 112, 115, 121, 129, 135, 136; MIDSTREAM: 14, 42, 46, 67, 87, 92, 104, 105, 108, 132, 134, 138; HELEN KELLER'S JOURNAL: 15, 30, 33, 45, 50, 85, 94, 119, 125, 128, 130; LET US HAVE FAITH: 17, 31, 36, 38, 48, 52, 53, 60, 68, 71, 76, 77, 78, 81, 83, 93, 98, 107, 110, 111, 114, 117, 123, 133.

I seal this little book to Anne Sullivan Macy
with an affection that knows my life
has breathed freely because of her

Foreword

Seventy years ago a seven-year-old child—blind, deaf, and mute—was dragged, bullied, baited, charmed, piqued, provoked, jolted, joked, titivated, cherished, and loved by a lion-hearted teacher into the world of thought. The child, of course, was Helen Keller. The dauntless teacher, Annie Sullivan, a twenty-one-year-old girl whose genius, rugged determination, and fierce, persisting love at last etched their message on the blank slate of Helen's brain. Annie awakened Helen's sleeping mind, gave it words with which to think, and for fifty years accompanied it on its famous journey into the hearts of men and women.

Today the name of Helen Keller is known by millions all over the world. But not because she is deaf and blind. Thousands have been, are, and will be deaf and blind. And not because, being deaf and blind, she learned to read and write and speak. But because *although* she is deaf and blind, she learned to think with a philosophical depth of understanding that reaches the minds and hearts of all, and because she learned to express those thoughts with a clarity all writers must envy.

Helen Keller is thought of as a phenomenon, a miracle, a humanitarian, and educator. That she is also a philosopher and a writer will be found, I believe, by those who read these excerpts from her several books, to which it is now my pleasure to commend you.

Katharine Cornell

The Open Door

WHEN ONE DOOR
of happiness closes, another opens; but often we look so long
at the closed door that we do not see the one which has been
opened for us.

RULY I HAVE
looked into the very heart of darkness, and refused to yield to
its paralyzing influence, but in spirit I am one of those who
walk the morning. What if all dark, discouraging moods of
the human mind come across my way as thick as the dry
leaves of autumn? Other feet have traveled that road before
me, and I know the desert leads to God as surely as the green,
refreshing fields and fruitful orchards. I, too, have been profoundly humiliated, and brought to realize my littleness amid
the immensity of creation. The more I learn, the less I think I
know, and the more I understand of my sense-experience, the
more I perceive its shortcomings and its inadequacy as a basis
of life. Sometimes the points of view of the optimist and the
pessimist are placed before me so skillfully balanced that only

by sheer force of spirit can I keep my hold upon a practical, livable philosophy of life. But I use my will, choose life and reject its opposite—nothingness.

$\mathcal{I}$F THERE WERE NO life beyond this earth-life, some people I have known would gain immortality by the nobility of our memory of them. With every friend I love who has been taken into the brown bosom of the earth a part of me has been buried there; but their contribution of happiness, strength, and understanding to my being remains to sustain me in an altered world.

CERTAINLY

I believe that God gave us life for happiness, not misery. Humanity, I am sure, will never be made lazy or indifferent by an excess of happiness. The order of nature will always necessitate pain, failure, separation, death; and these will probably become more menacing as the complexities and dangerous experiments of a vast world civilization increase. The delicate task will remain ours to ensure God's gift—joy—to His children. Many persons have a wrong idea of what constitutes true happiness. It is not attained through self-gratification but through fidelity to a worthy purpose. Happiness should be a means of accomplishment, like health, not an end in itself. Every human being has undeniable rights which, respected, render happiness possible—the right to live his own life as far as may be, to choose his own creed, to develop his capabilities; but no one has a right to consume happiness without producing it or to lay his burden upon other shoulders merely to fulfill a personal desire.

ECURITY IS
mostly a superstition. It does not exist in nature, nor do the children of men as a whole experience it. God Himself is not secure, having given man dominion over His works! Avoiding danger is no safer in the long run than outright exposure. The fearful are caught as often as the bold. Faith alone defends. Life is either a daring adventure or nothing. To keep our faces toward change and behave like free spirits in the presence of fate is strength undefeatable.

Serious harm, I am afraid, has been wrought to our generation by fostering the idea that they would live secure in a permanent order of things. It has tended to weaken imagination and self-equipment and unfit them for independent steering of their destinies. Now they are staggered by apocalyptic events and wrecked illusions. They have expected stability and find none within themselves or in their universe. Before it is too late they must learn and teach others that only by brave acceptance of change and all-time crisis-ethics can they rise to the height of superlative responsibility.

THE HIGHEST RESULT of education is tolerance. Long ago men fought and died for their faith; but it took ages to teach them the other kind of courage—the courage to recognize the faiths of their brethren and their rights of conscience. Tolerance is the first principle of community; it is the spirit which conserves the best that all men think. No loss by flood and lightning, no destruction of cities and temples by the hostile forces of nature, has deprived man of so many noble lives and impulses as those which his intolerance has destroyed.

SIMPLE, CHILDLIKE
faith in a Divine Friend solves all the problems that come to
us by land or sea. Difficulties meet us at every turn. They
are the accompaniment of life. They result from combina-
tions of character and individual idiosyncrasies. The surest
way to meet them is to assume that we are immortal and that
we have a Friend who "slumbers not, nor sleeps," and who
watches over us and guides us—if we but let Him. With this
thought strongly entrenched in our inmost being, we can do
almost anything we wish and need not limit the things we
think. We may help ourselves to all the beauty of the universe that we can hold. For every hurt there is recompense of
tender sympathy. Out of pain grow the violets of patience
and sweetness, the vision of the Holy Fire that touched the
lips of Isaiah and kindled his life into spirit, and the contentment that comes with the evening star. The marvelous rich-

ness of human experience would lose something of rewarding joy if there were no limitations to overcome. The hill-
top hour would not be half so wonderful if there were no
dark valley to traverse.

IT IS BEYOND A doubt that everyone should have time for some special delight, if only five minutes each day to seek out a lovely flower or cloud or a star, or learn a verse or brighten another's dull task. What is the use of such terrible diligence as many tire themselves out with, if they always postpone their exchange of smiles with Beauty and Joy to cling to irksome duties and relations? Unless they admit these fair, fresh, and eternal presences into their lives as they can, they must needs shut themselves out of heaven, and a gray dust settles on all existence. That the sky is brighter than the earth means little unless the earth itself is appreciated and enjoyed. Its beauty loved gives the right to aspire to the radiance of the sunrise and the stars.

I AM TOO HAPPY
in this world to think much about the future, except to
remember that I have cherished friends awaiting me there
in God's beautiful Somewhere. In spite of the lapse of years,
they seem so close to me that I should not think it strange if
at any moment they should clasp my hand and speak words
of endearment as they used to before they went away.

*I*T IS AMAZING how prodigiously men have written and talked about regeneration and yet how little they have said to the purpose. Self-culture has been loudly and boastfully proclaimed as sufficient for all our ideals of perfection. But if we listen to the best men and women everywhere, they will answer with a decided negative. Some of them have amassed vast treasures of knowledge, and they will say that science may have found a cure for most evils; but it has found no remedy for the worst of them all—the apathy of human beings.

*H*OLD OUT YOUR HANDS
to feel the luxury of the sunbeams. Press the soft blossoms
against your cheek, and finger their graces of form, their
delicate mutability of shape, their pliancy and freshness. Expose your face to the aerial floods that sweep the heavens,
"inhale great draughts of space," wonder, wonder at the
wind's unwearied activity. Pile note on note the infinite
music that flows increasingly to your soul from the tactual
sonorities of a thousand branches and tumbling waters. How
can the world be shriveled when this most profound, emotional sense, touch, is faithful to its service? I am sure that
if a fairy bade me choose between the sense of sight and that
of touch, I would not part with the warm, endearing contact
of human hands or the wealth of form, the mobility and
fullness that press into my palms.

I KNOW WHAT EVIL
is. Once or twice I have wrestled with it and for a time felt
its chilly touch on my life; so I speak with knowledge when
I say that evil is of no consequence, except as a sort of mental
gymnastic. For the very reason that I have come in contact
with it, I am more truly an optimist. I can say with conviction
that the struggle which evil necessitates is one of the greatest
blessings. It makes us strong, patient, helpful men and
women. It lets us into the soul of things and teaches us that
although the world is full of suffering, it is also full of over-
coming of it. My optimism, then, does not rest on the absence
of evil, but on a glad belief in the preponderance of good
and a willing effort always to co-operate with the good, that
it may prevail. I try to increase the power God has given me
to see the best in everything and every one, and make that

best a part of my life. The world is sown with good; but unless I turn my glad thoughts into practical living and till my own field, I cannot reap a kernel of the good.

NYONE WHO, out of goodness of his heart, speaks a helpful word, gives a cheering smile, or smooths over a rough place in another's path knows that the delight he feels is so intimate a part of himself that he lives by it. The joy of surmounting obstacles which once seemed unremovable, and pushing the frontier of accomplishment further—what joy is there like unto it? .If those who seek happiness would only stop one little minute and think, they would see that the delights they really experience are as countless as the grasses at their feet or the dewdrops sparkling upon the morning flowers.

HEN THE SUN of consciousness first shone upon me, behold a miracle! The stock of my young life which had perished, steeped in the waters of knowledge grew again, budded again, was sweet again with the blossoms of childhood! Down in the depths of my being I cried, "It is good to be alive!" I held out two trembling hands to life, and in vain silence would impose dumbness upon me henceforth! The world to which I awoke was still mysterious; but there were hope and love and God in it, and nothing else mattered. Is it not possible that our entrance into heaven may be like this experience of mine?

MPATIENT WITH frustration, we ask ourselves why terrible obstacles should be placed in our path! We cannot but wonder at times why we cannot have smooth sailing instead of being compelled always to fight against adverse winds and rough seas. No doubt the reason is that character cannot be developed in ease and quiet. Only through experiences of trial and suffering can the soul be strengthened, vision cleared, ambition inspired, and success achieved. Most of the men and women honored in history for their service to mankind were acquainted with "the uses of adversity." They triumphed because they refused to be turned aside by difficulties or opposition. These obstructions called forth their latent energies and the determination that carried them far beyond any goal to which they would otherwise have aspired.

OR YEARS TO come the debris of a convulsed world will beset our steps. It will require a purpose stronger than any man and worthy of all men to calm and inspirit us. A sane society whose riches are happy children, men and women, beautiful with peace and creative activity, is not going to be ordained for us. We must make it ourselves. Our destiny is our responsibility, and without faith we cannot meet it competently. Long enough have we been told that faith is impracticable, that we must trim our sails to whatever winds that blow. Now the truth is burning in us that indifference and compromise are chaos.

HEN I WAS A young girl at college I wrote my creed thus: "I believe in God, I believe in Man, I believe in the power of the spirit. I believe it is a sacred duty to encourage ourselves and others; to hold the tongue from any unhappy word against God's world, because no man has any right to complain of a universe which God made good, and which thousands of men have striven to keep good." It is many years since I wrote these words, and I have suffered many a bereavement and many a sorrow, but I see no reason to change my creed. Any human being who believes in God, in Man, and in the spirit is fundamentally, I think, an optimist. No matter what pain comes to him, he knows that good is the dominant power of the universe and feels himself surrounded by it and by God's love.

WHAT EARTHLY consolation is there for one like me, whom fate has denied a husband and the joy of motherhood? At the moment my loneliness seems a void that will always be immense. Fortunately I have much work to do—more than ever before, in fact —and while doing it I shall have confidence as always that my unfulfilled longings will be gloriously satisfied in a world where eyes never grow dim nor ears dull.

WE INVITE
needless suffering when we entertain an exaggerated idea of
our own suffering. Why should we be spared the chastening
rod which all mortals pass under? Instead of comparing our
lot with that of those who are more fortunate than we are,
we should compare it with the lot of the great majority of our
fellow men. It then appears that we are among the privileged.

S SELFISHNESS

and complaint pervert and cloud the mind, so love with its joy clears and sharpens the vision. It gives the delicacy of perception to see wonders in what before seemed dull and trivial. It replenishes the springs of inspiration, and its joy sends a new river of lifelike blood through the matter-clogged faculties.

*L*IBERTY NOT joined to faith is already half dead. Americans have for the most part not had faith enough in themselves to demand a decisive share in rearing the structure of the government. Rarely have they gone to the trouble of choosing men of high politics who would truly represent their interests. They have shirked their responsibility, and faith, the friendly, unitive force, has been left to preachers, "dreamers," and invalids when it should have been communicated throughout society.

B

Y LEARNING THE
sufferings and burdens of men, I became aware as never before of the life-power that has survived the forces of darkness, the power which, though never completely victorious, is continuously conquering. The very fact that we are still here carrying on the contest against the hosts of annihilation proves that on the whole the battle has gone for humanity. The world's great heart has proved equal to the prodigious undertaking which God set it. Rebuffed, but always persevering; self-reproached, but ever regaining faith; undaunted, tenacious, the heart of man labors toward immeasurably distant goals. Discouraged not by difficulties without, or the anguish of ages within, the heart listens to a secret voice that whispers: "Be not dismayed; in the future lies the Promised Land."

WE HEAR ON all sides a summons to return to religion. There is an encouraging ring of sincerity in the cry, but is it not a bit confusing to say "return to religion" when religion means "return to faith"? Religion is the fruit of faith, and to ask for religion without faith is like asking for the flower without the seed. Many religions have spread inspiring hope upon earth, but one Faith has been their tree, just as good will is the one root of all truly beneficent activities. It has crossed my mind that religion may perhaps be man's despair in not finding God, while faith is hope—God's searching for man.

DAILY I PLACE implicit faith in my friends with eyes and ears, and they tell me how often their senses deceive and lead them astray. Yet out of their evidence I gather countless precious truths with which I build my world, and my soul is enabled to picture the beauty of the sky and listen to the songs of birds. All about me may be silence and darkness, yet within me, in the spirit, is music and brightness, and color flashes through all my thoughts.

TO THE HAND OF the world belongs the best, the noblest, the most stupendous task, the subjection of all the forces of nature to the mind of man, the subjection of physical strength to the might of the spirit. We are still far from this loftiest of triumphs of the hand. Its forces are still to be disciplined and organized. The limbs of the world must first be restored. In order that no limb may suffer, and that none may keep the others in bondage, the will of the many must become self-conscious and intelligently united. Then the hand—the living power of man, the hewer of the world—will be laid with undisputed sway upon the machine with which it has so long been confounded. There will be abundance for all, and no hands will cry out any more against the arm of the mighty. The hand of the world will then have achieved what it now obscurely symbolizes—the uplifting and regeneration of the race, all that is highest, all that is creative, in man.

*I*T HAS BEEN SAID that life has treated me harshly; and sometimes I have complained in my heart because many pleasures of human experience have been withheld from me, but when I recollect the treasure of friendship that has been bestowed upon me I withdraw all charges against life. If much has been denied me, much, very much has been given me. So long as the memory of certain beloved friends lives in my heart I shall say that life is good.

I TRUST, AND nothing that happens disturbs my trust. I recognize the beneficence of the power which we all worship as supreme—Order, Fate, the Great Spirit, Nature, God. I recognize this power in the sun that makes all things grow and keeps life afoot. I make a friend of this indefinable force, and straightway I feel glad, brave, and ready for any lot Heaven may decree for me. This is my religion of optimism.

OW I AM AS
much up in arms against needless poverty and degrading influences as anyone else, but, at the same time, I believe human experience teaches that if we cannot succeed in our present position, we could not succeed in any other. Unless, like the lily, we can rise pure and strong above sordid surroundings, we would probably be moral weaklings in any situation. Unless we can help the world where we are, we could not help it if we were somewhere else. The most important question is not the sort of environment we have but the kind of thoughts we think every day, the kind of ideals we are following; in a word, the kind of men and women we really are. The Arab proverb is admirably true: "That is thy world wherein thou findest thyself."

VEN MORE AMAZING than the wonders of nature are the powers of the spirit. Instead of having dumb thoughts or conventional phrases about another world, why can we not take unto ourselves wings of imagination and traverse unafraid vast immensities of the unknown into the joyous, human yet divine warmth that is heaven?

I LOVE MY COUNTRY. To say that is like saying I love my family. I did not choose my country any more than I chose my parents, but I am her daughter just as truly as I am the child of my southern mother and father. What I am my country has made me. She has fostered the spirit which made my education possible. Neither Greece nor Rome, nor all China, nor Germany, nor Great Britain has surrounded a deaf-blind child with the devotion and skill and resources which have been mine in America.

But my love for America is not blind. Perhaps I am more conscious of her faults because I love her so deeply. Nor am I blind to my own faults. It is easy to see that there is little virtue in the old formulas, and that new ones must be found, but even after one has decided this, it is not easy to hold a steady course in a changing world.

AS MY EXPERIENCES broadened and deepened, the indeterminate, poetic feelings of childhood began to fix themselves in definite thoughts. Nature—the world I could touch—was folded and filled with myself. I am inclined to believe those philosophers who declare that we know nothing but our own feelings and ideas. With a little ingenious reasoning one may see in the material world simply a mirror, an image of permanent mental sensations. In either sphere self-knowledge is the condition and the limit of our consciousness. That is why, perhaps, many people know so little about what is beyond their short range of experience. They look within themselves—and find nothing! Therefore they conclude that there is nothing outside themselves, either.

WE BETRAY OURSELVES
into smallness when we think the little choices of each day
are trivial. Drama and risk are needed to vitalize every commonplace act or lesson or posture. The personalities which
heal and urge forward are the beautiful quintessence of this
daily, hourly practice grown natural like breathing. Every day
we should do a little more than is required. If we exert ourselves at some task we would rather not perform, provided we
are not overworked horses going around in a blind circle, we
shall find that soon or late our trained personalities will leap
exultantly to the test. Inuring ourselves each day to resolute
volition and spontaneous self-expression is like a plunge into
the brine. Its benefits may not show at the time, but the salty-
sweet virtue soaks into our fibers and is stored for the coming
victory.

POET ONCE SAID
I must be happy because I did not see the bare, cold present,
but lived in a beautiful dream. I do live in a beautiful dream;
but that dream is the actual, the present—not cold, but warm;
not bare, but furnished with a thousand blessings. The very
evil which the poet supposed would be a cruel disillusion-
ment is necessary to the fullest knowledge of joy. Only by
contact with evil could I have learned to feel by contrast the
beauty of truth and love and goodness.

HE WHO DOES
not see that joy is an important force in the world misses the
essence of life. Joy is a spiritual element that gives vicissitudes
unity and significance. Belief in the triumph of good vitalizes
a race; enlightened optimism fosters in man a constructive
purpose and frees him from fears which fetter his thought.
Pessimism or *passive* resignation weakens the spirit and top-
ples society to ruin, while *determined* resignation is a force.
The first is but a regret; the other is a possession, for it is
faith, a motive power. Optimism is Jehovah's lightning, clearing a fate-befogged atmosphere.

OMETIMES, IT
is true, a sense of isolation enfolds me like a cold mist as I sit
alone and wait at life's shut gate. Beyond there is light, and
music, and sweet companionship; but I may not enter. Fate,
silent, pitiless, bars the way. Fain would I question his im-
perious decree; for my heart is still undisciplined and passionate; but my tongue will not utter the bitter, futile words
that rise to my lips, and they fall back into my heart like un-
shed tears. Silence sits immense upon my soul. Then comes
hope with a smile and whispers, "There is joy in self-forget-
fulness." So I try to make the light in others' eyes my sun,
the music in others' ears my symphony, the smile on others'
lips my happiness.

*I*T NEED NOT discourage us if we are full of doubts. Healthy questions keep faith dynamic. In fact, unless we start with doubts we cannot have a deep-rooted faith. One who believes lightly and unthinkingly has not much of a belief. He who has a faith which is not to be shaken has won it through blood and tears —has worked his way from doubt to truth as one who reaches a clearing through a thicket of brambles and thorns.

ANOTHER FACT
I do not forget is the tendency of the beliefs which fire one generation to grow chill in the next. As enthusiasm cools the spontaneity and joy of communing with the Divine are lost. Ideas of life and conduct are accepted without investigation. True religion is obscured by sects, rites and legal codes. The dead weight of the letter killeth, and faith, the song that "turns a stone and starts a wing," ceases at the approach of dull-eared orthodoxy. Revolt is needed to rekindle the spirit that giveth life. But this very ebb and flow shows how unsubduable are faith and the freedom it reincarnates. In all ages faith renews man's impulse to penetrate the splendors of creation; it reveals a power working within him and apart from him and directs him toward new objectives.

*F*ACE YOUR
deficiencies and acknowledge them; but do not let them
master you. Let them teach you patience, sweetness, insight.
True education combines intellect, beauty, goodness, and the
greatest of these is goodness. When we do the best that we
can, we never know what miracle is wrought in our life, or in
the life of another.

HEN WE ARE
born of the flesh, we are utterly helpless and dependent, while in the spiritual birth we are active, and in a sense creators. We have nothing to do with our birth into existences; for we must exist before we can make anything of ourselves. On the other hand, our birth into life is a matter of choice, we have a very direct share in it; for no real spiritual life can be thrust upon us against our will.

This is the meaning of the Lord's constant, loving invitation through His Word to all of us, to come unto Him and choose life, and be ever on our guard against the evils which would rob us of the chosen life. Only by exercising our powers of thought and keeping our hearts always warm and pure do we become truly alive. But this beautiful work of re-creation cometh not by observation, it is wrought in the quiet depths of the soul. For, as the Lord says, "The wind bloweth where it listeth, and thou hearest the sound thereof, but canst not tell whence it cometh, and whither it goeth: so is everyone that is born of the Spirit."

WHAT IS SO SWEET as to awake from a troubled dream and behold a beloved face smiling upon you? I love to believe that such shall be our awakening from earth to heaven. My faith never wavers that each dear friend I have "lost" is a new link between this world and the happier land beyond the morn. My soul is for the moment bowed down with grief when I cease to feel the touch of their hands or hear a tender word from them; but the light of faith never fades from my sky, and I take heart again, glad that they are free. I cannot understand why anyone should fear death. Life here is more cruel than death—life divides and estranges, while death, which at heart is life eternal, reunites and reconciles. I believe that when the eyes within my physical eyes shall open upon the world to come, I shall simply be consciously living in the country of my heart. My steadfast thought rises above the treason of my eyes to follow sight beyond all temporal seeing! Suppose there are a million chances against that one that my loved ones who have gone are alive. What of it? I will take that one chance and risk mistake, rather than let any doubts sadden their souls, and find out afterward. Since there is that one chance of immortality, I will endeavor not to cast a shadow upon the joy of the departed. I sometimes wonder who needs cheer most, the one who gropes on here below or the one who is perhaps just learning truly to see in God's light. How real is the darkness to one who only guesses in the shadows of earth at an unseen sun! But how well worth the effort it is to keep spiritually in touch with those who have loved us to their last moment upon earth! Certainly it is one of our sweetest experiences that when we are touched by some noble affection or pure joy, we remember the dead most tenderly, and feel powerfully drawn to them. And always the consciousness of such faith has the power to change the face of mortality, make adversity a winning fight, and set up a beacon of encouragement for those whose last support of joy seems taken from them. There is no such thing as "other worldliness" when we are convinced that heaven is not beyond us, but within us. We are only urged so much the more to act, to love, to hope against hope and resolutely to tinge the darkness about us with the beautiful hues of our indwelling heaven, Here and Now.

THERE IS NO occasion for trepidation at the word "crisis." It is not necessarily a tragic finality. It may be a choice between lesser and greater light or between outworn values and progressive good. The courage to decide remains always the royalty of man. Ordinary choices are critical; simple words are decisive. Each time we break bread one with another has the appealing humanity of the last time if we look at it discerningly. Herein when someone dies lies the cause of self-reproach for appreciation held back and failure to help. Our joy is too limited to squander on the low planes of mediocrity when we are endowed sufficiently to stay at our best every day. Vicissitudes are too numerous and disorganizing for us to be perfunctory or careless about our inner defenses.

FTEN WHEN THE heart is torn with sorrow, spiritually we wander like a traveler lost in a deep wood. We grow frightened, lose all sense of direction, batter ourselves against trees and rocks in our attempt to find a path. All the while there is a path—the path of Faith—that leads straight out of the dense tangle of our difficulties into the open road we are seeking.

WHEN I THINK of all the wonders that the hand of man has wrought, I rejoice, and am lifted up. It seems the image and agent of the Hand that upholds us all. We are its creatures, its triumphs, remade by it in the ages since the birth of the race. Nothing on earth is so thrilling, so terrifying, as the power of our own hands to keep us or mar us. All that man does is the hand alive, the hand manifest, creating and destroying, itself the instrument of order and demolition. It moves a stone, and the universe undergoes a readjustment. It breaks a clod, and new beauty bursts forth in fruits and flowers, and the sea of fertility flows over the desert.

ANCIENT PHILOSOPHY
offers an argument which seems still valid. There is in the
blind as in the seeing an Absolute which gives truth to what
we know to be true, order to what is orderly, beauty to the
beautiful, touchableness to what is tangible. If this is granted,
it follows that this Absolute is not imperfect, incomplete,
partial. It must needs go beyond the limited evidence of our
sensations, and also give light to what is invisible, music to
the musical that silence dulls. Thus mind itself compels us to
acknowledge that we are in a world of intellectual order,
beauty, and harmony. The essences, or absolutes of these
ideas, necessarily dispel their opposites which belong with
evil, disorder, and discord. Thus deafness and blindness do
not exist in the immaterial mind, which is philosophically
the real world, but are banished with the perishable material
senses. Reality, of which visible things are the symbol, shines

before my mind. While I walk about my chamber with unsteady steps, my spirit sweeps skyward on eagle wings and looks out with unquenchable vision upon the world of eternal beauty.

OW, LIMITATIONS

of all kinds are forms of chastening to encourage self-development and true freedom. They are tools put into our hands to hew away the stone and flint which keep the higher gifts hidden away in our being. They tear away the bandage of indifference from our eyes, and we behold the burdens others are carrying, and we learn to help them by yielding to the dictates of a pitying heart.

*L*ET PESSIMISM
once take hold of the mind, and life is all topsy-turvy, all
vanity and vexation of spirit. There is no cure for individual
or social disorder, except in forgetfulness and annihilation.
"Let us eat, drink and be merry," says the pessimist, "for
tomorrow we die." If I regarded my life from the point of
view of the pessimist, I should be undone. I should seek in
vain for the light that does not visit my eyes and the music
that does not ring in my ears. I should beg night and day and
never be satisfied. I should sit apart in awful solitude, a prey
to fear and despair. But since I consider it a duty to myself
and to others to be happy, I escape a misery worse than any
physical deprivation.

I DO NOT PRETEND
that I know the whole solution of the world's problems, but
I am burdened with a puritanical sense of obligation to set
the world to rights. I feel responsible for many enterprises
that are not really my business at all, but many times I have
kept silence on issues that interested me deeply through the
fear that others would be blamed for my opinions. I have
never been willing to believe that human nature cannot be
changed; but even if it cannot, I am sure it can be curbed and
led into channels of usefulness. I believe that life, not wealth,
is the aim of existence—life including all its attributes of love,
happiness, and joyful labor. I believe war is the inevitable
fruit of our economic system, but even if I am wrong I believe that truth can lose nothing by agitation but may gain all.

O UR WILL TO ACT becomes vigorous in proportion to the frequency and definiteness of our actions, and the brain grows to its exercise. Then truly it implements faith. When we let a resolution or a fine emotion dissipate without results, it means more than lost opportunity; it actually retards the fulfillment of future purposes and chills sensibility. There is plenty of courage among us for the abstract but not enough for the concrete, because we allow our daily bits of bravery to evaporate.

OR THREE THINGS
I thank God every day of my life—that He has vouchsafed me knowledge of His Works, deep thanks that He has set in my darkness the lamp of faith, deep, deepest thanks that I have another life to look forward to—a life joyous with light and flowers and heavenly song.

THE INFINITE wonders of the universe are revealed to us in exact measure as we are capable of receiving them. The keenness of our vision depends not on how much we can see, but on how much we feel. Nor yet does mere knowledge create beauty. Nature sings her most exquisite songs to those who love her. She does not unfold her secrets to those who come only to gratify their desire of analysis, to gather facts, but to those who see in her manifold phenomena suggestions of lofty, delicate sentiments.

THE OLD PRECEPT —and who can improve upon it?—is, "Depart from evil, and do good." Anyone who looks into himself can see which of his desires tend toward his own well-being and that of his fellow creatures. Some people know this intuitively, but regrettably many people lack intuition. Still, patient scrutiny will reveal to them their imperfections, faults, vices—call them what you will—and they will find motives and methods for removing these shackles upon their freer and happier life.

THOSE ARE RED-LETTER days in our lives when we meet people who thrill us like a fine poem, people whose handshake is brimful of unspoken sympathy, and whose sweet, rich natures impart to our eager, impatient spirits a wonderful restfulness which, in its essence, is divine. The perplexities, irritations, and worries that have absorbed us pass like unpleasant dreams, and we wake to see with new eyes and hear with new ears the beauty and harmony of God's real world. The solemn nothings that fill our everyday life blossom suddenly into bright possibilities. In a word, while such friends are near us we feel that all is well. Perhaps we never saw them before, and they may never cross our life's path again; but the influence of their calm, mellow natures is a libation poured upon our discontent, and we feel its healing touch, as the ocean feels the mountain stream freshening its brine.

ACCORDING TO all art, all nature, all coherent human thought, we know that order, proportion, form are essential elements of beauty. Now order, proportion, and form are palpable to the touch. But beauty and rhythm are deeper than sense. They are like love and faith. They spring out of a spiritual process only slightly dependent upon sensations. Order, proportion, form cannot generate in the mind the abstract idea of beauty, unless there is already a soul-intelligence to breathe life into the elements. Many persons, having perfect eyes, are blind in their perceptions. Many persons, having perfect ears, are emotionally deaf. Yet these are the very ones who dare to set limits to the vision of those who, lacking a sense or two, have will, soul, passion, imagination. Faith is a mockery if it teaches us not that we may construct a world unspeakably more complete and beautiful than the material world. And

I, too, may construct my better world, for I am a child of God, an inheritor of a fragment of the Mind that created all worlds.

*L*OOK WHERE WE
will, we find the hand in time and history, working, building, inventing, bringing civilization out of barbarism. The hand symbolizes power and the excellence of work. The mechanic's hand, that minister of elemental forces, the hand that hews, saws, cuts, builds, is useful in the world equally with the delicate hand that paints a wild flower or molds a Grecian urn, or the hand of a statesman that writes a law. The eye cannot say to the hand, "I have no need of thee." Blessed be the hand! Thrice blessed be the hands that work!

*L*IFE DOES NOT derive its whole vigor from the past. With the birth of each child nature lays aside all traditions, except those man imposes. There are no traditions according to which the child shall breathe or think or speak or strengthen his limbs in the struggle for existence. Let us find out if the traditions bewailed are crutches for indolent minds or wills grown soft, and if so, let us cease to bolster them. Our task is rather to leave behind us stimulating lives that shall nerve posterity to higher goals, sloughing off our imperfect vision, our half-knowledge and half-gods, our ailments of mind and body. Disappearing landmarks are not our chief peril, but propaganda backed by neither good will nor faith.

I HAVE AN unshakable belief that mankind's higher nature is on the whole still dormant. The greatest souls reveal excellencies of mind and heart which their lesser fellows possess—hidden, it is true, but there all the same. That inborn goodness renders it possible for most people to recognize nobility when they see it, as the latent poet in a reader enables him to appreciate a fine poem.

AITH WELCOMES
the thoughts and clasps the hands of other nations. No nation is wise enough to rule another. That is why empires have fallen and are still falling. Differences in language make it well-nigh impossible to understand an alien culture, which is a people's way of thinking, especially when they try to communicate through prejudice, neither hearing nor wanting to hear the other's mind. No two individuals are alike, and no two ever completely understand one another. Even the most intimate friends do not really know each other, but each gains from the other stimulating hints of potency and new varieties of truth. In the same way one nation can give to another whatever spiritual learning and culture it has, humbly receiving the other nation's point of view, which is often a different kind of wisdom garnered from totally different experiences.

Then the two nations can seek a harmony in which their faiths blend and ring true. This has already been done in some instances, and faith will spread this world Pentecost.

PRING AND autumn; seedtime and harvest; rain and sun; winter's cold and summer's heat—everything changes. Observing the transience of all things, why should we dwell on the ultimateness of death? Why should we not face life and death alike, unafraid?

A THOUGHT HAS
often hung round me, the truth of which I am surer as I read and listen. Our vocabulary is not commensurate yet with inner progress. It looks to me as if faults and evil propensities have a whole lexicon to themselves and positive qualities only a brief page. Perhaps the reason is that good refuses to be dissected and labeled as evil is. However the case may be, I have not come across a word for good-finding to offset fault-finding. To permit one helpful concept to go unidentified is as wasteful as losing the tiny yet powerful units of radio-activity. Faith must have more working words as well as the uncountable beauties within for the nascent world that is to emerge from our untapped resources.

UR BLINDNESS
changes not a whit the course of inner realities. Of us it is as
true as it is of the seeing that the most beautiful world is always entered through the imagination. If you wish to be
something that you are not—something fine, noble, good—
you shut your eyes, and for one dreamy moment you are that
which you long to be.

WE ARE HEIRS of the most magnificent mechanical equipment in history. Proudly bequeathing it to another age, we have forgotten that civilization is not human or humane unless it is rethought and relived with heart and soul. Implements can be handed down, not minds and personalities. Our latest blunder, which we must prevent from turning to a Balaklava, is to worship tools, deserting the One and Only that can draw the imponderable loveliness they conceal and lift them as vapor into His Firmament for stores of refreshing joy. We are spirits, not things—and for that matter "things" are another kind of spirit dumbly begging to rise again as ideas and impulses of creation. Poetry is their speech translated, their prayer. There are no deputies for our souls, and we are only mediators for a stupendous machine crying for a soul.

HE LEGEND
tells that when Jesus was born the sun danced in the sky, the
aged trees straightened themselves and put on leaves and sent
forth the fragrance of blossoms once more. These are the sym-
bols of what takes place in our hearts when the Christchild
is born anew each year. Blessed by the Christmas sunshine,
our natures, perhaps long leafless, bring forth new love, new
kindness, new mercy, new compassion. As the birth of Jesus
was the beginning of the Christian life, so the unselfish joy at
Christmas shall start the spirit that is to rule the new year.

How often the thought saddens me that my limitations prevent me from rendering larger service to the poor, the overladen, the ignorant! But why murmur over my bowl of longing, as the Japanese would say?

I realize that mortals are only tiny drops lost in an ocean of time. The most any race or individual can do is to enter a little more deeply into the purpose of the Divine Mind. That race, that individual, fulfills the highest destiny that is the best medium to transmit the current of good will through the ages.

There is another sustaining belief for me—that a watchful Providence guides equally the planet's course and the flight of the sparrow, marks human affairs and strengthens endeavor. This faith that God is "personally" interested in us gives a fairer aspect to the weary old world where we live as strangers and enemies. It imparts to those who can believe a consciousness of power. It lets them be sure that mankind can prevail against the snares, machinations and greed of the wicked. Knowing that the hosts of the Lord encamp about them, they fear not armies or navies or lines of defense. Confidently they tell themselves that one day all men will be lovers and human calamities will vanish in the sunshine of peace and good will upon earth.

I am aware that this conception of the Creator seems antiquated to many. Occasionally I fail to hear His voice within me, and doubts overwhelm my mind; but I cannot let this belief go, for then I should have no light through the darkness of the world.

Y LIFE IS
"a chronicle of friendship." My friends—all those about me—
create my world anew each day. Without their loving care all
the courage I could summon would not suffice to keep my
heart strong for life. But, like Stevenson, I know it is better
to do things than to imagine them.

$\mathcal{S}$ TUDY THE HAND, and you shall find in it the true picture of man, the story of human growth, the measure of the world's greatness and weakness. Its courage, its steadfastness, its pertinacity make all the welfare of the human race. Upon the trustworthiness of strong, toil-hardened hands rests the life of each and all. Every day thousands of people enter the railway train and trust their lives to the hand that grasps the throttle of the locomotive. Such responsibility kindles the imagination! But more profound is the thought that the destiny and the daily life of mankind depend upon countless obscure hands that are never lifted up in any dramatic gesture to remind the world of their existence.

XPERIENCING A
great sorrow is like entering a cave. We are overwhelmed by
the darkness, the loneliness, the homesickness. Sad thoughts,
like bats, flutter about us in the gloom. We feel that there is
no escape from the prison house of pain. But God in His
Loving-kindness has set on the invisible wall the Lamp of
Faith—whose beams shall guide us back to the sunlit world
where work and friends and service await us.

KNOWLEDGE IS power." Rather, knowledge is happiness, because to have knowledge—broad, deep knowledge—is to know true ends from false, and lofty things from low. To know the thoughts and deeds that have marked man's progress is to feel the great heart throbs of humanity through the centuries; and if one does not feel in these pulsations a heavenward striving, one must indeed be deaf to the harmonies of life.

THE CALAMITY
of the blind is immense, irreparable. But it does not take away our share of the things that count—service, friendship, humor, imagination, wisdom. It is the secret inner will that controls one's fate. We are capable of willing to be good, of loving and being loved, of thinking to the end that we may be wiser. We possess these spirit-born forces equally with all God's children. Therefore we, too, see the lightnings and hear the thunders of Sinai. We, too, march through the wilderness and the solitary place that shall be glad for us, and as we pass, God maketh the desert to blossom like the rose. We, too, go unto the Promised Land to possess the treasures of the spirit, the unseen permanence of life and nature.

IT IS NOT POSSIBLE for civilization to flow backward while there is youth in the world. Youth may be headstrong, but it will advance its allotted length. Through the ages in the battle with the powers of evil—with poverty, misery, ignorance, war, ugliness, and slavery, youth has steadily gained on the enemy. That is why I never turn away from the new generation impatiently because of its knowingness. Through it alone shall salvation come.

EXPERIMENTS IN the enrichment of the heritage of the human mind are only just beginning. The utmost faith at our command is needed to carry them out. As matters now stand, we are too near the abyss of a returning dark world to let such experiments lapse through want of faith. If we keep gazing into the abyss it will gaze back into us and we shall be engulfed. This pernicious habit must be broken. It prolongs mind-blighting traditions and prevents the worshiper from being a participant in the whole of his own faith. Generous risks must be taken for progress.

𝕴F THE HIGHER
ideals we pursue are threatened with repression or extinction
they can be obscured only locally and for a time. They will
grow through the ineradicable might of the Divinity which
transformed a few timid, unknown, simple disciples into a
constructive power for good that made history both in the
ideals and the temporal affairs of the race. I believe it is because these very ideals are pushing their way to the front
harder than ever that the world is in such commotion. They
are rousing fiercer opposition in the forces they are to cast out
—greed and hate, fear and prejudice and intolerance. Today
it is as in the beginning—Darkness is upon the face of the
deep. And the Spirit of God is moving upon the face of the
water. In time the light shall shine more and more into a true
Easter, and in that light we shall behold a heaven-upon-earth
civilization. . . .

URELY WE WOULD not weep if some beloved friend had the good fortune to move from a humble and uncomfortable house to a mansion into which the sunlight streamed, and whose grounds are a never-ending maze of beauty and wonder and delight. We would say that that was a fortunate friend, and, a bit wistfully, we would look forward to the time when we too might leave the burden of our daily tasks and join him in his house of beauty and light.

T HE POETS HAVE taught us how full of wonders is the night; and the night of blindness has its wonders, too. The only lightless dark is the night of ignorance and insensibility. We differ, blind and seeing, one from another, not in our senses, but in the use we make of them, in the imagination and courage with which we seek wisdom beyond our senses.

*I*T IS NECESSARY for the endurableness of life that we should believe that the uncertainty, the darkness in which we are struggling, shall one day be illumined by the light of solution; and even now we possess signs and traces of the knowledge which shall come when we see that Light face to face.

CIENCE ITSELF, which to the unthinking may seem far removed from faith, is a constant challenge to us not to live like pygmies. For what is science but faith staking everything on imaginative hypotheses so that it may retrieve larger hopes for the race from the unknown? Its courage and activity in piling up inventions and benefits, its implacable war upon ill-health are among the most inspiring records of man's struggle upward. If simple faith can thus spur science to open up one immensity after another of natural truth, how much more can a thoughtful, all-round faith win great dominions in the soul of man!

Yet how are we moderns behaving toward such annals of faith? Moping and despairing on the shore of a continent upon which we are just setting foot. I did not think I would live to see such nervous collapse of a people—such utter breakdown of fundamentals. Spiritual helplessness is unworthy of us who feel ourselves men and companions equally with the stars and the atoms.

SINCE WE ARE all too prone to live selfishly, it is necessary that there should be something within us to offset this tendency. The choice of a better life which we are to make involves some previous knowledge of such a life. What could save us from becoming more and more like animals, if there were not present with us other tendencies of a nobler kind? We cannot freely and wisely choose the right way for ourselves unless we know both good and evil.

I AM BLIND AND have never seen a rainbow, but I have been told of its beauty. I know that its beauty is always broken and incomplete. Never does it stretch across the heavens in full perfection. So it is with all things as we know them here below. Life itself is as imperfect and broken for every one of us as the span of a rainbow. Not until we have taken the step from life into Eternity, shall we understand the meaning of Browning's words: "On the earth the broken arcs; in the heaven, a perfect round."

FEARS AND REGRETS have no place in the vocabulary of youth, whose spirit sets its white and shining wings toward the purple shores of the Promised Land. Be happy, talk happiness. Happiness calls out responsive gladness in others. There is enough sadness in the world without yours. Rebel against the hardness and injustice of things as much as you like. It is always well to keep your fighting edge keen to smite wrongs wherever you meet them. But never doubt the excellence and permanence of what is yet to be. Never doubt that this is God's world, and that it is brought nearer to Him by the right work of the least of His children no less than by the mighty works of genius. You are no less necessary to the world's uplifting than Luther and Lincoln.

Join the great company of those who make the barren places of life fruitful with kindness. Carry a vision of heaven in your souls, and you shall make your home, your college, the world correspond to that vision. Your success and happiness lie in you. External conditions are the accidents of life, its outer trappings. The great, enduring realities are love and service. Joy is the holy fire that keeps our purpose warm and our intelligence aglow. Work without joy shall be as nothing. Resolve to keep happy, and your joy and you shall form an invincible host against difficulties.

THE PROCESS OF the emancipation of mankind from old ideas is very slow. The human race does not take to new ways of living readily, but I do not feel discouraged. Personally, I am impeded by physical difficulties which generate forces powerful enough to carry me over the barriers. This is true of the world's problems, too. It is for us to work with all our might to unite the spiritual power of good against the material power of evil.

It is for us to pray not for tasks equal to our powers, but for powers equal to our tasks, to go forward with a great desire forever beating at the door of our hearts as we travel toward the distant goal.

IT IS SELDOM now that I think of my deprivations, and they never sadden me as they once did when I had bitter moments of rebellion because I must sit at life's shut gate and fight down the passionate impulses of my nature. I know that a great many people pity me because I can show so little visible proof of living. They are often supercilious and sometimes contemptuous of the "poor thing" who is so shut out from everything they know. Meeting me in one of the noisy arenas of commerce, they are as startled as if they had encountered a ghost on Broadway. At such times I smile inwardly and gather my dreams about me. My reason for living would be lost if the reality they think they see did not hide her cruel face from me under a veil of pleasant illusions—if they are illusions. One will not quarrel over definitions if one has the substance, and I feel that, since I have found existence rich in happiness and interest, I have the substance.

FAITH DOES NOT oblige us to be unusually endowed, but receptive. To say others may have it but we cannot is wanton self-limitation. To be alert for whatever surprises may glow within us is to have at our command a zest for living which outweighs all material possessions. Stepping inward softly so as not to crush shy dreams and impulses, we shall marvel as our minds little by little disclose the completeness and oneness we potentially are. We shall, as I can testify after fifty years' unbroken experience, grow longer wings as we draw from superficial living into our happiness. To me the only satisfactory definition of happiness is wholeness—a blending in harmony of all one's feelings, visions, skills with the world of unfoldment waiting to be scrutinized and claimed.

T IS NO USE trying to reconcile the multitude of egos that compose me. I cannot fathom myself. I ask myself questions that I cannot answer. I find my heart aching when I expected to find it rejoicing, tears flow from my eyes when my lips were formed to smile. I preach love, brotherhood, and peace, but I am conscious of antagonisms, and lo! I find myself brandishing a sword and making ready for battle.

I think that every honest belief should be treated with fairness, yet I cry out against people who uphold the empire of gold. I am aware of moods when the perfect state of peace, brotherhood, and universal love seems so far off that I turn to division, pugnacity, and the pageant of war. I am just like St. Paul when he says, "I delight in the law of God after the inward man: But I see another law in my members, warring against the law of my mind. . . ." I am perfectly

sure that love will bring everything right in the end, but I
cannot help sympathizing with the oppressed who feel driven
to use force to gain the rights that belong to them.

HE FACTS WHICH equip most lives for labor and learning are as numerous as the sands of the sea, but it is faith which lights us into sustaining realities beyond those perceived by the physical senses. Faith, like philosophy, endows me with a unity I miss in the chaos of material experience devoid of sight or hearing. But like everyone else I have eyes in my soul. Through faith I create the world I gaze upon; I make my own day and night, tint the clouds with iridescent fires, and behold! a midnight is strewn with other stars.

Proof is not my concern. Can anything really be proved—goodness or beauty or joy? You cannot define happiness any more than you can define health, but you know them when you feel them. What I want is to live. Not letting faith breathe in me would be death.

DEFEAT IS A gateway to mental adventure that makes humdrum days piquant, causes the blood to sing, and may even invest drudgery with grace. That is the meaning of Walt Whitman's song that victory is great, but defeat, if necessary, is greater.

THE EYE GROWS by learning to see more in particular objects. To man's physical sight the earth looks flat, and the stars are the same to us that they were to the ancients. Yet science has opened up infinite new wonders and glories in these phenomena! A child sees in the things about him only what he wants or does not want, but when a Newton recognizes the falling of the apple as the expression of a universal force in Nature, he sees far beyond ordinary sight. It is the same with our spirits. We grow as we discern more fully the possibilities of new life wrapped up in daily contacts. But when we forget or ignore this vital fact, the senses lead us astray. That is why limitations are necessary to bring before us the greatness of inner life offered us in the circumstances of our lives, and show us our God-given opportunities.

$\mathcal{A}$LL THE AEONS
and aeons of time before we were born, before the spirit
awoke to its present consciousness—where were we then? All
the aeons and aeons of time after we are dead, after the spirit
has sunk again to sleep from its present consciousness, where
then shall we be? Vain questions; vain wondering. But if the
spirit is eternal, we have no more reason to dread the future of
the spirit than to shudder at its past. Rather, it is better to
consider this, our life, merely as "a gleam of time between two
Eternities," and to believe that most of the truth, most of the
beauty, most of the real splendor and fulfillment lies rather
in those eternities than in the here-and-now.

I KNOW THERE ARE people who are bored with spiritual ideas. They are bored because they do not know their own capacities and consequently miss the multitude of bright, illuminating interests that would come if they learned to think inwardly. A bored person is one who is unacquainted with himself and God. God is never a bore to those who know and love Him.

*T*HE SEEING ARE apt to conclude that the world of the blind—and especially the deaf-blind person—is quite unlike the sunlit, blooming world they know, that his feelings and sensations are essentially different from their own, and that his mental consciousness is fundamentally affected by his infirmities. They blunder still further, and imagine that he is shut out from all beauty of color, music, and shape. They need to be told over and over innumerable times that the elements of beauty, order, form, and proportion are tangible for the blind, and that beauty and rhythm are the result of a spiritual law deeper than sense. Yet how many people with eyes do take this truth to heart? How many of them take the trouble to ascertain for themselves the fact that the deaf-blind inherit their brain from a seeing and hearing race fitted for five senses, and the spirit fills the silent darkness with its own sunshine and harmony?

*P*OWER, NOT COMFORT, is my demand upon faith. Living faith is discomforting to the last degree. It does not offer an escape from life and its evils, but it gives a more abundant life despite all obstacles and all hardships. Faith, rightly understood, is active, not passive. Passive faith is no more a force than sight is in an eye that does not look or search out. Active faith knows no fear. It denies that God has betrayed His creatures and given the world over to darkness. It denies that men are to be judged after the appearance of race, color and opinion instead of according to the Law of Life. It denies that a society in which good will shall replace hate and intelligent co-operation supplant armed force is unattainable. It denies despair. Defeat is simply a signal to press onward. Reinforced by faith, the weakest mortal is mightier than disaster. The God within braces him against the universe; his soul is whole and equal to any emergency.

OMETIMES I WISH
these too, too solid limitations would melt; I feel positively
bruised with their impacts! Day and night, in torrents of
letters, under an avalanche of compliments I am reminded
that I cannot see or hear when I know perfectly well that in
the eternal sense I do. The spirit, like the sea, is greater than
any island or continent of sense-experience within its waters.
It has an infinite horizon of ideas that bring new facts and a
way of living in accordance with them. My deep-rooted feeling that I am not deaf or blind is like the feeling that I am in
the body but not of it. Of course I know that outwardly I am
a "deaf and blind" Helen Keller. That is a transitory ego, and
the few dark, silent years I shall be here do not matter. I use
my limitations as tools, not as my real self. If others are helped
through them that is the seventh heaven of happiness for me.
The rub comes with the everlasting absorption in problems

of deafness and blindness that keeps me from oftener looking out upon the universe through book windows or listening to the many-voiced course of things. . . .

ICK OR WELL, blind or seeing, bond or free, we are here for a purpose and however we are situated, we please God better with useful deeds than with many prayers or pious resignation. The temple or church is empty unless the good of life fills it. It is not the stone walls that make it small or large, but the brave soul's light shining round about. The altar is holy if only it represents the altar of our heart upon which we offer the only sacrifices ever commanded—the love that is stronger than hate and the faith that overcometh doubt.

I T IS OFTEN said that usefulness is the end of life; and so it is. But happiness creates and inspires usefulness. If you have many gifts and the power to understand, even if you meditate night and day how to promote the welfare of the world, it shall all profit you little if you have not joy.

I N DAYS LIKE
these to believe that Good is the dominant principle is an
ordeal as by fire, but for me it would be much harder to surrender that faith. All too well do I realize that the bitterest
fears of modern thinkers did not envisage the ruin into which
we are now being hurled. So much more then is faith imperative to pour healing upon blinding anguish and deafen-
ing fear. Heaven and earth, it has been affirmed, are mirages
rising from the deserts of man's despair. Picturesque indeed
would despair be if it could perform such a miracle. But to
everyone with faith his own world is real, no matter what it
may appear to be to others, and happiness—its fundamental
meaning is a free breathing of the soul—has also a share in the
mirage. From the delight of young animals in simply being

alive, from children at play, from youth risking all for love, from the triumphs that follow long effort—from all these, faith gathers materials for her Temple to form a bulwark against the storm.

I WONDER WHY farewells, even for a short time, are depressing? The emotion, I imagine, is akin to the regret when first love's celestial dream fades, the mother's wistfulness, recalling the joyous moment when she sees her baby taking its first steps or hears his first word. Few pleasures there are indeed without an aftertouch of pain, but that is the preservation which keeps them sweet.

**T IS A DAY** bright with sunshine. Then, from somewhere, unexpected, comes a veil of mist and then another, until the face of the sun is hid from us, and all is dark before our eyes. Yet we never doubt for a moment the sun is still there. Some poet has said that Life itself is "A wisp of fog betwixt us and the sun." I think that is true; I think that we—that the spirit-part of us—is eternal, that the Sun of true love and happiness is eternal, and that life, with its hurry, its bustle, its materialism, comes between us and the Sun, like a wisp of fog, a veiling cloud.

OMORROW!"
What possibilities there are in that word. No matter how discouraging today, how gloomy with dark clouds, with terrors
and illness and death, there's always Tomorrow, with its
promise of better things. Let us think then of Death as but
one more tomorrow, filled with infinite promise and fulfillment.

OTHING HAS
happened today outwardly; but for me there is never a dull
day. There is in me an ego that observes, examines, and phi-
losophizes constantly. I cannot look out of the window or see
the expression of a face or catch the tone of a voice; and yet
what a wealth of experience is within my reach! Every gesture
of the hand, every footfall, every joy is examined and weighed
and noted in my mind. Only when I have said as clearly as I
can the best I discern in human beings am I satisfied.

NCE AFFLICTION
was looked upon as a punishment from God—a burden to be borne passively and piously. The only idea of helping the victims of misfortune was to shelter them and leave them to meditate and live as contentedly as possible in the valley of the shadow. But now we understand that a sequestered life without aspiration enfeebles the spirit. It is exactly the same as with the body. The muscles must be used, or they lose their strength. If we do not go out of our limited experience somehow and use our memory, understanding, and sympathy, they become inactive. It is by fighting the limitations, temptations, and failures of the world that we reach our highest possibilities.

HANGE MAY BE
the vitalizing wind blowing through the house of life, but it is not an abiding force. We need permanent things to soak peace into us as well as progress—the beauty of the earth, seedtime and harvest, the smiles of lovers, the joy of the young in being alive, pride in craftsmanship. Why, oh, why must we let ourselves forget these lasting treasures in an age of consuming ambition, speed-madness, and accumulated goods that leave us no chance to live? If we cannot be contented with a little no wealth will ever satisfy us. Only from simple beginnings can creation go on unchecked. . . .

WHAT WE HAVE once enjoyed we can never lose. A sunset, a mountain bathed in moonlight, the ocean in calm and in storm—we see these, love their beauty, hold the vision to our hearts. All that we love deeply becomes a part of us. Our beloved ones are no more lost to us when they die than if they were still laughing and loving and working and playing at our side. Truly, life is overlord of Death and Love can never lose its own.

TIME INVARIABLY disintegrates the substance of most experiences and reduces them to intellectual abstractions. Many of the poignant details elude any attempt to restate them. It is not merely the difficulty of recapturing emotions, it is almost equally difficult to define attitudes, or to describe their effects upon others. They are, as it were, in solution, or if they do crystallize, they appear different to the persons concerned. It seems to me it is impossible to analyze honestly the subtle motives of those who have influenced our lives, because we cannot complete the creative process with the freshness of the situation clinging to it. Analysis is as destructive of emotion as of the flower which the botanist pulls to pieces.

I BELIEVE IN
immortality as instinctively as the fruit tree in the seed and quite as growingly, but that is not faith, except as it shines among its aggregate of nerving truths. Without immortality faith would still count it a magnificent vision to look upon God's face a brief while, to hold a beloved mortal's hand, to receive a child's kiss, and look through a glass millions of miles to other universes.

O ONE KNOWS
—no one can know—the bitter denials of limitation better than I do. I am not deceived about my situation. It is not true that I am never sad or rebellious; but long ago I determined not to complain. The mortally wounded must strive to live out their days cheerfully for the sake of others. That is what religion is for—to keep the hearts brave to fight out to the end with a smiling face. This may not be a very lofty ambition, but it is a far cry from surrendering to fate. But to get the better of fate even to this extent one must have work and the solace of friendship and an unwavering faith in God's Plan of Good.

FEW PEOPLE ARE saints or geniuses; but there is always this much of hope in all men—every pure delight they cherish is a "focus of good will," and every lovely scene they dwell on, every harmony they listen to, every graceful or tender thing they touch with reverent hand starts on the wing a flock of sweet thoughts which neither care nor poverty nor pain can destroy. Joy is the voice of the love and faith that shall at last pronounce the word of eternal life—"Well done!"

As I WANDER
through the dark, encountering difficulties, I am aware of
encouraging voices that murmur from the spirit realm. I sense
a holy passion pouring down from the springs of Infinity. I
thrill to music that beats with the pulses of God. Bound to
suns and planets by invisible cords, I feel the flame of eternity
in my soul. Here, in the midst of the everyday air, I sense the
rush of ethereal rains. I am conscious of the splendor that
binds all things of earth to all things of heaven—immured by
silence and darkness, I possess the light which shall give me
vision a thousandfold when death sets me free.

NOT ONLY ARE
the senses deceptive, but numerous usages in our language
indicate that people who have five senses find it difficult to
keep their functions distinct. I understand that we hear views,
see tones, taste music. I am told that voices have color. Tact,
which I had supposed to be a matter of nice perception, turns
out to be a matter of taste. Judging from the large use of the
word, taste appears to be the most important of all the senses.
Taste governs the great and small conventions of life. Certainly the language of the senses is full of contradictions, and
my fellows who have five doors to their house are not more
surely at home in themselves than I.

I BELIEVE THAT

we can live on earth according to the teachings of Jesus, and that the greatest happiness will come to the world when man obeys His commandment, that "ye love one another."

I believe that every question between man and man is a religious question, and that every social wrong is a moral wrong.

I believe that we can live on earth according to the fulfillment of God's will, and that when the will of God is done on earth as it is in heaven, every man will love his fellow men and act toward them as he desires they should act toward him. I believe that the welfare of each is bound up in the welfare of all.

I believe that life is given us so we may grow in love, and I believe that God is in me as the sun is in the color and fragrance of a flower—the Light in my darkness, the Voice in my silence.

I believe that only in broken gleams has the Sun of Truth yet shone upon men. I believe that love will finally establish the Kingdom of God on earth, and that the corner-stones of that Kingdom will be Liberty, Truth, Brotherhood, and Service.

I believe that no good shall be lost, and that all man has willed or hoped or dreamed of good shall exist forever.

I believe in the immortality of the soul because I have within me immortal longings. I believe that the state we enter after death is wrought of our own motives, thoughts, and deeds. I believe that in the life to come I shall have the senses I have not had here, and that my home there will be beautiful with color, music, and speech of flowers and faces I love.

Without this faith there would be little meaning in my life. I should be "a mere pillar of darkness in the dark." Observers in the full enjoyment of their bodily senses pity me, but it is because they do not see the golden chamber in my life where I dwell delighted; for, dark as my path may seem to them, I carry a magic light in my heart. Faith, the spiritual strong searchlight, illumines the way, and although sinister doubts lurk in the shadow, I walk unafraid toward the Enchanted Wood where the foliage is always green, where joy abides, where nightingales nest and sing, and where life and death are one in the Presence of the Lord.